RED OR GREEN CHILE BIBLE

Love at First Bite

Traditional and Original New Mexico Recipes

RED OR GREEN CHILE BIBLE

Love at First Bite

Traditional and Original New Mexico Recipes

Harmon Houghton

Clear Light Publishing
Santa Fe, New Mexico

Clear Light Publishing
823 Don Diego
Santa Fe, New Mexico 87505
www.clearlightbooks.com
Printed in the United States of America

Disclaimer:
The preparation of foods with fresh ingredients requires that sanitary
guidelines for food preparation, refrigeration, and cooking temperatures be
followed to prevent any cross contamination or spoilage that can occur if
guidelines are not followed.

Library of Congress Cataloging-in-Publication Data. Houghton, Harmon,
1945- author.
   Red or Green Chile Bible: Love at First Bite.250 Traditional & Original
New Mexico Recipes: Includes Chilenista Degree / by Harmon Houghton.
-- First edition.
      pages 392
   Includes bibliographical references and index.
   ISBN 978-1-57416-108-3 (alk. paper)
   1. Cooking Chile (Pepper)--New Mexico. 2. Cooking, American--
Southwestern style. 3. Cooking--New Mexico. I. Title.

   TX819.P3H68 2014
   641.6'384--dc23

                              2014025715

ISBN 9781574161083 $14.95

Contents

CHAPTER 8—RED OR GREEN CHILE STEWS,   215
SOUPS & CHOWDERS

STEWS

SOUPS   224

CHOWDERS   235

CHAPTER 9–RED OR GREEN CHILE ENTRÉE RECIPES   239

ACKNOWLEDGEMENTS

I would like to dedicate this book to all Chilenistas, chileholics, chile-lovers, chile growers and supporters who have made the publication of this book possible.

I would like to thank Tony Trinkaus, one of the original chefs in the Waldorf Hotel kitchen in the 1920s and '30s while they were still on 34th Street at a time when chefs were called on to use their culinary skills to create recipes and prepare food for their discriminating clientele.

I would also like to thank Nawang Tenzin, a chef for the Dalai Lama in the Potala Kitchen for his knowledge of ingredients, spices, and blending the tastes of sweet, sour, salty, bitter, pungent and aromatic that makes eating a sensory experience. Both of them taught me to respect food and use my creative ability to bring vegetables, grains, meats, herbs and spices together.

I would also like to thank the many friends who have endured the experimenting and tasting of many recipes that did not work as expected but were fun to eat anyway.

I thank my wife, Marcia Keegan, who first introduced me to the tastes and smells of New Mexico chile through her monumental Southwest Indian Cookbook, an R.T. French Tastemaker Award winner.

I also thank all of the contributors to the Green Chile Bible for their favorite family recipes and inspiring me to fall in love with chile.

Additional gratitude goes to Kathleen Hansel and Audrey Jenkins, authors of the Red Chile Bible who introduced the subtle flavor of chile into mainstream recipes and its use as a condiment, Robert Strautins for his patient encouragement of my writing this book, and above all to the Creator that has provided us with the bounty of food, spices and flavors that made this book possible.

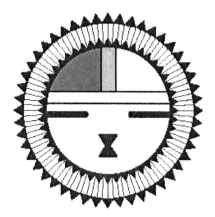

INTRODUCTION TO THE CHILE CUISINE

If you are a chileholic, chilenista or just plain chile-lover, this is the book for you. Chile, red or green is like a romance that once nurtured, becomes a love affair. I have been preparing and cooking chile for over thirty years and am still amazed at the versatility, popularity and ethnicity that chile has in almost every cuisine around the world. Perhaps it is the endorphins. Perhaps it is the variety. I happen to think that it is all about the taste from mild and sweet to super-hot and blistering. I would like to share with you my love affair with chile both red and green.

The first thing to learn about chile is that it is a fruit,[1] and as such, has the fragrance, aroma and flavor that can enhance any recipe. There are literally hundreds of varieties of chiles throughout the world. We have been blessed in New Mexico with a variety of chiles ranging from the mild New Mexican, Anaheim or Big Jim to the blistering Habanero. I have chosen the most popular chiles that can be used to prepare any recipe in this book to the desired Scoville Heat Unit (SHU) level can range from 500 (SHU) to 300,000 (SHU). The choice is yours. See our commonly used Chili Pepper List in Chapter 1 (p.32).

Chile can be used as a spice in powder form similar to salt and pepper, fresh as a garnish in salads and dishes to both decorate and refresh the palate, or as a main ingredient when roasted or made into a sauce. Chile can be used in stews, soups, casseroles, BBQ and an endless variety of entrées. Chile is probably one of the most popular ingredients in the world.

Cooking and eating are two sides of the same coin: They are both at the same time essential and pleasurable. Cooking gives you an immediate gratification of completing a task that pleases yourself as well as others. Eating and feeding others provide a euphoria that not only nourishes the body but also gratifies the soul.

Many scientific studies have shown that preparing and eating chile, which is laden with capsaicin, stimulates the natural endorphins in your body. This makes you feel good, and has a reputation for helping to ward off illnesses such as cancer and viruses, promotes blood circulation, assists in relieving arthritic pain, promotes weight loss and supports healthy body functions.

If you Google "medicinal properties of chile," you will get over 12 thousand documents expounding the benefits of consuming chile. The Red or Green Chile Bible will not only guide you through the cuisine of New Mexico chile but will also provide you with a Culinary Chilenista degree (CCD).

---

1 The scientific definition of a fruit is any structure that develops from the fertilized ovary of a **flower** and contains seeds of a plant. It is legally a vegetable in the U.S., but botanically, it is a fruit.

Please visit our website, www.redorgreenchilebible.com to register your degree. In order to receive your degree you have to pledge to enjoy life, cook and serve with the following:

Attitude
Always cook with a positive frame of mind and cook for those you love. Forget about the stresses of the day. The stove and your kitchen are your sanctuary, the ingredients are your sacraments and good thoughts your devotionals. Dedicate the meal to all who are in need and say a few good words as you stir. The magic ingredient in any dish is your positive attitude, people will taste the difference.

Joyful Eating
Eating is a celebration of the harvest and the bounty that nature has provided as sustenance for our well-being. The chile diet is truly a balance of all of the food groups—grains, meats vegetables, fruits, nuts and dairy— that provides all of the proteins, fiber and vitamins required to maintain a healthy body and mind. It is also important to experience the joy of cooking and eating through the many smells, tastes, textures and sights of the many ingredients that go into the recipes in this book. By eating joyfully, your digestion, health and vitality will improve to support all of your other pursuits in life.

Celebration of Life
The chile cuisine is one of the oldest on our planet with a cultural legacy that goes back thousands of years to the Aztec, Mayan and Native American cuisines that have been evolving through, trade, farming, hunting, fishing and the introduction of ingredients brought from Europe that were incorporated into food preparation. The breads, cheeses, chiles, condiments, herbs, spices and sweeteners are all part of the chile cuisine palate of taste, color, smell and texture. Come join us on a culinary journey of New Mexico chile.

GIVING THANKS—PRAYERS AND BLESSINGS FOR FOOD

Every culture, society and religion throughout history has evolved prayers and rituals to bless food and thank the Creator for the bounty that has been provided to sustain us. The following prayers and blessings all have one common theme: to consecrate the food we eat irrespective of our religions or beliefs. I recommend that you make prayers part of your ingredient list in the preparation of the recipes and meals you are about to serve.

Native American
Creator, Earth Mother, we thank you for our lives and this beautiful day. Thank you for the bright sun and the rain we received last night. Thank you for this circle of friends and the opportunity to be together. We want to thank all of the people that have been responsible for bringing this bounty to our table. We want to thank all of the animals, vegetables and grains that have made this meal possible. We thank them for giving of their lives so we may continue our lives through this great blessing. Please help us honor them through how we live our lives.

Christian
Bless us, O Lord, and these your gifts, which we're about to receive from your bounty. Through Christ our Lord, Amen.

Buddhist
(Serving the food) in this food I see clearly the presence of the entire universe supporting my existence.
(Looking at the plate of food) All living beings are struggling for life, may they all have enough food to eat today.
(Just before eating) The plate is filled with food. I am aware that each morsel is the fruit of much hard work by those who produced it.

(Beginning to eat) With the first taste, I promise to practice loving kindness. With the second, I promise to relieve the suffering of others. With the third, I promise to see others' joy as my own. With the fourth, I promise to learn the way of nonattachment and equanimity.
(After the meal) The plate is empty. My hunger is satisfied. I vow to live for the benefit of all living beings.

Hindu
Affirmation to My Body
I recognize you are the temple in which my spirit and creative energy dwell. I have created you from my need to have my spirit manifested on earth so that I may have this time to learn and grow. I offer you this food so that you may continue to sustain my creative energy, my spirit, my soul. I offer this food to you with love and a sincere desire for you to remain free from disease and disharmony. I accept you as my own creation. I need you. I love you.

Islamic
In the name of the compassionate and beneficent God. Allah be praised.

Judaic
Blessed art Thou, O Lord our God, King of the Universe, who creates many living beings and the things they need. For all that Thou hast created to sustain the life of every living being, blessed be Thou, the Life of the universe.

Christian (Gaelic)
God to enfold me, God to surround me, God in my speaking, God in my thinking, God in my sleeping, God in my waking, God in my watching, God in my hoping, God in my life, God in my lips, God in my soul, God in my heart.
God in my sufficing, God in my slumber, God in my mine ever-lasting soul, God in mine serenity.

A Cowboy's Prayer
Rub-u-dub, dear God, pass the grub. Thank you.

ABOUT CHILES

For some reason, chile pepper names change from when they are green and on the vine to when they ripen, turn red and are dried. Their Scoville Heat Units remain the same whether fresh, dried as pods or ground into powder. Some of the most common and available chiles are grown in the Southwest and Mexico and are available at most supermarkets or online.

Fresh green chiles are available year-round at the produce case or can be found frozen or canned. Chapter 13 lists over 100 varieties of chile peppers that are available ranging from regular bell peppers at 0 SHU to the Trinidad Scorpion at 2 million SHU. Pure capsaicin extract is also available with up to 16 million SHU. (You have to sign a release before it will be shipped.)

A comfortable heat range for most Chilenistas is 500 SHU to 1,200 SHU, which will flavor and spice up any recipe without overwhelming the other flavors. It is not unusual for the more seasoned Chilenistas to prefer an SHU range of 1,200 to 2,500 and push to over 5,000 SHU for dips and appetizers.

What You Need to Know about Green Chile

Commercial chile growers will harvest, roast, flash-freeze or can fresh green chile in mild, medium or hot flavors for distribution through supermarkets and specialty stores. The amazing quality of green chile is that it keeps its taste and can be used in any recipe in this book. (Needless to say fresh or freshly-roasted is best.) Some growers will dry and grind green chile into a powder that is available through most chile catalogs. Ground green chile serves as a condiment in almost any recipe to replace black pepper and enhances the taste of any recipe as a garnish. Please look at ESSENTIAL RECIPES (p. 31) for the many ways to prepare green chile for use in your recipes and at (p. 42) for a list of essential green chiles and their SHU ratings.

What You Need to Know about Red Chile

Red chile is green chile that has been allowed to ripen. It is often dried and ground into a powder. Some Chilenistas will state that red chile is a bit sweeter than green chile, a view that is open to discussion. Powdered red chile is easier to handle and can be stored in a dark, cool, dry space for years with no loss of taste, ready for use in a paste, sauce or as a dry powder. I prefer to make a quart of red chile paste, place it in a container and store in the fridge so that I have a spoonful or cupful ready for use at any time.

Please look at ESSENTIAL RECIPES (p. 31) for the many ways to prepare red chile for use in your recipes. I keep a spice jar of red chile powder on my spice shelf to use as a substitute for pepper and to garnish any recipe in this book. You can also freeze red chile paste in an ice cube container and have frozen chile balls that can be used year round.

Please look at the list bellow of some of the most popular chile varieties of New Mexico and Southwest chiles along with their Scoville Heat Units. You can refer to these ratings in preparing your recipes from mild and sweet to XXXX-hot and tongue-scorching. The great diversity of chile will allow you the flexibility to please everyone at the table. See the list of essential red chile recipes and their SHU rating (p. 32).

New Mexico Chile Properties
For all of the recipes in this book, I have used the basic eight varieties of chiles available in the Southwest in their fresh, frozen, canned, dried and powdered forms. The taste and heat levels vary from a mild and fruity to a blistering heat that can bring tears to your eyes and all points in between.

New Mexican /Anaheim / Big Jim—New Mexico Red Chile Dried Pod or Ground Powder
New Mexican / Anaheim / Big Jim New Mexico chile is the standard for the New Mexico Chilenista cuisine. It has a sweet, fruity flavor that can be used in any green chile recipe either raw or roasted. Anaheim chile is called "New Mexico Red" when dried and ground. It is used in almost every red chile recipe. (Sweet flavor with an undertone of fruit, acidity and a hint of dried cherries.)

Mild	500–800 SHU
Medium	800–1,200 SHU
Hot	1,200–1,800 SHU
X Hot	1,800–2,500 SHU
XX Hot	2,500–5,000 SHU
NM Scorpion	1,200,000 SHU

Cayenne Chile Pepper Powder
Cayenne chile is said by many to have medicinal powers because of its sweat-inducing powers. It makes a great garnish for any recipe and can be used in a shaker to spice up any dish. (Sweat-producing heat). Use sparingly. Keep some milk, crema and tortillas close by.)

Medium	35,000–40,000 SHU
Hot	80,000–90,000 SHU

Chilaca Chile—Pasilla Dried Pod or Ground Powder
Chilaca chiles when available fresh are a favorite because of the taste and flavor that they can add to any recipe. Most often found in dried form as Pasilla dried chile pods, they can be crushed or rehydrated to use in any red chile paste or sauce recipe. (Pungent but with a rich flavor and herb-like undertones.)
1,000–2,000 SHU

De Arbol—Chile and Powder
De Arbol chile pods are the small, bright-red chiles that enhance the look of your recipe and infuse it with their, grassy, nutty flavor. If you wish to add heat and looks to any dish, just drop three to six de Arbol chile pods into your recipe while cooking (dried or fresh). (Hot, bold, grassy flavor with a hint of nuttiness.)
15,000–30,000 SHU

Habanero—Chile and Ground Powder
The best way to describe habanero chiles is "HOT." They are readily available in either fresh or dried pods and add a bright yellow color to your dishes along with the heat. (Blistering heat, use sparingly.) Keep a beer or margarita ready.
150,000–300,000 SHU

Jalapeño Green Chile—Chipotle Chile Dried Pod or Ground Powder
Green jalapeño, often synonymous with hot chile pepper, is often eaten raw or chopped as a garnish to top many foods. Its fresh, grassy, fruity taste makes it a favorite. In its dried form, jalapeño changes its name to chipotle and is often smoked to dry it and impart a unique, smoky flavor. Chipotle is also available in a canned pickle variety that adds sparkle to any dish as a condiment. (Smoky with a slightly spicy, grassy fruitiness.)
5,000–8,000 SHU

Poblano Green Chile—Ancho Chile Dried Pod or Ground Powder
Poblano chile has one of the largest pods of the chile family and is one of my favorite chiles to cook with. It can be chopped, fresh-roasted, stuffed and used as a substitute for the common bell pepper to provide a chile kick. In its dried form it is called "ancho chile pods" and is rehydrated to make any chile paste or sauce. Its thin skin and thick meat make excellent flavor chunks when chopped and placed in any recipe. Poblano chile pods are also pickled and stored as a garnish. (Mild fruity flavor with undertones of plum, raisin, tobacco and a slight earthy bitterness.)
1,000–2,000 SHU

Serrano Green Chile—Chile Seco Dried Pod or Ground Powder
Serrano chile can be used to kick up any recipe that calls for jalapeño with an additional SHU burst of heat. (Smoky, fruity flavor.)
8,000–18,000 SHU

The above list of chiles is your palate of flavor and heat for making any chile dish in this cookbook as well as any dish you may be able to dream up by yourself.

Varying the Heat Level
Capsaicin is ultimately oil stored in the veins and seeds of chile pods and is how the plant protects itself from insects, birds and animals. The only way to dissipate the heat is by adding milk, sour cream, cheese, oils and alcoholic beverages to help dissolve the burn. Water and soda will only make it worse.

ESSENTIAL INGREDIENTS
Some of the most frequently used ingredients used in the Chilinista cuisine are:

Adobo Spice Mix
Adobo Spice Mix gives chile an aromatic flavor with a combination of equal parts ground oregano, garlic, coriander and cumin with ⅛ part clove powder as the "secret" aromatic ingredient. Adobo powder is used in the Chilenista cuisine as a universal spice to enhance the flavor of chile. I have found that it is easier to prepare the Adobo Spice Mix by mixing a cup at a time and placing it in a container on my spice shelf.

Some Chilenistas will add ground piloncillo for sweetness or annatto powder for a tart taste. Commercial adobo powder is available, however, if you read the label, it will contain mostly salt and sometimes MSG. Homemade Adobo Spice Mix will reflect your taste sensibility and your guests will wonder what makes your chile so special. See Adobo Spice Mix recipe (p. 83).

Crema
Crema is the Mexican version of sour cream that is often available in several forms in your grocer's cheese case, or you can make it yourself out of sour cream and buttermilk. Crema is a universal garnish for any chile dish. It cuts down the SHU level of chile, refreshes your tongue for the next bite or creates a creamy version of your chile paste. Please look at (p. 359) for ways to prepare and store crema.

Sweetener
Most Chilenistas, including myself, love sweets. When a recipe calls for a sweetener, the first instinct is to reach for the sugar. I have over the years learned that the choice for sweeteners in the Chilenista cuisine can be combined with aromatics to give a full flavor not available in refined sugar. Try using any of the liquid nectars, such as guava, papaya, guanabana, pear and apricot, available on your grocer's shelf or pastes such as guava paste, quince (membrillo) paste, honey, agave paste or piloncillo (cane sugar).

By expanding your sweetener choices, you are enriching the subtle aromatic undertones that define a great chile. A word of caution is to use small amounts of sweetener. No one likes sweet chile (I think.) Please look at (pp 85) for ways to prepare and store sweeteners.

Tortillas
No Chilenista meal is complete without a tortilla on the side. Whether made from cornmeal, flour or masa; as a gordita or burrito size; baked, fried or made into chips and used as an appetizer; burrito or side, the tortilla will complement and enhance any recipe. Please look at (p. 113) for ways to prepare tortillas.

YOUR PANTRY & WHAT YOU WILL NEED

The well-stocked pantry will allow you the freedom of taste expression similar to how artists choose their colors. Whenever you are inspired to prepare a recipe the following ingredients will allow you to start without having to run to the store first.

Beans, Grains & Pasta

Beans (fresh or canned), bread crumbs, cornmeal, flour (unbleached), masa harina, nachos, orzo, pasta, quinoa, rice, rice noodles, risotto, taco shells, corn tortillas and flour tortillas.

Canned Goods

Beans (black, kidney, pinto and white), corn, diced tomatoes (salt-free), garbanzos, hominy, posole, refried beans, tomato paste and tomato sauce.

Condiments

Annatto, achiote, adobo, bouillon cubes (beef, chicken, garlic, tomato), canned chile (all varieties), cilantro, pesto, ketchup, lime juice, lemon juice, mole, mole verde, recaito or sofrito, recado, sun-dried tomatoes and vinegar (balsamic, cider, white and wine).

Dairy

Yogurt, milk, butter, ricotta cheese, cream cheese, crema and sour cream.

Flour, Thickeners & Coating

Baking powder, cornmeal, corn starch, flour (unbleached, masa harina, rice flour and flour pre-mixes (sopapilla and tortilla).

Fresh Vegetables & Herbs

Bell pepper, corn, cucumber, eggplant, garlic, ginger, leafy greens, lemon, lime, onion, oregano, squash, tomatoes and zucchini.

Fish

Fruiti de Mare (seasonal fresh or frozen). Clams, mussels octopus, scallops, shrimp, squid and whitefish fillets (tilapia, pollock and cod).

Herbs

Cilantro, cinnamon, clove, coriander, cumin, oregano, parsley, rosemary, sage and thyme.

Meats

Beef shoulder cuts, brisket, chicken, chile-ground pork, flank steak, ground beef, lamb, pork shoulder cuts, sausage and game meat.

Oil

Butter, lard, olive oil, vegetable oil and liquid butter substitute. Lard has about half as much saturated fat as butter but about double the saturated fat found in olive oil.

Spices

Adobo Spice Mix, coriander, cumin, garlic powder and oregano (crushed). For aromatic blends, you can add clove or nutmeg. You will see Adobo Spice Mix used in many recipes in this book, as it is an essential for the chile cuisine.

Rather than adding the spices individually, I suggest that you make your own Adobo Spice Mix by combining equal parts of coriander, cumin, garlic and oregano powder. (I rub whole-leaf, dry Mexican oregano in my palms to crush it.) Store it in a jar along with your other spices.

You can also customize the mixture by blending a pinch of clove powder or nutmeg to give it a sweet, nutty taste. See (p. 83 for an Adobo Spice Mix recipe.

Try to not use store-bought adobo, as it is usually blended from salt and MSG as the prime ingredients.

Sweeteners

Sweeteners consist of brown sugar, corn syrup, fruit nectars, guava paste, quince (membrillo) paste, honey, maple syrup, piloncillo, and sugar.

Fruit nectars, apricot, guava, guanabana, papaya and tamarind, are the natural sweeteners for the chile cuisine and give a subtle, sweet taste that is aromatic and will enhance the natural taste of the other ingredients rather without overwhelming them with sweet. Fruit nectars can used straight from the can as a sweetener in a 4:1 ratio to sugar

Guava and quince paste are the perfect sweeteners for the Chilenista cuisine. Guava imparts a fruitiness and sweetness that will not overwhelm the other ingredients.

Piloncillo is pure cane sugar syrup that is dried and shaped into cones. The best way to use piloncillo is to grate it or place it in a microwave and break it apart with a fork when it starts to melt. (You will never want to use refined sugar again.)

Utensils

Blender, crockpot, cast-iron skillets, Dutch oven, comal, stockpots, saucepans, measuring cup and spoons, meat thermometer, mixing bowl, hand blender stick, stirring spoons, strainer, storage containers and freezer bags.

COOKING TECHNIQUES, TEMPERATURE & DURATION

There are many cooking techniques used in the chile kitchen and each can enhance the flavor of our beloved chile and ingredients that we use for each dish. A recipe is a guideline and road map toward a desired end. You are at all times the driver and in control of the outcome. In today's Internet world you can use Google or Bing like a GPS to help find the answers to any questions that you may have about food. What makes this book valuable is that it can spark your imagination about chile dishes from knowing how they have been prepared for generations as well as how original recipes take on the fusion of a modern cuisine.

Turning on the Heat

The range, oven, grill, microwave or open campfire can provide enough heat to start cooking. Fundamentally, there are only two methods you need: dry heat cooking and wet heat cooking.

Heat, whether direct or indirect, is at the source of all cooking techniques. Learning how to control the temperature and time is the secret skill that most chefs learn from experience. They have also developed a sixth sense and know when the food and ingredients are at their peak of flavor and texture and are ready to serve. I have included cooking times and temperature guidelines as part of the recipes in this book; however, your own senses of smell, sight and taste will tell you when a recipe is done and ready to serve. The tasting is a part of the joy of cooking.

In dry cooking the heat is transferred from the flame or heat source directly into ingredients. In wet cooking, water or steam transfers the heat into the ingredients.

Dry Heat Cooking

Dry cooking comprises baking, barbecuing, broiling, frying, roasting, microwaving, sautéing and searing. This method allows you a much greater control of the temperature from 190^0F to 425^0F, which sears in the flavors. In dry heat cooking only the air and flame from your heat source touch the ingredients, which requires a fair amount of attentiveness to make sure that the food does not dry out the natural moisture of the food. Marinating, searing and dry rubs will help keep the moisture inside. Time and attention to dry cooking is important, especially at the higher heat levels. Ingredients can dry and burn very quickly.

Oven Roasting

Oven roasting is ideal for cooking meats because you can have control of an even temperature from 170^0F to 450^0F. The flexibility of a consistent heat source will allow you to pan-roast or slow cook any ingredient. In an unsupervised manner, all you have to do is "pop" into the oven and let the heat do the work.

Baking

Placing food inside of an oven can give you the utmost degree of temperature and time control. You generally have a temperature selection from 300^0F to 350^0F and can control the time or duration of cooking down to the minute. Baking in an oven is the most convenient of all cooking methods. Baking is usually preferred for casseroles, roasts, bread and pastry items.

Barbecuing

Barbecuing introduces heat to your ingredients from the bottom and is the best method for slow cooking meats with an indirect heat. You can vary the heat by placing the ingredients away from the flame or adding wood chips to introduce smoke and you can inject water to generate steam. By lowering the flame and temperature, you can slow cook and marinate your food as it is cooking. Most barbecue masters will cook their meat for 6 to 8 hours with a low heat of 225^0F to 250^0F. A covered barbecue grill is the most versatile of all of the cooking methods, however, it will generate smoke and is best used outdoors. Barbecue is best for cooking meats.

Pan-Roasting (Iron Skillet)

Pan-roasting gives a new meaning to the phrase "jumping from the pan into the fire." By heating an iron skillet in very high heat you can sear the flavor into meat, chicken, fish and veggies in a very short amount of time and continue roasting in the oven, either covered to create a Dutch oven or open, to further cook the ingredients.

Pan-roasting is one of the professional chef's favorite cooking methods: It is quick, versatile and retains the flavor of the ingredients. Pan-roasting puts the sizzle in your food.

Broiling

Broiling introduces the heat from the top of the ingredients with an open flame. Broiling can quickly sear meat, create crusts or melt cheese and is ideal for cooking chicken, fish and the tender meat cuts that require a high direct heat. Since broiling will dry out food very quickly, you may wish to marinate your food for 1 to 2 hours before cooking or, in some cases, overnight in the refrigerator.

Grilling

Grilling is often confused with barbecuing. Grilling is the opposite of broiling because the heat source is introduced as an open flame from the bottom. Barbecue grills are an excellent way to grill meats and some vegetables to a crisp or char on the outside, leaving the inside moist and juicy. Grilling will dry out food very quickly. You may wish to marinate your food for 1 to 2 hours before cooking or overnight in the refrigerator. Grilling needs attention, so be prepared to make it an occasion. You have many grilling tools available, such as rotisseries, smokers, skewers, cages and racks, to assist you in preparing the food.

Searing

Searing is a technique of browning the surface of any meat prior to braising or slow cooking. It seals the natural juices and enhances the flavor. To sear a cut of meat, super-heat a heavy pan with a little oil on its surface, place the cut in the pan until the sizzle stops and flip the meat to its other side. When the sizzle stops remove the meat and braise, barbecue or slow cook to completion.

Sautéing

Sautéing is the most dramatic of all cooking techniques. We have all seen French chefs skillfully flipping their sautés in the air or pouring a bit of cognac into a hot pan to flambé the ingredients in a show of sizzle and anticipation of what is going to come next. Sautéing is flash-frying, only with very little oil and a lot of heat. It allows ingredients to simultaneously sear and brown on the outside while keeping the entire flavor inside. The key to great sautéing is high heat and not overcrowding the pan. You can only sauté one layer of food at a time and flip either with a spatula or by tossing in the pan to get both sides browned. The flambé finale with brandy or high-proof alcohol will not only impress your friends but also imparts a fruity sweetness and glaze to the sauté.

Frying

Believe it or not, frying is a dry-heat source for your food and when properly used, it will not impart any greasy coating to your food. The key to great non-greasy frying is temperature control and not letting the temperature of your oil drop below 350^0F. There are two methods of frying: deep-fat frying and pan-frying. In both cases, you should use a heavy skillet or pot (preferably cast-iron). Never overcrowd your fryer, allow a minimum of one-half inch between each piece you are frying to allow the oil to impart its heat. The larger and heavier the pot, the more heat it will retain and impart to the food.

Always compensate for the heat drop that will occur the minute you place the food into the hot oil. Place food items into the frying pan or pot, moving away from the side nearest you one at a time, to allow the heat of the oil to catch up and prevent flare-ups. For pan-frying, do not turn the pieces over too many times. Let the heat do the work.

For deep-frying, poke or stir the food once or twice with a wooden spoon to prevent the pieces from sticking together. At all times do not leave frying foods unattended. Flare-up can happen at any time, so have a cover or towel handy to smother any flames.

When the individual pieces are a golden brown, remove them from the oil with a tong or serrated spoon and place on a cooling rack that has been placed on top of a baking pan. This is the time to sprinkle chile powder, salt or any other spice to infuse the flavor into the coating. If you are doing a large quantity of frying, place the rack in your oven at 200^0F to 225^0F to keep the food warm while your next batch gets ready. There is an adage that everything tastes better fried.

Microwave

The microwave is one of the most useful tools for defrosting, warming and heating any ingredient with an indirect heat source. It tends to dry foods out, however. Microwave pots can be used to seal moisture in. Since the microwave cooks by activating the molecules of the ingredient from the inside out, you have to be careful to poke holes into the item so that moisture in the food does not explode it, as happens with potatoes. I have found the best use of a microwave is in heating sauces and leftovers.

Wet or Moist Heat Cooking

Wet cooking (boiling, braising, crockpot, Dutch oven, poaching, pressure-cooking and steaming) allows you more time for other preparations and requires less attention. Wet cooking hydrates and retains the natural juices of your ingredients at a temperature range of 135^0F to 212^0F over time. Vegetables are best when steamed and meats reach fall-off-the-bone tenderness when slow cooked. In wet cooking techniques, the ingredients are surrounded by water, steam, stock or any liquid that imparts the heat to the ingredients. The temperature can range from a simmer at 195^0F to boiling at 212^0F or steaming at over 212^0F. The only exception is in pressure-cooking where you can introduce temperatures as high as 250^0F at 15 psi.

Boiling

Anyone can boil a pot of water, which is admittedly the easiest of all cooking methods. Bring a pot of water to a boil, insert the ingredients and watch them cook. Be careful to watch the time, as over-boiling will turn your ingredients into a tasteless mush.

Braising

Braising is a combination of boiling and roasting, when the ingredients cook in their own juices or in a marinade to gain flavor. Generally, braising is best for larger, tough cuts of meat like shoulder steak or rump steak. In a heavy roasting pan, place ⅛ inch of oil and heat over the range until very hot. Carefully place the meat to sear the surfaces, top, sides and bottom. (Turn with two forks.) When the meat is seared all around, fill the pan half-way to the top of the meat with any liquid stock, some wine and aromatic spices such as bay leaf, Adobo Spice Mix, chile powder or achiote powder and then cover the pan with a lid or aluminum foil and place in the oven at 290^0F to 300^0F degrees for a length of time until the connective tissue starts to break down and reaches an internal temperature of 160^0F. (Generally, 1 hour per pound of beef.) Lower the heat to between 190^0F and 200^0F to further soften the meat until it is tender enough to drop off the bone. You can make the drippings into gravy or use as a marinade.

Vegetables can be braised in a deep pan over the stove with enough water to cover them to one-half their height. Bring the water to a boil, reduce to a simmer and cover the pan with a lid. In 30 minutes you will have firm braised vegetables.

Crockpot

Crockpot cooking is the ultimate no-muss, no-fuss cooking technique. You fill your crockpot with water, place the meat, vegetables and spices inside, plug it in and 6 to 8 hours later you have a meal. It is an excellent way to cook stews and soups. The low temperature of a crockpot is around 200^0F and the high temperature is around 250^0F.

Dutch Oven (Slow Cooking)

Dutch oven cooking has roots in the open campfire, fireplace hook, cast-iron pot and more recently, the covered enamel roasting pan. It is one of the oldest techniques of cooking in that it uses the ingredients' own juices and steam to cook drop-off-the-bone, melt-in-your-mouth recipes. The principle is to surround the ingredients with heat and let them cook. This needs very little or no attending. By placing a rack on the bottom of the pan, putting in ½ inch water to cover the bottom of the pan, placing the spices, herbs and aromatics in the water, placing the meat on top of the rack, covering the pan and placing it in the center of the oven at 220^0F to 230^0F for 6 to 8 hours, you will cook the tenderest brisket, pot roast or pork shoulder that you have ever tasted. (Please look at the dynamics of slow cooking below.) You may wish to use a dry rub of red or green chile powder, Adobo Spice Mix, garlic powder or any spice or herb to infuse your meat with flavor. You can also start a BBQ side of beef or ribs in a Dutch oven and then transfer it to a grill to sear-finish the outside with BBQ sauce.

Poaching

Poaching is the equivalent of pan-frying only with water or stock. Poaching is used to prepare very delicate dishes such as eggs, fruits and fish. You heat a shallow layer of water in a pan to between 140^0F and 180^0F until small bubbles form on the bottom of the pan. Gently place your ingredient in the pan and slow cook.

Pressure Cooking

Pressure cooking is the ultimate in steam-cooking because it is fast and tasty. In most cases, you place 1 to 2 cups of water in the pressure cooker, put in the ingredients, seal the top and in 5 to 10 or more minutes, the food is cooked. Vegetables, meats, grains and beans can all be prepared using a pressure cooker. For example, unsoaked beans are ready in 15 minutes versus in 3 to 4 hours of boiling. The taste is all there and the drippings can be used as a soup base.

Steaming

Steaming is best for vegetables and fish because the steam surrounds the ingredients and cooks at a gentle 212^0F. Steaming, the healthiest of all the cooking methods, leaves the nutrients and taste in their natural state. You will require a pot with a steam basket to keep the ingredients from touching the water.

REMEMBER—it is the internal temperature that dictates when a recipe is done, not the cooking temperature. Nothing tastes worse than an undercooked chicken or an overcooked enchilada. Generally, meats should have an internal temperature of a least 160^0F.

Slow Cooking

Slow cooking is an integral part of the chile cuisine. Most cuts of beef and pork used in the majority of chile recipes, such as brisket, rump roast, shoulder steak, pork picnic and butt cuts are fairly tough, have a high level of fat and are the best tasting and least expensive. The best way to prepare these cuts of meat and have them fall off the bone is to use slow cooking with a Dutch oven or heavy, covered pot. I would recommend using a slow cook temperature between 225^0F to 240^0F for optimal results over a 6 to 8 hour period. At an internal temperature of 105^0F to 120^0F degrees the meat starts its aging process and the enzymes in the meat start to decompose some of the connective tissue around the meat cells. From 120^0F to 140^0F, the meat starts to coagulate, turns pink and starts to push out water molecules from the cell. This would be considered rare and if cut, the meat will release juices. Between 140^0F to 150^0F, the meat begins to lose a lot of the liquids stored in its cells, starts to shrink and toughen up and turns from pink to brown-grey. This is when it is at its toughest. If you have ever had shoe-leather tough meat, it was because the internal temperature did not go above 150^0F.

From 150^0F to 160^0F, the heat starts to dissolve the connective tissue (toughness) from the meat cells and turns them into a gelatinous liquid that will ultimately become your gravy. At 160^0F to 170^0F degrees internal temperature, the meat reaches its fall-off-the-bone-tenderness. Remove the meat from the oven and let it cool for 5 to 10 minutes. This will set all of the gelatin and tenderness so the meat is ready for shredding, slicing or cubing depending on what your recipe calls for.

Slow cooked meat will freeze well for up to six months. I put the meat into sandwich bags in 1-lb. portions, pour in a bit of gravy, squeeze out the air and place them into a larger gallon freezer bags for freezing. This will prevent freezer burn or air leaking into the meat. I always have a supply of fall-off-the-bone sweetness for any recipe.
See Chapter13 The Chemistry of Slow Cooking (p.377)

RECIPE RATING

I have established an easy-to-use recipe rating system to allow you to evaluate the degree of difficulty and time that will be required to prepare any recipe in this book.

EZ: Less than 30 minutes.
Prep and cook 1 to 3 ingredients.

COOK: 30 minutes to 1 hour.
Prep and cook 2 to 5 ingredients.

SLOW: 30 minutes to 1 hour prep.
Slow cook 2 to 8 hours.
The oven or crockpot does the work.

CHEF: 1 to 4 hours prep and cook,
multiple steps.
Get creative and enjoy the cooking experience.

CHAPTER 1 ESSENTIAL RECIPES:

ESSENTIAL RECIPES are those you wish you had learned from your mother or grandmother. They are the soul of cooking. If you give an ingredient to a chef, he or she will immediately think of numerous ways to prepare it, what cooking technique to use, what sauces will blend well, what spices to use and how to serve it. It is not that chefs have a cookbook memorized, but rather they have ESSENTIAL RECIPES that they use over and over again to prepare food and meals.

In the Red or Green Chile Bible, I have attempted to present the essential things you must know to prepare red and green chile, as well as, the ingredients, spices and cooking techniques that make the chile cuisine one of the worlds most popular.

The chile cuisine has many essential recipes, spices and ingredients that are prerequisites for the Chilenista palate. First and foremost is the preparation of chile for subsequent use with every recipe in this book. Your choice of chiles that are available is the most important decision that you will have to make. Fresh chiles, whether green or red, are seasonal and can be prepared and frozen at harvest time for use during the entire year. This is especially true for the New Mexico Anaheim chile varieties available from the beginning of August through the middle of September. The Hatch Chile Festival celebrates the fall harvest at this time. Chile roasters pop up all over the Southwest, permeating the air with the aroma of chiles roasting.

Chile is often unpredictable in regard to how hot it becomes. The amount of capsaicin that is stored in its pod is determined by the soil conditions, humidity and sun that the chile plant receives during its growing cycle. Harvesting and labeling are not an exact science; each batch of chiles grown has its own unique flavor and SHU characteristics. In order to prepare and cook with chile, you have to determine how hot and aromatic you want to make your chile recipes.

I have developed numerous essential recipes for red and green chile that will show you how to prepare and store chile, for immediate and subsequent use.

RED CHILE ESSENTIAL RECIPES

Red chile is the fruit of the vine that has been allowed to ripen and bask in the late sunlight of the Southwest. Its mellow taste and sweetness is often preferred by Chilenistas in stews, salsas and condiments. The following ESSENTIAL RECIPES will allow you to prepare and store red chiles and red chile powders for use in all of the recipes throughout this Red or Green Chile Bible.

What I mean by ESSENTIAL RECIPES is just that. The flavor, texture and consistency of preparing red chile are the same for all recipes. By preparing and storing ground or dried chile pods in a paste, you will be able to progress and flavor it for any subsequent use in your appetizers salsas, side dishes, stews and entrée recipes. The choices of red chiles for taste and Scoville Heat Units are listed in the chart below. You can make an enchilada sauce or stew using any chile flavor you wish and I encourage you to try them all. The beauty of chile is the broad spectrum of flavors, heat levels and consistency of the sauce you can make.

Red Chile SHU / Flavor Chart

PODS / GROUND POWDER	SHU	TASTE	PODS/ CUP
Anaheim Red			
-Mild	500–800	Sweet, fruity, nutty	4/
-Medium Hot	800–1,200	Sweet, fruity, nutty	4/
-Hot	1,200–1,800	Pungent, fruity, nutty	4/
-X Hot	1,800–2,500+	Pungent, fruity, nutty	4/
Ancho	1,000–2,000	Sweet, fruity	4/
Pasilla	1,000–2,000	Pungent, herbal	6/
Chipotle	5,000–8,000	Smoky, grassy	10/
Chile Seco	8,000–18,000	Smoky, fruity	10/
De Arbol	15,000–30,000	Hot, grassy, nutty	Powder
Cayenne	80,000–90,000	Sweat-producing	Powder
Habanero	150,000– 300,000	Blistering heat	Powder

Each red chile variety has its own unique flavor and Scoville Heat rating and is available in most supermarkets or online. Chile stores as pods or as a ground powder.

RED CHILE PASTE
MADE FROM RED CHILE POWDER

Complexity Code: EZ   Origin: New Mexico
Cooking Method: Re-Hydrate / Simmer

About the Recipe: Preparing your Red Chile Paste for subsequent use in recipes is the key to great cooking. You will be using these prepared and stored ESSENTIAL RECIPES throughout the book, rather than having to make them every time you cook.

Essential Recipe: Adobo Spice Mix (p. 83)

Ingredient	Measure	Spices	Measure
Red chile powder SHU to taste See chart (pg. 32)	2 cups	Adobo Spice Mix (p. 83)	1 Tbsp.
Water or broth stock	4 cups	Sweetener (pg. 85)	2 Tbsp.
Vegetable oil, butter or lard	½ cup		

Prep Instructions

The secret to consistently preparing any red chile recipe is control of the heat level of the chile itself. When chile is harvested, the grower estimates the SHU heat level for processing. The art of chile grading varies by the season and supply. Mild chile can be mixed in with medium and hot, or vice versa.

The only way to accurately use chile powder is to make a paste by hydrating 1 cup of chile powder to 2 cups of water. The chile will take about 1 hour to hydrate by itself or you can put it in a quart saucepan over a very low heat.

Taste the paste. If too mild, put in the next higher SHU powder, one tablespoon at a time. If too hot, use a tablespoon of melted butter or a small can of tomato sauce.

Chile paste is ideal for flavoring with coriander, cumin, oregano, garlic powder, parsley, rosemary, sage and thyme. Add 1 teaspoon at a time. You may also add sweetener such as guava paste, piloncillo, sugar, honey or maple syrup, by the tablespoon. I find that the Adobo Spice Mix recipe is an ideal flavor enhancer for almost any chile recipe. There are no rules. Your taste buds are the best judge of the right levels of heat and taste.

Label and store the chile paste in 1-pint containers. (Yogurt containers are excellent for this.) Store in your refrigerator for up to four weeks or freeze for subsequent use. Some people use an ice cube tray to freeze the paste into balls and then store in a plastic bag. This way you always have chile ready whenever you need a fix.

All of the red chile recipes in this book will refer to this prepared chile paste recipe.

Servings: 1 pt. You can scale up the recipe by using a 1 cup red chile powder to 2 cups of water.

RED CHILE PASTE
MADE FROM FRESH RED CHILE PODS

Complexity Code: EZ   Origin: New Mexico
Cooking Method: Boil / Simmer

About the Recipe: If you are fortunate and can get fresh red chile pods in season, use this recipe for Red Chile Paste that you can freeze and use year-round. Served fresh, it is the ultimate Chilenista rush. You can spoon it on a cracker or add it to any recipe.
Essential Recipe: Adobo Spice Mix (p. 83)

Ingredient	Measure	Ingredient	Measure
Red chile pods SHU to taste See Chart (p. 42)	4 cups, 2–18 pods, depending on size	Adobo Spice Mix (p.83)	2 Tbsp.
Water or broth stock	1 cup	Sweetener (p. 85)	4 Tbsp.
		Balsamic vinegar	2 Tbsp.

Prep Instructions

Fire-roast chile pods over open flame until the skins starts to bubble. Line your stovetop with aluminum foil to catch any seeds that may spill out, or
Preheat your oven to 400^{0}F. Roast the chiles in a roasting pan under the broiler. Use a tong to turn and broil both sides until the skin starts to bubble.
Place roasted pods in a large plastic bag to sweat the skin off.
Cooking Instructions
When cool, peel the skins, rinse out the seeds and place in a saucepan.
Boil chiles for 10 minutes in water or stock.
Place chiles in a blender; add Adobo Spice Mix, sweetener and vinegar, and purée until you have a paste-like consistency.
Place chile paste in a jar, 1-pint container or Ziploc bag and refrigerate for subsequent use.

Suggested Complementary Dishes: Red Chile Paste can be progressed and used in any recipe calling for red chile sauce, soup, enchilada, condiment or garnish.

Servings: 4 cups

RED CHILE ROUX (FLOUR PASTE)

Complexity Code: COOK   Origin: New Mexico
Cooking Method: Pan roast / Simmer

About the Recipe: Many family red chile recipes in Northern New Mexico prefer thicker, hardier chile stews made with varieties of beans, meats and vegetables. This recipe is a hearty base for any red chile stew main course. In many traditional kitchens you will find a pot of chile stew on the stove that lasts for days. It may be the original fast-food. Roux can also be frozen in 1-pint containers.

Essential Recipe: Adobo Spice Mix (p. 83).

Ingredient	Measure	Ingredient	Measure
Red chile powder SHU to taste See Chart (p. 32)	1 cup	Adobo Spice Mix (p.83)	2 Tbsp.
Masa harina, corn flour, flour (unbleached)	½ cup	Water or broth stock	4+ cups
Oil	½ cup	Sweetener (p. 85)	1 Tbsp.

Prep Instructions

Start with ½ cup of any vegetable oil, rendered fat or lard in a 3- to 4-quart stockpot. Heat to 300^0F or until it is almost ready to bubble. (Drop a pinch of flour into the oil and if it starts to bubble, the oil is ready.)

Cooking Instructions

Put in flour and immediately turn the heat to low. Stir quickly to keep the flour from scorching as it absorbs the oil. Keep stirring until you smell the flour cooking and see it turning color. (The longer you cook flour, the darker it gets and the more pronounced the flavor.)

Add 4 cups of water or soup stock to the roux to thin it out and add 1 cup of red chile powder, (mild, medium or hot), constantly stirring until the roux, liquid and chile powder are blended.

Bring the roux and chile mixture to a simmer and add an additional 3 to 4 cups of water or soup stock one cup at a time until the chile is as thick or thin as you like.

Taste the chile paste. If too mild, add the next higher SHU powder, one tablespoon at a time. If too hot, add a tablespoon of crema or cream cheese, milk or a small can of tomato sauce to cut the heat. Personalize your chile by adding your preferred spices and herbs. Use coriander, cumin, oregano, garlic powder, cilantro, parsley, rosemary, sage or thyme, a pinch of clove or nutmeg and a tablespoon of sweetener such as guava paste, piloncillo or sugar.

You can store, freeze and use your Red Chile Roux for any recipe in the book. Or if I may suggest, the red chile roux is now ready for the main event.

Suggested Complementary Dishes: Use the roux in any recipe that calls for a thick red chile sauce. Servings: 1 qt. You can scale up the amount by doubling the ingredients.

RED CHILE SAUCE

Complexity Code: EZ   Origin: New Mexico
Cooking Method: Simmer

About the Recipe: When someone tells you "I need a bowl of red," it is more than likely they are referring to this recipe. Everything else is a frill. This is the basic red chile recipe for making red chile sauce for any dish.
Essential Recipe: Red Chile Paste (p. 33). Red Chile Roux Paste (p. 35). Red Chile Pod Paste (p. 34),

Ingredient	Measure	Ingredient	Measure
Red Chile Paste (p. 32) SHU to taste	1 cup	Adobo Spice Mix (p.83)	1 Tbsp.
Water, broth, or meat drippings*	1–2 cups	Sweetener (p. 85)	2 Tbsp.
		Red chile powder	To taste

*Whenever possible use the natural (au jus) drippings from the meat dish that you are preparing as a substitute for water, or use a canned clear broth from a can. You can also add a bouillon cube, chicken, beef, or tomato to the water.

Prep Instructions
Blend 1 cup of chile paste with water to get the sauce consistency that you want. In most cases it should be a creamy soup to cover and stick to the entrée that you are making or garnishing. Some people like their chile the consistency of ketchup so it sticks to the dish. There are no rules. Add spices for aroma, sweetener and additional chile to kick up the SHU.

Cooking Instructions
Warm the chile paste over a low flame to a slight simmer for 15 to 20 minutes and stir to make sure that the chile does not burn. You can also warm the chile in a microwave 2 to 3 minutes or warm it in a 210^{0}F oven for 30 minutes to 1 hour in a covered pot. I have found that the oven method of slow cooking gives you the best flavor texture. You can also use a crockpot to get the same results.

RED CHILE TOMATO SAUCE

Complexity Code: EZ   Origin: New Mexico
Cooking Method: Simmer

About the Recipe: This great all around red chile tomato sauce can be used in almost every recipe. You can use this recipe as your spaghetti sauce, pizza topping, shrimp dip, enchilada sauce, ketchup replacement and in any recipe that calls for tomato sauce. You may never go back to having plain tomato sauce again.
Essential Recipe: Red Chile Paste (p. 33).

Ingredient	Measure	Ingredient	Measure
Tomatoes (preferably salt-free)	(2) 16-oz. cans chopped	Adobo Spice Mix (p.83)	2 Tbsp.
Tomato paste	(1) 6-oz. can	Garlic powder	1 Tbsp.
Olive oil	¼ cup	Oregano	1 Tbsp. ground
Red Chile Paste SHU to taste	1 cup	Sweetener (p. 85)	2 Tbsp.

Cooking Instructions

In a small 2- to 3-quart saucepan, line the bottom with olive oil and place on medium heat, empty 2 cans of salt-free chopped tomatoes, 2 Tbsp. of dry Adobo Spice Mix, and then garlic powder, crushed oregano and sweetener. Simmer over medium heat for 30 minutes

Purée tomato sauce with a blender stick, add 1 can of tomato paste, 1 cup of red chile paste and stir to blend all ingredients. Adjust to taste. If it needs more sweetening, add 1 to 2 Tbsp. of sweetener. Add additional chile powder to increase heat level.

Simmer in a crockpot or oven at low heat of 250^0F for 1 to 2 hours or in a covered pot or over low heat for 30 minutes to 1 hour, stirring frequently. Store red chile tomato sauce in 8-ounce containers for freezing or subsequent use.

To give an extra kick to this recipe, rehydrate 2 large pasilla or ancho chiles. Cut chile pods into ¼-inch square pieces and add to the sauce while simmering. Each chunk of chile in the sauce will give a burst of fruit flavor. Use a chipotle chile for a smoky flavor.

Suggested Complementary Dishes: Any recipe that requires a red sauce, pasta, enchiladas, tacos and as ingredients in salsa dishes or Red Chile Stew.

Servings: 48 oz.

CREAMY RED CHILE SAUCE

Complexity: COOK   Origin: New Mexico
Cooking Method: Sauté

About the Recipe: Creamy Red Chile Sauce brings velvety lusciousness
and texture to any red chile dish by combining the sweetness of crema
with pungent chile. It is a base recipe for use with almost any recipe that
calls for red chile, stews, sauce and toppings as a recipe ingredient.
Creamy Red Chile Sauce can be made in advance and used as needed.
You can refrigerate or freeze it in pint containers or Ziploc bags to have it
available when a chile emergency arises. You can also freeze the sauce in
an Ice cube tray and have red chile sauce balls if you wish to place one on
top of an egg, salad or other recipe.
Essential Recipe: Red Chile Paste (p. 33). Red Chile Roux Paste (p. 35).
Red Chile Pod Paste (p. 34).

Ingredient	Measure	Ingredient	Measure
Red chile paste	1 cups	Adobo Spice Mix (p.83)	1 Tbsp.
Crema or cream cheese	1 cup.	Garlic	1 tsp
Oil	¼ cup	Sweetener (p. 85)	1 Tbsp.
Flour	¼ cup	Red chile Powder	To taste

Prep Instructions

Blend 1 cup of chile paste with 1 cup crema to the consistency that you
want. In most cases it should be a creamy soup to cover and stick to the
entrée that you are making or garnishing. Some people like their chile
the consistency of ketchup so it sticks to the dish. There are no rules. Add
spices for aroma, sweetener and additional chile to kick up the SHU.

Cooking Instructions

Heat mixture over low heat until it starts to bubble, slowly adding crema or
cream cheese. Stir to blend and reduce the heat to low.
Prepare roux in a small saucepan by adding oil and heating to a frying
point of 350^{0}F.
Add flour to the oil and immediately reduce heat to medium at 200^{0}F,
stirring vigorously to prevent the roux from burning.
When the roux starts to turn color and thicken, carefully pour it into the
green chile sauce and increase the heat to a slow bubble. Stir until the roux
is completely blended into the chile sauce.

Reduce the heat to low and let the red chile simmer for about 15 to 20 minutes.

Taste the chile, add 1 Tbsp. of sweetener. Add coriander to give it a nutty taste. Add garlic or red chile powder to kick up the heat if you wish.

Suggested Complementary Dishes: Red chile stew, Red chile topping, Red chile condiment for tacos, enchiladas, chile relleno, pasta and any recipe that calls for a reds chile sauce.

Servings: 32 oz. that can be put into 8-oz. containers or Ziploc bags for subsequent use in any red chile recipe.

REHYDRATED RED CHILE PODS

Complexity Code: EZ   Origin: New Mexico
Cooking Method: Re-hydrate

About the Recipe: Dried red chile pods are available at most supermarkets or online stores. (See Vendors and Suppliers Index.) Rehydrate the pods by soaking in warm water for 1 to 2 hours until they are tender and flexible. Any of the chiles below can be rehydrated for your recipes.

Ingredient	SHU*	Taste	Pods/Cup
Anaheim Red			
-Mild	500–1,000	Sweet, fruity, nutty	6/
-Medium hot	800–1,200	Sweet, fruity, nutty	6/
-Hot	1,200–1,800	Pungent, fruity, nutty	6/
-X Hot	1,800–2,500+	Pungent, fruity, nutty	6/
Ancho	1,000–2,000	Sweet, fruity	8/
Pasilla	1,000–2,000	Pungent, herbal	10/
Chipotle	5,000–8,000	Smoky, grassy	20/
Chile Seco	8,000–18,000	Smoky, fruity	20/
De Arbol	15,000–30,000	Hot, grassy, nutty	Powder
Cayenne	80,000–90,000	Sweat-producing	Powder
Habanero	150,000–300,000	Blistering heat	Powder

*Be sure to wear gloves when processing or handling the hotter chile pods.

Prep Instructions

Cut tops of red chiles and remove stems and seeds. Hydrate your chiles in a bowl of warm water for 1 to 2 hours until soft. (Overnight in the refrigerator will also work.) Remove hydrated chiles from the water. Discard soaking water. Cut chiles into ¼- to ½-inch squares. You can use a scissor or knife.

Rehydrated Chopped Red Chile Pods (Flavor Chunks)
Cut hydrated chile pods enhance the texture of any recipe when mixed into ingredients as chile flavor chunks that do not alter the ingredients' taste. (Think of putting raisins or blueberries into muffins.) They give a sudden burst of flavor while eating the food. The heat level and taste is your choice. New Mexico red chile pods give sweetness. Ancho chile has a fruity quality and pasilla has an herbal taste, chipotle has a smoky taste, chile seco to habanero have a burst of heat from sweet to blistering hot. It is always best to use moderation. Use optional flavoring as

above. (Anaheim chiles have a very tough skin when dried. I would not recommend using them for chopped red chile recipes.)

Red Chile Paste Made from Rehydrated Pods
To progress your rehydrated chile pods into a paste, place them into a blender or use a blender stick with ½ cup of water for every 10 to 20 chile pods and purée. The chile paste is now ready for use or store in containers or Ziploc bags. (Make sure to label.)

Red Chile Sauce Made from Rehydrated Pods
Add water or broth to thin paste into a sauce.
Add 1 Tbsp. Adobo Spice Mix, 1 tsp. vinegar, 1 Tbsp. sweetener, add red chile powder to increase the SHU or make thicker, add a pinch of clove or nutmeg to impart an aromatic flavor and salt to taste. (You can store the chile sauce in containers or Ziploc bags. (Make sure to label them.)

Red Chile Roux Made from Rehydrated Pods
Heat ¼ cup oil in a fry pan, add ¼ cup masa harina, corn flour or unbleached flour, and reduce the heat to a medium heat.
Add chile paste or cut hydrated chile pods into the roux mixture.
Keep stirring the roux mixture until the flour starts to turn color.
Add your favorite spices, garlic, coriander, oregano, etc., 1 teaspoon at a time.
Add 1 cup of water or soup stock, reduce heat to a simmer and cook for 15 to 20 minutes. Stir occasionally but make sure that the heat is low enough so that the roux does not bubble. You can sweeten it a bit if you wish.
You are now ready to progress your roux into gravy, chile topping or chile stew for use in almost every recipe in this book. Refrigerated, it will hold for over a week.

GREEN CHILE ESSENTIAL RECIPES

Green chiles are the fruit of the vine in its freshest state. They have the fruitiness, juiciness, energy and vibrancy of youth. Whether you eat them raw, roasted or sautéed, the flavor cannot be duplicated.

Green Chile SHU / Flavor Chart

PODS/GROUND POWDER	SHU	Taste	PODS /Cup
Anaheim Green			
-Mild	500–800	Sweet, fruity, nutty	6/
-Medium	800–1,200	Sweet, fruity, nutty	6/
-Hot	1,200–1,800	Sweet, fruity	6/
-X Hot	1,800–5,000	Sweet, pungent	6/
-XX Hot	5,000–70,000	Very pungent	6/
Poblano	1,000–2,000	Mild, fruity flavor Slight earthy/bitter	4/
Chilaca	1,000–2,000	Pungent, herbal undertones	10/
Jalapeño	5,000–8,000	Smoky and slightly spicy, grassy, fruity	10/
Serrano	8,000–18,000	Smoky, fruity	10/
Habanero	150,000– 300,000	Very pungent	15/
NM Scorpion	1,200,000	Blistering pungent	15/

GREEN CHILE PASTE
MADE FROM FRESH GREEN CHILE PODS

Complexity Code: EZ: Origin: New Mexico
Cooking Method: Fire-roast

About the Recipe: If you are fortunate enough to be able to get fresh
green chile pods, this is the recipe for Green Chile Paste. Served fresh, it
is the ultimate chilenista rush. You can spoon it on a cracker or add it to
any recipe to get your chile fix.
Essential Recipe: Adobo Spice Mix (p. 83).

Ingredient	Measure	Ingredient	Measure
Fresh Green chile SHU to taste Chart (p. 42)	6–24, depends on size chopped	Adobo Spice Mix (p.83)	2 Tbsp.
Water or broth stock	1 cup	Sweetener (p. 85)	2 Tbsp.
		Balsamic vinegar	2 Tbsp.

Prep Instructions
Fire-roast chile pods over open flame until the skin starts to bubble. (Line
your stovetop with aluminum foil to catch any seeds that spill out.)

OR
Preheat your oven to 425^0F and roast the chiles in a roasting pan under
the broiler. Use a tong to turn the chile over and broil both sides until the
skin starts to bubble. (Use oven mitts.)
When the chile pods are roasted, place them in a large plastic bag to sweat
the skins off.
When cool enough, peel the skins off, rinse out the seeds and place in a
saucepan.
Place water into saucepan and boil chiles for 10 minutes.
Place chiles in a blender. Add Adobo Spice Mix, sweetener and vinegar.
Purée until you have a paste-like consistency.

Suggested Complementary Dishes: Green Chile Paste can be
progressed and used in any recipe calling for Green Chile Sauce, soup,
enchilada, condiment, garnish or dip.

Servings: 4 cups.

FRESH GREEN CHILE

Complexity Code: EZ   Origin: New Mexico
Cooking Method: Raw, Blanch, Roast, Sauté, Steam

About the Recipe: For many years I passed the fresh chile counter of my grocery store with the popular belief that green chiles had to be fire-roasted over an open flame, skinned and refrigerated or frozen prior to use. BOY WAS I WRONG. After some experimenting and research I have found that fresh chiles are not only as flavorful as roasted chiles but also retain more of the capsaicin to be transferred to your recipe. Raw green chiles can be cut into strips, chopped and used raw as a garnish, in salads and side dishes, as well as sautéed as a side dish to enhance the flavor of any ingredient. They are also stuffed and used as a main dish.
The next time you are at your grocer, select a few meaty chile pods from the produce counter and try them. YOU WILL LIKE THEM!

Ingredient	Measure
Green chile pods (fresh) SHU to taste See chart (p. 42)	Any quantity

Prep Instructions

Wash green chile pods, cut off the top stems, scoop out the seed pods and cut in half. Remove the veins and any leftover seeds.
Cut chile in strips, for toppings, quarters for sautés or chop in ¼- or ½-inch squares for use in your recipe. It is that easy. No defrosting and no cans to open.

Variations

Raw green Chile, whether Anaheim, Poblano, Jalapeno or hotter varieties can be chopped, sliced into strips and added to any recipe as a garnish or ingredient to add bursts of flavor to any recipe.
Try pickling the raw chile as a condiment to enhance any dish. (Careful—it is addictive.)

Blanched Chile, Place in boiling water for 1 to 2 minutes until it starts to soften, remove and strain in a colander under cool water. You can use the chile in your recipe or purée it to make a paste, add adobo, some sweetener (guava paste, piloncillo, sugar) and salt to taste. Blanched chile is the fresh alternative to canned chile without any preservatives.

Oven-roasted Chile, is as close to flame-roasted as you can get. Preheat your oven to 425°F. Place chiles in oven for 15 to 20 minutes until they are soft. Peel the skin and serve as a vegetable, side dish or use in your recipe.

Sautéed Chile, is an easy stovetop recipe to prepare fresh chile in strips or chopped. Place 2–4 Tbsp. of oil in a sauté pan. On high heat sauté chile to the texture that you wish. Add Adobo Spice Mix and sweetener to flavor for your taste. You can also sauté chile with onion, squash, tomato and zucchini. Add beans, rice or pasta and you can create an endless variety of easy-to-make side dishes.

Steamed Chile, place whole chiles that have been seeded in a steamer for 5–6 minutes and you will have a steamed whole chile that can garnish your recipes or be progressed into any recipe.

Chile In a Hurry: Many recipes call for chopped green chile to be added as an ingredient within the recipe. I have found that if you are in an extreme hurry and are willing to sacrifice some flavor, **NUKE IT** in a microwave as a substitute for blanched OR Roasted chiles. You can microwave your chiles (Anaheim, poblano, jalapeño or serrano) a few pods at a time, use frozen chiles that were prepared with ESSENTIAL RECIPE Roasting Chiles (p. 32) or you can use whole, canned chiles that have been rinsed well. Wash chiles, cut in half, remove stems, seeds and veins. Cut chile pod into strips or ½-inch squares. Place chopped chile into a microwaveable mixing bowl. Pour 1 cup water on top of chiles. Microwave for 3 to 5 minutes until chiles are soft. You are now ready to place the chopped green chile into your recipe or use it as a garnish.
Preparing chile does not have to be a whole day affair.

FLAME-ROASTED GREEN CHILE

Complexity Code: EZ   Origin: New Mexico
Cooking Method: Flame Roasting

About The Recipe: Every year starting in mid-August and for most
of September, it is chile-roasting time in New Mexico. Almost every
supermarket takes on the unmistakable aroma of fresh chiles roasting.
Usually the chiles come in 20-lb. sacks fresh from the farm. Anaheim and
Big Jim chiles are graded as mild, medium, hot and XX hot. The season
crescendos during the first week in September at the Hatch Chile Festival
where Chilenistas from all over the world come to get their chile fix and
supply of roasted chiles for the rest of the year.
It is possible to roast your own, but it is not as much fun.

Ingredient	Measure
Anaheim – Big Jim Chiles	20-lb. sack
SHU to taste	

Prep Instructions

Purchased fresh-roasted chiles: Let roasted chiles cool and sweat in
the plastic bag for about a half-hour. Pull out a few chiles at a time and
peel the skins off by rubbing the chiles in your hands. A plastic glove is
suggested if you have delicate skin. Rinse the chiles under cold water if you
are having problems peeling them. Cut off the stems and remove as many
of the seeds as you can from inside the chile. Rinsing will help. Place the
chiles inside a one-gallon Ziploc bag and position the chiles next to each
other, ready to freeze.
Squeeze as much of the air as you can out of the bag and zip it. I can
generally get 12 chiles in a bag and use them year-round.

Cooking Instructions

Roast your own: There are many techniques for roasting your own
chiles. Each one is messy, so I recommend that you line your range top
with aluminum wrap, leaving a cut-out for the flame. This will not work on
electric or induction stoves.
Unless you want to roast each chile one at a time with a tong, I would
recommend that you place 6 to 12 chiles in a flat BBQ grill basket, hold
it over an open flame and char the skins of the chile until each starts to
bubble. You can do the same over an open flame of your stove, broiler or
BBQ grill.
When the chiles are charred, put them into a plastic bag to sweat for 15
minutes to ½ hour and peel the skin as above. You are now ready to use
the chiles to make Chile Relleno, Stew, Green Chile Sauce or sauté them
as a side dish.

Other Green Chile Options:

Frozen green chile: Anaheim or Big Jim: You can purchase frozen green chile that is already chopped at most super markets. When defrosted, it can be used in any recipe.

Canned green chile: Canned green chile is used in making stews and sauces, however, it does not have the texture of fresh or frozen. Make sure you rinse out all of the preservatives that are used to extend the life of the canned green chile before you use it.

Green chile powder: The powder is used as a spice to sprinkle over food or is reconstituted as a paste for use in recipes. Make sure you taste-check the SHU of any chile powder. You can use the same recipes to make Green Chile Paste or Red Chile Paste for your recipes.

NOTE: Chili powder that is available in the grocer's spice rack is a blend of many spices and is not real chile.

Poblano and jalapeño chiles are generally not roasted. They are used within the recipes or as a garnish to add zest to any meal. You can roast these chiles, however, and use them in place of the Anaheim chiles.

BLANCHED GREEN CHILE (CHOPPED)

Complexity Code: EZ   Origin: New Mexico
Cooking Method: Blanch / Sauté

About the Recipe: Many recipes call for chopped green chile added
as an ingredient within the recipe. I have found that blanched chile is
an easy substitute for roasted chiles. It can be cooked to order without
having to roast chiles over an open flame and can give you the flexibility of
determining the SHU heat level that you wish to add to the recipe—from
mild to blistering hot.
You can blanch your chiles (Anaheim, poblano, jalapeño or serrano) a few
pods at a time, use frozen chiles that were prepared with
Essential Recipe: roasted (Chiles (p. 44) or you can use whole canned
chiles that have been rinsed well.

Ingredient	Measure	Ingredient	Measure
Fresh Green Chile SHU to taste Chart (p. 42)		Oil, butter or lard	2 Tbsp.
Anaheim or Big Jim Mild -Medium -Hot- -X-Hot	4–6 pods/1 cup chopped		
Poblano	2–3 pods/1 cup chopped		
Jalapeño	8–12 pods/1 cup chopped		
Serrano	12–18 pods/ 1 cup chopped		

Prep Instructions

Wash chiles, cut in half, remove stems, seeds and veins. Cut chile pod into
strips or ½-inch squares.

Cooking Instructions

Coat the bottom of a heavy frying pan with vegetable oil, butter or lard.
Heat pan over high flame to 400°F.
Place chopped chile into the hot oil and stir until it starts to smell and
slightly pop (about 3 to 5 minutes). Pour ½ cup water into pan and let
steam 2 to 3 minutes until soft.
You are now ready to place the chopped green chile into your recipe or
use it as a garnish.

GREEN CHILE ROUX (FLOUR PASTE)

Complexity Code: COOK   Origin: New Mexico
Cooking Method: Sauté

About the Recipe: Many family chile recipes in Northern New Mexico prefer a thicker, hardier chile that is used in stews with many varieties of beans, meats and vegetables that are seasonably available as a main course. In many traditional homes you will find a pot of chile stew on the stove that can last for days. It may be the original fast-food. It can also be frozen in 1-pint containers to have a chile fix any time you need it.
Essential Recipe: Green Chile Paste (p. 43).

Ingredient	Measure	Ingredient	Measure
Green Chile Paste Or	2 cup	Adobo Spice Mix (p.83)	2 Tbsp.
Green chile powder SHU to taste See Chart (p. 42)	½ cup		
Flour	½ cup	Water or broth stock	4 cups
Oil	½ cup	Sweetener (p. 85)	2 Tbsp.
		Optional herbs to taste	

Cooking Instructions

Start making your roux by placing a ½ cup of any vegetable oil, rendered fat or lard into a large frying pan. Heat the oil or lard until it is viscous and almost ready to bubble (300°F). Drop a pinch of flour into the oil; if it starts to bubble, the oil is ready.
Immediately lower the heat to medium (200°F degrees). Put in ½ cup of flour and stir as fast as you can to keep the flour from scorching as it absorbs the oil. Keep stirring until you can smell the flour cooking and see it turning color. (The longer you cook the flour, the darker it will get and the more pronounced flavor it will have.)
Add 4 cups of water or broth stock to the roux to thin it. Add 2 cups green chile paste or ½ cup green chile powder, constantly stirring until the roux, liquid and chile are blended together.
Bring the roux and chile mixture to a simmer and add 3 to 4 cups of water or broth stock one cup at a time to bring the chile to the consistency you like. Taste the chile in its paste form. If it is too mild, put in a few tablespoons of the next higher SHU powder. If it is too hot, put in a tablespoon of crema or cream cheese, milk or a small can of tomato sauce to cut the heat level down.

You are now ready to add your spices and herbs. Use Adobo Spice Mix, or optionally, cilantro, parsley, rosemary, sage or thyme and a tablespoon of sweetener (guava paste, piloncillo, sugar or maple syrup).

You can store, freeze or use your Green Chile Roux for any of the recipes in the book. Or, if I may suggest, the Green Chile Roux is now ready for the main event.

Suggested Complementary Dishes: You can use Green Chile Roux in any recipe that calls for a thick, Green Chile Sauce, or thin it for soups, stews, sauces, garnishes or dips.

Servings: 1 qt. Double the ingredients to scale up the serving size.

GREEN CHILE SAUCE

Complexity Code: EZ   Origin: New Mexico
Cooking Method: Sauté

About the Recipe: Green Chile Sauce can complement and spice up almost any dish or recipe and can be used from mild to extra hot to please any palate.

Essential Recipe: Roasted, blanched, frozen or canned Fresh Green Chile, (p. 44).

Ingredient	Measure	Ingredient	Measure
Fresh Green Chile Anaheim, Big Jim, Poblano, Jalapeño, Serrano SHU to taste	1 cup chopped	Adobo Spice Mix (p.83)	2 Tbsp.
Onion	½ cup chopped	Garlic clove or Powdered garlic	1 ½ Tbsp.
Water, broth or meat drippings*	2 cups+	Sweetener (p. 85)	1 Tbsp.
Flour	2 Tbsp.	Vegetable oil, butter	¼ cup

*Whenever possible use the natural (au jus) drippings from the meat dish that you are preparing as a substitute for water, or use a clear broth from a can. You can also add a bouillon cube, chicken, beef, or tomato, to the water.

Prep Instructions

Chop fresh or frozen chile or well-rinsed, canned chile. (Rinse well to remove the preservatives used in canned chiles.)
Chop a medium onion into ¼-inch squares. Chop or mince garlic clove.

Cooking Instructions

In a medium saucepan, sauté the onion and garlic in the oil over medium-high heat until tender.
Stir in the flour to make a paste, making sure that you keep stirring over a low heat until the oil and flour are blended.
Add chopped chile, water and spices and bring the mixture to a simmer while stirring. If you want a smooth consistency, you can blend the sauce with a blender stick. Add additional water if you want the sauce thinner.

Suggested Complementary Dishes: You can use this chile sauce for any green chile dish as a stew, topping, dip or ingredient for any entrée.

Servings: 4-6 cups

CREAMY GREEN CHILE SAUCE

Complexity: COOK   Origin: New Mexico
Cooking Method: Sauté

About the Recipe: Creamy Green Chile Sauce brings lusciousness to any green chile dish by combining the sweetness of crema with pungent chile. It is a basic recipe for use with almost any recipe that calls for green chile, stews, sauce and toppings as a recipe ingredient.

Creamy Green Chile Sauce can be made in advance and used as needed. You can refrigerate or freeze it in pint containers or Ziploc bags to have it available when a chile emergency arises. You can also freeze the sauce in an Ice cube tray and have green chile sauce balls if you wish to place one on top of an egg, salad or other recipe.

Essential Recipe: Roasted, blanched, frozen or canned Fresh Green Chile (p. 44).

Ingredient	Measure	Ingredient	Measure
Fresh Green Chile	2 cups chopped	Adobo Spice Mix (p.83)	1 Tbsp.
Crema or cream cheese	½ cup.	Garlic	1 tsp
Water	½ cup	Sweetener (p. 85)	1 Tbsp.
Oil	¼ cup		
Flour	¼ cup		

Prep Instructions

Chop fresh chiles into ¼-inch squares. Use blanched, steamed, roasted or canned as per the above ESSENTIAL RECIPES. (If you are using a canned chile, make sure to rinse and strain out all of the preservatives.) Place chiles in a quart saucepan, add water and purée to a coarse consistency with a hand stick blender.

Cooking Instructions

Heat mixture over medium heat until it starts to bubble, slowly adding crema or cream cheese. Stir to blend and reduce the heat to low.

Prepare roux in a small saucepan by adding oil and heating to a frying point of 350^0F.

Add flour to the oil and immediately reduce heat to medium at 200^0F, stirring vigorously to prevent the roux from burning.

When the roux starts to turn color and thicken, carefully pour it into the green chile sauce and increase the heat to a slow bubble. Stir until the roux is completely blended into the chile sauce.

Reduce the heat to low and let the green chile simmer for about 15 to 20 minutes.

Taste the chile. If it is too sour (as some canned chiles are), add 1 Tbsp. of sweetener. Add coriander to give it a nutty taste. Add garlic or green chile powder to kick up the heat if you wish.

Suggested Complementary Dishes: Green chile stew, green chile topping, green chile condiment for tacos, enchiladas, chile relleno, pasta and any recipe that calls for a green chile sauce.
Servings: 32 oz. that can be put into 8-oz. containers or Ziploc bags for subsequent use in any green chile recipe.

GREEN CHILE SAUTÉ

Complexity Code: EZ   Origin: New Mexico
Cooking Method: Sauté

About the Recipe: Sautéed green chile will allow you to use strips or chopped chiles for any sandwich, burrito, entrée, salad, sauce or dip. Although best used fresh, it can be frozen or stored and used as needed.
Essential Recipe: Oven-roasted, blanched Fresh Green Chili (p. 44), or frozen or canned chopped green chile.

Ingredient	Measure	Ingredient	Measure
Fresh Green chile pods	6 -8	Adobo Spice Mix (p.83)	1 Tbsp.
Butter, oil	¼ cup	Sweetener (p. 85)	1 tsp.
Water	¼ cup		

Prep Instructions
Place butter or oil in frying pan or skillet and heat to melt.

Cooking Instructions
Place chile pods in heated butter or oil, reduce to a low heat, add water and spices and cover pan. Sauté for 10 to 15 minutes. Turn chiles in pan to absorb spices and soak.
Remove chiles from pan and cut into strips or chop into squares.

Suggested Complementary Dishes: Use sautéed chile to complement any dish as a topping, condiment or ingredient. Eggs, sandwiches, salads, soups, entrées, sauces and dips—everything tastes better with green chile on it.
Servings: 2-4 cups

MEAT ESSENTIAL RECIPES

There are many ways to prepare meat, beef, pork, poultry and fish for the chilenista cuisine, either red or green. The following recipes will guide you in making even the toughest meat into a fall-off-the-bone tenderness to combine with your favorite chile recipe. Whether you are preparing the meat for stews, enchiladas or your main dish, it is important that the meat reaches the proper internal temperature to be safe for serving.

CHORIZOS

Complexity Code: EZ   Origin: New Mexico
Cooking Method: Pan-Fry

About the Recipe: Chorizos are a perfect accompaniment to any egg breakfast recipe as a side or as an ingredient for scrambled eggs or migas.
Essential Recipe: Red Chile Sauce (p. 36).

Ingredient	Measure	Ingredient	Measure
Chile-ground pork (coarse ground) OR Italian sausages	1 lb.	Adobo Spice Mix (p.83)	4 Tbsp.
Red Chile Sauce SHU to taste	½ cup	Caraway seed*	1 tsp.
Tomato sauce or ketchup	¼ cup	Cilantro	1 cup
Vinegar (balsamic or wine)	2 Tbsp.	Sweetener (p. 85)	2 Tbsp.
Oil or butter	¼ cup	Hot sauce*	To taste
Water	2 Tbsp.	Clove*	Pinch to taste
Flour	2 Tbsp.	Nutmeg*	Pinch to taste

*Optional

Prep Instructions

If using Italian sausages remove the casing and then place in a 3- to 4-quart mixing bowl.
In a mixing bowl combine chile-ground pork with red chile sauce, tomato sauce, vinegar and water, Adobo Spice Mix, cilantro and sweetener. Add hot sauce and aromatic spices to taste.
Mix well until all ingredients are thoroughly blended.
Add oil to a heavy skillet and preheat to very hot.

Cooking Instructions

Place chile-ground pork mixture into fry pan in small pinches of ½ inch each and cover bottom of pan with meat.
Occasionally turn meat over with a spatula. Cook until meat starts to brown.Place 2 Tbsp. of flour on top of meat and turn with a spatula until the flour is absorbed by the juices on the bottom of the pan.
Remove from heat and let cool for 5 minutes.

Suggested Complementary Dishes: Serve chorizos on the side of eggs.
Serves: 4 to 6 people

CHICKEN (WET COOK)

Complexity Code: EZ   Origin: Original
Cooking Method: Fast Cook / Slow Cook / Crockpot / Parboil

About the Recipe: "It tastes just like chicken" is one of the most widely stated misconceptions that I have ever heard. It is true, however, that improperly cooked chicken will often dry out and taste like a substance devoid of its own flavor.
Chicken is one of the mainstays of the chilenista's diet, and this recipe allows you to prepare chicken for any recipe in this book.
I would highly recommend selecting chicken thighs, for they are the tastiest and meatiest of all parts of a chicken, however chicken breasts will also work well.

Ingredient	Measure	Ingredient	Measure
Chicken thighs Boned or whole	8–12	Red or Green Chile powder	Rub top and bottom
Water	¼» on bottom of pan	Garlic powder	As above
		Coriander powder	As above
		Rosemary	As Above
		Thyme	As above

Prep Instructions
Remove skin and fat from chicken thigh.
Remove bone and fillet thigh, if desired. (You can cook the thigh with the bone in. It will fall out when it is cooked.)
Rub spices on both top and bottom.
Pour ¼ inch water into pan or Dutch oven.
Place chicken skins on bottom of pan. (This will add flavor to the au jus sauce.)
Place rack on bottom of pan.
Cover pan with aluminum foil tent, making sure that there is enough air around the chicken.

Cooking Instructions
Fast Cook
Preheat oven to 350^{0}F.
Place cooking pan into center of oven for 45 to 50 minutes. The chicken will be ready when the internal temperature reaches 165^{0}F. Remove chicken from the oven and let cool for 15 to 30 minutes. You can then shred, cube or filet.
Slow Cook
Reduce the oven heat to 235^{0}F.

Place pan in oven for 3 hours until the internal temperature reaches 165^{0}F.

Remove chicken from the oven and let cool for 15 to 30 minutes.

Drain the liquid into a bowl for subsequent use as a broth, au jus sauce or gravy.* (This makes an excellent au jus for making red chile or green chile sauce.)

You can now shred, cube or filet the chicken for your entrée.

Crockpot

Place chicken into a crockpot, add spices and water on low setting. The chicken thighs will be ready in 5 to 6 hours and in 3 to 4 hours at high heat.

Servings: Approximately 4–6 oz. per person.

Par-boil Steaming

You can prepare chicken for subsequent sautéing or frying in recipes by parboiling or steaming, allowing the meat to cool and then storing for use.

Place whole, half or quartered chicken into a steamer or a crockpot with a steaming basket on the bottom.

Bring pot to a boil for 15 to 20 minutes until the chicken is soft and reaches an internal temperature of 165^{0}F. Remove chicken from the steamer and let cool.

Drain the liquid into a bowl for subsequent use as a broth, au jus sauce or gravy.*

Debone the chicken and store in plastic bags or freeze to have chicken meat as you need it for any recipe. I have found that the steaming retains all of the chicken taste and enhances it.

You can also coat the parboiled chicken with rice flour for subsequent super-crispy frying.

*Broth or au jus sauce from chicken drippings

Drain the drippings from the Dutch oven or pan into a bowl and place in the refrigerator to solidify the fat. Once you see the fat form on the surface, skim it off. The remaining juices make an ideal base for any red or green chile sauce and can also be used as a liquid for masa and any other dough or filling recipe.

You can also progress the au jus as a gravy for any dish. You can store the juices (gravy) in a jar in the refrigerator or freeze them in a container. I much prefer the natural au jus to prepared or canned broth.

Suggested Complementary Dishes: Any meat recipe in this book.

PORK BUTT (WET COOK)

Complexity Code: EZ   Origin: Original
Cooking Method: Dutch oven or covered roasting pan (Wet Cooking)

About the Recipe: Pork butt and picnic cuts are two of the sweetest meats that you can use for your chile recipes. They are a bit fattier and lend themselves to slow cooking. Pork should reach an internal temperature of 160^0F. The longer the cook time, the tenderer the meat becomes.
Pork butt is an ideal meat for enchiladas, tamales, tacos, burritos and any recipe that calls for shredded pork. It can be subsequently pan-fried as filling for burritos, enchiladas and tamales or cut in cubes to be used in either red or green chile stews.

Ingredient	Measure	Ingredient	Measure
Shoulder picnic and pork butt	4–6 lbs.	Red or green chile powder	Rub top and bottom
Water	Depending on cooking method (see below)	Garlic powder	As above
		Garlic clove	
		Coriander	As above
		Sugar or honey	As above

Prep Instructions
Remove meat from wrapper, Cryovac or supermarket packaging.
Rinse meat to get rid of any blood or preservatives. Towel-dry surface.
Rub chile powder, garlic powder, coriander and sugar around all sides of the pork butt.
Place a rack on the bottom of a Dutch oven or pan; pour ¼ inch of water on the bottom.
Place pork butt on rack skin side up. Place a whole garlic bulb along inside edge of pan.
Cover Dutch oven or place an aluminum foil tent over the pan, seal the edges and allow plenty of room for air to circulate.
Preheat oven to 350^0F and place Dutch oven or pan in the middle of the oven.

Cooking Instructions

High Heat, Fast Cook
You can cook a pork butt for about 45 minutes per pound at 350^0F until it reaches an internal temperature of 160^0F.
Note: The meat will be fairly tough but useable for most recipes.
Low Heat Slow Cook (Preferred Method)

Lower the heat in the oven to 230°F. Allow about 1 to 2 hours cooking time per pound until the internal temperature of 160°F is reached.

Remove from the oven and drain the gravy into a bowl for subsequent use. This makes an excellent au jus for making red chile or green chile sauce.*

Let the meat sit and cool in the pan for about 30 minutes, so the juices do not run out when you cut or shred the meat. If you wish, you can broil the meat for a few minutes to brown the top.

Cut any excess fat from the roast. You are now ready to cut, pull and cube the meat for your recipe.

Overnight Cooking

To cook the pork butt overnight, set your oven at 225°F and go to sleep. In the morning, or after 8 to 12 hours, you will have the tenderest pork that you have ever cooked or tasted. Most professional BBQ chefs prefer this cooking method.

Crockpot Cooking

For smaller cuts of pork butt (2–3 lbs.) you can calculate from 2 to 3 hours per pound on the low setting and 1½ to 2 hours per pound on the medium setting.

Place the pork butt in the crockpot, pour in 1 to 2 cups of water based on weight and add the desired spices.

When fully cooked, shred the pork butt using two forks to split the meat into shreds.

The excess meat can be easily frozen in sandwich bags for subsequent use.

Suggested Complementary Dishes: Any meat recipe in this book. Servings: Approximately 4–6 oz. per person.

Broth or Au Jus Sauce From Pork Butt Drippings

Drain the drippings from the Dutch oven or pan into a bowl and place in the refrigerator to solidify the fat. Once you see the fat form on the surface, skim it off.

The remaining juices make an ideal base for any red or green chile sauce and as a liquid for masa and any other dough or filling recipe.

You can also progress the au jus as a gravy for any dish. Store the juices (gravy) in a jar in the refrigerator or freezer. I much prefer the natural au jus to prepared or canned broth.

ROAST BEEF (WET COOK)

Complexity Code: EZ   Origin: Original
Cooking Method: Dutch oven or covered pan roasting (Wet Cooking)

About the Recipe: For chile recipes that call for beef, you can use the less expensive cuts such as brisket and shoulder cuts, which are a bit tougher and fattier and for the most part tastier when properly cooked. Slow cooking is the key, and the variable is time. The more time you allow the more tender the meat becomes as the collagen and connective tissues break down to a gelatinous taste treat so the meat will fall off the bone. The secret is the internal temperature of 140^0F to 160^0F and keeping the moisture in the meat.
Brisket is an ideal meat for enchiladas, tamales, tacos, burritos and any recipe that calls for shredded beef. It can be subsequently pan fried or cut in cubes to be used in either red or green chile stews.

Ingredient	Measure	Ingredient	Measure
Brisket, pot roast, rump roast	3–5 lbs.	Red chile	Rub on both sides
Water	Cover bottom of pan 1/4 "	Garlic powder	As above
		Coriander	As above
		Oregano	As above
		Salt (Use sparingly)	As above
		Whole garlic bulb	

Prep Instructions

Remove meat from wrapper, Cryovac or supermarket packaging.
Rinse meat to get rid of any blood or preservatives. Towel-dry surface.
Rub red chile, garlic powder, coriander, oregano and salt (use sparingly) on all sides of roast.
Place a rack on the bottom of a Dutch oven or pan. Pour ¼ inch of water on the bottom.
Place roast on rack skin or fat side up. Place a whole garlic bulb on side of pan.
Cover Dutch oven or place an aluminum foil tent over the pan and seal the edges and allow plenty of room for air to circulate.
Preheat oven to 325^0F and place Dutch oven or pan in the middle of the oven.

Cooking Instructions

High Heat, Fast Cook

If you are in a hurry, let roast cook for about 20 minutes per pound at 325^0F until it reaches an internal temperature of 145^0F

Note: The meat will be fairly tough but useable for most recipes if shredded.

Low Heat Slow Cook (Preferred Method)

Lower the heat in the oven to 235^0F. Allow about 1 to 2 hours cooking time per pound until the internal temperature of 145^0F is reached. Stick a toothpick into the meat and if it goes in without any resistance, the meat is tender. If the meat is at all hard, cook for an additional hour.

Remove from the oven and drain the gravy into a bowl for subsequent use. This makes an excellent au jus for making red chile or green chile sauce.*

Let the meat sit and cool in the pan for about 30 minutes, so the juices do not run out when you cut or shred the meat.

If you wish, you can broil the meat for a few minutes to brown the top. Cut any excess fat from the roast.

You are now ready to cut, shred, pull and or cube the meat for your recipe.

You can freeze the meat in sandwich bags for subsequent use.

Overnight Cooking

To cook the brisket overnight, set your oven at 225^0F and go to sleep. In the morning or in 8 to 12 hours, you will have the tenderest meat that you have ever tasted.

Crockpot Cooking

For smaller cuts of roast beef (2–3 lbs.) you can calculate from 2 to 3 hours per pound on the low setting and $1\frac{1}{2}$ to 2 hours per pound on the medium setting.

Place the roast in the crockpot, pour in 1 to 2 cups of water based on weight and add desired spices.

Suggested Complementary Dishes: Any meat recipe in this book. Servings: Approximately 4–6 oz. per person.

When fully cooked shred the beef using two forks to split the meat into shreds.

The excess meat can be easily frozen in sandwich bags for subsequent use.

*Broth or au jus sauce from meat drippings

Drain the drippings from the Dutch oven or pan into a bowl and place in the refrigerator to solidify the fat. Once you see the fat form on the surface, skim it off.

The remaining juices make an ideal base for any red or green chile sauce and as a liquid for masa and any other dough or filling recipe.

You can also progress the au jus as a gravy for any dish. You can store the juices (gravy) in a jar in the refrigerator or freeze. I much prefer the natural au jus to prepared or canned broth.

TACO GROUND BEEF (GREEN CHILE)

Complexity Code: EZ   Origin: New Mexico
Cooking Method: Sauté

About the Recipe: A great ground beef mixture will bring instant goodness to any carne dish from tacos, to burritos, enchiladas, chile con carne or even eaten á la carte on a tortilla or hamburger bun. This recipe has been time-tested and stored in a container or frozen for use with any meal or recipe.

Essential Recipe: Green Chile Sauce (p. 50). Roasted Green Chile (p. 46).

Ingredient	Measure	Ingredient	Measure
Lean ground beef	1 lb.	Adobo Spice Mix (p.83)	2 Tbsp.
Chile-ground pork (coarse ground) or Italian sausages	½ lb.	Green chile powder	2 Tbsp.
Green Chile Sauce	1 cup	Cilantro	1 cup chopped
Roasted Fresh Green Chile	1 cup chopped	Oil or butter	¼ cup

*Select the (SHU units of heat that you would like to blend into the ground beef mix from the charts (p. 40, p. 42). You will find basic chile properties in this chapter (p. 8) and in extensive detail in chapter 13 (p. 365).

Prep Instructions

If using Italian sausages, remove the casing from the sausage and then place in a 3- to 4-quart mixing bowl.

Place ground beef into mixing bowl; add adobo mix, green chile powder and blend pork and ground beef well.

Let sit for 15 to 30 minutes for the flavors to infuse into each other.

Cooking Instructions

Place oil or butter in heavy skillet over high heat.

Place ground beef mixture into skillet in ¼- to ½-inch clumps and sauté.

Move cooked beef to side of skillet as you are placing new meat into skillet. (Keep turning the meat so it does not burn.)

Turn heat to simmer for 15 to 20 minutes.

Add green chile sauce, chopped green chiles and chopped cilantro.

Simmer until all flavors have blended.

Add additional green chile powder for additional SHU to taste.

Suggested Complementary Dishes: Any carne dish in this book.

Servings: (4) 6-oz. servings.

TACO GROUND BEEF (RED CHILE)

Complexity Code: EZ   Origin: Original
Cooking Method: Sauté

About the Recipe: A great ground beef mixture will bring instant goodness to any carne dish from tacos to burritos, enchiladas, chile con carne or even eaten á la carte on a tortilla or hamburger bun. This recipe has been time-tested and can be stored in a container or frozen for use with any meal or recipe.

Essential Recipe: Red Chile Sauce (p. 36) Rehydrated Red Chile pods (p. 40).

Ingredient	Measure	Ingredient	Measure
Lean ground beef	1 lb.	Adobo Spice Mix (p.83)	2 Tbsp.
Chile-ground pork (coarse ground) or Italian sausages	½ lb.	Ketchup or tomato paste	½ cup
Red Chile Sauce	1 cup	Cilantro	1 cup chopped
Rehydrated Red Chile Pods Ancho, Pasilla, Chipotle SHU to taste	1 cup	Oil or lard	¼ cup

Prep Instructions

If using Italian sausages, remove the casing before placing in a 3- to 4-quart mixing bowl.

Chop Rehydrated Red Chile Podsinto ¼-inch squares (removing stems and seeds).

Place ground beef into mixing bowl. Add Adobo Spice Mix and tomato paste.

Blend pork and ground beef well.

Let sit for 15 to 30 minutes for the flavors to infuse into each other.

Cooking Instructions

Place oil or lard in heavy skillet over high heat.

Place ground beef mixture into skillet in ¼- to ½-inch clumps and sauté. Move cooked beef to the side of skillet as you are placing new meat into skillet. (Keep turning the meat so it does not burn.)

Turn heat to simmer for 15 to 20 minutes. Taste and add Red Chile Sauce, chopped red chiles and chopped cilantro.

Simmer meat under low heat for spices to blend. Add additional hot sauce for additional heat and any additional spices that you may want.

Suggested Complementary Dishes: Any carne dish in this book.
Servings: (4) 6-oz. servings.

SAUTÉED BEEF, CHICKEN OR PORK, RED OR GREEN

Complexity Code: EZ   Origin: New Mexico
Cooking Method: Sauté

About the Recipe: A great recipe that can be prepared in very little time to create and awesome meal for tacos, burritos, enchiladas, chile con carne or even eaten á la carte on a tortilla or hamburger bun. This recipe has been time-tested and stored in a container or frozen for use with any meal or recipe.

Essential Recipe: Green Chile Sauce (p. 50), Roasted Green Chile (p. 46) OR Red Chile Sauce (p.36), Rehydrated Chile Pods (p.40).

Ingredient	Measure	Ingredient	Measure
Any cut of Beef pork or chicken	1 -2 lb.	Adobo Spice Mix (p.83)	2 Tbsp.
Green or Red Chile Sauce SHU to taste	1 cup	Green or Red chile powder	2 Tbsp.
Roasted Green Chile OR Rehydrated Red Chile Pods SHU to taste	1 cup chopped	Cilantro	1 cup chopped
		Oil	¼ - ½ cup

Prep Instructions

Cut beef, pork or chicken into ¼" strip across the grain. You may also cube meat into ¼" cubes for use in tacos, or burritos.
Pre-heat heavy skillet with oil to very hot. 360^0 +

Cooking Instructions

Place strips or cubes of beef, chicken or pork cubes into skillet and sauté. 3-5 minutes per side
Turn heat in skillet to simmer.
Add Red or Green chile sauce, chopped chiles, chopped cilantro. Simmer until all flavors have blended.
Add additionalRed or Green chile powder for additional SHU to taste.

Suggested Complementary Dishes: Any Burrito, Enchilada, Meat filling, Taco recipe or Meat topping.
Servings: (4) 6-oz. servings.

MARINADES, SAUCES, SPICES & SWEETENER ESSENTIAL RECIPES

New Mexico won its independence from Mexico in 1850, however, the many cultural ties with the Spanish colonials still endure today, especially in the local cuisine.

What makes the chile cuisine different from all others are the many marinades, sauces & spices that have been incorporated into the Chilenista cuisine.

Pay special attention to the Adobo Spice Mix and Sweeteners (p. 85) for they are often the key ingredients to providing your recipes with a personalized taste that will make your food outstanding.

MARINADES

Marinades are used to infuse flavor into meats, chicken and fish. The combination of herbs, spices and liquids will give you the finesse of a chemist in a Chilenista kitchen. You can marinade any ingredient from 30 minutes to overnight to flavor and tenderize your meats. In all recipes in this book, chile is one of the main ingredients. I would recommend using either red or green chile powder to blend into the other ingredients. The SHU is under your control from mild and sweet to blistering hot.

ASADA MARINADE—RED OR GREEN

Complexity Code: EZ   Origin: New Mexico
Cooking Method: When ingredients are marinated, use in any recipe

About the Recipe: This is the basic marinade recipe for any meat,
chicken or fish. The aromatic flavor of the nectar juice, sour of the lime,
nuttiness of the adobo and pungency of the chile will infuse your meat with
flavor that will last for the entire cooking process. All you need is the time
and refrigerator space.

Ingredient	Measure	Ingredient	Measure
Sweetener: Fruit nectar (p. 85) Apricot, guava, guanabana, papaya and tamarind or orange Juice	2 cups	Adobo Spice Mix (p.83)	2 Tbsp.
Lime juice	½ cup	Red chile powder or green chile powder SHU to taste	2 Tbsp.
		Optional Herbs: Cilantro, oregano, sage, rosemary, thyme Use to taste	2 Tbsp.

Prep Instructions

In a 3-quart mixing bowl blend nectar, lime juice, Adobo Spice Mix and
chile powder. Stir until all the ingredients are blended.
Stir the herbs into the marinade alone or in a combination to infuse the
desired flavor into the marinade.
Let the marinade stand for 30 minutes to 1 hour for all flavors to blend.
Place meat in the marinade and store in your refrigerator.
Beef, pork, lamb 4 to 6 hours. Chicken 3 to 4 hours. Fish: Whitefish,
shrimp, shellfish 1 hour.

CARNE ADOVADO MARINADE—RED CHILE

Complexity Code: EZ   Origin: New Mexico

About the Recipe: Carne Adovado is a Chilenista mainstay for spicing up any meat.

Ingredient	Measure	Ingredient	Measure
Red Chile Paste SHU to taste	2 cups	Adobo spice mix (p. 83)	2–4 Tbsp.
Sweetener: Fruit nectar (p. 85)	½ cup	Vegetable oil	2 Tbsp.
Red chile flakes	¼ cup	Salt	1 Tbsp.

Prep Instructions

In a 3-quart mixing bowl blend red chile paste, sweetener, red chile flakes, Adobo Spice Mix, oil and salt. Stir all ingredients until thoroughly blended.
Let the marinade stand for 30 minutes to 1 hour for all flavors to blend.
Taste and make any adjustments.
Place meat into mixing bowl and stir until all meat is covered.
Store in the refrigerator for 4 to 6 hours. Overnight is okay.
When ingredients are marinated and infused with flavor use in any recipe.

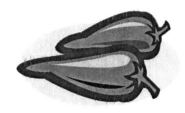

CERVESA MARINADE—RED OR GREEN

Complexity Code: EZ   Origin: Original

About the Recipe: The hearty taste of cerveza combined with the pungency of chile will prepare any meat for a BBQ grill. This marinade is bold and perfect for barbecue.

Ingredient	Measure	Ingredient	Measure
Cerveza	2 cups	Adobo Spice Mix (p.83)	2 Tbsp.
Lime Juice	½ cup	Garlic powder	1 tsp.
Vegetable oil	¼ cup	Red chile powder or Green chile powder SHU to taste	¼ cup

Prep Instructions

In a 3-quart mixing bowl blend cerveza, lime juice, vegetable oil, Adobo Spice Mix, garlic powder and chile powder. Stir all ingredients until thoroughly blended.

Let the marinade stand for 30 minutes to 1 hour for all flavors to blend. Taste and make any adjustments.

Place chops, steak, chicken, fish or shrimp into mixing bowl and stir. Marinate in your refrigerator. Beef, pork, lamb 4 to 6 hours. Chicken 3 to 4 hours. Fish: Whitefish, shrimp, shellfish 1 hour.

When ingredients are marinated and infused with flavor use for your favorite broiling or BBQ.

CHIPOTLE MARINADE—RED CHILE

Complexity Code: EZ   Origin: Original

About the Recipe: This is the hot one that Chilenistas will thank you for and come back for more. It is ideal for beef and pork dishes.
Essential Recipe: Red Chile Paste (p. 33).

Ingredient	Measure	Ingredient	Measure
Red Chile Paste SHU to taste	1 cup	Adobo Spice Mix (p. 83)	2 Tbsp.
Canned chipotle chiles	6–8	Balsamic vinegar	¼ cup
Sweetener: Fruit nectar (p. 85)	1 cup	Red chile flakes	¼ cup

Prep Instructions

In a 3-quart mixing bowl blend red chile paste, chipotle chiles, nectar, Adobo Spice Mix, vinegar and red chile flake. Stir all ingredients until thoroughly blended. (Use a blender stick.)
Let the marinade stand for 30 minutes to 1 hour for all flavors to blend. Taste and make any adjustments.
Place beef, pork, lamb or chicken, or into mixing bowl and stir.
Marinate in the refrigerator. Beef, pork, lamb 4 to 6 hours. Chicken 3 to 4 hours.
When ingredients are marinated and infused with flavor, use in recipe.
Have some crema or cerveza on the side.

FAJITA MARINADE—RED OR GREEN CHILE

Complexity Code: EZ   Origin: New Mexico

About The Recipe: The sizzle of a great fajita cannot help but arouse anyones tastebuds. The old adage "you sell the sizzle and not the meat" must have been developed to describe a great Fajita dinner.

Ingredient	Measure	Ingredient	Measure
Sweetener: Fruit nectar (p. 85) Apricot, guava, guanabana, papaya, and tamarind or orange juice	2 cups	Adobo Spice Mix (p.83)	2 Tbsp.
Lime juice	¼ cup	Cilantro	½ cup chopped
Soy sauce	¼ cup	Green onion	½ cup chopped
Vegetable oil	1 ½ cups	Red chile powder or Green chile powder SHU to taste	¼ cup
		Salt	1 Tbsp.

Prep Instructions

In a 3-quart mixing bowl blend nectar, lime juice, soy sauce, vegetable oil, Adobo Spice Mix, chopped cilantro, chopped green onion and chile powder and salt.

Stir all ingredients until thoroughly blended. Let the marinade stand for 30 minutes to 1 hour for all flavors to blend. Taste and make any adjustments. Place meat into mixing bowl and stir until all meat is covered. Store in a refrigerator for 4 to 6 hours. Overnight is okay.

When ingredients are marinated and infused with flavor, use in any fajita recipe.

MARGARITA MARINADE SAUCE

Complexity Code: EZ   Origin: Original

About The Recipe: The tanginess of margaritas along with the pungency of chile can be infused into any fish or chicken recipe. While making this marinade, make a margarita for your self.

Ingredient	Measure	Ingredient	Measure
Sweetener: Fruit nectar(p. 85) Apricot, guava, guanabana, papaya, and tamarind or orange juice	1 cup	Red chile powder or Green chile powder SHU to taste	½ cup
Tequila	1 cup	Adobo Spice Mix (p.83)	2 Tbsp.
Triple Sec	½ cup	Chopped green onion	½ cup
Lime juice	½ cup	Chopped cilantro	½ cup
Soy Sauce	¼ cup	Vegetable oil	2 Tbsp.

Prep Instructions

In a 3-quart mixing bowl blend nectar, lime juice, soy sauce, vegetable oil, Adobo Spice Mix, chopped cilantro, chopped green onion and chile powder and salt. Stir all ingredients until thoroughly blended.
Let the marinade stand for 30 minutes to 1 hour for all flavors to blend. Taste and make any adjustments.
Place chicken, fish or shrimp into mixing bowl and stir. Store in a refrigerator for 30 minutes to 1 hour.
When ingredients are marinated and infused with flavor they are ready for use in your recipe.

SAUCES

While marinades infuse their tastes from the inside; sauces infuse their taste from the outside.

When any one says finger liking good, they are talking about the sauces. Try some of these recipes, for a finger liking experience that you and your guest will not soon forget. Have wet toweletts or lemon water handy for the end of the meal

BBQ Sauce—Red Chile

Complexity Code: EZ   Origin: Original
Cooking Method: Simmer / Bake

About The Recipe: A BBQ is only as good as its sauce and although there are many variations for a great sauce, they all have a regional flavor that works well: North Carolina vinegar sauce, KC sticky sauce, Texas blistering hot sauce and our choice. New Mexico Sweet and tangy red chile sauce.

Essential Recipe: Red Chile Sauce (p. 36). Beef, pork or chicken drippings from Slow Cook Meat (p. 56, 58, 60) or canned broth.

Ingredient	Measure	Ingredient	Measure
Red Chile Sauce SHU to taste	2 cups	Adobo Spice Mix (p.83)	2 Tbsp.
Tomato paste	1 cup	Honey or molasses 1/2 – 1/2 blend okay	2 cups
Drippings or broth	1/2 cup	Sweetener, fruit nectar (p. 85) (Aromatic flavor)	1/2 cup
Butter, oil or lard	1/2 cup	Garlic powder	1–2 Tbsp.
Peanut butter Or Tahini sauce*. (Nutty taste)	1/2 cup	Vinegar (balsamic)	1/2 cup
Tequila* *Optional	1/2 cup		

Prep Instructions

Preheat oven 250°F. In a 2- to 3-quart stockpot, blend red chile paste, tomato paste, broth, butter, Adobo Spice Mix, honey or molasses and fruit nectar. Stir until well blended.

Cooking Instructions

Place stockpot in preheated oven or simmer over low flame for 30 to 45 minutes. (Do not cover pot.) The BBQ sauce should have a consistency of pancake syrup. If too thick, add some fruit nectar and if too thin, add some red chile sauce and simmer for an additional 15 minutes. If you want it a bit stickier add an additional cup of honey.

Suggested Complementary Dishes: Any slow cooked meat, chicken wings.

Servings: 6–8 cups.

CHIPOTLE CREAM SAUCE

Complexity Code: EZ   Origin: Original
Cooking Method: Simmer

About The Recipe: Chipotle cream sauce makes a perfect condiment with any dish to give it a pungent, smoky, aromatic, sour taste that can enhance the flavor of any dish as a topping or condiment.

Ingredient	Measure	Ingredient	Measure
Pickled Chipotle (canned or pickled)	1 cup	Balsamic vinegar	1 cup
Crema	1 cup		
Cilantro	½ cup		

Prep Instructions
Soak 6 to 9 dried chipotle peppers in a small saucepan and bring to a simmer over low heat until the chipotle is soft and pliable. (You can use canned chipotles.) Allow to cool.

Cooking Instructions
Add crema and cilantro into saucepan and blend with a blender stick or mixer to a smooth consistency. Store Chipotle Cream Sauce in a jar for future use.

Suggested Complementary Dishes: Use the Chipotle Cream Sauce on any meat dish to kick it up a notch (great on hotdogs, hamburgers and fried chicken).

Servings: 2–3 cups.

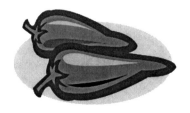

CILANTRO PESTO (RECAITO)

Complexity Code: EZ   Origin: Mexico

About The Recipe: Cilantro pesto is one of the most aromatic condiments that you can make and offers a counter part to the pungent chile recipes. You can use it as a condiment or topping for any vegetable, chicken or fish dish.

Essential Recipe: Fresh Green Chile (p. 44).

Ingredient	Measure	Ingredient	Measure
Cilantro tightly packed	2 cups chopped	Sweetener: Fruit nectar (p.85)	¼ cup
Garlic	4 cloves	Lime juice	¼ cup
Fresh Green Chile	1 cup chopped	Olive oil	¼ cup

Prep Instructions

Place cilantro (stems and leaves), garlic, green chile, sweetener, lime juice and olive oil into blender and blend in chop mode until all ingredients are blended and you can still see some small chunks.

Remove from blender and place in a container or jar for immediate use or store in refrigerator for future use.

Suggested Complementary Dishes: Condiment or topping for any vegetable, fish or chicken dish.

Servings: 3–4 cups.

ENCHILADA SAUCE—GREEN CHILE

Complexity Code: EZ   Origin: New Mexico / Mexico
Cooking Method: Sauté

About The Recipe: Green chile enchilada sauce can be used to spice up
and flavor almost any dish, however, it comes to life in its native enchilada.
I prepare a few pints and refrigerate them ready for use with any dish. It
complements any fish dishes or poultry dishes.
Essential Recipe: Green Chile Sauce (p. 50).

Ingredient	Measure	Ingredient	Measure
Green Chile Sauce	4 cups	Adobo Spice Mix (p.83)	2 Tbsp.
Onion	½ cup Fine chopped	Flour	2 Tbsp.
Tomato	1 cup Fine chopped	Oil	2 Tbsp.
		Sweetener Fruit nectar (p. 85)	¼ cup

Prep Instructions

In a medium saucepan place oil and heat, add flour and stir to make a
roux.
Add green chile sauce, onion, tomatoes, Adobo Spice Mix and sweetener.
Stir to blend all ingredients.

Cooking Instructions

Heat sauté pan with medium heat and stir until it starts to
bubble. Lower the heat to low and simmer for ½ hour, let cool
and place in a storage jar for future use.
Servings: Makes 1 qt. that can be stored for future use.

ENCHILADA SAUCE—RED CHILE

Complexity Code: EZ   Origin: New Mexico
Cooking Method: Simmer in oven, crockpot or stovetop

About The Recipe: A great enchilada sauce can be used on almost any
dish from Huevos Rancheros, hamburgers and steaks and as a topping for
almost any dish that needs to be spiced up, as well as enchiladas. I make it
the consistency of a pancake batter and can thin it or thicken it at any time
with water or with roux (p. 35). I always keep a few pint containers in the
refrigerator or frozen for any occasion.
Essential Recipe: Red Chile Paste (p. 33), Rehydrated Red Chile pods
(p. 40).

Ingredient	Measure	Ingredient	Measure
Red Chile Paste	2 cups	Adobo Spice Mix (p.83)	2 Tbsp.
Tomato sauce	1 cup	Sweetener, fruit nectar (p. 85)	2 cups
Rehydrated Red Chile Pods Ancho, Pasilla, Chipotle or Chile Seco SHU to taste	1 cup chopped	Water or chicken stock	1 cup
Butter or vegetable oil	¼ cup		

Prep Instructions

Mix red chile paste, tomato sauce, water and oil in a 2-quart bowl until it
is smooth and blended. It should have the consistency of a pancake batter.
Add additional water to thin down or some roux or flour to thicken.
Add the Adobo Spice Mix; sweetener and other powdered spices.
(To make your enchilada sauce more aromatic add rosemary, thyme, sage
and cilantro. To make it real exotic add a pinch of clove or nutmeg.)

Cooking Instructions

Place the mixture in the oven or crockpot at low heat about 190^0F degrees
and let the sauce simmer for at least 1 to 2 hours. If you are in a hurry you
can heat it on the stovetop in a low simmer for 30 minutes being careful
to stir often. Red chile will scorch or burn and give it a bitter taste.
Suggested Complementary Dishes: Any recipe in this book calling for red
chile sauce.
Servings: Makes 1 qt. that can be stored for future use.

MOLE SAUCE—RED CHILE

Complexity Code: COOK
Cooking Method: Simmer

Origin: Aztec / Mayan /Mexico

About The Recipe: Mole is considered by some as the food of the Gods and should be prepared as if it were an offering. It almost always is found at celebrations and takes on the festive flavor of fruit, nuts spices and heat level that is desired to enhance any dish or eaten plain with rice to savor the taste of chocolate and chile combined.

Essential Recipe: Red Chile Paste (p. 33). Rehydrated Red Chile pods (p. 40).

Ingredient	Measure	Ingredient	Measure
Red Chile Paste	2 cups	Adobo Spice Mix (p.83)	¼ cup
Rehydrated Red Chile Pods Ancho, Pasilla, Chipotle or Chile Seco (SHU to taste)	2 cups chopped	Achiote paste	2 Tbsp.
Dark chocolate (More if you wish)	2–4 oz.	Sesame seeds or Tahini paste	2 Tbsp.
Tomatoes (fresh or canned)	1 cup chopped	Ground nuts, Walnut, almond, peanut, pinion	½ cup
Sweetener: Fruit nectar (p. 85)	1 cup		
Corn tortilla or ½ cup masa thinned with ½ cup water	1 cup shredded	Clove	¼ tsp.
Olive oil	¼ cup	Cinnamon	¼ tsp.
		OPTIONAL: Tequila	2 Tbsp. or more

Prep Instructions

Rehydrate red chile pods in your favorite liquid, (water, fruit nectar, tequila). Chop into ¼-inch squares.

Combine all ingredients into a blender and blend until fully blended with a sticky consistency. (Add more liquid if too thick, more chocolate or corn tortilla if too thin.)

Cooking Instructions

Pour blend into a double boiler or thick covered saucepan and simmer for 30 minutes. On low heat stir occasionally to make sure that the bottom does not burn.

As an alternative method of cooking, place the covered saucepan into your oven at 225°F for 30 minutes, let cool, place Red Chile Mole Sauce on a glass jar and use as needed.

You can also freeze the mole sauce in an ice cube tray, store in a plastic freezer bag and use a cube at a time as needed.

Suggested Complementary Dishes: Can be used in any recipe calling for enchilada sauce, chicken, fish, vegetable dish, enchiladas and tamales. (Some people spoon it straight from the sauce pan).

Servings: 6–8 cups.

MOLE SAUCE—GREEN CHILE CHOCOLATE

Complexity Code: EZ   Origin: New Mexico
Cooking Method: Simmer

About The Recipe: Green chile mole sauce is the Chilenistas and chocoholics ultimate sauce, combining the pungency of green chile, sweetness of chocolate and nuttiness of nuts into a heavenly eating experience.
Essential Recipe: Roasted Green Chile (p. 46).

Ingredient	Measure	Ingredient	Measure
Roasted Green Chile (fresh or frozen) SHU to taste	4 cups chopped	Adobo Spice Mix (p.83)	¼ cup
Tomatillos	1 cup chopped	Sweetener: Fruit nectar (p. 85)	1 cup
Dark chocolate	2– 4 oz.	Ground nuts, Walnut, Almond, Peanut, Pinion	1 cup
Crema or heavy cream	1 cup	Sesame seeds or Tahini paste	2 Tbsp.
Corn tortilla (shredded) or ½ cup masa thinned with ½ cup water	1 cup	Clove	¼ tsp.
		Cinnamon	¼ tsp.
		OPTIONAL: Tequila	2 Tbsp. or more

Prep Instructions

Combine all ingredients into a blender and blend until fully blended and has a sticky consistency. (Add more liquid if too thick, more chocolate or corn tortilla if too thin.)

Cooking Instructions

Pour blend into a double boiler or thick covered saucepan and simmer for 30 minutes. On low heat stir occasionally to make sure that the bottom does not burn.

As an alternative method of cooking place the covered saucepan into your oven at 225^0F for 30 minutes, let cool, place green chile mole sauce in a glass jar and use as needed. You can also freeze the mole sauce in an ice cube tray, store in a plastic freezer bag and use a cube at a time as needed.

Suggested Complementary Dishes: Any meat fish or fowl dish Can be used in any recipe calling for enchilada sauce, chicken, fish, vegetable dish, enchiladas and tamales.
Servings: 6–8 cups.

MOLE VERDE—GREEN CHILE

Complexity Code: EZ   Origin: New Mexico
Cooking Method: Simmer
About The Recipe: Green Chile Mole from New Mexico is an inspired sauce that omits the chocolate which was very hard to come by in the early days.
Essential Recipe: Roasted Green Chile (p. 46).

Ingredient	Measure	Ingredient	Measure
Roasted Fresh Green Chile (fresh or frozen) SHU to taste	4 cups chopped	Adobo Spice Mix (p. 83)	¼ cup
Tomatillos	1 cup chopped	Sweetener: Fruit Nectar (p. 85)	1 cup
Corn tortilla or ½ cup masa thinned with ½ cup water	1 cup shredded	Ground nuts, Walnut, Almond, Peanut, Pinion	1 cup
Cilantro	1 cup chopped	Sesame seeds or Tahini paste	2 Tbsp.
Onion	1 cup chopped	Clove	¼ tsp.
		Cinnamon	¼ tsp.

Prep Instructions

Combine all ingredients into a blender and blend until fully blended and has a sticky consistency. (Add more liquid if too thick, more corn tortilla or masa if too thin.)

Cooking Instructions

Pour blend into a double boiler or thick covered saucepan and simmer for 30 minutes. On low heat stir occasionally to make sure that the bottom does not burn. As an alternative method of cooking place the covered saucepan into your oven at 225°F for 30 minutes, let cool, place green chile mole verde sauce in a glass jar and use as needed. You can also freeze the mole sauce in an ice cube tray, store in a plastic freezer bag and use a cube at a time as needed.

Suggested Complementary Dishes: Can be used in any recipe calling for enchilada sauce, chicken, fish, vegetable dish, enchiladas and tamales.
Servings: 6–8 cups

POBLANO GREEN CHILE GINGER SAUCE

Complexity Code: Cook   Origin: New Mexico
Cooking Method: Sauté

About The Recipe: Oriental inspired green chile sauce.
Essential Recipe: Roasted Green Chile (p. 46). Red Chile Sauce (p. 36).

Ingredient	Measure		Measure
Roasted Fresh Green Chile (Poblano preferred)	1 cup chopped	Olive or vegetable oil	4 Tbsp.
Crushed red chile Ancho, Pasilla, Chipotle, or Chile Seco SHU to taste	1 cup	Red Chile Sauce SHU to taste Commercial red chile sauce	½ cup
Ginger (fresh)	½ cup	Tomato paste or ketchup	¼ cup
Jicama	½ cup	Sweetener (p. 85) Guava paste	½ cup
Garlic fresh or minced	4 cloves	Water	¼ cup
Scallions	½ cup	Corn starch (use as a thickener)	1 tsp.

Prep Instructions

Roast Poblano chile pods.
Coat heat heavy skillet with oil and bring to low-to-medium heat (215°F).
Chop roasted chile into ¼-inch squares and place into skillet to sauté.
Peel and cut ginger and cut jicama into ⅛-inch thick, 1-by-⅛-inch strips and place into skillet.
Crush red chile pods into ¼-inch to ½-inch flakes, seeds included, and place into skillet.
Crush garlic cloves and mince into ⅛-inch cubes and place into skillet to sauté.
Chop scallions into ½-inch strips; place into skillet to sauté.
Increase heat to boil, add cornstarch, stir skillet to blend all ingredients 3 to 5 minutes, reduce heat to low and allow to sauté for 5 to 10 minutes.
Serve warm or refrigerate.

Cooking Instructions

Sauté all of the above ingredients under medium heat. Add red chile sauce, tomato paste, sweetener and water.

Suggested Complementary Dishes: Any fish or fried food will be enhanced. Serve it as a condiment or pour on top.
Servings: 3–4 cups.

SPICES

The New World was accidently encountered by spice trade merchants looking for a shorter ocean routes between India and Europe.
We are fortunate today to find an endless variety of spices, seeds and condiments that satisfy any taste at our local supermarkets. The Chilenista's spice shelf can be found on (p. 361). There are however, several spice combinations that make the chile cuisine what it is today, and the frequently used spices described below will enhance your cooking with a distinctive taste.

ADOBO SPICE MIX

Complexity Code: EZ   Origin: Traditional
Cooking Method: Grind, Blend

About The Recipe: Adobo Spice Mix used in many recipes in the chilenista cuisine, as an essential ingredient consisting of coriander, cumin, garlic, and oregano.
Rather than adding the spices individually, I would suggest that you make your own adobo mix by combining equal parts of coriander, cumin, garlic and oregano powder. Rub whole-leaf, dry Mexican oregano in your palms to crush it. Store it in a jar along with your other spices. You can also customize the mixture by blending a pinch of clove powder or nutmeg to give it a sweet, nutty taste. You can vary your blend by increasing or decreasing these ingredients to your taste preferences.
Try to not use store-bought adobo because it is usually blended with salt and MSG as the prime ingredients. (Read the label.)

Essential Recipe:

Ingredient	Measure
Coriander	1 Tbsp.
Cumin	1 Tbsp.
Garlic	1 Tbsp.
Oregano	1 Tbsp.
Clove powder	Pinch
Nutmeg	Pinch

Prep Instructions

In a mixing bowl, place ground coriander, cumin, garlic powder and ground oregano in equal parts. Stir all ingredients to blend and place in a 4-, 8- or 16-ounce lidded container, (an empty spice jar) and store for future use in your recipes.

Suggested Complementary Dishes: Any red or green chile recipe that you may wish to prepare.

Servings: ¼ cup

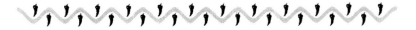

ANNATTO / ACHIOTE PASTE

Complexity Code: EZ

About The Recipe: Annatto / Achiote paste consists of a blend of ground annatto seeds (red color) cumin, peppercorns, allspice, cloves, chile powder, garlic, vinegar and fruit nectar that have been blended into a paste. There are many commercial paste blocks available that can be purchased.
The primary function of achiote paste is to give food a red color and an astringent, earthy, slightly bitter taste.

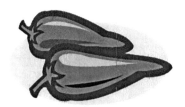

SWEETENERS

Complexity: Code EZ   Origin: Original / Personal

Brown sugar, corn syrup, fruit nectars, guava paste, quince paste, piloncillo, honey, maple syrup, molasses and refined white sugar.

About The Recipe: The "sweetness factor" of your recipes is a very personal touch that can improve the flavor. A heavy hand will drown out some of the more delicate spices. Sweetener used in trace or small amounts will give an innuendo or flavor character that enhances the flavor of any ingredient or recipe. With the concern for diabetes and sugar-free recipes, I prefer to use nectars, pastes and piloncillo (unrefined sugar) as excellent substitutes for refined sugar that offer aromatic additions to your recipes.

As a rule, the sweeteners made from nectar are one-fourth the sweetness of raw sugar and offer maximum aromatic flavor. Nectars are available as canned fruit juice drinks. Sweeteners made from paste are half the sweetness of raw sugar and offer the same aromatic flavor. Sweeteners made from piloncillo have the same sweetness of raw sugar and offer a nutty/ woody taste. Sweeteners made from refined sugar offer the optimal sweetness and in moderation can be used in your recipes.
Honey, maple syrup and molasses all impart unique flavors to your recipes and used interchangeably, enhance and customize the "sweetness factor."

Ingredient	Measure	Ingredient	Measure
Fruit nectar: Apricot, guava, guanabana, papaya and tamarind	4 Tbsp.	Honey	1 Tbsp.
Fruit paste: Guava, quince	2 Tbsp.	Maple Syrup	1 Tbsp.
Piloncillo: Unrefined brown sugar	1 Tbsp.	Molasses	1 Tbsp.
Refined Sugar	1 Tbsp.		

Prep Instructions

Fruit nectars can be used straight from the can as a sweetener in a 4:1 ratio to sugar. They are the natural sweeteners of the chile cuisine and give a soft, sweet aromatic taste that enhances the natural taste of the other ingredients but does not overwhelm with sweet.

Pastes need to be liquefied for use in most recipes in a 1:1 ratio with water. I prepare one cup at a time and keep it in the refrigerator to use as needed. Guava or quince pastes are perfect for the Chilenista cuisine.

Guava imparts a fruitiness and sweetness that will not overwhelm.I have found that it is best to liquefy guava paste bars by cutting into cubes and placing in a small microwaveable bowl with an equal amount of water. Microwave the paste for 2 minutes (until it starts to bubble), stir it to liquefy any remaining lumps and pour the liquefied guava into a container for future use. Keep the container in the refrigerator and pour out as needed for your recipe.

Piloncillo usually comes dried in cones or as unrefined brown sugar. You can break down the cones in a microwave by heating them for 15 to 20 seconds or until they start to melt and splitting the cones with a fork. You can store in a sugar container for use as needed.

Caramelized Sugar or Piloncillo

Caramelized sugar is the Cadillac of all sweeteners and acquires a nutty taste that substitutes nicely for raw sugar. It takes a little time to prepare but it is well worth the effort, especially in the desserts.

Ingredient	Measure	Ingredient	Measure
Refined sugar	1 cup	Water	2 Tbsp.
Unrefined sugar	1 cup		
Brown sugar	1 cup		
Piloncillo	1 cup		

Prep Instructions
Place sugar in a heavy skillet under high heat and add 2 Tbsp. of water.

Cooking Instructions
Stir vigorously until sugar starts to melt. (Sugar melts at 320^0F.)
Reduce heat once the sugar has melted and boil for an additional 5 to 10 minutes until the sugar starts to brown.
Reduce heat to simmer until ready to use.
Servings: 1 cup

CHAPTER 2: APPETIZERS

Finger food may have been invented for the chile cuisine. The many chiles, sauces, salsas, cheeses and spices can satisfy any taste experience of sweet, sour, salty, pungent and bitter on top of a tiny tortilla chip. Your imagination and creativity are the only limits to what you can create. Below are a few red and green chile appetizer recipes to use or modify to please your family and guests for any occasion, Sunday football, party, reception, re-union or just a snack.

"Apetizers are the little things you keep eating until you lose your appetite"   Joe Moore

BBQ BUFFALO WINGS
RED CHILE ORIGINAL RECIPE

Complexity Code: EZ   Origin: Buffalo, New York
Cooking Method: Pan-Fry / Deep-Fry

About the Recipe: This is the original recipe for chicken wings with a slight Southwest flavor enhancement of using real red chile sauce. You can always use a commercial hot sauce, but fresh is best.
Essential Recipe: Red Chile BBQ Sauce (p. 73), Red Chile Sauce (p. 36) Roasted Green Chile (p. 46).

Ingredient	Measure	Ingredient	Measure
Chicken wings Winglets and drumlets	1 lb. 20–24	Oil for frying	1 qt.
		Green Chile Blue Cheese Dip	
Red Chile BBQ Sauce			
Red Chile Sauce:* Ancho, Pasilla, Chipotle or Chile Seco	2 cups	Crema	1 cup
Tomato paste	1 cup	Crumbled blue cheese	1 cup
Molasses or honey	1 cup	Mayonnaise	½ cup
Butter	4 Tbsp.	Garlic powder	1 Tbsp.
Vinegar (balsamic or wine)	½ cup	Green chile powder	1 Tbsp.
OPTIONAL: Tequila	¼ cup	Fresh Green Chile (roasted or frozen)	½ cup chopped

* You can use a ready-made hot sauce.

Prep Instructions
Wash chicken wings, cut winglets from drumlets at joints. Towel-dry wings.
Red Chile BBQ Sauce
Melt butter in a small saucepan (low heat), add red chile sauce, tomato paste, honey and vinegar, then stir to blend and keep warm. (Do not boil.)
Green Chile Blue Cheese Dip
Mix crema, crumbled blue cheese, mayonnaise, garlic powder, green chile powder and Fresh Green Chile in a small mixing bowl and blend well.
Preheat oil in heavy skillet or deep-fryer to 375°F.

Cooking Instructions
Pan-Fry
Place chicken wings into frying pan; fry chicken wings 4 to 5 minutes per side in skillet until light brown.

Deep-Fry

Place chicken wings into deep fryer; fry chicken wings for 10 minutes until light brown.

Place wings on a cooling rack to drain any excess oil and place in a large mixing bowl or 1-gallon plastic bag.

Pour BBQ sauce into mixing bowl or plastic bag and stir / shake until all chicken wings are coated.

VARIATION

You can place the coated chicken wings into a preheated oven at 400^0F for 15 minutes to glaze the hot sauce and crisp the wings.

Plate on a large platter with a bowl of Blue Cheese dip, Red Chile Sauce, Green Chile Sauce or BBQ Sauce for dipping.

Servings: 20–24 wings.

BURRITO PINWHEELS

Complexity Code: EZ   Origin: New Mexico

About the Recipe: Burrito Pinwheels are a great finger food that you can create in minutes as an appetizer or meal. A tortilla and your imagination are the only limitations.

Essential Recipe: Red Chile Sauce (p. 36), Green Chile Sauce (p. 50), Fresh Green Chile (p. 44), Rehydrated Red Chile pods (p. 40), Red Chile Tomato Sauce (p. 37), Sautéed Beef, Chicken or Pork (p.64), Slow Cooked Beef, Chicken, or Pork (p. 56,58,60)

Ingredient	Measure	Ingredient	Measure
Tortilla (burrito size) thin if available	4–6	Shredded cheese blend Asadero, Cheddar, Jack, Queso Quesadilla, or Cheddar only	2 cups
Lettuce	4–6 leaves	Crema or Mayonnaise	¼ cup
Red chile powder	2 Tbsp.	Green chile powder	2 Tbsp.
SUGGESTED FILLINGS:			
Fresh Green Chile Anaheim, Poblano, Jalapeño (fresh or frozen) SHU to taste	2 cup chopped	Rehydrated Red Chile Pods Ancho, Pasilla, Chipotle or Chile Seco SHU to taste	2 cup chopped
Onion	2 cup chopped	Shredded Beef	2 cups
Cilantro	1 cup chopped	Taco Ground Beef or Sauteed beef	2 cups
Guacamole	2 cups	Shredded Chicken	2 cups
Crema	1 cup	Red Chile Sauce	2 cups
Beans or refried beans	1 cup	Green Chile Sauce	2 cups
Red Chile Tomato Sauce	1 cup	Shrimp	2 cups
Salsa	1 cups	Cold cuts	½ lb.

Prep Instructions

Place a tortilla on a flat surface, coat the end nearest to you with crema or mayonnaise and place a 1-inch strip of cheese on top of mayonnaise. Cover cheese with any ingredients or cold cuts that you may have available or prepared from the above suggested list.

Place a leaf of lettuce on top of filling and roll up burrito. You can moisten the edge of the burrito to seal the tortilla or place a toothpick to hold it closed. Place crease side down on a plate and roll the rest of the tortillas. With a sharp knife cut burrito straight across or diagonally in 1-inch pieces. Place a toothpick through the burrito pieces to make them easy to serve and eat.

Servings: 32–48 pieces.

CANDIED RED CHILE BACON

Complexity Code: EZ   Origin: New Mexico
Cooking Method: Bake (slow cook)

About the Recipe: This is the ultimate bacon appetizer, tart, sweet and crunchy. The only problem is making enough to meet your demand.

Ingredient	Measure	Ingredient	Measure
Bacon (thick cut)	1 lb.	Piloncillo or unrefined sugar	¼ lb.
		Red chile powder SHU to taste	½ cup

Prep Instructions
Preheat oven 250°F.
Cut bacon strips in half. (They will be easier to handle.)
Lay bacon strips on a large baking pan. (You may need two.)
Coat top with red chile powder and then unrefined sugar. Flip bacon strips over and coat second side with red chile and unrefined sugar.
Place baking pan(s) in center of oven.

Cooking Instructions
Bake bacon for 1 to 2 hours until sugar caramelizes and bacon strips are starting to get crisp.
Remove from oven. Let cool. Start second batch.

Suggested Complementary Dishes: Tortilla chips, duros, crackers, crema.

Servings: 18–24 strips.

CHICKEN WINGS (BAKED)

Complexity Code: EZ   Origin: Original
Cooking Method: Bake

About the Recipe: Frying is often very daunting or impossible. If you do not have the proper equipment, this recipe is the next best thing to making the original recipe chicken wings.
Essential Recipe: Red Chile Sauce (p. 36).

Ingredient	Measure	Ingredient	Measure
Chicken wings, Winglets and drumlets	1 lb. 20–24	Adobo Dry Spice Mix (p. 83)	2 Tbsp.
Unbleached flour, rice flour or corn flour	1 cup	Red chile or green chile powder	2 tbsp.
Red Chile Sauce* SHU to taste	1 cup	Butter	1 stick
		Honey or molasses	½ cup
		Vinegar (balsamic or wine)	1 Tbsp.

* You can use a readymade hot sauce.

Prep Instructions

Wash chicken wings and cut winglets from drumlets at joints. Towel-dry.
Mix flour, Adobo Spice Mix and chile powder in a shallow bowl.
Dredge chicken wings through flour and place in plastic bag or storage container in refrigerator to chill for 30 minutes.
Melt the butter under low heat; add honey, Red Chile Sauce, vinegar, Adobo Spice Mix and chile powder. Blend well.
Preheat the oven to 425⁰F.
After wings have been cooled in refrigerator, place them on a greased baking sheet with space around each wing. (Do not crowd the wings.)

Cooking Instructions

Place chicken wings in center of oven for 45 minutes; turn the wings over after 20 minutes to brown both sides.
When the wings are crispy on the outside, place them into a large mixing bowl, pour the Red Chile Sauce on top of the wings and toss with a serving spoon to completely cover each wing.
Variation:
To glaze the chile-coated chicken wings, return them to baking pan and bake for an additional 15 minutes.
Plate on a large platter with a bowl of Red Chile Sauce, Green Chile Sauce or BBQ Sauce for dipping.

Servings: 20–24 wings.

CHILE CHICKEN WINGS
(FRIED–RED OR GREEN)

Complexity Code: EZ   Origin: Original
Cooking Method: Pan-Fry / Deep-Fry

About the Recipe: Chicken wings have become synonymous with
Sunday football, picnics, beer fests and any other occasion where people
gather to celebrate. This recipe will bring all the taste and pleasure of fried
chicken wings without the sticky finger problem, making it ideal for stand-
up and more formal occasions.

Essential Recipe: Red Chile BBQ Sauce (p. 73), Green Chile Blue
Cheese Dip (p. 126), Red Chile Sauce (p. 36) OR Green Chile Sauce (p.
50).

Ingredient	Measure	Ingredient	Measure
Chicken wings, Winglets and drumlets	1 lb. 20–24	Adobo Dry Spice Mix (p. 83)	2 Tbsp.
Rice Flour (Harina de Arroz)	1–2 cups	Oil	1 qt.
Red Chile BBQ Sauce	1 cup	Crema	1 cup
Green Chile Blue Cheese Dip	1 cup	Red chile or green chile powder	2 Tbsp.

Prep Instructions

Wash chicken wings, cut winglets from drumlets at joints and towel-dry
wings.
Mix rice flour and Adobo Spice Mix in a shallow bowl.
Dredge wings through rice flour and place in plastic bag or storage
container in refrigerator to cool 30 minutes. (For extra crispy, leave in
refrigerator overnight.)
Preheat oil in heavy skillet or deep fryer to 375°F.

Cooking Instructions

Shake excess rice flour from wings and place in hot oil.
Pan-fry 4 to 5 minutes per side in skillet until a light brown or deep-fry 8
to 10 minutes in a deep fryer until light brown.
Place wings on a cooling rack or towel to drain any excess oil and sprinkle
with red chile or green chile powder.
Plate on a large platter with a bowl of Red Chile Sauce, Green Chile Sauce
or BBQ Sauce for dipping.

Servings: 20–24 wings.

DUROS (PINWHEELS)

Complexity Code: EZ
Cooking Method: Deep-Fry

Origin: Mexico

About the Recipe: Duros are the Mexican equivalent of potato chips and come in pinwheel or flat shapes. They have a nutty, crisp flavor that will enhance any dip or salsa. You can get them at almost any Mexican grocer or online.

Ingredient	Measure	Ingredient	Measure
Duros	1 lb.	Oil	1 qt.
		Red chile powder	SHU to taste
		Green chile powder	SHU to taste
		Salt	To taste

Prep Instructions

In a large skillet or deep-fat fryer heat oil to 375°F.

Cooking Instructions

Drop duros pieces into the hot oil one at a time. They will sink to the bottom and then expand to float to the top. Place duros on a paper towel to drain excess oil and sprinkle red chile or green chile powder or salt to taste. You can store the duros in a dry bag for future use.

Suggested Complementary Dishes: Any dip or salsa.

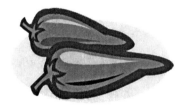

FLAUTAS–BAKED OR FRIED TAQUITOS

Complexity Code: EZ   Origin: New Mexico / Mexico
Cooking Method: Deep-Fry / Bake

About the Recipe: Flautas are named for their resemblance to flutes and, like their namesake, are music to your mouth. They are the perfect finger food and are usually the first to disappear from the appetizer plate.
Essential Recipe: Slow cooked Beef (p. 60), Slow cooked Chicken (p. 56) or Slow cooked Pork (p. 58) Red Chile Sauce (p. 36).

Ingredient	Measure	Ingredient	Measure
Corn tortilla 6" or Gordita (thin)	12–24	Adobo Dry Spice Mix (p. 83)	2 Tbsp.
Shredded Beef, Chicken or Pork	2–4 cups	Red Chile Sauce SHU to taste	1 cup
		Oil for frying	2 cups

Prep Instructions

In a mixing bowl shred Beef, Chicken or Pork and add Adobo Spice Mix. Soften tortillas, wrapping 4 to 6 at a time in a wet towel, and microwave at defrost mode for 15 seconds.
Place softened tortilla on a flat surface, coat with Red Chile Sauce and place shredded meat on tortilla (2–3 Tbsp.). Roll tortilla into a tube ¾ to 1 inch in diameter and place toothpicks at both ends to hold together.
For frying, preheat oil in heavy skillet at 360°F with at least 2" of oil. For baking preheat oven to 400°F.

Cooking Instructions

Frying
Place rolled tortillas into the skillet and fry for 3 to 4 minutes until golden brown. (Do not overcrowd the skillet.) Fry 4 to 6 flautas at a time.
Remove the flautas from the oil, remove toothpicks and place on a towel or baking rack to drain excess oil. Place flautas in a warm oven of 200°F until the entire batch is fried.

Baking
Place rolled tortillas in a baking pan with plenty of space around each one. Place baking tray in hot oven for 15 to 20 minutes until tortillas are golden brown and crisp.
Remove toothpicks from flautas and let cool for 5 to 10 minutes.

Suggested Complementary Dishes: Crema, salsa, melted cheese.

Servings: 12–24 pieces.

GREEN CHILE EGG ROLLS (CHIMICHANGA)

Complexity Code: COOK   Origin: Original
Cooking Method: Sauté / Fry

About the Recipe: The ever popular egg roll has been given a New
Mexico Chile makeover for a delicious meal or appetizer. You can use
either egg roll skins available at most supermarkets or thin, taco-style soft
tortillas. You can also use a large, thin burrito-style tortilla and cut it in
quarters. Green Chile Egg Rolls are a perfect appetizer accompaniment to
chicken wings and tacos.

Essential Recipe: Roasted Green Chile (p. 46), Green Chile Paste (p.
43), Slow Cooked Chicken (p. 56), Taco Ground Beef (p. 62), Pulled
Pork (p. 58), Sautéed Beef, Chicken or Pork (p.64), Calabacitas (p. 330),
Enchilada Sauce (p. 76).

Ingredient	Measure	Ingredient	Measure
Egg roll wraps (available at most groceries)	12	Green Chile Paste	¼ cup
Coleslaw mix	2 cups	Soy sauce	2 Tbsp.
Bean sprouts	2 cups	Vinegar	1 Tbsp.
Roasted Fresh Green Chile	1 cup chopped	Sweetener (p. 85)	2 Tbsp.
Green onion	1 cup chopped	Garlic powder	1 Tbsp.
Sliced celery	½ cup	Coriander	1 tsp.
Choose main ingredient Chicken, chorizo, ground beef, pulled pork, fish, shrimp, veggie (calabacitas)	1 lb.	Oil, pan, or deep-fry*	
		Green chile powder	2 Tbsp.

*Recommended

Prep Instructions

Combine coleslaw, bean sprouts, green onion, chopped celery, garlic
powder, soy sauce, vinegar, sweetener and coriander in a mixing bowl and
mix.
Prepare filling as per the ESSENTIAL RECIPES or your own recipe. If you
are preparing fish, you can use any firm whitefish such as tilapia.
Lightly whip 2 eggs, scramble-fry and set aside.

Cooking Instructions

Sauté

In a large frying pan, coat bottom with oil, heat and sauté vegetables until they are soft but not fully cooked. Place vegetables back into mixing bowl. Prepare the meat filling as per the ESSENTIAL RECIPE or your own recipe. Shred meat. Cut fish and shrimp into ½-inch squares. Add scrambled eggs and mix until all ingredients are blended.

Make Egg Rolls

Place egg roll wrap or large burrito cut into quarters on a flat surface with pointed edge away from you.

Place vegetables (1–2 oz.) on the egg roll 1 inch from the bottom and 1 ½ inches from the sides (as if you were making a burrito). Place meat filling on top of veggies (1–2 oz.) and fold the sides over the mixture (about 1 ½-inch round). Roll the bottom of the egg roll over the top and roll toward the front. (Make sure the sides are closed). You can wet the top of the roll to make sure that the roll holds together and place a toothpick in the middle to hold it together.

Place egg rolls on a plate ready to fry.

Cooking Instructions

Frying

In a large skillet or deep-fryer heat oil to at least 360°F. Place Egg Rolls seam side down into hot oil and fry for about 2 to 3 minutes per side until golden brown, 3 to 4 at a time.

Place fried egg rolls on a plate with some paper towels to absorb any excess oil and sprinkle the top with red or green chile powder (SHU level to your liking).

Suggested Complementary Dishes: Enchilada sauce, salsa, duck sauce, cole slaw.

Servings: 12.

JALAPEÑO PEPPER POPPERS & MORE

Complexity Code: EZ   Origin: New Mexico
Cooking Method: Bake or Fry

About the Recipe: Jalapeño peppers have become synonymous with hot chilies and are a favorite appetizer popper. They are easy to make baked, fried or raw, with numerous fillings and toppings.

Essential Recipe: Fresh Green Chile (p. 44), Chopped Green Chile (p. 48).

Ingredient	Measure	Ingredient	Measure
Jalapeño peppers	12	Adobo Dry Spice Mix (p. 83)	2 Tbsp.
Shredded cheese blend Asadero, Cheddar, Jack, Queso Quesadilla, or Cheddar only	2 cups	Bread crumbs or cornmeal stuffing (Fine)	1 cup
Crema or whipped cream cheese	1 cups	Corn dog frying mix (pre-mix)	
SUGGESTED ADDITIONS			
Pignola nuts		Corn	
Rehydrated Red Chiles	chopped	Beans or refried beans	
Roasted Green Chile	chopped	Raisins or craisins	
Tomato	chopped		

Prep Instructions

Cut jalapeño peppers in half, scooping out all the seeds and veins.
Blend shredded cheese, crema and Adobo Spice Mix in a mixing bowl. Add any suggested additional ingredients.
Stuff jalapeño with cheese blend. Top with breadcrumbs or cornmeal stuffing.
Lightly grease baking pan and place stuffed jalapeño halves.

Cooking Instructions

Baking

Preheat oven at 350°F. Bake for 30 minutes, remove baking tray and allow cooling.

Frying
Preheat fryer to 360°F.
Prepare corn dog frying mix as per instructions on the box in a
3-quart mixing bowl. Dip stuffed jalapeño halves into corn dog
batter to cover entire piece. (Use a tong or toothpick.)
Gently place jalapeño into fryer and fry for 3 to 5 minutes until
batter turns golden brown.
Remove with a serrated spoon or tong and place on a towel-draped
plate to cool. Sprinkle red or green chile powder for extra zest.

Suggested Complementary Dishes: Chips and salsa.

Servings: 24 pieces.

MEATBALL POPPERS–RED OR GREEN

Complexity Code: COOK   Origin: Original
COOKING METHOD: Bake / Fry

About the Recipe: Green or Red chile meatball poppers are a
Chilenista's candy. They are guaranteed to win accolades from guests and
be the center of the party.

Essential Recipe: Taco Ground Beef Mix (p. 62), Roasted Green Chile
((p. 46), or Rehydrated Red Chile pods (p. 40), Enchilada Sauce (p. 77).

Ingredients	Measure	Ingredient	Measure
Lean ground beef	1 lb.	Adobo Spice Mix (p. 83)	1 Tbsp.
Ground pork or sausage meat	½ lb.	Cilantro	¼ cup chopped
Roasted Green Chile Anaheim, Poblano, Jalapeño SHU to taste	1 cup chopped	Enchilada Sauce or ketchup	¼ cup
OR Rehydrated Red Chile Pods Ancho, Pasilla, Chipotle or Chile Seco SHU to taste	1 cup chopped	Rice flour or unbleached flour	1 cup
Bread crumbs	½ cup	Green chile powder	SHU to taste
Vegetable oil	¼ cup	Red chile powder	SHU to taste

Prep Instructions

Mix ground beef and ground pork in a mixing bowl and add
cilantro, Adobo Spice Mix, garlic, Enchilada Sauce, Roasted Green
Chile or Rehydrated Red Chile and bread crumbs. Blend mixture
well.
Coat bottom of a 10-by-15-inch baking pan with vegetable oil.
Place flour in a deep bowl. (Rice flour will give you a better crust.)

Form meatball ¾-inch round in the palm of your hand and roll
meatball in flour mix to coat entire surface.
Place on baking pan in even rows, leaving ¼ inch space around
each one.

Cooking Instructions

Baking

Preheat oven to 400^0F, place baking pan in heated oven and lower the temperature to 350^0F. This will create a thin crust on the meatball and keep all the juices in. Bake for about 30 minutes. Take out and let cool. Sprinkle any SHU level of chile powder on top to give the meatballs an extra burst of flavor.

Frying

Preheat a frying pan with about ¾ inch oil to 350^0F. Place coated meatballs in the oil and fry until the surface turns a brownish color. You will have to turn the meatballs every 3 minutes until all sides are evenly done. They should be cooked in about 15 to 20 minutes.

Place cooked meat balls on a paper towel to absorb extra oil and sprinkle with red or green chile powder, garlic powder or salt to give an extra burst of flavor.

Servings: 36 meatballs.

POTATO POPPERS—GREEN CHILE

Complexity Code: COOK   Origin: Original
Cooking Method: Pan-Fry / Bake

About the Recipe: Green Chile Potato Poppers will leave them asking for more.

Essential Recipe: Roasted Green Chile (p. 46).

Ingredient	Measure	Ingredient	Measure
Potatoes (medium Russet)	3–4	Adobo Spice Mix (p. 83)	2 Tbsp.
Roasted Green Chile Anaheim, Poblano, Jalapeño SHU to taste	1 cups chopped	Potato or cornstarch	2 Tbsp.
Eggs	2–3	Vegetable oil (frying)	2 cups
Scallions	Fine chopped	Red or green chile powder	½ cup
		Potato flour, mashed potato mix or unbleached flour	2 cups

Prep Instructions

Peel and grate potatoes with a hand grater (fine strips) or food processor with grating attachment (or use frozen hash brown mix) and place in 3- to 4-quart mixing bowl.

Strain excess liquid from shredded potatoes using a strainer by pressing down, or squeeze the water out with a cheese cloth wrapped around shredded potatoes.

Chop green chile into ¼-inch squares. Chop green scallion into ¼-inch rounds.

Beat eggs and add Adobo Spice Mix and potato starch.

Pour egg mixture and chopped green chile into mixing bowl. Mix potatoes, eggs and green chile until thoroughly blended.

Place flour on a plate or bowl (for dredging poppers). Form potato balls 1- to 1 ½-inch round. Flatten to ½-inch thick, dredge flattened potato balls in flour to coat all sides and place on a plate for frying. Let sit for 3 to 5 minutes.

Cooking Instructions

Pan-frying

Pour oil into large frying pan and bring to 375°F.
Gently place flattened potato balls into frying pan and fry each side for approximately 4 to 5 minutes until brown. (Do not overcrowd.) Place potato balls on a paper towel to drain, sprinkle with green chile powder or red chile powder.

Baking

Preheat oven to 375°F.
Place flatted potato balls on a greased baking pan and bake 4 to 5 minutes per side until brown.

Suggested Complementary Dishes: Crema dip, salsa, Red or Green Chile Sauce.

Servings: 24–30 potato poppers.

QUESADILLA (CRISPY & DIY VARIATIONS)

Complexity Code: EZ   Origin: New Mexico
Cooking Method: Fry and Bake

About the Recipe: Quesadillas are extremely easy to make and can let your imagination and creative ability concoct the perfect appetizer, based on the ingredients that you have. There are no rules. All you absolutely need is a tortilla and some cheese. The spices, sauces and fillings come from your own imagination and the suggested toppings.

Essential Recipe: Red Chile Sauce (p. 36), Green Chile Sauce (p. 50), Red Chile Tomato Sauce (p. 37), Taco Ground Beef (p.63), Sautéed Beef, Chicken or Pork (p.64).

Ingredient	Measure	Ingredient	Measure
Gordita (small tortillas 6") or thin burrito tortilla (9")	8–12	Shredded cheese blend. Asadero, Cheddar, Jack, Queso Quesadilla, or Cheddar only	2–4 cups
Red chile powder	To taste	Green chile powder	To taste
		Vegetable oil	2 Tbsp. (As needed)
SUGGESTED TOPPINGS Choose one or all			
Fresh Green Chile. Anaheim, Poblano, Jalapeño (fresh or roasted) SHU to taste	2 cups chopped	Rehydrated Red Chile Pods. Ancho, Pasilla, Chipotle or Chile Seco SHU to taste	2 cups
Onion	2 cups chopped	Shrimp	2 cups
Cilantro	1 cups chopped	Taco ground beef or Sauteed beef	2 cups
Guacamole	2 cups	Shredded chicken	2 cups
Crema	1 cup	Red Chile Sauce	2 cups
Beans or refried beans	1 cup	Green Chile Sauce	2 cups
Red Chile Tomato Sauce	1 cup	Salsa	2 cups
		Cold cuts	½ lb.

Prep Instructions

Prepare filling. (See suggestions above.)
Preheat heavy skillet with oil.360^{0}F.
Prepare a flat baking pan with a cooling rack on top. Preheat oven 350^{0}F.

Cooking Instructions

Fry gorditas or tortillas 15 to 20 seconds on each side until crispy.
Place fried gorditas (or tortillas) on the baking pan rack to drain the oil.
Sprinkle red or green chile powder to taste on top.
Spread ⅛-inch cheese layer or more on gordita. You can use cheddar
or cotija cheese to sharpen the taste. Place a layer(s) of fillings from the
above-suggested list on top of the cheese.
Cover fillings with a gordita. (Think of a quesadilla as a covered mini
pizza.) Place quesadilla on a flat baking pan.
Place quesadillas into center of 350^{0}F oven for 10 to 15 minutes to melt
cheese and blend fillings.
Cut into 4 pieces and plate.

Suggested Complementary Dishes: Crema, salsa and guacamole.

Servings: 32–64 pieces.

TOSTADA CON QUESO & MORE

Complexity Code: EZ   Origin: New Mexico
Cooking Method: Fry / Broil

About the Recipe: Freshly made tostadas are the ultimate appetizer,
snack or meal for any occasion. Tostadas are made in a few easy steps
with multiple toppings from simple melted cheese to a topping filled with
do-it-yourself delights. You can make the tostadas and have the toppings in
individual bowls for your guests and family to make their own.
Essential Recipe: Salsa (p. 142), Rehydrated Red Chile pods (p. 40),
Fresh Green Chile (p. 44), Ground Beef Mix (p. 62), Shredded Beef, Pork,
Chicken (p. 64).

Ingredient	Measure	Ingredient	Measure
Corn tortilla, gorditas or packaged tostadas	6–8 or more	Shredded cheese blend Asadero, Cheddar, Jack, Queso Quesadilla, or Cheddar only	2 cups
		Oil for frying	2 cups
TOPPINGS			
Crema		Fresh Green Chile	chopped
Salsa		Rehydrated Red Chile Pods	chopped
Shredded lettuce		Tomato	chopped
Refried beans		Onion	chopped
Shredded, Beef, Pork, Chicken		Cilantro	chopped
Ground Beef Mix			

Prep Instructions
Dry corn tortillas in a 250^{0}F oven for 10 minutes.
Preheat oil in a heavy skillet to 360^{0}F.

Prepare condiments and place in individual bowls.

Cooking Instructions
Fry corn tortillas or gorditas in hot oil about 3 to 5 seconds per side until
golden brown.
Place gordita (tortilla, tostada) in a baking pan with a rack to drain excess
oil. Place in 250^{0}F oven to keep warm.
If you wish to melt cheese on the gordita or tortilla, do so before placing
in oven by spreading the cheese mix on top and then broiling for 15 to 30
seconds.
Remove gorditas (tortillas, tostadas) from the oven, place on a large
serving plate and start placing the toppings.

Servings: 6-8 people

Chapter 3–BREADS & CHIPS

Bread is a staple of the Chilenista cuisine and serves as the underpinning of any great meal. Tortillas, gorditas, fry bread, pan bread, bolillos and sopapillas are all fairly easy to make. All you need is a tortilla press and a comal (flat pan). Although commercially available in almost every supermarket, nothing beats the taste of homemade breads.

"All sorrows are less with bread"   Cerauntes

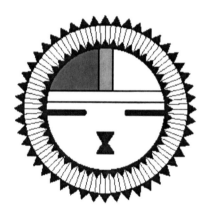

BOLILLOS

Complexity Code: Cook Origin: Mexico / New Mexico
Cooking Method: Bake

About the Recipe: Bolillos are the quick breads of the Chilenista cuisine and can be easily made, even though they do require a bit of attention. The first smell of fresh cooked bolillos will convince you they are worth the time; after one taste you will want to do it all over again.

Ingredient	Measure	Ingredient	Measure
Unbleached flour	6 cups	Active dry yeast	1 package
Warm water	2 cups	Sugar	2 Tsp.

Prep Instructions

In a 3- to 4-quart mixing bowl, mix yeast and sugar in two cups of warm water and stir well to blend.
Add salt and gradually add flour while stirring until the dough stiffens.
Place dough ball on a floured flat surface and continue to knead while adding all the flour for about 8 to 10 minutes until the dough is smooth and springy.
Place dough ball into a greased mixing bowl and cover with a wet towel. Let the dough rise until it doubles in size (about 1 hour). Punch the dough down and cover with wet towel until it doubles in size again.
Form dough ball into football-shape rolls about 3 inches long and twist each end closed.
Place rolls on a lightly floured baking pan(s) leaving 2 inches around each piece. Cut a small incision on top of the roll with a paring knife. Let the rolls rise once again to double in size. Brush top of roll with some melted butter.

Cooking Instructions

Preheat oven to 400°F. Place baking pan in center of oven and bake for 20 to 30 minutes until the top starts to brown. Remove from oven and let cool for 10 minutes.

Suggested Complementary Dishes: Butter, honey or any ingredient that you may wish to fill it with or just keep it plain.

Servings: 24–30 rolls.

CORNBREAD GREEN CHILE

Complexity Code: EZ   Origin: New Mexico
Cooking Method: Bake

About the Recipe: Once you taste or smell fresh green chile cornbread you will be hooked for life. This recipe will keep you and your guests coming back for more.
Essential Recipe: Roasted Green Chile (p. 46).

Ingredient	Measure	Ingredient	Measure
Cornmeal*	1 cup	Butter	1 stick
Unbleached flour	1 cup	Crema	½ cup
Baking soda	1 Tsp.	Sweetener (p. 85)	¼ cup
Eggs	2	Clove powder	pinch
Roasted Green Chile	2 cups	Vanilla extract	4 drops
Corn	1 cup	**OPTIONAL:**	
Milk	1 ½ cups	Optional Cheddar cheese	1 cup

*You can use a corn bread mix if you wish for the dry ingredients.

Prep Instructions

Preheat oven to 400°F.
Mix cornmeal, flour and baking soda in a 3- to 4 quart mixing bowl. Stir well to blend.
Soften butter in a microwave (defrost cycle 15 to 20 seconds) until almost melted.
In a separate mixing bowl beat eggs, add softened butter, milk, crema, clove powder and vanilla and blend well. Add liquid mixture to flour slowly and mix until all ingredients are blended. Add corn and green chile. Stir the batter until all the ingredients are well mixed. (Optionally add cheddar cheese.)
Pour batter into a greased 8-by-12-inch baking dish.

Cooking Instructions

Place baking dish in center of oven and bake for 30 to 40 minutes until the top is golden brown.
Insert a toothpick into the center of the cornbread; if it comes out dry, the cornbread is done.
Remove from oven and let cool for 15 to 20 minutes.

Suggested Complementary Dishes: Any soup, stew, meat, fish or vegetable dish. Serve with butter or crema.

Servings: 12 pieces.

FRY BREAD

Complexity Code: EZ   Origin: New Mexico
Cooking Method: Deep-fat frying

About the Recipe: Fry bread power is seen on many T-shirts, as it almost has a cult following. It is of one of the tastiest of all breads that you can easily make for any occasion. It is the ultimate in comfort food, eaten plain, as a desert or a meal with toppings.

Ingredient	Measure	Ingredient	Measure
Unbleached flour	2 cups	Baking powder	1 Tbsp.
Warm water	1 cup	Salt	1 Tsp.
Lard or vegetable oil	4 cups	**OPTIONAL:** Powdered milk	2 Tbsp.
Extra flour			

Prep Instructions

Preheat oil in a heavy skillet to 360^0F.

In a 3- 4-quart mixing bowl combine flour, baking powder, salt and blend well. (Add powdered milk for a touch of sweetness to the dough.) Pour water into flour and mix well until all the water is absorbed and dough is sticky.

Form a dough ball, place on a flat surface and coat with extra flour. Let dough sit for 5 minutes. (Do not knead.) Form 3- to 5-inch balls from the dough, flour outside to keep from sticking (inside should be sticky), flatten dough ball into a 5- to 7-inch round and immediately place in hot oil.

Cooking Instructions

Fry dough until it is golden brown and has puffed up. Place fry bread on a paper towel or baking rack to drain excess oil. Place in a warm oven 225^0F to keep warm until the fry bread is cooked.

Suggested Complementary Dishes: Eat plain with any dish, coat with powdered sugar and cinnamon for dessert or make an Indian Taco with lettuce, beans, red chile, onions, cheese, lettuce and ground beef with salsa on top.

Servings: 6–8 fry breads.

PAN BREAD–GREEN CHILE

Complexity Code: EZ   Origin: New Mexico / Mexico
Cooking Method: Bake

About the Recipe: This is as easy as it gets to make an excellent bread dish without any muss or fuss.
Essential Recipe: Roasted Green Chile (p. 46).

Ingredient	Measure	Ingredient	Measure
Cornmeal	2 cups	Garlic flakes or granulated powder	1 Tbsp.
Warm water	1 ½ cups	Onion flakes	¼ cup
Roasted Fresh Green Chile Anaheim, Poblano, Jalapeño. SHU to taste	1 cup chopped	Shredded cheese blend Asadero, cheddar, Jack, queso quesadilla	1 cup

Prep Instructions

Preheat oven to 350°F.
Mix cornmeal, garlic flakes and onion flakes in a mixing bowl. Add warm water and blend all ingredients. Add Roasted Green Chile and shredded cheese. Stir well.
Pour cornmeal batter into a greased heavy skillet.

Cooking Instructions

Place skillet into center of oven and bake for 15 to 20 minutes until it crusts. (You can check the center of the pan bread with a toothpick to make sure it is solid.)
Remove from oven, let cool for 5 minutes and serve.

Suggested Complementary Dishes: Beans, Red or Green Chile Stew and soups.

Servings: 4–6.

SOPAPILLA

Complexity Code: EZ   Origin: New Mexico
Cooking Method: Deep-fat fry

About the Recipe: Sopapillas are synonymous with New Mexico's chile cuisine. The fry bread concoction can be served with almost any dish forming a pocket for honey to be eaten with the hottest of chile dishes or stuffed with meats to make it a meal. Prepared sopapilla flour mixes are available at your supermarket

Ingredient	Measure	Ingredient	Measure
Unbleached flour	4 cups	Baking powder	2 Tsp.
Shortening or lard	4 Tbsp.	Salt	1 Tsp.
Warm milk	1½ cups	Lard or vegetable oil	4 cups

Prep Instructions

Preheat oil or butter in deep-fat fryer or heavy skillet with at least 2 to 3 inches of oil to 375^0F.

In a 3- to 4-quart mixing bowl, mix flour, baking powder and salt.

Pour 1 ½ cups of milk and shortening into a small microwaveable mixing bowl and warm under the defrost cycle for 1 to 2 minutes. (Do not bring to a boil.) Blend the liquefied shortening and milk and slowly pour into the flour and stir until a dough ball is formed.

Place the dough ball on a well-floured flat surface and knead the dough, folding it in half from all sides and pushing it together until the dough ball is soft and no longer sticky.

Cover the dough ball with a wet towel and let it rest for 15 to 20 minutes.

Cut the dough ball in half and roll out a flat strip of dough ¼-inch thick on a floured surface. Work fast so that the dough will not dry out.

With a sharp knife or pizza cutter cut the dough into 4-inch squares.

Cover the dough with a wet towel to keep the squares moist until ready to fry.

Cooking Instructions

Carefully place the sopapilla dough into the fryer and fry for about 1 to 2 minutes per side until golden brown. Place sopapilla on a towel or rack to drain, keep warm in an oven at 200^0F until all of the sopapillas are fried and ready to serve.

Suggested Complementary Dishes: Rip one corner of the sopapilla and pour honey into the middle. Serve with any chile dish, stew, soup or have one ready for desert.

Servings 18–24.

TORTILLAS (CORN)

Complexity Code: EZ   Origin: Mexico, New Mexico
Cooking Method: Pan-fry (dry)

About the Recipe: While corn tortillas are available in almost every grocery in many varieties and shapes, nothing beats fresh made corn tortillas for their smell, texture and taste. They are very simple to make and take very little time.

Ingredient	Measure		Measure
Masa Flour (Masa Harina), Blue cornmeal or yellow cornmeal	2 cups	Baking powder	1 Tbsp.
Shortening or lard	1 cup	Salt	2 Tsp.
Warm water	1 cup		

Prep Instructions

Mix flour, baking soda and salt in a 2-quart mixing bowl.

Soften shortening or lard in a microwave using the defrost cycle for 20–30 seconds in a small mixing bowl.

Add softened shortening into the masa and blend with a fork or your hands. Gradually pour warm water while blending to form a dough ball. The dough should be soft, stretchy and not sticky. Add some additional flour or water if necessary. Cover the mixing bowl with a wet towel and let the dough rest for about ½ hour.

Place dough ball on a flat floured surface and cut into 1 ½-inch balls. If you do not have a tortilla press which is available at all Mexican groceries, you can flatten balls with a rolling pin to about 1/8-inch thick and 6-inch round. If you want perfectly round tortillas, place a 6-inch plate over the flattened bough ball and cut the edges with a sharp knife.

Preheat an iron skillet or comal to medium heat.

Cooking Instructions

Place each tortilla on a skillet or comal and pan fry for 1 to 2 minutes per side. (Do not overcook.)

Suggested Complementary Dishes: Fresh tortillas will complement any dish

Servings: 12–15 tortillas.

TORTILLAS OR GORDITAS (FLOUR)

Complexity Code: EZ   Origin: Mexico, New Mexico
Cooking Method: Pan-fry (dry)

About the Recipe: While store bought tortillas are available in almost every grocery in many varieties and shapes, nothing beats fresh made tortillas for their smell, texture and taste. They are very simple to make and take very little time.

Ingredient	Measure	Ingredient	Measure
Unbleached flour	4 cups	Baking powder	1 Tbsp.
Shortening or lard	1 cup	Salt	2 Tsp.
Warm water	1 cup		

Prep Instructions

Mix flour, baking soda and salt in a 3- to 4-quart mixing bowl.
Soften shortening or oil in a microwave using the defrost cycle for 20 to 30 seconds in a small mixing bowl.
Add softened shortening into the flour and blend with a fork or your hands. Gradually pour warm water while blending to form a dough ball. The dough should be soft, stretchy and not sticky. Add some additional flour or water if necessary. Cover the mixing bowl with a wet towel and let the dough rest for about 1 hour.
Place dough ball on a flat floured surface and cut 2-inch balls. If you do not have a tortilla press which is available at all Mexican groceries, you can flatten balls with a rolling pin to about 1/8-inch thick and 9-inch round. If you want perfectly round tortillas, place a 9-inch plate over the flattened bough ball and cut the edges with a sharp knife. Use a 6-inch plate to make gorditas.
Preheat an iron skillet or comal to medium heat.

Cooking Instructions

Place each tortilla on skillet or comal and pan fry for 1 to 2 minutes per side. (Do not overcook.)

Suggested Complementary Dishes: Fresh tortillas will complement any dish

Servings: 12–15 9-inch tortillas, 18–24 gorditas.

TORTILLAS (FRIED)

Complexity Code: EZ
Cooking Method: Pan-fry

Origin: New Mexico

About the Recipe: Also known as the lazy man's fry bread, you can fry up a tortilla in less than 3 minutes to satisfy the urge for fry bread.

Ingredient	Measure	Ingredient	Measure
Flour Tortillas	4–8	Red chile powder	To taste
Vegetable oil	2 Tbsp.	Green chile powder	To taste
		Honey	To taste

Prep Instructions

Coat bottom of heavy skillet with oil.
Preheat a heavy skillet to high heat.

Cooking Instructions

Place a tortilla into the skillet and pan-fry for 1 to 2 minutes until it bubbles, flip and pan-fry second side.
Remove tortilla from skillet and place on a paper towel or drying rack to drain.
Sprinkle red chile or green chile powder to taste.
Place tortilla on a paper towel or rack to drain, keep warm in an oven at 200°F until all of the tortillas are fried and ready to serve.

Suggested Complementary Dishes: Eat plain with a dip of honey while warm.

Servings 4–8.

TORTILLAS (STEAMED)

Complexity Code: EZ
Cooking Method: Microwave / Oven

Origin: New Mexico

About the Recipe: Steamed tortillas can be the ultimate comfort food. Soft, warm and juicy, tortillas can be topped or folded with almost any ingredient.

Ingredient	Measure	Ingredient	Measure
Tortilla or gordita	4–8	Butter	To taste
(Store-bought is okay)		Crema	To taste
Wet towel		Green chile	To taste
		Red chile	To taste
		Any meat, chicken, fish	To taste

Prep Instructions

Wet a clean kitchen towel.
Moisten tortillas and wrap moist towel around 2 to 4 tortillas.

Cooking Instructions

Place moist towel into microwave. Set microwave to defrost cycle for 20 to 30 seconds or place in a warm oven at 250^0F until all of the tortillas are steamed.
Remove tortillas from towel. Separate if they have stuck together

Suggested Complementary Dishes: A soft tortilla can be used to wrap any filling or eaten with a meal.

Servings 4–8.

CHIPS

An endless variety of packaged chips can be purchased: white corn chips, yellow corn chips, blue corn chips, tostadas and scooping chips. I like to use locally produced chips whenever possible, as they are generally fresher, have less additives and seem to taste better. It is always wise to taste-test your chips before you serve them. Many a great dip or salsa has been bypassed because the chips were not fresh or tasted stale.

DUROS (CHIPS)

Complexity Code: EZ   Origin: Mexico
Cooking Method: Deep-fry

About the Recipe: Duros are the Mexican equivalent of potato chips and come in pinwheel or flat shapes. They have a nutty, crisp flavor that will enhance any dip or salsa. You can get them at almost any Mexican grocer or online.

Ingredient	Measure		Measure
Duros chips	1 lb.	Oil	1 qt.
		Red chile powder	To taste
		Green chile powder	To taste
		Salt	To taste

Prep Instructions
In a large skillet or deep-fat fryer heat oil to 375^{0}F.

Cooking Instructions
Drop duros pieces into the hot oil one at a time. They will sink to the bottom and then expand to float to the top.
Place duros on a paper towel to drain excess oil and sprinkle red chile or green chile powder or salt to taste. You can store the duros in a dry bag for future use.

Suggested Complementary Dishes: Any dip or salsa.

FRIED TORTILLA CHIPS

Complexity Code: EZ   Origin: New Mexico

About the Recipe: Although there are numerous store-bought tortilla chips available in many shapes and varieties, none can compare to freshly-made tortillas.

Ingredient	Measure		Measure
Flour or corn tortillas	4–8	Red chile powder	To taste
Vegetable oil	2 Tbsp.	Green chile powder	To taste
		Honey	To taste

Prep Instructions
Coat bottom of heavy skillet with oil and preheat to high.
Cut tortilla into strips, squares or triangles. (Using scissors is okay.)

Cooking Instructions
Place a tortilla into the skillet, fry for 1 to 2 minutes until it bubbles, flip, and pan-fry second side.
Remove tortilla from skillet and place on a paper towel or drying rack to drain.
Keep warm in an oven at 200^0F until all of the tortillas are fried and ready to serve.

Suggested Complementary Dishes: Any dip or accompaniment for any dish.

Servings: 4–8.

Chapter 4–DIPS

You will find an endless variety of dips in the Chilenista cuisine, consisting of the ever-popular chile con queso to numerous other concoctions. Crema, cream cheese, asadero, cheddar, Monterey Jack, queso quesadilla and Mexican cheese blends are available in most dairy cases to suit any taste. Please look at the glossary cheese section (p. 353) for additional cheese selections.

Melted cheeses and a variety of vegetables can be shredded, chopped puréed and flavored with chile, garlic, onion, cilantro, lime juice, lemon juice, nectars, Adobo Spice Mix, coriander, cumin, crushed oregano, red chile and green chile powder to create your own best dip ever.

Most dips can be used as condiments to enhance a meal or as a side dish to refresh the palate.

Please look at the serving suggestions for recommendations.

CHILE CON QUESO

Complexity Code: EZ   Origin: New Mexico / Mexico

About the Recipe: Chile con queso is the basic warm melted cheese dip that can be adapted to any taste—hot, mild, sweet, sour or bland. This recipe will give you the ESSENTIAL RECIPE that you can adapt to make your own creation. Your imagination and taste buds should be your guide in making your con queso. The great thing is that you can eat your mistakes.

Essential Recipe: Fresh Green Chile (p. 44), Rehydrated Red Chile pods (p. 40).

Ingredient	Measure	Ingredient	Measure
Shredded cheese blend Asadero, cheddar, Jack, queso quesadilla	2 cups		
		OPTIONAL:	
Half-and-half or heavy cream	1 cup	Tomato	¼ cup chopped
Butter or oil	2 Tbsp.	Onion	¼ cup chopped
Rehydrated Red Chile Pods Ancho, Pasilla, Chipotle or Chile Seco SHU to taste	1 cup chopped	Cilantro	¼ cup chopped
Tomato sauce	¼ cup	Raisins (hydrated)	¼ cup
Sweetener (p. 85)	2 Tbsp.	Adobo Spice Mix (p. 83)	1 Tbsp.
Balsamic or wine vinegar	2 Tbsp.	Pinion nuts, peanuts or other chopped nuts	¼ cup
Green chile powder or red chile powder SHU to taste	1 Tbsp. at a time		

Prep Instructions

Combine half-and-half, cheese and butter into a 2- to 3-quart saucepan or microwavable bowl.

Cooking Instructions

Under low heat or defrost mode in your microwave, heat cheese until it starts to melt.

Blend milk and cheese to a thick consistency so that it will stick to a tortilla chip. (Add additional cheese or milk to get the right consistency.)

Add chopped red or green chile, tomato sauce, sweetener, balsamic vinegar and blend well. Add red or green chile powder to heat up the chile dip to your desired taste and SHU level. (Use 1 tsp. at a time and blend before you taste.

Add additional chile powder until desired heat level is reached. You may wish to split the mixture into two batches, mild and hot, to suit the taste of different individuals from wimp to macho.

Optional Ingredients

Chopped tomato for flavor chunks. Chopped onion for flavor chunks. Chopped cilantro for an aromatic herbal flavor.

Adobo Spice Mix or individual portions of 1 Tsp. each of garlic, coriander, cumin and oregano for a tart and aromatic spice flavor.

Pinion nuts, peanuts or other chopped nuts for a nutty, crunchy texture.

Suggested Complementary Dishes: Serve warm with chips, celery stalks, or bell pepper strips.

Servings 3–4 cups. Serves: 6–8 people.

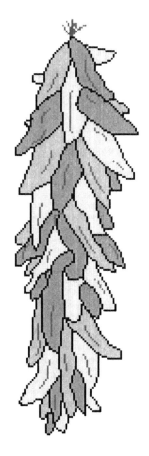

CREMA CHILE CHEESE DIP–RED OR GREEN

Complexity Code: EZ   Origin: Original

About the Recipe: This is the universal cheese dip that can be flavored, spiced and served for any occasion. The basic recipe allows an infinite assortment of flavors, spices and ingredients tailored to your family's or guests' taste. Make two batches mild and hot to please everyone.
Essential Recipe: Fresh Green Chile (p. 44), Chopped Rehydrated Red Chile (p. 40).

Ingredient	Measure	Ingredient	Measure
Crema or sour cream	1 cup	**OPTIONAL:**	
Whipped cream cheese	1 cup	Chopped pimento pepper	¼ cup
Red or Green Chile (fresh or roasted) SHU to taste	1 cup chopped	Tomato	¼ cup chopped
Sweetener (p. 85)	2 Tbsp.	Onion or scallions	¼ cup chopped
Fruit Nectar Mango, guava, papaya or lime juice	2 Tbsp.	Cilantro	¼ cup
Balsamic or wine vinegar	2 Tbsp.	Crumbled cheese: Cheddar, cotija, blue cheese, queso fresca	½ cup
Adobo Spice Mix (p. 83)	1 Tbsp.	Pinion or other nuts	¼ cup
Green chile powder or red chile powder SHU to taste	1 tsp. at a time	Additional garlic, oregano, cumin, coriander to taste	1Tbsp. at a time

Prep Instructions

Blend crema and whipped cream cheese in a mixing bowl to a thick consistency that will not drip off of a chip, and add chopped red or green chile for flavor chunks, sweetener, nectar to give a sweet fruitiness, lime juice, and balsamic vinegar for a sweet and sour aftertaste.
Add Adobo Spice Mix or individual portions of 1 Tsp. each of garlic, coriander, cumin and oregano for tart and aromatic spice flavor. Add red or green chile powder to heat up the chile dip to your desired taste and SHU level. (Use 1 Tbsp. at a time and blend in; taste and add additional chile powder until desired heat level is reached.) You may wish to split the mixture into two batches, mild and hot to suite the taste of different individuals.

Optional Ingredients

Chopped pimento peppers to add color and pimento pepper taste.
Chopped tomato for flavor chunks. Chopped onion for flavor chunks.
Chopped cilantro for an aromatic herbal flavor.
Crumbled cheese for tart cheese flavor chunks. Pinion nuts or other nuts
for a nutty, crunchy texture.
Your imagination and taste buds should be your guide in making your
cheese dip.

Suggested Complementary Dishes: Garnish with green scallions.
Serve with chips, celery stalks, jalapeño strips and bell pepper strips.

Servings: 3–4 cups. Serves: 6–8 people.

CUCUMBER / DILL CHILE DIP

Complexity Code: EZ   Origin: Original
Cooking Method: Blender

About the Recipe: This dip offers a taste change of pace that renews your taste buds. It is as refreshing as brushing your teeth and cleaning your mouth. It will enhance the taste of any dish you may prepare. Use it as a dip, garnish or condiment between dishes.

Essential Recipe: Fresh Green Chile (p. 44).

Ingredient	Measure	Ingredient	Measure
Crema or sour cream	1 cup	Adobo Spice Mix (p. 83)	1 tsp.
Whipped cream cheese	1 cup	Sweetener: (Nectar) (p. 85) Mango, guava, papaya	2 Tbsp.
Fresh Green Chile Anaheim, Poblano, Jalapeño (fresh or roasted) SHU to taste	1 cup	Lime juice	2 Tbsp.
Cucumber	2 cups	Green chile powder SHU to taste	1 tsp.
Dill (dried or fresh)	1 cup		

Prep Instructions

Blend crema and whipped cream cheese in a mixing bowl to a thick consistency that will not drip off of a chip. Add sweetener (nectar to give a sweet fruitiness to the cheese dip) and lime juice for a sweet and sour aftertaste. Place in blender.

Chop green chile and dill and place in blender. Peel and seed cumbers and cut into 1-inch chunks. Place in blender.

Add Adobo Spice mixture and green chile powder into blender.

Cooking Instructions

Blend all ingredients in the chop mode to leave a few chunks in the mixture.

Suggested Complementary Dishes: Chips or any dish as a condiment or side dish.

Servings: 3–4 cups. Serves: 6–8 people.

GREEN CHILE BEAN DIP (NEW MEXICO CAVIAR)

Complexity Code: EZ   Origin: New Mexico
Cooking Method: Stir / blend

About the Recipe: New Mexico caviar can be served as an alternate to refried beans to give a fresh, tart taste as a dip, condiment or side dish for any meal.
Essential Recipe: Fresh Green Chile (p. 44).

Ingredient	Measure	Ingredient	Measure
Crema or sour cream	1 cup	Adobo Spice Mix (p. 83)	1 Tbsp.
Whipped cream cheese	1 cup	Sweetener (Nectar) (p. 85) Mango, guava, papaya	¼ cup
Fresh Green Chile Anaheim, Poblano, Jalapeño, Roasted or fresh SHU to taste	1 cup	Lime juice	¼ cup
Pinto beans (canned okay)	2 cup	Balsamic or wine vinegar	2 Tbsp.
Cilantro	1 cup	Green chile powder SHU to taste	1 Tbsp.
Chopped onion	½ cup		

Prep Instructions

Blend crema and whipped cream cheese in a mixing bowl to a thick consistency that will not drip off of a chip. Add sweetener (nectar to give a sweet fruitiness) and lime juice for a sweet and sour aftertaste.
Rinse a can of pinto beans of all preservatives, crush ½ cup of beans into a paste, place beans into mixing bowl.
Chop green chile, onion and cilantro into ¼" squares.

Cooking Instructions

Add Adobo Spice mixture into bowl along with green chile powder and balsamic vinegar. Stir mixture until all ingredients are blended. Taste and adjust as you would like with additional garlic, coriander, cumin, oregano or green chile powder 1 tsp. at a time.

Suggested Complementary Dishes: Chips or any dish as a condiment or side dish.

Servings: 4–6 cups. Serves: 8–12 people.

GREEN CHILE BLUE CHEESE DIP

Complexity Code: EZ   Origin: Original
Cooking Method: Stir / Blend

About the Recipe: Something magical happens when blue cheese and green chile get together. The combination of the two tastes explodes in your mouth with a euphoric blend that is almost addictive.
Essential Recipe: Roasted Green Chile (p. 46).

Ingredient	Measure	Ingredient	Measure
Crema or sour cream	1 cup	Sweetener (Nectar) (p. 85) Mango, guava, papaya	¼ cup
Crumbled blue cheese	1 cup	Garlic powder	1 Tbsp.
Mayonnaise	½ cup	Green chile powder	1 Tbsp.
Roasted Green Chile (fresh or frozen)	½ cup	Balsamic or wine vinegar	2 Tbsp.

Prep Instructions

Blend crema, blue cheese mayonnaise, vinegar and fresh Green Chile in a mixing bowl to a thick consistency. Add green chile powder, vinegar and sweetener and blend all ingredients.
If it is too thin, add some additional crumbled blue cheese, and if it is too thick add some additional sweetener.

Servings: 3–4 cups.

GREEN CHILE REFRIED BEAN DIP

Complexity Code: EZ   Origin: Original
Cooking Method: Stir / Blend

About the Recipe: Refried beans combined with green chile can be served as dip, condiment or side dish for any meal or occasion. You will get compliments every time.

Essential Recipe: Fresh Green Chile (p. 44) OR Roasted Green Chile (p.46)

Ingredient	Measure	Ingredient	Measure
Crema or sour cream	1 cup	Adobo Spice Mix (p. 83)	1 Tbsp.
Refried beans (canned OK)	2 cup	Sweetener (Nectar) (p. 85) Mango, guava, papaya	¼ cup
Fresh Green Chile Anaheim, Poblano, Jalapeño (fresh or roasted) SHU to taste	1 cup	Lime juice	¼ cup
Cilantro	1 cup	Balsamic or wine vinegar	2 Tbsp.
Onion	½ cup chopped	Green chile powder SHU to taste	1 Tbsp.

Prep Instructions

Blend crema and refried beans in a mixing bowl to a thick consistency that will not drip off of a chip. Add sweetener (nectar for a sweet fruitiness) and lime juice for a sweet and sour aftertaste. If the mixture is too thick, blend some milk or half-and-half to thin out.

Chop green chile, onion and cilantro into ¼-inch squares.

Cooking Instructions

Add Adobo Spice mixture into mixing bowl along with green chile powder and balsamic vinegar. Stir mixture until all ingredients are blended. Taste and adjust as you would like with additional garlic, coriander, cumin, oregano or green chile powder, 1 tsp. at a time.

Suggested Complementary Dishes: Chips or any dish as a condiment or side dish.

Servings: 4–6 cups. Serves: 8–12 people.

GREEN CHILE CLAM, CRAB OR FISH DIP

Complexity Code: EZ   Origin: New Mexico
Cooking Method: Stir / Blend

About the Recipe: For seafood lovers this is the change of pace dip. You can use clams, crabs or any whitefish to create your own fish dip.
Essential Recipe: Fresh Green Chile (p. 44) OR Roasted Green Chile (p.46)

Ingredient	Measure	Ingredient	Measure
Crema or sour cream	1 cup	Adobo Spice Mix (p. 83)	1 Tbsp.
Whipped cream cheese	1 cup	Sweetener (Nectar) (p. 85) Mango, guava, papaya	¼ cup
Chopped clams, crab, fish blend or any cooked whitefish	2 cup	Lime juice	¼ cup
Fresh Green Chile Anaheim, Poblano, Jalapeño (fresh or roasted) SHU to taste	1 cup	Balsamic or wine vinegar	1 tsp.
Cilantro	1 cup	Green chile powder SHU to taste	1 tsp.
Clam juice	½ cup		
Red bell pepper	½ cup		

Prep Instructions

Blend crema, whipped cream cheese in a mixing bowl to a thick consistency that will not drip off of a chip. Add sweetener (nectar gives a sweet fruitiness) and lime juice for a sweet and sour aftertaste.
Chop clams or crab mix, bell pepper and cilantro into ¼-inch squares. You may use canned clams or imitation blend crab.

Cooking Instructions

Add Adobo Spice mixture into a bowl along with hot green chile powder and balsamic vinegar. Stir mixture until all ingredients are blended. Taste and adjust as you would like with additional garlic, coriander, cumin, oregano or green chile powder 1 tsp. at a time.

Suggested Complementary Dishes: Chips or any dish as a condiment to spice it up.

Servings: 4–6 cups.

GREEN CHILE CORN DIP

Complexity Code: EZ   Origin: New Mexico
Cooking Method: Stir / Blend

About the Recipe: Corn is the perfect complement to any dish or recipe, this green chile corn dip will enhance any party or meal.
Essential Recipe: Fresh Green Chile (p. 44) OR Roasted Green Chile (p.46)

Ingredient	Measure	Ingredient	Measure
Crema or sour cream	1 cup	Adobo Spice Mix (p. 83)	1 Tbsp.
Corn (frozen okay)	2 cup	Sweetener (Nectar) (p. 85) Mango, guava, papaya	¼ cup
Fresh Green Chile Anaheim, Poblano, Jalapeño (fresh or roasted) SHU to taste	1 cup	Lime juice	¼ cup
Cilantro	1 cup	Balsamic or wine vinegar	2 Tbsp.
Onion	½ cup chopped	Green chile powder SHU to taste	1 Tbsp.
Red bell pepper	½ cup chopped		

Prep Instructions
Blend crema and corn in a mixing bowl to a thick consistency that will not drip off of a chip. Add sweetener (nectar to give a sweet fruitiness to the cheese dip) and lime juice for a sweet and sour aftertaste. If the mixture is too thick, blend some milk or half-and-half to thin out.
Chop green chile, onion bell pepper and cilantro into ¼-inch squares.

Cooking Instructions
Add Adobo Spice mixture into mixing bowl along with green chile powder and balsamic vinegar. Stir mixture until all ingredients are blended. Taste and adjust as you would like with additional garlic, coriander, cumin, oregano and green chile powder, 1 tsp. at a time.

Suggested Complementary Dishes: Chips or any dish as a condiment or side dish.

Servings: 4–6 cups. Serves: 8–12 people.

GREEN CHILE–SALSA DIP (CHUNKY OR PASTE)

Complexity Code: EZ   Origin: New Mexico

About the Recipe: Green chile salsa is an authentic New Mexico tradition that blends the great green chile taste with any dish as an appetizer with chips, a condiment or side dish.

Essential Recipe: Fresh Green Chile (p. 44) OR Roasted Green Chile (p.46)

Ingredient	Measure	Ingredient	Measure
Fresh Green Chile Anaheim, Poblano, Jalapeño (fresh or roasted) SHU to taste	2 cups	Adobo Spice Mix (p. 83)	1 Tbsp.
Tomato fresh or canned (drained)	1 cups chopped	Sweetener (p. 85)	2 Tbsp.
Onion	½ cup chopped	Lime juice	¼ cup
Cilantro	1 cup chopped	Tomato paste	1 Tbsp.
Tomatillo (finely chopped or puréed)	½ cup	Olive oil	2 Tbsp.
		Balsamic or wine vinegar	1 Tbsp.

Prep Instructions

Variations

Coarse Green Chile Salsa

(To be served as a dip with chips.) Chop green chile, tomato, onion and cilantro into ¼-inch squares or less and place in a mixing bowl.

Blend tomatillo, sweetener, lime juice, Adobo Spice Mix, tomato paste, olive oil and vinegar in a blender or use a blending stick.

Pour in sweetener, blend over chopped chile mixture and stir all ingredients. Taste and adjust to add additional ingredients (garlic, green chile powder, a pinch of clove). Add more sweetener or tomato paste to thicken. Place in a refrigerator to cool ½ to 1 hour.

Green Chile Salsa Paste

(To be served as a garnish with chips before a meal.) Chop green chile, tomato and onion into ¼-inch squares or less and place in a blender. Chop cilantro and add. Add tomatillo, sweetener, Adobo Spice Mix, tomato paste, olive oil and vinegar and blend in a chop mode to leave some chunks in the paste. Pour green chile salsa paste into a mixing bowl. Taste and make adjustments as above, chill and serve.

Suggested Complementary Dishes: Chips, wine, guacamole.

Servings: 3–4 cups. Serves: 6–8 people.

GUACAMOLE

Complexity Code: EZ   Origin: New Mexico / Mexico
Cooking Method: Mix / Blend

About the Recipe: Guacamole is one of the most popular of all Mexican
sauces (mole) that is used as a dip, salsa or side dishes. To prepare it best,
select ripe guacamoles that you can easily mash with a fork. Its delicate
fruit-like taste and buttery texture are easily overwhelmed by other more
powerful spices, so use them sparingly.
Essential Recipe: Fresh Green Chile (p. 44) OR Roasted Green Chile
(p.46)

Ingredient	Measure	Ingredient	Measure
Avocado (large) ripe	2 cups	Tomato	¼ cup chopped
Fresh Green Chile Anaheim, Poblano, Jalapeño, (Fresh or roasted) SHU to taste	1 cup	Cilantro	¼ cup chopped
Lime juice	¼ cup	Cumin	¼ tsp.
Onion	¼ cup fine chopped	Garlic powder	1 Tbsp.
Green onion	¼ cup chopped	Olive oil	2 Tbsp.

Prep Instructions
Peel avocado and scoop out the meat with a spoon into a mixing bowl.
Add lime juice, chopped green onion, chopped onion, chopped tomato,
chopped cilantro, cumin, garlic and olive oil.
With a potato masher or fork, mash and blend ingredients. Leave a few
chunks of avocado for texture and taste.

Cooking Instructions
Cover mixing bowl and refrigerate avocado mixture for ½ to 1 hour.

Suggested Complementary Dishes: Chips or side dish for any meal.

Servings: 3–4 cups. Serves: 6–8 people.

JALAPEÑO OR HABANERO FIRE EATERS DIP

Complexity Code: EZ
Cooking Method: Stir / Blend

Origin: New Mexico

About the Recipe: This is the XXXX chile dip that will separate the men or women from the wimps. (Please have some cream cheese, milk or tequila ready for the gringos.)
Essential Recipe: Fresh Green Chile (p. 44).

Ingredient	Measure	Ingredient	Measure
Crema or sour cream	1 cup	Adobo Spice Mix (p. 83)	1 Tbsp.
Whipped cream cheese	1 cup	Sweetener (Nectar) (p. 85) Mango, guava, papaya	¼ cup
Jalapeño or better still Habanero chiles SHU to XXXX taste	2 cups chopped	Lime juice	¼ cup
Cilantro	1 cup	Balsamic or wine vinegar	2 Tbsp.
		Green chile powder SHU to taste	2 Tbsp.

Prep Instructions
Blend crema, whipped cream cheese in a mixing bowl to a thick consistency that will not drip off of a chip. Add nectar to give a sweet fruitiness and lime juice for a sweet and sour aftertaste.
Chop jalapeño or habanero chiles, or blend of both, into ¼-inch squares. Chop cilantro.

Cooking Instructions
Add Adobo Spice mixture into mixing bowl along with hot green chile powder and balsamic vinegar. Stir mixture until all ingredients are blended. Taste and adjust with additional garlic, coriander, cumin, oregano and green chile powder 1 tsp. at a time.

Suggested Complementary Dishes: Chips or any dish as a condiment to spice it up.

Servings: 4–6 cups.

RED CHILE HAM, SPAM OR MEAT DIP

Complexity Code: EZ   Origin: New Mexico
Cooking Method: Blender

About the Recipe: For meat-lovers this is the ultimate chile dip that will satisfy the carnivore in the room.
Essential Recipe: Rehydrated Red Chile pods (p. 40).

Ingredient	Measure	Ingredient	Measure
Crema or sour cream	1 cup	Adobo Spice Mix (p. 83)	1Tbsp.
Whipped cream cheese	1 cup	Sweetener (Nectar) (p. 85) Mango, guava, papaya	¼ cup
Chopped ham, spam or any cooked meat.	2 cup	Lime juice chopped	¼ cup
Rehydrated Red Chile Pods Ancho, Pasilla, Chipotle or Chile Seco SHU to taste	1 cup chopped	Balsamic or wine vinegar	1 tsp.
Cilantro	1 cup	Red chile powder SHU to taste	1 tsp.
Tomato sauce or ketchup	½ cup		
Red bell pepper	½ cup		

Prep Instructions

Blend crema and whipped cream cheese in a mixing bowl to a thick consistency that will not drip off of a chip. Add nectar to give a sweet fruitiness to the cheese dip and lime juice for a sweet and sour aftertaste. Place in blender.
Chop ham, spam or meat into squares and place in blender.
Add Adobo Spice mixture and red chile powder into blender.

Cooking Instructions

Blend all ingredients in the chop mode to leave a few chunks in the mixture.

Suggested Complementary Dishes: Chips or any dish as a condiment or side dish.

Servings: 3–4 cups. Serves: 6–8 people.

RED CHILE SALSA DIP (CHUNKY OR PASTE)

Complexity Code: EZ   Origin: New Mexico

About the Recipe: Red Chile Salsa is served with almost every meal in an authentic New Mexico kitchen. It can be used as a dip, condiment or side dish to complement any meal.
Cooking Method: Blender
Essential Recipe: Rehydrated Red Chile pods (p. 40), Red Chile Sauce (p. 36).

Ingredient	Measure	Ingredient	Measure
Rehydrated Red Chile Pods Ancho, Pasilla, Chipotle or Chile Seco SHU to taste	1 cup chopped	Adobo Spice Mix (p. 83)	1 Tbsp.
Red Chile Sauce SHU to taste	1 cup	Sweetener (p. 85)	2 Tbsp.
Tomato fresh or canned (drained)	1 cups chopped	Lime juice	¼ cup
Onion	½ cup chopped	Tomato paste	1 Tbsp.
Cilantro	½ cup chopped	Olive oil	2 Tbsp.
Tomatillo (finely chopped or puréed)	½ cup	Balsamic or wine vinegar	1 Tbsp.

Prep Instructions

Coarse Red Chile Salsa
(To be served as a dip with chips.)
Chop Rehydrated Red Chile Pods, tomato and onion into ¼-inch squares or less and place in a mixing bowl. Add chopped cilantro.
Blend tomatillo, sweetener, lime juice, Adobo Spice Mix, tomato paste, olive oil and vinegar in a blender or with a blending stick.
Pour sweetener, blend over chopped chile mixture and stir all ingredients. Taste and adjust. Add additional ingredients: garlic, red chile powder, a pinch of clove. Add more sweetener or tomato paste to thicken. Place in a refrigerator to cool one-half to 1 hour.

Red Chile Salsa Paste
(To be served as a garnish with chips before a meal.)
Chop Rehydrated red chile pods, tomato and onion and into ¼-inch squares or less and place in a blender. Add chopped cilantro. Blend tomatillo, sweetener, Adobo Spice Mix, tomato paste, olive oil and vinegar in a chop mode to leave some chunks in the paste. Pour Red Chile Salsa Paste into a mixing bowl. Taste and make adjustments as above, chill and serve.

Suggested Complementary Dishes: Chips, wine, guacamole.

Servings: 3–4 cups. Serves: 6-8 people.

SALSA VERDE–GREEN CHILE DIP

Complexity Code: EZ   Origin: New Mexico / Mexico
Cooking Method: Blend

About the Recipe: Salsa Verde will add a piquant, semi-sour taste to any dish and can be served alongside any other dips or condiments to give you a refreshing taste.

Essential Recipe: Fresh Green Chile (p. 44).Roasted Green Chile (p. 46)

Ingredient	Measure	Ingredient	Measure
Tomatillo	2 cups	Adobo Spice Mix (p. 83)	1 Tbsp.
Fresh Green Chile Anaheim, Poblano, Jalapeño (fresh or roasted) SHU to taste	1 cup	Sweetener (p. 85)	2 Tbsp.
Onion	½ cup chopped	Lime juice	¼ cup
Cilantro	1 cup chopped	Olive oil	2 Tbsp.

Prep Instructions

Clean tomatillo and quarter and place in a blender along with Fresh Green Chile, chopped onion, chopped cilantro, sweetener, lime juice and Adobo Spice Mix.

Cooking Instructions

Blend all ingredients with chop mode to leave a few chunks in salsa verde. Pour blend in a serving bowl and garnish with a few green chile squares and cilantro.

Suggested Complementary Dishes: Chips and condiment for main dishes or side dishes.

Servings: 3–4 cups. Serves: 6–8 people.

Chapter 5—SALSAS

Chilenistas love their salsas almost as much as their meals. The first thing that you will be served in any traditional home is chips and salsa. Every celebration, event or get together will feature a variety of salsas served with great pride.

Almost all salsas are a secret blend of red or green chile that can range from a mild sweet condiment to a tongue-blistering experience that XXXX aficionados vie for. The Scoville Heat Units are under your control, and you can blend the salsa that you make to be mild, medium, hot or XXXX for any occasion. Salsa-making is the best place to show off your skill in selecting and using the many chile varieties that are available, either green or red. I have several recipe suggestions, but the blending of heat levels is your choice.

My recommendation is to make two batches—mild and hot or XXXX—for each recipe to satisfy all of your family or guest preferences.

GREEN CHILE EGGPLANT SALSA

Complexity Code: COOK   Origin: New Mexico
Cooking Method: Bake / Chop, Mix, Marinate

About the Recipe: The tangy buttery taste of eggplant combined with
the pungency of green chile will produce an excellent salsa that can be
served as a dip, side dish or condiment with any recipe.
Essential Recipe: Roasted Green Chile (p. 46).

Ingredient	Measure	Ingredient	Measure
Eggplant	2–4 cups	Adobo Spice Mix (p. 83)	1 Tbsp.
Roasted Green Chile, Anaheim (8), Poblano (4) SHU to taste	2 cup chopped	Olive oil	2 Tbsp.
Tomato (canned okay)	2 cup chopped	Lime juice	¼ cup
Cilantro	¼ cup chopped	Tomato juice (from canned tomatoes)	¼ cup
		Garlic	2 cloves chopped

Prep Instructions

Preheat oven to 400^{0}F.
Brush eggplant with oil and place in baking pan. Brush Anaheim or
poblano chiles with oil and place in baking pan.
Drain one can of tomatoes. (Save tomato juice.)
Finely chop 2 cloves of garlic (or more).

Cooking Instructions

BAKING
Place baking pan in center of oven for 20 to 30 minutes until eggplant and
chile are tender.
Remove baking pan from oven and place eggplant and chile into a large
1-gallon resealable plastic bag to sweat for 15 to 20 minutes.
Peel off skin from eggplant and chiles. Cut into ¼-inch cubes and place
into a mixing bowl.
MIX MARINADE
Place chopped eggplant, chiles, tomato, cilantro, Adobo Spice Mix,
lime juice, tomato juice and chopped garlic into a mixing bowl. Mix well
to blend all ingredients. Place mixing bowl in refrigerator to cool and
marinate 2 to 4 hours.
Suggested Complementary Dishes: Chips, or serve as a condiment or
side dish.

Servings: 8–10 cups.

GREEN CHILE JICAMA SALSA

Complexity Code: EZ   Origin: New Mexico
Cooking Method: Chop, Mix, Marinate

About the Recipe: Green Chile Jicama Salsa combines the crunchiness and refreshing taste of jicama with pungent and fruity green chile to create a flavor explosion in your mouth. It is the perfect accompaniment for any green chile dish such as a dip, condiment or side dish and is best prepared on the mild side to let the flavors of the jicama green chile through.
Essential Recipe: Fresh Green Chile (p. 44).

Ingredient	Measure	Ingredient	Measure
Fresh Green Chile Anaheim, Poblano SHU to taste	1 cup chopped	Adobo Spice Mix (p. 83)	1 Tbsp.
Jicama	2 cups chopped	Lime juice	½ cup
Tomato	1 cup chopped	Sweetener (Nectar) (p. 85)	¼ cup
Onion	1 cup chopped	Green chile powder SHU to taste	1 tsp.
Cilantro	½–1 cup chopped To taste	**OPTIONAL:** Pinion or other nuts	½ cup

Prep Instructions

Chop green chile, jicama, tomato and onion into ¼-inch squares and place in a 3- to 4-quart mixing bowl. Add chopped cilantro.
Pour Adobo Spice Mix, sweetener and lime juice into the mixing bowl and blend ingredients.
(For additional SHU heat, add green chile powder 1 tsp. at a time.)
Place in refrigerator to chill and marinate for 1 to 2 hours.

Suggested Complementary Dishes: Chips or any dish as a garnish or side dish.

Servings: 3–4 cups.

GREEN CHILE SALSA (PICO DE GALLO)

Complexity Code: EZ   Origin: New Mexico
Cooking Method: Chop, Mix, Marinate

About the Recipe: Pico de Gallo is the perfect accompaniment of any green chile dish as a dip, condiment or side dish to refresh the palate and enhance the taste of any dish. This recipe can be prepared to the XXXX level by using habanero chiles. Have some crema ready on the side.
Essential Recipe: Fresh Green Chile (p. 44) OR Roasted Green Chile (p.46)

Ingredient	Measure	Ingredient	Measure
Fresh Green Chile Anaheim, Poblano, Jalapeño Serrano, Habanero SHU to taste	1 cup chopped	Adobo Spice Mix (p. 83)	1 Tbsp.
Tomato	1 cup chopped	Sweetener (Nectar) (p. 85)	¼ cup
Onion	½ cup chopped	Lime juice	¼ cup
Cilantro	½ - 1 cup chopped	Green chile powder SHU to taste	1 tsp.
Jicama	½ cup chopped	**OPTIONAL:** Clove powder	1 pinch
Tomato sauce	½ cup		

Prep Instructions
Chop green chile (fresh or roasted) and put into a 3- to 4-quart mixing bowl. See green chile chart for SHU ratings and flavor qualities of green chile pods (p. 32).
Chop tomato and onion into ¼-inch squares and place in the mixing bowl. Add chopped cilantro.
Pour tomato sauce, Adobo Spice Mix, sweetener, lime juice and a pinch of clove into mixing bowl and blend. (For additional SHU heat, add one tsp. green chile powder at a time.)
Place in refrigerator to chill and marinate for 1 to 2 hours.

Suggested Complementary Dishes: Chips or serve as a relish, condiment or side dish with any recipe.

Servings: 3–4 cups.

GREEN CHILE CORN SALSA

Complexity Code: EZ   Origin: New Mexico
Cooking Method: Chop, Mix, Marinate

About the Recipe: Green Chile Corn Salsa is extremely easy to make
and familiar to everyone's taste. Make it for your next event or gathering.

Essential Recipe: Fresh Green Chile (p. 44) OR Roasted Green Chile
(p. 46)

Ingredient	Measure	Ingredient	Measure
Fresh Green Chile (fresh or roasted) Anaheim, Poblano SHU to taste	1 cup chopped	Lime juice	¼ cup
Corn (frozen – thawed okay)	2 cups	Sweetener (Nectar) (p. 85)	¼ cup
Onion	¼ cup	Green chile powder (to taste)	1 tsp. at a time
Cilantro	¼ cup chopped		

Prep Instructions

Chop green chile and onion into ¼-inch squares. Chop cilantro. Place into
a 2- to 3-quart mixing bowl.
Place corn, lime juice, sweetener and green chile powder into mixing bowl.
Stir vigorously to blend all ingredients.
Place in refrigerator to chill and marinate for 1 to 2 hours.

Suggested Complementary Dishes: Chips or serve as a relish,
condiment or side dish.

Servings: 3–4 cups.

RED CHILE, SALSA ROJO

Complexity Code: EZ   Origin: New Mexico
Cooking Method: Chop, Mix, Marinate

About the Recipe: Red Chile Salsa is the standard for all other salsas; this recipe will also put you on top of the list. Serve as a relish, condiment or side dish.
Essential Recipes: Red Chile Sauce (p.36) or Enchilada Sauce (p.77).

Ingredient	Measure	Ingredient	Measure
Red Chile Sauce or Enchilada Sauce SHU to taste	2 cups	Adobo Spice Mix (p. 83)	2 Tbsp.
Red chile flakes, Ancho, Pasilla, Chipotle or Chile Seco SHU to taste	1 cup	Lime juice	¼ cup
Tomato	2 cups	Lemon juice	¼ cup
Jicama	½ cup Chopped	Sweetener (Nectar) (p. 85)	½ cup
Onion	½ cup chopped	Red chile powder To taste	1 tsp. at a time
Cilantro	½ cup chopped		

Prep Instructions

Crush dried red chile pods into ¼-inch to ½-inch squares and place in a 2- to 3-quart mixing bowl. (See Red Chile Chart for SHU and flavor qualities of red chile pods p. 42.)
Add Adobo Spice Mix, lime juice, lemon juice and sweetener into mixing bowl.
Stir ingredients to blend.
Place in refrigerator to chill and marinate 3 to 4 hours (for chile flakes to hydrate).
Chop tomato, jicama, onion and cilantro into ¼-inch squares.
Pour Red Chili Sauce into mixing bowl with hydrated chile flakes, and add Tomatoes, jicama, onion and cilantro.
Stir mixture until all ingredients are thoroughly mixed.
(For additional SHU units, add red chile powder 1 tsp. at a time.)
Place in a refrigerator to marinate until ready to serve.

Suggested Complementary Dishes: Chips or serve as a relish, condiment or side dish with any recipe.

Servings: 4 cups.

GREEN CHILE SALSA (SALSA VERDE)

Complexity Code: EZ   Origin: New Mexico
Cooking Method: Chop, Mix, Marinate

About the Recipe: Salsa verde is the green chile purist's answer to the perfect salsa and makes an excellent accompaniment for any green chile dish or as a dip, condiment or side dish.
You can prepare Salsa Verde with jalapeño, serrano or habanero chiles to create a hot to XXXX-hot salsa. Have some crema ready on the side.
Essential Recipe: Fresh Green Chile (p. 44).

Ingredient	Measure	Ingredient	Measure
Fresh Green Chile Anaheim, Poblano, Jalapeño, Serrano, Habanero (fresh or roasted) SHU to taste	1 cup chopped	Adobo Spice Mix (p. 83)	1 Tbsp.
Tomatillo (fine chopped or puréed)	5–6 1 cup	Sweetener (Nectar) (p. 85)	¼ cup
Onion	1 cup	Lime juice	¼ cup
Cilantro	½–1 cup chopped	Green chile powder SHU to taste	1 tsp.
		OPTIONAL: Clove powder	1 pinch

Prep Instructions

Chop Fresh Green Chile (fresh or roasted) and place into a 3- to 4-quart mixing bowl. See green chile chart for SHU ratings and flavor qualities of green chile pods (p. 32).
Chop onion into ¼-inch squares and place in a mixing bowl. Add chopped cilantro.
Chop or purée 5 to 6 tomatillos in a blender or with a blender stick. (Yields 1+ cup.)
Pour tomatillo purée, Adobo Spice Mix, sweetener, lime juice and a pinch of clove into mixing bowl and blend ingredients. (For additional SHU heat, add one tsp. green chile powder at a time.)
Place in refrigerator to chill and marinate for 1 to 2 hours.

Suggested Complementary Dishes: Chips or any dish as a garnish or side dish.

Servings: 3–4 cups.

MANGO OR PAPAYA SALSA

Complexity Code: EZ   Origin: New Mexico
Cooking Method: Chop, Mix, Marinate

About the Recipe: The sweetness of mango or papaya infused with red chile is a taste delight that has to be experienced.

Ingredient	Measure	Ingredient	Measure
Red chile flakes, Ancho, Pasilla, Chipotle or Chile Seco SHU to taste	¼ cup	Lime juice	¼ cup
Chopped mango or papaya	2 cups	Green onion	½ cup chopped
Jicama	1 cup chopped	Chopped cilantro	½ cup
		Red chile powder (to taste)	1 tsp. at a time

Prep Instructions

Crumble dried red chile pods into ¼-inch to ½-inch squares and place into a 2- to 3-quart mixing bowl.
Peel and remove stem and seeds from mango or papaya, chop into ¼-inch squares and place in mixing bowl.
Peel and chop jicama into ¼-inch squares and place in mixing bowl.
Pour lime juice, onion, cilantro and red chile powder into mixing bowl.
Stir vigorously to blend all ingredients.
Place in refrigerator to chill. Marinate and hydrate red chile flakes 3 to 4 hours.

Suggested Complementary Dishes: Chips, or serve as relish, condiment or side dish with any recipe.

Servings: 3–4 cups.

NEW MEXICO CAVIAR

Complexity Code: EZ   Origin: New Mexico

Cooking Method: Chop, Mix, Marinate.

About the Recipe: Pinto beans and green chile are the official
New Mexico state vegetables. This recipe can be proudly served for
any occasion in the Land of Enchantment because it is the taste of
enchantment. It is best served with mild chile to allow the flavors of the
beans to blend.
Essential Recipe: Fresh Green Chile (p. 44).

Ingredient	Measure	Ingredient	Measure
Fresh Green Chile Anaheim, Poblano SHU to taste	1 cup chopped	Adobo Spice Mix (p. 83)	2 Tbsp.
Pinto beans	2 cups	Crema or sour cream	1 cup
Onion	1 cup	Sweetener (Nectar) (p. 85)	½ cup
Tomato	1 cup	Lime juice	¼ cup
Corn	½ cup	Olive oil	¼ cup
Cilantro	½ cup or More chopped	Green chile powder SHU to taste	1 tsp. at a time
		Salt to taste	1 tsp.

Prep Instructions

Chop green chile, onions, tomato and cilantro into ¼-inch squares and
place into a 3- to 4-quart mixing bowl.
Drain and rinse one can of pinto beans, mash ½ cup and place into
mixing bowl.
Place corn, Adobo Spice Mix, crema, sweetener, lime juice and olive oil
into mixing bowl.
(For additional SHU heat, add 1 tsp. green chile powder at a time.)
Stir to blend all ingredients and place in refrigerator to cool and marinate 1
to 2 hours.

Suggested Complementary Dishes: Chips or use as condiment or
side dish for any recipe.

Servings: 4–6 cups.

PICKLED POBLANO OR JALAPENO PEPPERS

Complexity Code: EZ   Origin: New Mexico

About the Recipe: Homemade poblano or jalapeño pickles combine the sour and pungent tastes to make a pickle that is served alone or chopped as a relish or salsa to enhance any meal.

Ingredient	Measure	Ingredient	Measure
Anaheim (10), Poblano (6) or jalapeño (16) (fresh) SHU to taste	2 cups	Piloncillo or unrefined cane sugar	1 cup
		Cider or balsamic vinegar	1 cup
		Garlic powder	½ cup
		Coriander	1 Tbsp.

Prep Instructions

Place sugar, vinegar, garlic and coriander into a 2- to 3-quart mixing bowl. Stir vigorously to blend all ingredients.

Clean and seed Anaheim, poblano or jalapeño chile peppers.

Cut into ½-by-1-inch strips and place into a mixing bowl. Stir to blend all ingredients and soak chile.

Pour contents of mixing bowl into a 1-quart jar or container, top off with water, shake container to make sure that the sugar has not settled and place in refrigerator to pickle overnight.

To serve as a relish, finely chop pickles, drain the liquid and serve.

Suggested Complementary Dishes: Serve as a relish or condiment for any dish.

Servings: 1 qt.

PICKLED POBLANO, RED CHILE GINGER SALSA

Complexity Code: COOK   Origin: Original
Cooking Method: Sauté

About the Recipe: This salsa is ideally suited to be served as a side or topping for seafood or vegetables. Its pungent, sweet and aromatic taste will have your guests eating it by the spoonful.
Essential Recipe: Fresh Red Chile (p. 34).

Ingredient	Measure	Ingredient	Measure
Fresh Red Chile Pods, Ancho, Pasilla, Chipotle or Chile Seco SHU to taste	1 cup chopped	Adobo Spice Mix (p. 83)	1 Tbsp.
Chopped Green Chile Anaheim, Poblano, Jalapeño SHU to taste	2 cups	Sweetener (p. 85)	½ cup
Chile de Arbol (whole pods)	4 pods	Balsamic vinegar	½ cup
Ginger	½ cup julienne	Olive oil or vegetable oil	¼ cup
Garlic	½ cup or more fine chopped		

Prep Instructions

Heat large skillet with oil to medium heat 275^0F.
Chop / flake red chile pods into ¼-inch squares and place into a mixing bowl with seeds.
Chop green chiles (remove stems) into ¼-inch squares and place into mixing bowl with seeds.
Remove stems from de arbol chiles, julienne ginger in ⅛-inch strips, mince garlic and place all into a mixing bowl.

Cooking Instructions

Place red chile flakes, green chile, ginger and garlic into skillet and sauté until soft (approx. 5 to 10 minutes).
Reduce heat to low 190^0F. Add sweetener, vinegar and sauté for 15 to 20 minutes for all ingredients to blend and soften.
Place salsa into a container and refrigerate for 4 to 6 hours.

Suggested Complementary Dishes: Chips, or fish or vegetable dishes as a garnish or side dish.

Servings: 3–4 cups.

PICKLED RED CHILE JICAMA

Complexity Code: EZ   Origin: Original
Cooking Method: Pickling

About the Recipe: Homemade jicama pickles are a refreshing intermezzo for any dish and are served as a relish or salsa.

Ingredient	Measure	Ingredient	Measure
Jicama (1 or 2)	2 cups	Piloncillo or Unrefined cane sugar	1 cup
Red chile flakes	1 cup	Cider or balsamic vinegar	1 cup
		Garlic powder	½ cup
		Coriander	1 Tbsp.

Prep Instructions

Place sugar, vinegar, garlic and coriander into a 2- to 3-quart mixing bowl. Stir vigorously to blend all ingredients.

Clean and peel jicama, cut off ends and cut into ¼-by-2-inch strips.

Crumble dried red chile pods into ¼-inch to ½-inch squares. (The chunks will rehydrate in the pickling juice.)

Place jicama and red chile into a mixing bowl and stir to blend all ingredients to soak.

Pour contents of mixing bowl into a 1-quart jar or container, top off with water, shake container to make sure that the sugar has not settled and place in refrigerator to pickle overnight.

Suggested Complementary Dishes: Serve as a relish or condiment for any dish.

Servings: 1 qt.

RED CHILE FRUIT SALSA

Complexity Code: EZ   Origin: New Mexico
Cooking Method: Chop, Mix, Marinate

About the Recipe: Fruits in season or canned fruit can be used for this
sweet salsa on a year-round basis. The red chile adds a zest to the natural
sweetness of the fruit.
Essential Recipe: Rehydrated Red Chile pods (p. 40).

Ingredient	Measure	Ingredient	Measure
Rehydrated Red Chile Pods Ancho, Pasilla, Chipotle or Chile Seco SHU level to taste	½ cup	Sweetener (Nectar) (p. 85)	½ cup
Fresh fruit (Apple, pear, peach)	1 cup chopped	Cilantro	½ cup Fine chopped
Tropical fruit (canned or fresh) Pineapple, mango, guava	1 cup	Lime juice	½ cup

Prep Instructions

Chop Rehydrated Chile into ¼-inch squares and place in mixing bowl.
Chop fresh fruits into ¼-inch squares and place in mixing bowl. Chop
tropical fruit into ¼-inch squares. (If using canned fruit, drain all juice in
can.) Place in mixing bowl.
Finely chop cilantro and place in mixing bowl.
Pour sweetener and lime juice into mixing bowl and stir until all ingredients
are blended.
Cover mixing bowl and place in refrigerator to chill and marinate 1 to 2
hours.

Suggested Complementary Dishes: Chips or use as a condiment or
side dish.

Servings: 3–4 cups.

RED CHILE TEQUILA SALSA

Complexity Code: EZ   Origin: New Mexico
Cooking Method: Chop, Mix, Marinate

About the Recipe: This recipe is the royalty of red chile salsa that will keep them coming back for more and earn points toward your certified Chilenista degree.

Essential Recipe: Red Chile Sauce (p. 36) or Enchilada Sauce (p.77).

Ingredient	Measure	Ingredient	Measure
Red Chile or Enchilada Sauce	2 cups	Adobo Spice Mix (p. 83)	2 Tbsp.
Red chile flakes Ancho, Pasilla, Chipotle or Chile Seco SHU to taste	1 cup	Sweetener (Nectar) Mango, guava, papaya	1 cup
Tomato	1 cups	Lime juice	½ cup
Jicama	1 cup chopped	Lemon juice	½ cup
Onion	½ cup chopped	Tequila	½ cup
Cilantro	1 cup chopped	Red chile powder (to taste)	1 tsp. at a time
Cheese (p.353) Queso fresco, cotija, Feta*	1 cup crumbled		

Prep Instructions

Crush dried red chile pods into ¼-inch to ½-inch squares and place in a 2- to 3-quart mixing bowl. See Red Chile Chart for SHU and flavor qualities of red chile pods (p. 42).

Add Adobo Spice Mix, lime juice, lemon juice, sweetener and Tequila into mixing bowl.

Stir ingredients to blend. Place in refrigerator to chill and marinate 3 to 4 hours (for chile flakes to hydrate).

Chop tomato, jicama and onion into ¼-inch squares. Chop cilantro. Crumble cheese. (See cheese chart Glossary section (p. 353.)

Pour red chile sauce into mixing bowl with hydrated chile flakes, add Tomatoes, jicama, onion and cilantro and crumbled cheese. Stir mixture until all ingredients are thoroughly mixed.

(For additional SHU units, add red chile powder 1 tsp. at a time.)

Place in a refrigerator to marinate until ready to serve.

Suggested Complementary Dishes: Chips or serve as relish, condiment or side dish.

Servings: 4–6 cups.

RED CHILE TOMATO, JICAMA SALSA

Complexity Code: EZ   Origin: New Mexico
Cooking Method: Chop, Mix Marinade

About the Recipe: Tomatoes combined with jicama and red chile flakes
will spice up any gathering. The crunchiness of jicama and smoothness
of tomato combined with the pungent taste of red chile will create a taste
explosion in your mouth. It can be served as a salsa or side dish with any
recipe.

Ingredient	Measure	Ingredient	Measure
Red chile flakes, Ancho, Pasilla, Chipotle or Chile Seco SHU to taste	¼ cup	Lime juice	¼ cup
Tomato	2 cups	Green onion	½ cup chopped
Jicama	1 cup chopped	Cilantro	½ cup chopped
		Red chile powder SHU to taste	1 tsp. at a time

Prep Instructions

Crumble dried red chile pods into ¼-inch to ½-inch squares and place into
a 2- to 3-quart mixing bowl.
Chop tomato into ¼-inch squares and place in mixing bowl.
Peel and chop jicama into ¼-inch squares and place in mixing bowl. Chop
cilantro.
Place lime juice, onion, cilantro and red chile powder into mixing bowl.
Stir vigorously to blend all ingredients.
Place in refrigerator to chill, marinate and hydrate red chile flakes, 3 to 4
hours.

Suggested Complementary Dishes: Chips or serve as relish,
condiment or side dish with any recipe.

Servings: 3–4 cups.

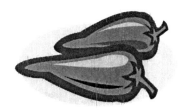

SWEET HABANERO / MANGO SALSA

Complexity Code: EZ
Cooking Method: Chops, Mix, Marinate

Origin: New Mexico

About the Recipe: Some like it hot and others like it hotter. This salsa is not for the teetotalers or faint-of-heart. It promises to satisfy even the most discriminating Chilenista.

Ingredient	Measure	Ingredient	Measure
Habanero chile	4–6 pods	Adobo Spice Mix (p. 83)	2 Tbsp.
Mango (2)	1 cup chopped	Sweetener (Nectar) Mango, guava, papaya	¼ cup
Jicama	½ cup chopped	Lime juice	¼ cup
Onion	½ cup chopped	Garlic	1 clove or more minced
Cilantro	½ cup chopped	**OPTIONAL:** Tequila	¼ cup

Prep Instructions

Peel and chop mango and onion into ¼-inch squares and place into a 3- to 4-quart mixing bowl. Add chopped cilantro.
Seed and chop habanero chile into ⅛-inch squares and place in mixing bowl.
Place Adobo Spice Mix, sweetener, lime juice, minced garlic and optionally Tequila into mixing bowl. Vigorously mix ingredients to blend.
Place mixing bowl in refrigerator to chill and marinate for 3 to 4 hours.

Suggested Complementary Dishes: Chips, serve as a relish, condiment or side dish

Servings: 3-4 cups. Serves: 6–8 people.

TOMATO, GREEN CHILE AND BLACK BEAN SALSA

Complexity Code: EZ   Origin: New Mexico
Cooking Method: Chop, Mix, Marinate

About the Recipe: What's red, green and black all over? This salsa
is a multi-colored feast for the eyes as well as your taste. It can be the
centerpiece of your hors d'oeuvre table.
Essential Recipe: Fresh Green Chile (p. 44) OR Roasted Green Chile
(p.46)

Ingredient	Measure	Ingredient	Measure
Fresh Green Chile Anaheim, Poblano (fresh or roasted) SHU to taste	1 cup	Adobo Spice Mix (p. 83)	2 Tbsp.
Tomato (large)	1 cup	Lime juice	¼ cup
Black beans (canned okay)	2 cups	Sweetener (Nectar) (p. 85)	¼ cup
Onion	1 cup chopped	Olive oil	2 Tbsp.
Corn (frozen – thawed okay)	1 cup	Garlic	2 cloves or more chopped
Cilantro	½ cup chopped		

Prep Instructions

Chop green chile, tomato and onion into ¼-inch squares and place in a 2-
to 3-quart mixing bowl. Add chopped cilantro.
Drain and rinse one can of black beans and place in mixing bowl.
Place corn, Adobo Spice Mix, lime juice, sweetener, olive oil and garlic
into mixing bowl. Stir vigorously to blend all ingredients.
Place in refrigerator to chill and marinate 1 to 2 hours.

Suggested Complementary Dishes: Chips, condiment or side dish for
any dish.

Servings: 4–6 cups.

Chapter 6—DRESSINGS & SALADS

About Dressings

Salad dressings have evolved from the brine oil and vinegar solutions that were used as preservatives to a gourmet art that can enhance any salad.

The secret behind any salad is the way you dress and garnish it. No one wants to start or end a meal with a naked salad. To appease even the most discriminating Chilenista, we have a variety of green chile and red chile dressing recipes from light vinaigrettes to hearty creamy dressings that complement any salad or dish. If you prepare your dressings ahead of time and store them in your refrigerator, you can have a healthy salad with the minimum of work at any time. Feel free to add herbs, nuts and spices to your dressings to personalize any of these recipes.

Vinaigrettes

Vinaigrettes consist primarily of olive oil, vinegar, sweetener and herbs. Vinaigrette offers a lighter fare for loose-leaf lettuce. Refer to the dressing section of this chapter for many dressing options. (Do not drown your salad with dressing.)

Creamy Dressings

Creamy dressings consist primarily of crema, milk or sour cream, vinegar, sweetener, herbs, spices, green chile, red chile and vegetables that are blended into a creamy mixture that offer a heartier flavor to head leaf lettuce and can make complete meals with meats, fish or vegetables. Creamy dressings should be made in advance and refrigerated to allow all of the flavors to blend.

Herbs

Basil, dill, oregano, rosemary, and tarragon will highlight your salad with herbal overtones and should be well tossed in the salad before serving. (Use sparingly.)

Nuts

Pinions, walnuts, pistachios, peanuts and sunflower seeds add crunchiness, texture, and nutty flavor to any salad. Toss well and add at the last minute to make sure that they do not get soggy with the salad dressing.

Spices

Salt, pepper, red chile powder, green chile powder, coriander, garlic powder, onion powder when properly tossed into the salad (in moderation) will coat the leaf and leave an overtone of flavor for each bite.

About Salads

Salads can be served as an appetizer, a meal or as an aperitif to complete a meal.

Salads derive their name from the Latin word "salata" meaning a brine solution consisting of salt, oil and vinegar used to preserve vegetables. Eventually the brine salt solution evolved as dressing or a coating for vegetables and leafy greens and have made their way into the Chilenista cuisine.

Leafy Salads

To make crispy leafy salads it is best to place the individual leaves of lettuce into a mixing bowl 1 to 2 hours before serving and cover with crushed ice or ice cubes. When ready to serve, you hand-cut the leaves and spin-dry or towel-dry whole leaves. The ice will crisp any salad to restaurant quality. Salad belongs on almost every Chilenista's table to refresh the palate and cool down the tongue with the vinaigrette or creamy dressings that complement any chile dish.

There are several readily available salad leaf and lettuce combinations that you can use as well as some pre-mixed varieties that allow you to get creative with your salad ingredients.

(When using pre-mixed salads, always wash and spin-dry the leaves to get rid of any preservatives that were used to keep them fresh.)

Full Head Lettuce

Full head lettuce like iceberg, romaine and Boston bibb are best served hand-cut or shredded and have a heavier, crispy texture that goes well with the creamy dressings.

Nuts raisins, tomatoes, cucumber and grated hard cheeses make an excellent pairing to highlight the crispiness of the lettuce.

Loose-Leaf Salads

Loose-leaf salad usually contains a mix of arugula, chicory, endive, escarole, radicchio and water cress, sometimes referred to as mesclun salad greens. Loose-leaf lettuce has an herbal flavor leaning toward the mildly bitter side. Tossed together they make light, airy salads and are best garnished with the lighter vinaigrette dressings.
Nuts, raisins, cranberries and some soft crumbled cheese make excellent additions to give texture and additional taste.

Bound Salads

Bound salad evolved from leftovers that were given a new life by coating them with a thick dressing such as mayonnaise and combining with other ingredients to freshen their taste. Some of the more popular bound salads are chicken salad, egg salad, pasta salad, potato salad and tuna salad. Combined with chopped chile, red or green, you can create a meal in a minute. Bound salads also make great burrito filling.

Main Course Salads

Main course salads are a no-brainer that you can make with any leafy salad, any leftover or simply grilled meat, chicken, fish or cold cuts, drizzled with a bit of dressing on top.

Fruit Salads

Fruit salads are in a league of their own and can be the highlight of any meal or used as a dessert. Cut whatever fruits are in season, marinate them in some fruit nectar and sprinkle a bit of chile powder on top. Try it and you will like it.

Salad Add-Ons

Cheese

Soft crumbled cheeses such as queso fresca, panela and requison go well with leafy salads.

For a shredded cheese blend, combine asadero, cheddar, jack or queso quesadilla, which are readily available in the grocer's cheese case and can be easily used to garnish any salad.

Hard grated cheeses like cotija, añejo, Parmesan and Romano go well with cut or shredded full head lettuce.

Vegetables

Vegetables such as avocados, bell peppers, carrots, celery, chiles, cilantro, , cucumbers, jicama, mushrooms, onions, radishes, scallions and tomatoes, can all be diced and used as salad ingredients to enhance the texture, color and taste of the leafy salads.

SALAD DRESSINGS

GREEN CHILE LIME VINAIGRETTE

About the Recipe: This dressing recipe goes with any salad as a light, low-cal dressing that is sure to please all of your guests and family.
Essential Recipe: Fresh Green Chile (p. 44)

Ingredient	Measure	Ingredient	Measure
Fresh Green Chile Anaheim, Poblano, Jalapeño. Choose your SHU level	1 cup Fine chopped	Adobo Spice Mix (p. 83)	1 Tbsp.
Balsamic vinegar	2 Tbsp.	Olive oil	½ cup
Lime juice	½ cup	Garlic powder	1 tsp.
Sweetener: Nectar Guava, mango, papaya, tamarind	½ cup		

Prep Instructions
Finely chop green chile into ¼-inch squares and place in mixing bowl. Add olive oil, lime juice, garlic, sweetener and vinegar. Stir dressing mixture vigorously and drizzle on salad.
Suggested Complementary Dishes: Any leafy salad.
Servings: 2 cups
Double the ingredients and put dressing into jar for future use. Keep refrigerated.

Variations

Green Chile Cilantro Lime Vinaigrette
ABOUT THE RECIPE: The aroma of cilantro will infuse into the dressing and merge with the chile to create a Chilenista favorite. Variation: Finely chop 1 cup cilantro and add to the rest of ingredients.

Green Chile Orange Vinaigrette
ABOUT THE RECIPE: The sweetness of orange combined with the warm piquant taste of chile will tantalize any Chilenista's taste buds. Variation: Grate 2 Tbsp. of orange zest; add ½ cup orange juice.

CREAMY GREEN CHILE VINAIGRETTE

About the Recipe: This creamy dressing recipe offers the aromatic herbal sweetness of green chile that will become a favorite.
Essential Recipe: Fresh Green Chile (p. 44) OR Roasted Green Chile (p.46)

Ingredient	Measure	Ingredient	Measure
Fresh Green Chile Anaheim, Poblano, Jalapeño (fresh or roasted) Choose your SHU level	1 cup	Adobo Spice Mix (p. 83)	1 Tbsp.
Crema or sour cream	1 cup	Olive oil	½ cup
Sweetener: Nectar Guava, mango, papaya, tamarind	½ cup	Garlic powder	1 tsp.
Lime juice	½ cup		1 pinch
Balsamic Vinegar	2 Tbsp.	**OPTIONAL:** Crumbled cheese Anejo, cotija, queso fresca	½ cup

Prep Instructions

Finely chop green chile into ¼-inch squares and place in mixing bowl.
Add olive oil, lime juice, garlic, sweetener and vinegar.
Blend dressing mixture with a blender stick or blender Add olive oil and stir mixture vigorously to blend all ingredients; stir in optional crumbled cheese and drizzle on salad.
Suggested Complementary Dishes: Any leafy salad.
Servings: 2 cups, (4) 4-oz.

Variations

Creamy Green Chile Cilantro Vinaigrette
ABOUT THE RECIPE: The aroma of cilantro will infuse into the dressing and merge with the chile to create a Chilenista favorite. Variation: Finely chop 1 cup cilantro and add to the rest of ingredients.

Creamy Green Chile Avocado Dressing
ABOUT THE RECIPE: Avocado will give your vinaigrette a creamy, nutty, herbal flavor. This recipe infuses your salad with great avocado taste and a touch of chile tartness. Variation: Chop 1 medium avocado into bite-size pieces and garnish salad.

GREEN CHILE BLUE CHEESE DRESSING

About the Recipe: Blue cheese dressing is one of the most beloved dressings and universally liked for its pungent taste. Add a bit of green chile and kick it up a notch.

Essential Recipe: Fresh Green Chile (p. 44) OR Roasted Green Chile (p.46)

Ingredient	Measure	Ingredient	Measure
Fresh Green Chile Anaheim, Poblano, Jalapeño (fresh or roasted) Choose your SHU level	1 cup	Sweetener: Nectar Guava, mango, papaya, tamarind	½ cup
Blue cheese	1 cup crumbled	Balsamic vinegar	1 Tbsp.
Mayonnaise	½ cup	Garlic powder	1 tsp.
Crema or sour cream	½ cup	Optional garnish: Croutons (	
Milk or half-and-half	¼ cup		

Prep Instructions

Finely chop or mince green chile into ¼ small squares. Place in mixing bowl.

Pour mayonnaise, blue cheese, crema, sweetener, vinegar and garlic powder into the mixing bowl.

Stir all ingredients vigorously. Add milk if needed to thin dressing.

Stir again to blend all ingredients. Place dressing in jar for storage in refrigerator.

Garnish salad with croutons

Suggested Complementary Dishes: Any leafy salad, Cob salad or salad with a meat topping.

Servings: 2 cups or (4) 4-oz.

GREEN CHILE CAESAR SALAD DRESSING

About the Recipe: Caesar salad is probably the best known of all salad dressings. This recipe raises the bar for taste by including green chile into the formula with or without anchovies.

Essential Recipe: Fresh Green Chile (p. 44) OR Roasted Green Chile (p.46)

Ingredient	Measure	Ingredient	Measure
Fresh Green Chile Anaheim, Poblano, Jalapeño (fresh or roasted) Choose your SHU level	1 cup	Sweetener: Nectar Guava, mango, papaya, tamarind	½ cup
Egg yolk	4	Oliver oil	1 cup
Garlic powder	2 tsp.	Cotija or Parmesan cheese grated (Garnish)	1 cup
Lemon juice	¼ cup	Optional garnish: Anchovies	6 fillets
Worcestershire sauce	1 tsp.	Optional garnish: Green Chile powder	1 tsp.

Prep Instructions

Chop green chile into ¼-inch squares. Place in mixing bowl.

Crack an egg and separate egg yolk from white, discard or freeze egg white for future use; place egg yolk into mixing bowl. Mince garlic and place in mixing bowl.

Add lemon juice, sweetener, olive oil, Worcestershire sauce, green chile powder (optional) and anchovies (optional).

Pour mixture into a blender or use a blender stick to purée and blend all ingredients. Drizzle on salad.

Pour Caesar dressing into a glass jar and refrigerate.

Garnish salad with cheese, anchovies or green chile powder.

Suggested Complementary Dishes: Romaine salad.

Servings: 3 cups, (6) 4-oz. (for large salads).

GREEN CHILE GODDESS DRESSING

About the Recipe: Green Chile Goddess Dressing brings the sweet aromatic taste of tarragon to the table. If you like sweet, pungent and aromatic flavor, this is a dressing you will love.

Essential Recipe: Fresh Green Chile (p. 44) OR Roasted Green Chile (p.46)

Ingredient	Measure	Ingredient	Measure
Fresh Green Chile Anaheim, Poblano, Jalapeño (Fresh or roasted) SHU to taste	1 cup Minced	Cilantro	¼ cup minced
Mayonnaise	1 cup	Green onion	¼ cup minced
Crema or sour cream	½ cup	Tarragon (fresh or dried)	1 Tbsp.
Milk or half-and-half	¼ cup	Garlic powder	1 tsp.
Sweetener: Nectar Guava, mango, papaya, tamarind	½ cup	Balsamic vinegar	2 Tbsp.

Prep Instructions

Finely chop or mince green chile and green onion into small squares. Place in mixing bowl.

Mince cilantro and add garlic powder) and place in a mixing bowl.

Pour mayonnaise, crema, vinegar, tarragon and sweetener into the mixing bowl.

Stir all ingredients vigorously. Add milk if needed to thin dressing. Stir again to blend all ingredients. Drizzle on salad.

Place extra dressing in jar for storage in refrigerator

Suggested Complementary Dishes: Any leafy salad, Cob salad or salad with a meat topping.

Servings: 2 cups, (4) 4-oz.

GREEN CHILE RANCH DRESSING

About the Recipe: Ranch dressing is the old standby for salads and can be made in minutes from ingredients that you already have in the refrigerator.

Ingredient	Measure	Ingredient	Measure
Mayonnaise	1 cup	Green chile powder SHU to taste	1 Tbsp. or more
Crema or sour cream	½ cup	Balsamic vinegar	1 Tbsp.
Milk or half-and-half	¼ cup	Sweetener: Nectar Guava, mango, papaya, tamarind	½ cup
Cilantro	¼ cup minced	Garlic powder	1 tsp.

Prep Instructions

Mince cilantro and add garlic powder; place in a mixing bowl.
Pour mayonnaise, crema, green chile powder, vinegar and sweetener into the mixing bowl.
Stir all ingredients vigorously. Add milk if needed to thin dressing. Stir again to blend all ingredients.
Place dressing in jar for storage in refrigerator or drizzle on salad.

Suggested Complementary Dishes: Any leafy salad, Cob salad or salad with a meat topping.

Servings: 2 cups, (4) 4-oz.

GREEN CHILE THOUSAND ISLAND DRESSING

About the Recipe: Green Chile Thousand Island Dressing can transport you to a tropical island setting where you taste a crisp lettuce salad as an appetizer, entrée or aperitif.

Essential Recipe: Fresh Green Chile (p. 44) OR Roasted Green Chile (p.46)

Ingredient	Measure	Ingredient	Measure
Fresh Green Chile Anaheim, Poblano, Jalapeño (Fresh or roasted) Choose your SHU level	1 cup minced	Cilantro	½ cup minced
Mayonnaise	1 cup	Garlic powder	1 tsp.
Crema or sour cream	½ cup	Balsamic vinegar	1 Tbsp.
Milk or half-and-half	¼ cup	Sweetener: Nectar Guava, mango, papaya, tamarind	½ cup

Prep Instructions

Finely chop or mince green chile into small squares. Place in mixing bowl.
Mince cilantro and garlic (very fine), place in a mixing bowl.
Pour mayonnaise, crema, green chile powder, vinegar and sweetener into the mixing bowl.
Stir all ingredients vigorously. Add milk if needed to thin dressing. Stir again to blend all ingredients.
Place dressing in jar for storage in refrigerator or drizzle on salad.

Suggested Complementary Dishes: Any leafy salad, Cob salad or salad with a meat topping.

Servings: 2 cups, (4) 4-oz.

RED CHILE VINAIGRETTE

About the Recipe: Red Chile Vinaigrette can be served with any salad to add a tangy, refreshing taste.
Essential Recipe: Rehydrated Red Chile pods (p. 40).

Ingredient	Measure	Ingredient	Measure
Rehydrated Red Chile Pods Ancho, Pasilla, Chipotle or Chile Seco SHU to taste	1 cup fine chopped	Adobo Spice Mix (p. 83)	1 Tbsp.
Lime juice	¼ cup	Olive oil	½ cup
Sweetener: Nectar Guava, mango, papaya, tamarind	½ cup	Garlic powder	1 tsp.
Balsamic vinegar	2 Tbsp.		

Prep Instructions
Finely chop red chile pods, (discard seeds) and place in mixing bowl.
Add lime juice, garlic, sweetener and vinegar. Allow red chile flakes to rehydrate 1 to 2 hours.
Add olive oil and blend dressing mixture in a blender or with a blender stick.
Place dressing in jar or storage container for red chile to soften, hydrate and infuse its flavor; place in refrigerator for 4 to 6 hours. When ready shake, stir and drizzle on salad.
Suggested Complementary Dishes: Any leafy salad.
Servings: 2 cups, (4) 4-oz.

Variations

Red Chile Tomato Vinaigrette
ABOUT THE RECIPE: This dressing matches the best of the sweetness of tomatoes and pungent taste of red chile to create a taste sensation for any salad.
Variation: Add Tomato juice 1 cup

Red Chile Tequila Vinaigrette
ABOUT THE RECIPE: This dressing is for the hardcore Chilenistas, as they may want to drink it out of the bowl before it gets to the salad.
Variation: Add ½ cup orange juice and ½ cup Tequila.

CREAMY RED CHILE VINAIGRETTE

About the Recipe: This creamy red chile dressing recipe offers the sweet and aged piquant taste of red chile in mild (Ancho), medium (Pasilla) smoky (Chipotle and hot (Seco) chilies to please almost all Chilenistas.
Essential Recipe: Rehydrated Red Chile pods (p. 40).

Ingredient	Measure	Ingredient	Measure
Rehydrated Red Chile Pods Ancho, Pasilla, Chipotle or Chile Seco SHU to taste	1 cup chopped	Adobo Spice Mix (p. 83)	1 Tbsp.
Lime juice	½ cup	Olive oil	½ cup
Sweetener: Nectar guava, papaya, tamarind	½ cup	Garlic powder	1 tsp.
Crema or sour cream	1 cup		
Balsamic Vinegar	2 Tbsp.	**OPTIONAL:** Cheese Añejo, cotija, queso fresca	1 cup crumbled

Prep Instructions

Finely chop red chile pods, (discard seeds) and place in mixing bowl.
Add lime juice, garlic, sweetener, vinegar and olive oil.
Place dressing in jar or storage container for red chile to soften, hydrate and infuse its flavor; place in refrigerator for 4 to 6 hours. When ready add crumbled cheese, shake, stir and drizzle on salad.
Suggested Complementary Dishes: Any leafy salad.
Servings: 2 cup, (4) 4-oz.

Variation

Creamy Red Chile Avocado Dressing
ABOUT THE RECIPE: Avocado will give your vinaigrette a creamy, nutty, herbal flavor. This recipe infuses your salad with the great avocado taste with a touch of chile tartness.
Variation: Chop 1 medium avocado into bite size pieces and garnish salad.

RED CHILE HONEY MUSTARD DRESSING

About the Recipe: Honey mustard red chile blended into a dressing not only awakens your taste buds but also creates a sensation for your guests and family.

Essential Recipe: Rehydrated Red Chile pods (p. 40).

Ingredient	Measure	Ingredient	Measure
Rehydrated Red Chile Pods Ancho, Pasilla, Chipotle or Chile Seco SHU to taste	1 cup chopped	Mustard	¼ cup
Mayonnaise	1 cup	Honey	1 cup
Crema or sour cream	½ cup	Garlic powder	1 tsp.
Milk or half-and-half	¼ cup	Balsamic vinegar	2 Tbsp.
Sweetener: Nectar Guava, mango, papaya, tamarind	½ cup	**OPTIONAL:** Tequila	½ cup

Prep Instructions

Crush red chile pods into ¼-inch pieces; place in mixing bowl.

Pour mayonnaise, mustard, honey, crema, sweetener, vinegar, garlic and Optional tequila into the mixing bowl.

Stir all ingredients vigorously. Add milk if needed to thin dressing. Stir again to blend all ingredients.

Place dressing in jar or storage container for red chile to soften, hydrate and infuse its flavor; place in refrigerator for 4 to 6 hours. When ready shake, stir and drizzle on salad.

Suggested Complementary Dishes: Any leafy salad, Cob salad or salad with a meat topping.

Servings: 2 cup, (4) 4-oz.

SALPICON DRESSING

About the Recipe: Salpicon is a hearty meat-lover's dressing used in any meat and salad combination.

Ingredient	Measure	Ingredient	Measure
Chipotle chile in adobo sauce (canned)	½ cup	Olive oil	¼ cup
Beef broth or Bovril	¼ cup 2 Tbsp.	Sweetener: Nectar Guava, mango, papaya, tamarind	½ cup
Lime juice	¼ cup	Onion powder	1 Tbsp.
Balsamic vinegar	2 Tbsp.	Garlic powder	1 Tbsp.
Tomato sauce	¼ cup		

Prep Instructions

Chop chipotle in adobo sauce into ¼-inch squares; pour adobo sauce and chipotle into mixing bowl.
Pour beef broth or Bovril into bowl.
Pour lime juice, vinegar and tomato sauce, oil, sweetener, onion powder and garlic powder into bowl. Stir vigorously to blend all ingredients.
Store in a glass jar or use in salad.

Suggested Complementary Dishes: Any combined meat salad.

Servings: 2–3 cups.

SALADS—ENSALADA

Salads can range from an appetizer to a complete meal from basic lettuce and tomato to the main course, side dish or aperitif or to aid digestion. The one thing all salads have in common is the dressing that adds their identity, flavor and ethnicity. Salads in the Chilenista cuisine all have one thing in common, red or green chile to enhance the flavors with the addition of capsaicin to stimulate the endorphins before, during and after the main course. Salads never tasted so good.

The recipes in this chapter initially focus on making the dressing and ways to use them on leafy, vegetable, fruit and meat salads.

BOSTON BIBB SALAD

About the Recipe: Boston Bibb lettuce has a smooth velvety texture that can be compared to a comfort food. The mixture of the lettuce with a light creamy dressing can be savored by itself or as an ideal appetizer.
Essential Recipe: Fresh Green Chile (p. 44) OR Roasted Green Chile (p.46)

Ingredient	Measure	Ingredient	Measure
Boston Bibb lettuce	1 head	Vinaigrette dressing	1 cup
Tomato diced, wedged or sliced	1 cup	**OPTIONAL:** Nuts	¼ cup
Cucumber sliced or diced	1 cup	**OPTIONAL:** Spices	1 Tbsp.
Green Chile (fresh or roasted)	¼ cup or more chopped	**OPTIONAL:** Soft cheese, Asadero, queso fresca, panela requesón	½ cup or more crumbled

Prep Instructions
It is always best to refrigerate Boston Bibb lettuce to keep its crispness and cut leaves for salad as needed. To give it an extra crispness, place leaves into a mixing bowl and cover with ice cubes or shaved ice for 1 hour prior to serving. The ice cubes will both crisp and hydrate the lettuce to give it a just picked consistency and crispness.

Variations

Whole Leaf Boston Bibb Salad
Tear the outer leaves and cut them into bite-size pieces; pick the inner small leaves whole to add to the salad. Pour a light vinaigrette or creamy vinaigrette on the lettuce leaves, and sprinkle with a grated hard cheese or crumbled soft cheese and serve.

Wilted Salad
Wilted salad allows for the vinaigrette dressing to saturate the lettuce leaves and produce a soft creamy salad that is unique.
Heat the dressing in a microwave, low setting for 15 to 20 seconds until the dressing is hot to the touch. Pour the hot dressing over the lettuce and toss. Add cheese, bacon bits, roasted chile, nuts and serve.

Suggested Dressings: Any vinaigrette.

Serves: 4–6 people.

COLE SLAW —RED OR GREEN

Complexity Code: EZ   Origin: New Mexico
Cooking Method: Blend / Marinate

About the Recipe: A New Mexico variation that will enhance any recipe served as a side dish or salad for any main dish.
Essential Recipe: Fresh Green Chile (p.44), or Rehydrated Red Chile pods (p. 46).

Ingredient	Measure	Ingredient	Measure
Green cabbage (Thinly sliced)	3 cups	Milk	¼ cup
Red cabbage (Thinly sliced)	3 cups	Vinegar	¼ cup
Shredded carrot	2 cups	Sweetener: Nectar Guava, papaya, tamarind	2 Tbsp.
Shredded jicama	2 cups	Olive Oil	2 Tbsp.
Fresh Green Chile Anaheim, Poblano, Jalapeño. SHU to taste	1 cup chopped	Mayonnaise	¼ cup
OR			
Rehydrated Red Chile Ancho, Pasilla, or Chipotle SHU to taste	1 cup chopped	Crema or sour cream	¼ cup
Cilantro	½ cup chopped	Raisins or Craisins	½ cup
Nuts (pinion, walnuts, pecan)	½ cup	Celery seed	1 Tbsp.

Prep Instructions

Thinly slice cabbage into 1/8-inch strips and place in mixing bowl.
Shred carrots and jicama with a grater and place in bowl.
Clean green chiles (removing stem, seeds and veins). Chop into ¼-inch squares and place in bowl.
Chop rehydrated red chile into ¼-inch squares (SHU units to taste) and place in bowl.
Chop cilantro and place in bowl.Add nuts, milk, vinegar, sweetener, olive oil, mayonnaise, crema, raisins and celery seeds to bowl.
Cooking Instructions

Mix all ingredients in mixing bowl and let marinate for 1 to 2 hours. Taste and make any corrections.
Add additional milk or crema to thin out or thicken.

Suggested Complementary Dishes: Any main dish will be enhanced with Red or Green Cole Slaw on the side.
Servings: 12–18 cups.

GARDEN SALAD

About the Recipe: As its name suggests, a garden salad is composed of what you can pick or what is fresh at your local grocer. There are many variations you can create; here is a healthy combination served as a salad or side dish.

Ingredient	Measure	Ingredient	Measure
Spinach leaves	6-8 cups	Bean sprouts	1 cup
Fresh Green Chile SHU to taste	1 cup chopped	Cilantro	1 cup chopped
Shredded jicama	1 cup	Chopped celery	1 cup
Shredded carrot	1 cup	Fresh snap peas or green beans	1 cup
Broccoli	1 cup		
		OPTIONAL: Walnuts, peanuts, pinion, sunflower seeds	1 cup

Prep Instructions

Clean and place fresh spinach in a mixing bowl.
Chop green chile in ¼-inch squares, chop cilantro and place in bowl.
Chop celery into thin, diagonal cuts.
Peel and shred carrots and jicama.
Chop broccoli florets into small pieces.
Wash bean sprouts.
Chop snap peas or green beans into ½-inch strips.
Toss and mix all ingredients in mixing bowl.
Optionally place nuts into the salad and stir right before serving.
Suggested Dressing: Any vinaigrette.

Suggested Complementary Dishes: Any meat or fish dish.

Servings: 6–8 people.

GREEN CHILE CUCUMBER SALAD

About the Recipe: Green chile and cucumber salad is one of the most refreshing combinations that you can pair for any meal.

Ingredient	Measure	Ingredient	Measure
Cucumber (2)	4 cups Chopped or sliced	Green Chile Vinaigrette (p. 158) or Creamy Green Chile Vinaigrette (p. 159)	1 cup
Chopped Fresh Green Chile SHU to taste	2 cups chopped		
Cilantro	1 cup chopped		

Prep Instructions

Chop into bite-size pieces or slice cucumber, chop green chile into ¼-inch squares and chop cilantro.

Place these ingredients with vinaigrette dressing in bowl and toss to coat all ingredients.

Suggested Complementary Dishes: Any dish as a salad or side dish.

Servings: 4–6 people

GREEN CHILE JICAMA MANGO SALAD
WITH TEQUILA LIME VINAIGRETTE

About the Recipe: Pungent green chile, crunchy jicama, sweet mango, tart leafy greens and Tequila Lime Vinaigrette. It doesn't get any better than this.

Essential Recipe: Fresh Green Chile (p. 44) OR Roasted Green Chile (p. 46)

Ingredient	Measure	Ingredient	Measure
Mesclun leafy salad mix: Arugula, chicory, endive, escarole radicchio	½ lb.	Fresh Green Chile Anaheim, Poblano, Jalapeño (fresh or roasted) SHU to taste	1 cup chopped
Jicama	1 cups	Tequila Lime Vinaigrette (p. 158)	1 cup
Mango	1 cups		
Nuts: Pinion, walnuts, pistachio, sunflower seeds	½ cup	**OPTIONAL:** Beef, pork chicken, fish	2 cups or more

Prep Instructions

Chop green chile into ¼-inch squares.
Peel and chop jicama into ¼-inch squares.
Peel and chop mango into ¼-inch squares.
Place these ingredients into a mixing bowl.
Wash, crisp and place leafy salad mix into bowl.
Pour Tequila Lime Vinaigrette (p. 158) into bowl. Add nuts.
Toss to coat all ingredients.
OPTIONAL: Add any meat to serve as a meal.

Suggested Complementary Dishes: Any chile dish as a salad or serve with meat topping as a salad meal.

Servings: 4-6 people

ICEBERG LETTUCE SALAD

About the Recipe: Iceberg lettuce is probably the most abundant and inexpensive of all the lettuce family and is available year-round. Its crisp taste appeals to all and makes a wonderful salad. It can be served in wedges, cut into squares, shredded and also used in whole leaf form as a base for other ingredients.

Ingredient	Measure	Ingredient	Measure
Iceberg lettuce	1 head	Creamy dressing or vinaigrette	1 cup
Tomato diced, wedged or sliced	1 cup	**OPTIONAL:** Nuts	¼ cup
Cucumber sliced or diced	1 cup	**OPTIONAL:** Spices	1 Tbsp.
Fresh Green Chile	¼ cup or more chopped	**OPTIONAL:** Soft cheese. Asadero, queso fresca, panela, requesón	½ cup or more crumbled

Prep Instructions

It is always best to refrigerate Iceberg lettuce to keep its crispness and then cut leaves for salad as needed.

Variations

Quartered Head of Iceberg Lettuce
Iceberg can be cut in quarters and served with a creamy dressing like blue cheese, green goddess, honey mustard, ranch or thousand island. Pour the creamy dressing over the top of the wedge and let it cool on the plate. Garnish plate with some nuts, cherry tomatoes, beans and spices to decorate and flavor.

Cut or Shred Iceberg Lettuce
Tear the head of the Iceberg lettuce into bite-size pieces or shred into ¼-inch strips and place in a bowl. Pour creamy or vinaigrette dressing on lettuce, then add tomato, cucumber, chopped chile and spices. Toss salad to evenly coat cut leaves. Serve in individual bowls before or during the meal.

Whole Leaf Bowl
Tear a whole leaf from the outside of the lettuce and fill with shredded beef, pork or chicken (2–3 oz.). Pour your favorite salsa or dressing on top of the meat, top with cheese and serve in a shallow plate as an appetizer.

Suggested Dressings: Any vinaigrette, creamy vinaigrette, green goddess, ranch, honey mustard, or thousand island dressing

Servings: 4–6 Servings

LAYERED ICEBERG CHILE SALAD
WITH VINAIGRETTE DRESSING

About the Recipe: Layered salads can be a meal unto themselves and include vegetables, meats or fish. They make a great midweek leftover meal.

Ingredient	Measure	Ingredient	Measure
Iceberg lettuce	6–10 cups	Shredded cheese blend Asadero, cheddar, Jack, queso quesadilla	1 cup
Fresh Green Chile SHU to taste	1 cup Chopped	Cilantro	1 cup chopped
Tomato	2 cup chopped	**OPTIONAL:**	
Black beans	2 cup	Taco Ground Beef	1 cup
Corn (fresh or frozen)	1 cup	Shredded Pork	1 cup
Onion	½ cup	Shredded Chicken	1 cup
Tortilla chips	2–3 cups	Shrimp or fish	1 cup
Vinaigrette dressing	1 cup		

Prep Instructions

Strip outer whole leaves from iceberg lettuce (one whole leaf per person). Cut lettuce in half lengthwise and cut strips of ¼-inch+ of lettuce for salad (6–8 cups). Place in a large mixing bowl.
Chop tomato in ¼-inch squares and place in bowl. (Save 1 cup for garnish.)
Chop onion in ¼-inch squares and place in bowl.
Chop cilantro and place in bowl. (Save ½ cup for garnish.)
Open can of black beans, rinse all preservatives and place (1) cup in bowl. (Save 1 cup for garnish.)
Place defrosted corn and 1 cup shredded cheese blend in bowl.
Pour vinaigrette dressing (your choice) in bowl and toss salad to coat all ingredients evenly.
Place any Optional ingredients on top of salad (beef, pork, fish or shrimp).
Cover top of salad with tortilla chips and garnish with tomato, black beans and cilantro.

Suggested Complementary Dishes: Any main course

Servings: 4–6 people

MESCLUN SALAD (LEAFY GREENS)

About the Recipe: Arugula, chicory, endive, escarole, radicchio and watercress are all available in the salad section of most supermarkets either individually or as a pre-mix. The combination of the different greens goes especially well with meat dishes prepared with sauces and chile.
Essential Recipe: Fresh Green Chile (p. 44) OR Roasted Green Chile (p.46)

Ingredient	Measure	Ingredient	Measure
Mesclun salad mix: Arugula, chicory, endive, escarole radicchio	½ lb.	Vinaigrette dressing	½ cup
Green Chile (fresh or roasted)	¼ cup or more	**OPTIONAL:** Nuts	¼ cup
		OPTIONAL: Spices	1 Tbsp.
		OPTIONAL: Soft cheese Asadero, queso fresca, panela, requesón	½ cup or more crumbled

Prep Instructions

It is always best to refrigerate the Mesclun lettuce leaf mix to keep its crispness. To give it an extra crispness, place leaves into a mixing bowl and cover with ice cubes or shaved ice for 1 hour prior to serving. The ice cubes will both crisp and hydrate the lettuce to give it a just-picked consistency and crispness.

Place leaves in a mixing bowl, pour a light vinaigrette dressing over the leaves and toss to lightly coat all leaves. Add crumbled cheese, chopped red or green chile and crumbled soft cheese.
Suggested Dressings: Any vinaigrette.

Suggested Complementary Dishes: Any fish, vegetable or light chile dish.

Servings: 4–6 people.

NOPALES (CACTUS) GREEN CHILE SALAD

About the Recipe: Nopales are a favorite of Mexican Chilenistas and make a novelty salad that will appeal to everyone; they can be eaten as an appetizer, salad or side dish.

Essential Recipe: Fresh Green Chile (p. 44) OR Roasted Green Chile (p.46)

Ingredient	Measure	Ingredient	Measure
Cactus Paddles or prepared nopales	2–4 cups	Green Chile Anaheim, Poblano, Jalapeño (Fresh or roasted) SHU to taste	1 cup chopped
Tomato	2 cups chopped	Adobo Dry Spice Mix (p. 83)	1 Tbsp.
Onion	½ cup chopped	Olive oil	½ cup
Cheese Asadero, queso fresca, panela, requesón	1 cup crumbled	Lemon juice	½ cup
Baking powder	2 Tbsp.	Sweetener: Nectar Guava, papaya, tamarind	½ cup

Prep Instructions

For fresh cactus paddles, burn off any spines or hairs; boil them with in water with 2 Tbsp. baking powder (to soften and preserve the green color) until tender. Cool off and cut into ¼-inch strips. Prepared nopales are available at most grocery stores. Place in mixing bowl.

Chop chile, tomato and onion into ¼-inch squares and place in mixing bowl.

Add Adobo Spice Mix, olive oil, lemon juice and sweetener into bowl. Toss to coat all ingredients.

Add crumbled cheese to bowl and stir to mix into salad.

Suggested Complementary Dishes: Serve as a salad or side dish for any recipe.

Serves: 4–6 people.

ROMAINE SALAD

About the Recipe: Romaine is one of the crispiest of all the lettuce family and has both a green leafy top and a broad crispy stem with a clean moist flavor that bursts in your mouth with each bite. You can also strip away the outer leaves and have a hearts of romaine salad.

Essential Recipe: Fresh Green Chile (p. 44)

Ingredient	Measure	Ingredient	Measure
Romaine lettuce	1 head	Creamy dressing or Vinaigrette	1 cup
Tomato diced, wedged or sliced	1 cup	**OPTIONAL:** Nuts	¼ cup
Cucumber sliced or diced	1 cup	**OPTIONAL:** Spices	1 Tbsp.
Fresh Green Chile	¼ cup or more chopped	**OPTIONAL:** Soft cheese Asadero, queso fresca, panela, requesón	½ cup or more crumbled

Prep Instructions

It is always best to refrigerate romaine lettuce to keep its crispness and cut leaves for salad as needed. To give it an extra crispness, place leaves into a mixing bowl and cover with ice cubes or shaved ice for 1 hour prior to serving. The ice cubes will both crisp and hydrate the lettuce.

Variations

Hearts of Romaine
Romaine hearts can be served with a creamy or vinaigrette dressing. Add some nuts, cherry tomatoes, slices of hard cheese on the plate to decorate and flavor.

Chopped Romaine Salad
Tear the leaves of the romaine lettuce and cut into bite-size pieces. Place in a bowl.
Pour any of the Suggested Dressings into the salad.
Toss salad to evenly coat cut leaves. Serve in individual bowls before or during the meal.

Suggested Dressings: blue cheese, Caesar, green goddess, honey mustard, ranch, thousand island dressing and salpicon are ideally suited for chopped romaine salad.

Serves: 4–6 people.

TOMATO & CUCUMBER SALAD
WITH CREAMY RED CHILE VINAIGRETTE

About the Recipe: Tomatoes and cucumbers combined with Creamy Red Chile Vinaigrette is as great a start to a meal as you can get.

Ingredient	Measure	Ingredient	Measure
Tomato chopped or sliced (4)	2 cups	Creamy Red Chile Vinaigrette (p. 166)	1 cup
Cucumber chopped or sliced (2)	2 cups	Red chile flake SHU to taste	¼ cup
Chopped basil	1 cup	**OPTIONAL:** Soft cheese Asadero, queso fresca, panela, requesón	1 cup crumbled

Prep Instructions

Slice or dice tomatoes and cucumbers and place in bowl.
Chop basil into ¼-inch squares and place in bowl.
Place red chile flakes in bowl.
Place Red Chile Vinaigrette in bowl and toss to cover all ingredients.
Place crumbled cheese in bowl and stir salad.

Suggested Complementary Dishes: Any meal as a salad or side dish.

Servings: 4-6 people

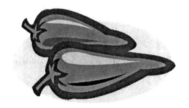

VEGETABLE FRUIT AND GRAIN SALADS

These are combination meal / salads that are served at any time or at festive occasions such as receptions. They also complement hors d'oeuvres, appetizers or side dishes.

PICO DE GALLO FRUIT SALAD

About the Recipe: Pico de Gallo is a standard for almost any meal and as a salad, it makes the meal memorable.
Essential Recipe: Fresh Green Chile (p. 44)

Ingredient	Measure	Ingredient	Measure
Jicama	2 cups chopped	Green Chile Orange Vinaigrette	1 cup
Cucumber	2 cups chopped	Cilantro	1 cup chopped
Fresh Green Chile Anaheim, Poblano, Jalapeño SHU to taste	2 cups chopped	Cut orange slices or canned mandarin oranges	2 cups

Prep Instructions

Peel and chop jicama into ¼-inch cubes and place in a mixing bowl.
Peel and seed cucumber, chop into ¼-inch cubes and place into bowl.
Clean and seed green chile, chop into ¼-inch squares and place into bowl.
Chop cilantro and place in top bowl.
Cut orange slices into ½-inch pieces (remove seeds) or drain a can of mandarin oranges and place into bowl.
Pour green chile orange vinaigrette into bowl and stir to coat all ingredients.
Let sit for 1 to 2 hours to marinate.

Suggested Complementary Dishes: Any dish as a salad, garnish or side dish.

Serves: 4–6 people.

RED CHILE GARBANZO SALAD

About the Recipe: Garbanzos, corn, tomato, beans and green chile is a festive, colorful dish that complements any recipe as a salad, side dish or main meal.

Ingredient	Measure	Ingredient	Measure
Garbanzo beans	1 cups	Red Chile Vinaigrette (p. 166)	½ cup
Corn (frozen okay)	1 cups	Fresh Green Chile SHU to taste	1 cup chopped
Tomato	½ cup chopped	Onion	1 cup chopped
Black, pinto or kidney beans	1 cup	Cilantro	½ cup chopped

Prep Instructions

Rinse and drain one can of garbanzo beans and one can of your chosen other beans and place in a mixing bowl.

Chop tomato, green chile and onion into ¼-inch squares and place in bowl. Add chopped cilantro.

Pour 1 cup of Red Chile Vinaigrette into bowl and stir to coat all ingredients.

Suggested Complementary Dishes: Any meat, or vegetable dish as a garnish or side.

Servings: 6–8 cups.

SALADS AS A MEAL

Meal salads are an excellent menu choice for a high-fiber, easy-to-prepare meal that can also incorporate leftovers and allow you to create distinctive meals on very short notice.

CHICKEN SALAD—RED OR GREEN

About the Recipe: Whether you like red or green this chicken salad recipe will make the perfect lunch, light dinner or sandwich.
Essential Recipe: Shredded Chicken (p. 64). Rehydrated Red Chile pods (p.40) OR Fresh Green Chile (p.44), Roasted Green Chile (p.46).

Ingredient	Measure	Ingredient	Measure
Shredded chicken	4 cups	Crema or sour cream	½ cup
Rehydrated Red Chile Pods Ancho, Pasilla, Chipotle or Chile Seco SHU to taste	1 cup chopped	Creamy Red Chile Vinaigrette (p. 166)	½ cup
Or Fresh Green Chile Anaheim, Poblano Jalapeño SHU to taste	1 cup	Or Creamy Green Chile Vinaigrette (p. 159)	½ cup
Green bell pepper for Red chile chicken salad	½ cup chopped	Adobo Spice Mix'(p. 83)	2 Tbsp.
Or chopped red bell pepper for green chile chicken salad	½ cup	Sweetener: Guava paste, piloncillo, sugar	2 Tbsp.
Cilantro	½ cup chopped	Onion	½ cup chopped

Prep Instructions

Shred chicken with a fork or by hand and place in a large mixing bowl.
Chop red or green chile pods, bell pepper and onion into ¼-inch squares and place in mixing bowl. Add chopped cilantro.
Add crema, creamy vinaigrette dressing, Adobo Spice Mix and sweetener into bowl.
Stir until all ingredients are blended. Refrigerate in sealable container and serve as needed.
Scale recipe up or down for small or large gatherings.

Suggested Complementary Dishes: You can have this as a meal, burrito or as a side dish.
Servings: 4–6 people

CREAMY RED CHILE SHRIMP SALAD

About the Recipe: Shrimp salad with a creamy red chile sauce can be served as an appetizer, side dish or spooned from a cocktail glass. Any way you serve it, it is bound to satisfy any Chilenista from mild to blistering hot.

Ingredient	Measure	Ingredient	Measure
Shrimp (cooked)	1 lb. (medium 41–50 per lb.)	Creamy Red Chile Vinaigrette (p. 166)	1 cup
Jicama	1 cup chopped	Or Red Chile Vinaigrette (p. 165)	1 cup
Tomato	1 cup chopped		
Romaine lettuce or Mesclun leafy salad mix	4–6 leaves ½ lb. or more	**OPTIONAL:** Chipotle chile w/ adobo sauce	3–4 slices
Cilantro	½ cup chopped	Soft cheese Asadero, queso fresca, panela, requesón	1 cup crumbled
		Pepitas (pumpkin seeds)	½ cup

Prep Instructions

Place medium cooked shrimp into a mixing bowl.
Chop jicama and tomato into ¼-inch squares and place into bowl. Chop cilantro.
Add Red Chile Vinaigrette to bowl and stir to coat ingredients.
Optionally chop chipotle in adobo sauce into ¼-inch squares. (Use more or less to taste.)
Plate salad, either romaine leaf or leafy salad mix, on plate. (Create an empty spot in the middle of the leaf.) Place shrimp salad mix on romaine leaf or center of leafy salad mix.
Garnish with chopped chipotle chile, crumbled cheese and pepitas.

Suggested Complementary Dishes: Serve as a meal dish with tostadas or tortillas.

Serves: 4–6 people.

EGG SALAD—RED OR GREEN

About the Recipe: Red or green this egg salad will spice up any salad, sandwich, dip or side dishes. Try it as a meal.
Essential Recipe: Rehydrated Red Chile Pod, (p. 40) OR Fresh Green Chile (p. 44)

Ingredients:	Measure	Spices	Measure
Boiled eggs	8–12	Mayonnaise	1 cup
Rehydrated Red Chile Pods Ancho, Pasilla, Chipotle or Chile Seco SHU to taste	1 cup chopped	Creamy Red Chile Vinaigrette (p. 166)	1 cup
Or Fresh Green Chile Anaheim, Poblano Jalapeño SHU to taste	1 cup chopped	Or Creamy Green Chile Vinaigrette (p. 159)	1 cup
Green bell pepper for Red Egg Salad	½ cup chopped	Adobo Spice Mix (p. 83)	2 Tbsp.
Or Red bell pepper for Green Egg Salad	½ cup chopped	Sweetener: Guava paste, piloncillo, sugar	2 Tbsp.
Cilantro	½ cup chopped	Onion	½ cup chopped

Prep Instructions

Boil eggs and mash with a fork or potato masher. Leave some chunks and place in a large mixing bowl.
Chop red or green chile pods, bell pepper and onion into ¼-inch squares and place in mixing bowl. Add chopped cilantro.
Add mayonnaise, creamy vinaigrette dressing, Adobo Spice Mix and sweetener into bowl.
Stir until all ingredients are blended. Refrigerate in sealable container and serve as needed.
Scale recipe up or down.

Suggested Complementary Dishes: You can serve it as a meal or side dish.

Servings: 6–8 cups

GREEN CHILE TACO SALAD

About the Recipe: Taco salad solves the problem of having a Taco spill on your shirt, the taco shell breaking in your hands or wanting to stuff more into the shell than it can hold.
This recipe will allow Chilenistas to enjoy their tacos without the mess of making them. Yes, you can spoon your taco with as many chiles as you wish.

Essential Recipe: Taco Ground Beef (p.63), Fresh Green Chile (p.44)

Ingredient	Measure	Ingredient	Measure
Taco Ground Beef	1–2 lbs.	Shredded cheese blend Asadero, cheddar, Jack, queso quesadilla	2 cups
Iceberg lettuce Shredded	4–6 cups	Creamy Red Chile Vinaigrette	1 cup
Fresh Green Chile Anaheim, Poblano, Jalapeño SHU to taste	1 cups	Adobo Dry Spice Mix (p. 83)	2 Tbsp.
Tomato	1 cup chopped	Crushed tostada or corn chips	2 cup or more
Cilantro	½ cup chopped	Crema (garnish)	2 cups
Onion	1cups chopped		

Prep Instructions

Prepare Taco Ground Beef and place in a mixing bowl.
Shred lettuce into ¼-inch strips and place into bowl.
Clean, seed, devein and chop green chile into ¼-inch squares and place into bowl.
Chop tomato and onion into ¼-inch squares and place into bowl. Add chopped cilantro.
Add cheese mix, Creamy Red Chile Vinaigrette and Adobo Spice Mix into bowl and toss all ingredients.
Prior to serving, add crushed tostada corn chips and toss. Plate salad into individual plates and garnish with crema.

Suggested Complementary Dishes: As a salad or main dish.

Servings: 6–8 people

GREEN CHILE MACARONI SALAD

About the Recipe: Macaroni is the universal favorite food, so why not serve it with green chile?

Ingredient	Measure	Ingredient	Measure
Elbow, shell or bow tie macaroni	6–8 oz.	Green Chile Vinaigrette (p.158)	½ cup
Fresh Green Chile Anaheim, Poblano Jalapeño SHU to taste	1 cup	Crema or sour cream (p.327)	½ cup
Chopped onion	½ cup	Shredded cheese blend Asadero, cheddar, Jack, queso quesadilla	1 cups
Corn	½ cup	Beans	½ cup

Prep Instructions

Boil elbow macaroni until tender, strain and cool under cold water. Place macaroni in a mixing bowl.
Chop green chile and onion into ¼-inch squares and place in bowl.
Pour green chile vinaigrette and crema into bowl.
Place corn and beans into bowl and add shredded cheese.
Stir contents to thoroughly mix.

Suggested Complementary Dishes: Serve with tortilla or as a side to your favorite meat recipe

Servings: 4–6 people

GREEN CHILE TUNA SALAD

About the Recipe: Tuna salad is a staple that can be served as a salad, meal, sandwich or just spooned from a bowl. This recipe combines the popularity of tuna with the taste of green chile to make a meal that will be requested time after time.

Essential Recipe: Creamy Green Chile sauce (p. 52), Fresh Green Chile (p. 44)

Ingredient	Measure	Ingredient	Measure
Canned Tuna	16 oz.	Creamy Green Chile Sauce	1 cup
Fresh Green Chile Anaheim, Poblano Jalapeño SHU to taste	1 cup	Or Green Chile Vinaigrette	1 cup
Onion	1 cup chopped		
Cilantro	½ cup chopped	**OPTIONAL:** Pinion nuts	½ cup
Romaine lettuce or Mesclun leafy salad mix	4–6 leaves ½ lb. or more		

Prep Instructions

Place drained tuna into a mixing bowl.

Chop green chile and onion into ¼-inch squares and place into bowl. Add chopped cilantro.

Add Green Chile Vinaigrette to bowl and stir to coat ingredients.

Plate salad, either romaine leaf or leafy salad mix. (Create an empty spot in the middle of the leaf.) Place tuna salad mix on romaine leaf or center of leafy salad mix. Garnish with pinion nuts.

Suggested Complementary Dishes: Serve as a meal dish with tostadas or tortillas.

Servings: 4-6 people

GRILLED CHICKEN JICAMA, GREEN CHILE, MANGO SALAD

About the Recipe: The soft, chewy texture of chicken combines with the crunchiness of jicama, pungent green chile and sweetness of mango. Cooking Method: Sauté

Ingredient	Measure	Ingredient	Measure
Chicken breast (skinless)	4 pieces	Green Chile Lime Vinaigrette (p. 158)	1 cups
Green Chile Jicama Mango Salad (p. 174)	6–8 cups	Olive oil	2–3 Tbsp.

Prep Instructions

Place chicken breasts in a 1-gallon plastic bag and pour Green Chile Vinaigrette into bag. Seal and marinate for 2 to 4 hours. Remove chicken from marinade.

Prepare Green Chile Jicama Mango Salad (p. 174).

Cooking Instructions

Place oil and heavy sauté pan and heat to high flame. Place chicken breast and sauté each side about 5 minutes until done.

Slice chicken into ½-inch strips.

Plate salad and place chicken on top.

Suggested Complementary Dishes: Serve with salsa, beans or corn.

Servings: 4–6 people.

POTATO SALAD—RED OR GREEN

About the Recipe: Red Chile or Green Chile Potato Salad goes with any meal, picnic, BBQ, sandwich or works by itself as a side dish.

Essential Recipe: Rehydrated Red Chile Pods, (p. 40). Fresh green chile (p. 44)

Ingredient	Measure	Spices	Measure
Potatoes	4 lbs.	Crema or sour cream	1 cup
Rehydrated Red Chile Pods, Ancho, Pasilla, Chipotle or Chile Seco SHU to taste	1 cup chopped	Creamy Red Chile Vinaigrette (p. 166)	1 cup
Or Fresh Green Chile Anaheim, Poblano Jalapeño SHU to taste	1 cup	Or Creamy Green Chile Vinaigrette (p. 158)	1 cup
Cilantro	½ cup chopped	Adobo Dry Spice Mix (p. 83)	2 Tbsp.
Onion	½ cup chopped	Sweetener: Guava paste, piloncillo, sugar	2 Tbsp.

Prep Instructions

Peel and boil potatoes until fork tender, drain water and let cool. Cut potatoes into ½-inch or ¾-inch squares and place in a large mixing bowl. Chop red or green chile pods and onion into ¼-inch squares and place in mixing bowl. Add chopped cilantro.

Add crema, creamy vinaigrette dressing, Adobo Spice Mix and sweetener into bowl.

Stir until all ingredients are blended. Refrigerate in sealable container and serve as needed.

Scale recipe up or down.

Suggested Complementary Dishes: Any dish goes well with potato salad.

Servings: 8–12 people

SALPICON (RED CHILE SPICY BEEF SALAD)

About the Recipe: This hearty recipe is a great winter food that can be served year-round.

Essential Recipe: Slow Cooked Brisket (p. 60), Rehydrated Red Chile pods (p. 40).

Ingredient	Measure	Ingredient	Measure
Beef brisket (shredded) (p. 60)	1 - 2 lbs.	Salpicon Dressing (p. 168)	2 cups
Chopped tomato	2 cups	Cilantro	1 cup chopped
Avocado (diced)	2 cups	Shredded cheese blend Asadero, cheddar, Jack, queso quesadilla	2 cups
Onion	1 cup chopped	Sweetener: Nectar Guava, papaya, tamarind	½ cup
Rehydrated Red Chile Pods Ancho, Pasilla, Chipotle or Chile Seco SHU to taste	½ cup chopped	Green onion	½ cup chopped

Prep Instructions
Prepare Slow Cooked Brisket and shred 1–2 lbs. Place in mixing bowl.
Peel, seed and dice avocado into ½-inch squares and place into mixing bowl.
Chop onion into ¼-inch squares and place into bowl. Add chopped cilantro.
Chop green onion into ½-inch strips and add.
Place shredded cheese into bowl.
Pour Salpicon Dressing and sweetener into bowl.
Toss salad until all ingredients are blended.
Plate on a serving dish and garnish with a green onion.

Suggested Complementary Dishes: Serve as an appetizer or as a meal

Servings: 4–6 people

Chapter 7
BREAKFAST RECIPES RED OR GREEN

There is no better way to start a new day than with a chile fix. Preparing the ESSENTIAL RECIPES for chile paste, chile sauce or creamy chile in advance and storing them in your fridge makes all of the recipes below quick and easy.

Quite a few of the following recipes can be made with either red or green chile, depending on your mood, taste preference and available ingredients. If you cannot decide which to make, try Christmas and get the best of both Red and Green.

"All happiness depends on a leisurly breakfast"
John Gunther

ATOLE PORRIDGE —RED OR GREEN

Complexity Code: EZ   Origin: New Mexico
Cooking Method: Boil / Simmer

About the Recipe: Atole is purported to have medicinal qualities and
should be eaten daily either as a porridge or a drink at any time. By adding
chile you can supercharge its potency by adding capsaicin to stimulate
endorphins. For sweet Atole, look at the desert (Postre) section (p.
341). Atole may be served with sugar as a beverage or served with milk,
sweetener and vanilla.
Essential Recipe: Creamy Red Chile Sauce (p.38) OR Green Chile
Sauce (p. 52).

Ingredient	Measure	Ingredient	Measure
Masa corn flour	1 cup	Baking powder	1 tsp.
Milk or water	4 cups	Butter	4 pats
Creamy Red or Green Chile Sauce	1 cup	Cilantro	1 sprig

Prep Instructions

Combine masa flour, with 2 cups milk and baking powder in a mixing bowl
and stir until it forms a smooth paste (no lumps).
Place 2 cups milk or water and chile sauce in a 2- to 3-quart saucepan.
Cooking Instructions
Bring saucepan with milk and chile sauce to a boil and immediately turn
heat down to simmer.
Add atole flour paste to milk and simmer under low flame, stirring until it
gains the porridge consistency you like. Turn heat down and serve.

Suggested Complementary Dishes: Garnish with a pat of butter or
crema top, or serve with eggs, chorizos and bacon.

Servings 4–6 cups.

CHILE QUICHE —RED OR GREEN

Complexity Code: COOK   Origin: New Mexico / Mexico
Cooking Method: Bake

About the Recipe: Quiche is one of the world's most popular breakfast or brunch recipes. By adding chile, we bring it home with a dish that is guaranteed to dish-appear the minute it is made. Better make two or more while you are at it. It will keep well in the fridge for a week, but I doubt that it will last that long.

Essential Recipe: Re-hydrated Red Chile Pods (p. 40), OR Roasted Green Chile (p. 46), Fresh Green Chile (p. 44).

Ingredient	Measure	Ingredient	Measure
Eggs	4	Heavy cream	1 cup
9" pie crust (frozen works best)	1		2 Tbsp.
Red Chile Pods Ancho, Pasilla, Chipotle, Serrano (Rehydrated or canned) SHU to taste	1 cup	Shredded cheese blend Asadero, cheddar, Jack, queso quesadilla	1 cup
Green Chile (finely chopped) Anaheim Poblano, Jalapeño Fresh or Roasted SHU to taste	1 cups fine chopped	Onion	1 small fine chopped
Sweetener (p. 85)	½ cup	Tomato	1 cup fine chopped
		Baking powder	½ tsp.

Prep Instructions

Preheat oven to 350^0F.

Defrost and bring pie crust to room temperature.

In a mixing bowl, crack eggs; blend in chopped chile, shredded cheese, sweetener, heavy cream, onion, tomato and baking powder. Whip eggs hard till bubbles form.

Place egg mixture into pie shell. (I recommend preparing 2 to 4 pie shells at a time.)

Cooking Instructions

Place pie shell in oven and bake for 15 to 20 minutes until eggs are firm. You can use a toothpick to test the quiche.

Suggested Complementary Garnishes: Salsa, crema, sparkling wine.

Servings: 4 cups.

BREAKFAST BURRITO —RED OR GREEN

Complexity Code: EZ   Origin: New Mexico
Cooking Method: Sauté

About the Recipe: A breakfast burrito is the breakfast of choice for anyone who is in a hurry, traveling or just savoring it with a cup of coffee. You can choose any topping or meat to roll into the burrito

Essential Recipe: Rehydrated Red Chile pods (p. 40), OR Roasted Green Chile (p.46), Fresh Green Chile (p. 44), Chorizos (p. 55), Taco Ground Meat (p. 63), Salsa (p. 142),

Ingredient	Measure	Ingredient	Measure
Eggs	6	Cilantro	½ cup or more chopped
Heavy cream or half-and-half	¼ cup	Vegetable oil	¼ cup
Dehydrated Red Chile Pods Ancho, Pasilla, Chipotle, Serrano (Rehydrated or canned) SHU to taste	1 cup chopped	Shredded cheese blend Asadero, cheddar, Jack, queso quesadilla	1 cup or more
Green Chile Pods Anaheim, Poblano, Jalapeño (fresh or roasted) SHU to taste	1 cup chopped	**OPTIONAL:** Bacon, chorizos, taco meat, salsa, chopped cilantro	To taste
Tortilla (Burrito size) Thin if available	4–6		

Prep Instructions

Chop chile pods into squares (removing stem and seeds).
Crack eggs in a mixing bowl, add heavy cream or half-and-half and beat well until bubbles form. Add chopped chile and cilantro, and beat eggs again until all the ingredients are well blended.
Soften burritos by placing them on the microwave defrost cycle 10 to 15 seconds.
Heat large skillet with oil.

Cooking Instructions

Place eggs into skillet and let the eggs sauté until the edges start to firm. Gently fold the edges toward the center of the skillet. The uncooked eggs will flow out of the center onto the pan. (DO NOT SCRAMBLE.) Let the eggs firm and repeat folding the edges toward the center until all of the eggs have firmed.

Place warm burrito on a flat pan; place a 1-inch row of eggs 2 inches from the edge. Place ½-inch row of cheese on top of the eggs and any optional meat topping, salsa, cilantro on top of the cheese. Tuck the right edge of the burrito in and roll the burrito towards the top. Place a toothpick to hold the roll together. To warm and melt the cheese, place the burrito in a microwave for 15 to 20 seconds.

Suggested Complementary Dishes: Chorizos, bacon, crema.

Serves: 4–6 people.

EGG ENCHILADAS
RED OR GREEN WITH CHORIZOS

Complexity Code: Cook

Origin: New Mexico

Cooking Method: Sauté / Bake

About the Recipe: Chile egg enchiladas with chorizos are a wonderful Sunday breakfast that can feed your family and guests and yield leftovers for breakfast during the week. You can also serve it for lunch or brunch or anytime you want a genuine New Mexico chile fix.

Essential Recipe: Rehydrated Red Chile pods (p. 40), Red Chile Enchilada Sauce (p. 77), OR Roasted Green Chile (p. 46), Green Chile Enchilada Sauce (p. 76), Chorizos (p. 55).

Ingredient	Measure	Ingredient	Measure
Eggs	12	Adobo Spice Mix (p.83)	2 Tbsp.
Chorizos*	6 oz.	Onion	1 small fine chopped
Red or Green Chile Enchilada Sauce*	4 cups	Shredded cheese blend Asadero, cheddar, Jack, queso quesadilla	3 cups
Rehydrated Red Chile Pods Ancho, Pasilla, Chipotle, Serrano (canned is okay) SHU to taste	½ cup	Tomato	1 cup fine chopped
Roasted Green Chile Anaheim, Poblano, Jalapeño SHU to taste	½ cup chopped	Sweetener (p. 85)	½ cup
		Vegetable oil	4 Tbsp.

*Store-bought is okay.

Prep Instructions

Phase 1:

Crack eggs in a mixing bowl; add half-and-half, Adobo Spice Mix, onion, tomato and sweetener. Whip eggs with a whisk or fork until small bubbles appear.

Moisten tortillas and warm in a microwave (defrost cycle 15 to 20 seconds) or oven at 175°F.

Preheat oven to 350°F.

Phase 2

Grease bottom of 9-by-13-inch casserole dish; place 2 cups of enchilada sauce on bottom of pan.

Place a warm tortilla on a plate; fill a layer 2 Tbsp. each of chorizos, egg, chopped chile and cheese on the front edge of the tortilla. Roll the tortilla, folding in the edges (as if you were making burritos). Place rolled tortilla in casserole dish seam side down. Repeat for all 12 tortillas. Pour the rest of the chile enchilada Sauce on top of the tortillas; sprinkle the shredded cheese mix on. Cover dish with aluminum foil. Place casserole dish in oven.

Cooking Instructions

Sauté:

Sauté chorizos in large skillet, remove from pan and allow to dry on a towel.

Remove most of the chorizos grease from the skillet and scrape the bottom of the skillet to de-glaze chorizos bits. Add 2–3 Tbsp. oil and heat skillet on high.

Pour egg mixture into skillet and let eggs cook till a bottom crust is partially formed and some bubbles appear. Push edges of eggs toward center to let loose eggs flow to the pan. (DO NOT SCRAMBLE.) When eggs are loose but firm remove from heat.

Bake:

Place casserole dish in center of oven and bake for 15 to 20 minutes, remove foil and place dish under the broiler for 5 minutes to crust the cheese.

Remove from oven let cool for 5 to 10 minutes. You are ready to serve the enchiladas.

Suggested Complementary Garnishes: Chopped tomatoes, cilantro, crema, salsa and avocado.

Servings 8–10 cups.

EGG OMELET —RED OR GREEN

Complexity Code: EZ
Cooking Method: Sauté

Origin: Original

About the Recipe: Omelets are the one of the easiest recipes to prepare and can serve many people in a short time. When guests pop in, think of omelets. This recipe has been time-tested to please everyone for breakfast, brunch, snack or meal and as a burrito filling.
Essential Recipe: Rehydrated Red Chile pods (p. 40). Fresh Green Chile (p. 44) OR Roasted Green Chile (p.46)

Ingredient	Measure	Ingredient	Measure
Eggs	6	Cilantro	½ cup or more chopped
Heavy cream or half-and-half	½ cup	Vegetable oil or butter	¼ cup
Rehydrated Red Chile Pods. Ancho, Pasilla, Chipotle, Serrano (canned is okay) SHU to taste	1 cup	Red chile powder	2 Tbsp.
Green Chile Anaheim, Poblano, Jalapeño (fresh or roasted) SHU to taste	1 cup chopped	Green chile powder	2 Tbsp.

Prep Instructions
Chop chile pods into ¼-inch squares. (Remove stem and seeds.)
Crack eggs in a mixing bowl, add heavy cream or half-and-half and beat well until bubbles form.
Add chopped chile, cilantro and beat eggs again until all the ingredients are well blended.
Heat large skillet with oil.

Cooking Instructions
Place eggs into skillet and let the eggs sauté until the edges start to firm. Gently fold the edges toward the center of the skillet. The uncooked eggs will flow out of the center onto the pan. (DO NOT SCRAMBLE.) Let the eggs firm and repeat to fold the edges toward the center. When all of the eggs have firmed, serve eggs on individual plates. Garnish with red or green chile powder.

Suggested Complementary Dishes: Chorizos, bacon, crema, tortilla burrito.
Serves: 4–6 people.

EGG OMELET CAKES
(TORTA) DIA DE LOS MUERTE

Complexity Code: COOK   Origin: New Mexico / Mexico
Cooking Method: Fry

About the Recipe: Many favorite recipes are prepared during the *Day of the Dead* to honor and feed those departed. This recipe creates miniature egg omelet cakes, which can be served year-round to honor our ancestors.
Essential Recipe: Red Chile Sauce (p. 36).

Ingredient	Measure	Ingredient	Measure
Eggs	4	Salt	½ tsp.
Red Chile Sauce	2 cups	Red chile powder	½ tsp.
Flour (Unbleached)	2 Tbsp.	Vegetable oil or lard (traditional)	2 cups
Sweetener: Honey, piloncillo, sugar	1 Tbsp.		

Prep Instructions
Separate egg whites into a mixing bowl and place yolk in a small bowl. Beat egg white with a whisk or mixing stick until bubbles form. (Do not harden whites.)
Stir in flour, sweetener, salt and red chile powder until well blended (no lumps).
In a heavy skillet place 1-inch of oil or lard (traditional) for frying.
Into a medium sauté pan pour red chile sauce.

Cooking Instructions
Heat red chile sauce to a low simmer (warm).
Heat oil in heavy skillet (high heat), drop a tablespoon full of eggs into the oil and fry until golden brown. Remove eggs (tortas) with a serrated spoon, shake off excess oil and place in the simmering red chile sauce.

Suggested Complementary Dishes: Salsa, tortilla, tostada, crema or sour cream.

Serves: 4–6 people.

MIGAS CASSEROLE —RED OR GREEN

Complexity Code: EZ   Origin: Original
Cooking Method: Bake

About the Recipe: Half egg and half cake, the migas casserole is for the hearty eater and an ideal brunch that will last for the balance of the day.

Essential Recipe: Rehydrated Red Chile pods (p. 40), Creamy Red Chile Sauce (p. 38), OR Roasted Green Chile Pods (p. 46), Creamy Green Chile Sauce (p. 52).

Ingredient	Measure		Measure
Eggs	12	Baking powder	1 tsp.
Masa or Flour (Unbleached)	1 cup	Tomatoes	1 cup chopped
Rehydrated Red Chile Pods, Ancho, Pasilla, Chipotle, Serrano (Rehydrated or canned) SHU to taste	1 cup	Shredded cheese blend, Asadero, cheddar, Jack, Quesadilla	4 cups
Roasted Green Chile Anaheim, Poblano, Jalapeño SHU to taste	1 cup chopped	Oregano powder	1 Tbsp.
Creamy Red or Green Chile Sauce		Scallions	4 sprigs chopped
		Cilantro	¼ cup fine chopped
		Crema or cottage cheese	2 cups

Prep Instructions

Preheat oven to 400°F.

Chop chile pods into ¼-inch squares (removing stem and seeds).

Crack eggs into a mixing bowl, add flour and baking powder, beat eggs with a whisk until all the flour and baking powder are blended well and a few bubbles appear in the mix.

Add 3 cups of shredded cheese, crema, tomatoes, red chile, oregano, scallions and cilantro.

Mix blend well. Pour eggs into a greased 9-by-13-inch baking pan.

Cooking Instructions

Place eggs in center of oven and immediately reduce the heat to 350°F and bake for approximately 45 minutes until the center of the casserole is firm. (Use a toothpick to check that it come out dry and clean.)

Sprinkle 1 cup of shredded cheese blend on top of casserole and place under the broiler to brown (3 to 5 minutes).

Remove casserole from oven, let cool approximately 5 to 10 minutes. Cut into squares.

Suggested Complementary Dishes: Salsa, crema, bacon, Chorizos, sausage on the side.

Serves: 8 people.

MIGAS OMELET - RED OR GREEN

Complexity Code: EZ   Origin: Original
Cooking Method: Fry

About the Recipe: Migas is a Spanish dish that combines eggs with tortillas and has become a favorite breakfast throughout the Southwest. It is easy to make and can incorporate the creative skills of any chef.

Essential Recipe: Rehydrated Red Chile pods (p. 40), OR Roasted Green Chile (p. 46).

Ingredient	Measure		Measure
Eggs	6	Red or green chile powder	2 Tbsp.
Cream or milk	¼ cup	Sweetener (p. 85)	1 Tbsp.
Corn Tortilla chips (Crushed)	1 cup	Garlic powder	½ tsp.
Rehydrated Red Chile Pods Ancho, Pasilla, Chipotle, Serrano (Rehydrated or canned) SHU to taste	½ cup	Vegetable oil or butter	2–3 Tbsp.
Roasted Green Chile. Anaheim, Poblano, Jalapeño SHU to taste	½ cup chopped	Tomatoes	½ cup diced
		Scallion	2 sprigs chopped
		Cilantro	¼ cup fine chopped

Prep Instructions

Chop chile pods into ¼-inch squares (removing stem and seeds).
Crack eggs in a mixing bowl; add cream or milk, crushed tortilla chips, chile powder, sweetener and garlic powder.
Whip eggs and spices with a whisk until it is thoroughly blended and a few bubbles appear. Let sit a few minutes for the Tortilla chips to soak.
Blend red chiles (canned or rehydrated), diced tomatoes and cilantro in a small bowl

Cooking Instructions

Coat bottom of frying pan with oil or butter, heat pan to high and lower to medium.

Pour the eggs into the pan to evenly coat the bottom of the frying pan.

Fry until the first bottom crust appears in the eggs. The edges will start to bubble.

Pour the blended chiles on top of the omelet and wait till the eggs firm up a bit.

With a spatula, gently fold half of the omelet over itself. Wait for 30 seconds and flip the omelet over. Wait for another 30 seconds. Garnish top of omelet with scallions.

Suggested Complementary Dishes: Salsa, tortilla chips, crema or sour cream, hot sauce,
bacon, Chorizos, sausage on the side.

Serves: 4 people.

MIGAS SOUFFLÉ (RED OR GREEN—CARNE)

Complexity Code: Cook
Cooking Method: Bake.

Origin: Original

About the Recipe: A migas soufflé can be prepared ahead of time, put into the refrigerator overnight and baked fresh in the morning.
Essential Recipes: Rehydrated Red Chile pods (p. 40), Creamy Red Chile Sauce (p. 38), OR Roasted Green Chile (p. 46), Creamy Green Chile Sauce (p. 52), Chorizos (p. 55) Taco Ground Beef (p. 62), Sautéed Beef, Chicken or Pork (p.64).

Ingredient	Measure	Ingredient	Measure
Eggs	8	Red or green chile powder	1 Tbsp.
Cream or milk	¼ Cup	Sweetener (p. 85)	1 Tbsp.
Tortilla chips	3 cups crushed	Cilantro	½ cup chopped
Shredded cheese blend Asadero, cheddar, Jack,	2 cups	Oil or Butter	¼ cup
Rehydrated Red Chile Pods Ancho, Pasilla, Chipotle, Serrano (or canned) SHU to taste	1 cup	Chorizos recipe (p. 55) or purchased Substitute or add chopped bacon, sausage. Taco Ground Beef, Sauteed Beef.	1–2 cups
Roasted Green Chile Anaheim, Poblano, Jalapeño SHU to taste	1 cup chopped		
Creamy Red or Green Chile Sauce	2 cups		

Prep Instructions

Chop chile pods into ¼-inch squares (removing stem and seeds).
Crack eggs in a mixing bowl; add cream or milk, chile powder and sweetener.
Whip eggs and spices with a whisk until it is thoroughly blended and a few bubbles appear. (You may use a blender stick if you have one.) Grease bottom of 9-by-13-inch pan with oil or butter.
Place crushed tortilla chips on bottom of pan. Spread Creamy Red Chile Sauce on top of tortilla and stir / mix well to coat the tortilla chips with chile sauce.

Spread 1 cup of shredded cheese on top of tortillas.

Spread chopped chiles on top of shredded cheese.

Spread chorizos or carne over cheese layer. Spread balance of shredded cheese (1 cup) on top of carne layer. (The cheese will melt over and through the carne when baked.)

Spread whipped eggs over cheese layer. (Gently shake the bake pan back and forth to allow the eggs to flow to the bottom.)

Cooking Instructions

Preheat oven to 350^0F. Place migas soufflé into center of oven, bake for a half-hour until firm and golden brown. Remove from oven and let sit for 5 minutes. Cut into 3-inch squares, garnish top of migas soufflé with cilantro and serve.

Suggested Complementary Dishes: Salsa, crema or sour cream, bacon, chorizos, sausage on the side.

Serves: 8–12 people.

MIGAS SOUFFLÉ (RED OR GREEN VEGGIE)

Complexity Code: Cook   Origin: Original
Cooking Method: Bake

About the Recipe: A migas soufflé is a culinary delight sure to please every egg-lover. It is light and fluffy and combines the flavors of chile, eggs and tortilla into a culinary delight. It has become the favorite of almost every Bed & Breakfast and breakfast buffet.
A migas soufflé can be prepared ahead of time, put into the refrigerator and baked fresh.

Essential Recipe: Rehydrated Red Chile (p. 40), Creamy Red Chile Sauce (p. 38) OR Roasted Green Chile (p. 46), Creamy Green Chile Sauce (p. 52).

Ingredient	Measure	Ingredient	Measure
Eggs	8	Red or green chile powder	2 Tbsp.
Cream or milk	¼ Cup	Sweetener (p. 85)	1 Tbsp.
Tortilla chips (Crushed)	3 cups	Cilantro	½ cup chopped
Rehydrated Red Chile Pods Ancho, Pasilla, Chipotle, Serrano (or canned) SHU to taste	1 cup	Oil or Butter	¼ cup
Roasted Green Chile Anaheim, Poblano, Jalapeño SHU to taste	1 cup chopped	Shredded cheese blend Asadero, cheddar, Jack,	2 cups
Creamy Red or Green Chile Sauce	2 cups		

Prep Instructions

Chop chile pods into ¼-inch squares (removing stem and seeds).
Crack eggs in a mixing bowl. Add cream or milk, chile powder and sweetener.
Whip eggs and spices with a whisk until it is thoroughly blended and a few bubbles appear. (You may use a blender stick if you have one.)
Grease bottom of 9-by-13-inch pan with oil or butter.
Place crushed tortilla chips on bottom of pan, spread creamy chile sauce on top of tortilla and stir / mix well to coat the tortilla chips with chile sauce. Spread 1 cup of shredded cheese on top of tortillas. Spread chopped chiles on top of shredded cheese.

Spread balance of shredded cheese (1 cup) on top of chile layer. (The cheese will melt over and through the chile when baked.) Spread whipped eggs over cheese layer. (Gently shake the bake pan back and forth to allow the eggs to flow to the bottom).

Cooking Instructions

Preheat oven to 350^0F. Place Migas Soufflé into center of oven and bake for a half-hour until
firm and golden brown. Remove from oven and let sit for 5 minutes. Cut into 3-inch squares, garnish top of Migas Soufflé with cilantro and serve.

Suggested Complementary Dishes: Salsa, crema or sour cream. bacon, chorizos, sausage on the side.

Serves: 8–12 people.

NEW MEXICAN EGG BAKE —RED OR GREEN

Complexity Code: EZ   Origin: New Mexico / Mexico
Cooking Method: Pan Fry / Bake
About the Recipe: If you are looking for a hearty breakfast, look no further.
Essential Recipe: Rehydrated Red Chile pods (p. 40), OR Roasted Green Chile (p. 46).

Ingredient	Measure	Ingredient	Measure
Eggs	12	Milk or half-and-half	1 cup
Sausage or Chorizos sausage	1 lb.	Adobo Dry Spice Mix (p. 83)	2 Tbsp.
Rehydrated Red Chile Pods. Ancho, Pasilla, Chipotle, Serrano (or canned) SHU to taste	1 cup	Shredded cheese blend Asadero, cheddar, Jack, queso quesadilla	2 cup
Roasted Green Chile, Anaheim Poblano, Jalapeño SHU to taste	1 cup chopped	Onion	1 small fine Chopped
		Tomato	1 cup fine chopped
		Potato (diced)* or Frozen hash brown potatoes	1 cup

Prep Instructions
Dice one large potato and pan-fry, or use 1 cup hash brown potatoes (defrost).
Pan-fry sausage or chorizos.
Crack eggs in mixing bowl; add half-and-half, beating briskly with a whisk or fork until bubbles form.
Add chopped chile, shredded cheese, adobo mixture, onion, tomato, potato and blend until all are covered by eggs.
Grease bottom of 9-by-13-inch baking pan. Pour eggs into pan.

Cooking Instructions
Preheat oven 350°F. Place baking pan in center of oven and bake for 30 to 45 minutes until eggs are firm. Remove from oven and cool for 5 minutes. Cut into 3-by-3-inch slices and serve.

Suggested Complementary Dishes: Salsa, crema, tortilla, tortilla chips, pickled green chile.

Serves: 10–12 people.

POACHED OR FRIED EGGS ON A RAFT
RED OR GREEN

Complexity Code: EZ   Origin: Original
Cooking Method: Fry /Poach / Broil

About the Recipe: This is an easy and dramatic dish to serve for Sunday breakfast.

Essential Recipe: Red Chile Sauce (p. 36) or Creamy Red Chile Sauce (p. 38), Rehydrated Red Chile pods (optional) (p. 40) OR Green Chile Sauce (p. 50), Creamy Green Chile Sauce (p. 52), Fresh Green Chile (p. 44).

Ingredient	Measure	Ingredient	Measure
Eggs	4	Oil, or butter	4 Tbsp.
Tortillas (Corn or Wheat)	4	Vegetable oil	¼ cup
Chile Sauce —Red or Green Creamy Chile Sauce, Red or Green	2 cups	Water	1 cup
Rehydrated Red Chile Pods Ancho, Pasilla, Chipotle, Serrano (or canned) SHU to taste	2 cups	**OPTIONAL:** Shredded cheese blend. Asadero, cheddar, Jack	1 cup
Fresh Green Chile, Anaheim, Poblano, Jalapeño (fresh or roasted) SHU to taste	2 cups chopped		

Prep Instructions

Preheat oven with broiler rack 6 to 8 inches from the flame.
Chop red or green chile pods into ¼-inch squares. (Remove stem and seeds.)
Grease bottom of a large cookie sheet or flat pan. Place 4 tortillas on pan, cover each tortilla with Red or Green Chile Sauce, place chopped chiles around edge of each tortilla, leave center blank, or optionally place ¼ cup shredded cheese blend in center.
Place vegetable oil into large frying pan and heat on range.

Cooking Instructions

Place flat pan with tortillas under broiler until chile sauce starts to bubble and cheese has melted. Turn off broiler and leave tortillas in oven until the eggs are poached.
Crack eggs and carefully place them in frying pan to not break the yolks. Let eggs fry until the egg whites firm up.
To poach eggs, pour 1 cup of water in frying pan and cover pan. (The steam will poach the egg yolk.) Turn heat off.
Remove tortillas from oven and place on individual plates with a spatula. Place poached eggs in the middle of the tortilla. You now have an egg essential piece.

Suggested Complementary Dishes: Bacon, chorizos, crema or sour cream.
Serves: 4 people.

HUEVOS RANCHEROS —RED OR GREEN

Complexity Code: Cook
Cooking Method: Fry / Poach / Broil

Origin: New Mexico

About the Recipe: Huevos Rancheros, the King of a New Mexico breakfast, and can be prepared with corn or wheat tortilla, and served with or without carne either red or green.

Essential Recipe: Red Chile Sauce (p. 36) or Creamy Red Chile Sauce (p. 38), Rehydrated Red Chile pods (optional) (p. 40), Green Chile Sauce (p. 50), Creamy Green Chile Sauce (p. 52), Fresh Green Chile (p. 44).

Ingredient	Measure	Ingredient	Measure
Eggs	4	Shredded cheese blend Asadero, cheddar, Jack	2 cups
Corn tortilla	4	Cilantro	½ cup chopped
Red Chile Sauce or Creamy Red Chile Sauce	2 cups	Rehydrated Red Chile Pods, Ancho, Pasilla, Chipotle, Serrano (or canned) SHU to taste	1 cup
Green Chile Sauce or Creamy Green Chile Sauce	2 cups	Fresh Green Chile (Chopped) Anaheim, Poblano, Jalapeño (fresh or roasted) SHU to taste	1 cup chopped
Water	½ cup	Chopped Tomato	½ cup
Oil, butter, lard	4 Tbsp.	Crema	½ cup

Prep Instructions

Preheat oven with broiler rack 6 to 8 inches from the flame.
Grease a 12-by-14-inch cookie pan with oil. Place 4 tortillas evenly spaced on the pan. Cover tortillas with a thin layer of the red or green chile sauce. Place chile sauce, shredded cheese and chopped chile in individual bowls.

Cooking Instructions

Place tortillas under broiler until the chile bubbles slightly. Remove from oven (leave oven on).
Crack eggs and carefully place them in frying pan to not break the yolks. Let eggs fry until the egg whites firm up.
To poach eggs, pour 1 cup of water in frying pan and cover pan for eggs to poach. (The steam will poach the egg yolk.)

With a spatula place each egg on top of a tortilla on the baking pan, cover egg with chile sauce on top of the yolk, and cover tortilla with shredded cheese.

Place baking pan under the broiler for 3 to 4 minutes until the cheese melts, remove from oven and voila!! You have huevos rancheros.

Plate each tortilla individually and garnish with cilantro, chile flakes and tomato.

Suggested Complementary Dishes: Salsa, bacon, Chorizos, sausage on the side.

Serves: 4 people.

Chapter 8—RED OR GREEN CHILE STEWS, SOUPS & CHOWDERS

For some red or green chile stew can be a religious experience. The delicate flavors of roasted chilies combined with fresh garden vegetables, beans and meats evokes a creative cooking and eating experience that some have described as the ultimate comfort food.

For New Mexicans, it the perfect way to celebrate a homecoming, a holiday, a celebration, and a gathering with friends and family. For a Chilinista it is the ultimate chile fix.

If there is one recipe that you need to know, this chapter will provide it.

"I need a bowl of chile" is the first thing a New Mexican says when returning to the Land of Enchantment.

RED CHILE STEW
(A BOWL OF RED FOR THE PURIST)

Complexity Code: EZ   Origin: New Mexico
Cooking Method: Boil, Simmer

About the Recipe: A bowl of red is the quintessential dish to come home
to. You can prepare and freeze this recipe and have it ready for any chile
emergency.
Essential Recipe: Red Chile Paste (p.33), Red Chile Roux (p.35),
Rehydrated Red Chile Pods, (p.40).

Ingredient	Measure	Ingredient	Measure
Red Chile Paste SHU to taste	2 cups	Adobo Spice Mix (p.83)	2 Tbsp.
OPTIONAL: Rehydrated Red Chile pods Ancho, Pasilla, Chipotle or Chile Seco SHU to taste	1 cup chopped	Sweetener (p. 85)	2 Tbsp.
Water or beef broth	2 cups	Masa, corn flour or flour (unbleached)	½ cup

Prep Instructions
Place red chile paste, chopped red chile pods and water into 3- to 4-quart
stockpot and stir to blend mixture.
In a small mixing bowl, add 1 cup red chile mixture and ½ cup flour
(masa preferred). Add Adobo Spice Mix and sweetener. Stir mixture to
completely blend and remove any lumps to create a Red Chile Roux.

Cooking Instructions
Bring red chile mixture to a slow boil (medium bubbles) and add Adobo
Spice Mix and sweetener. Boil for 5 to 10 minutes.
Reduce heat to a simmer and slowly add the Red Chile Roux into red chile
stockpot. Stir and simmer for 15 to 20 minutes. If the chile is too thin, you
may add some additional flour mixture. If it is too thick, add water.

Suggested Complementary Dishes: Tortilla, fry bread.

Servings: 4–6.

GREEN CHILE STEW
(A BOWL OF GREEN FOR THE PURIST)

Complexity Code: Cook   Origin: New Mexico
Cooking Method: Boil, Simmer

About the Recipe: A " bowl of green" is the standard-bearer for the
Chilenista cuisine and the basis for most Feast Day or Sunday dinners.
Essential Recipe: Roasted Green Chile (p.46), Green Chile Sauce (p.50).

Ingredient	Measure	Ingredient	Measure
Roasted Green Chile, Anaheim, Poblano, Jalapeño SHU to taste	8 cups chopped	Adobo Spice Mix (p. 83)	¼ cup
Tomatoes (Canned okay)	2 cups chopped	Sweetener (p. 85)	¼ cup
Green Chile Sauce SHU to taste	1 cup	Vegetable oil, butter	¼ cup
Water or beef broth	8 cups	Salt (To taste)	1 Tbsp.
		OPTIONAL: Beans, garbanzo or posole (from scratch or canned)	4 cups

Prep Instructions
Place 8 cups (2 quarts) of water in 3- to 4-quart stockpot and bring to a
boil.
Chop Roasted Green Chile into ¼-inch squares.
Chop tomatoes into ¼-inch cubes. If using canned chile or veggies, drain
cans and rinse and strain to remove preservatives and additives.

Cooking Instructions
Add Fresh Green Chile, tomatoes, Green Chile Sauce, Adobo Spice Mix,
Sweetener,   vegetable oil and salt and reduce heat to a simmer (slow
bubbles). Stir and simmer for 1 hour.
Add optional cooked or canned beans and simmer for an additional 10 to
15 minutes.

Suggested Complementary Dishes: Tortillas, tortilla chips.

Serves: 6–8 people.

BEAN, GARBANZO OR POSOLE STEW
RED OR GREEN

Complexity Code: Cook   Origin: New Mexico
Cooking Method: Boil, Simmer

About the Recipe: This is a traditional recipe. Posole may be the world's
oldest processed food going back to 1500 B.C. and was used by the Aztec
and Native people in Central and South America. Posole is made out
of corn that has been soaked in lye to remove the hull and germs from
the corn kernel and puffing it up three to four times its size. It is more
digestible than corn. You can use any legumes that you wish from what is
available.

Essential Recipe: Beans, Garbanzos, Posole (p.304), Red Chile Paste
(p.33), Red Chile Roux (p.35), Rehydrated Red Chile Pods, (p.40), OR
Green Chile Paste (p.43), Green Chile Roux (p.49), Roasted Green Chile
(p.46).

Ingredient	Measure	Ingredient	Measure
Beans, Garbanzo or Posole (from scratch or canned)	4 cups	Adobo Spice Mix (p.83)	1 Tbsp.
Rehydrated Red Chile Pods Ancho, Pasilla, Chipotle or Chile Seco SHU to taste	2 cups chopped	Water, pork or beef broth	8 cups
OR Roasted green chile, Anaheim, Poblano, Jalapeño SHU to taste	2 cups chopped	Sweetener (p.85)	2 Tbsp.
Red or Green Chile Paste	2 cups	**OPTIONAL:** Beef or pork cubes (boiled)	1–2 lbs.
Red or Green Chile Roux	½ cup		

Prep Instructions

Drain and rinse canned beans, garbanzos or posole.
Cut pork into 1-inch cubes.
Boil pork in 8 cups of water until tender, 30 to 45 minutes. (Use broth
for the stew base). Drain broth with a colander and place 8 cups in 3- to
4-quart stockpot.
Set pork aside for later use.
Chop Rehydrated Red Chile pods into ¼-inch squares. (Remove stems and
seeds.)
Chop Roasted Green Chile into ¼-inch squares. (Remove stems and
seeds.)
Place 8 cups of water or beef broth in 3- to 4-quart stockpot.
Prepare Red or Green Chile Roux.

Cooking Instructions

Bring water in the stockpot to a slow boil, add chile-ground pork (optional), chile paste, Adobo Spice Mix, sweetener and chile roux and boil for 15 to 20 minutes.

Reduce heat to a simmer (gentle bubbles), add beans, garbanzos, or posole, red chile roux, pork cubes and chopped chile pods.

Simmer for 30 minutes pot cover off or longer. (The longer, the tenderer the meat will become.)

If the stew is too thin, you may add some additional Red Chile Paste or Red Chile Roux until it thickens to a light gravy consistency. You may substitute mashed potato mix as a thickener.

Suggested Complementary Dishes: Tortillas, bread, fry bread.

Servings: 4–6 people

CHICO STEW—RED OR GREEN

Complexity Code: Cook   Origin: New Mexico / Mexico
Cooking Method: Boil, Simmer

About the Recipe: Chico Stew is an ancient recipe that provided nourishment to the Native Americans long before Columbus landed in the New World. Corn was harvested, dried and stored for the long winters as well as long trips. It could be ground into atole, the predecessor of cereal, made into masa (corn flour), as well as rehydrated and made into a stew. Today chicos are served on Feast Days at the Pueblos in New Mexico and are a great complementary dish to any recipe.

Essential Recipe: Red Chile Paste (p.33), Red Chile Roux (p.35), Rehydrated Red Chile Pods (optional) (p.40) OR Green Chile Paste (p. 43), Roasted Green Chile (p.46), Green Chile Roux (p.49).

Ingredient	Measure	Ingredient	Measure
Chicos or frozen corn	4 cups	Adobo Spice Mix (p.83)	1 Tbsp.
Pork cubed or chile-ground pork	1-2 lbs.	Water for soaking	8 cups
Rehydrated red chile pods, Ancho, Pasilla, Chipotle or Chile Seco SHU to taste	2 cups chopped	Water for pork broth	10 cups
OR Roasted green chile, Anaheim, Poblano, Jalapeño SHU to taste	2 cups chopped	Beef bouillon or Bovril (Optional for water)	2 Tbsp.
Red or Green Chile Paste	2 cups	Sweetener (p.85)	1 Tbsp.
Red or Green Chile Roux	¼ cup		

Prep Instructions

Soak chicos (dried corn) in 8 cups of water overnight until tender. You can use frozen corn as a substitute.

Boil pork in 10 cups of water until tender, 30 to 45 minutes. (Use broth for the stew base.) Drain broth with a colander and place broth in 3- to 4-quart stockpot.

Set pork aside for later use.

Chop optional rehydrated red chile pods into ¼-inch squares. (Remove stem and seeds.)

Chop roasted green chile pods into ¼-inch squares. (Remove stem and seeds.)

Place 8 cups of water or beef broth in 3- to 4-quart stockpot.

Prepare Red or Green Chile Roux.

Cooking Instructions

Bring water in the stockpot to a slow boil; add chile paste, Adobo Spice Mix, sweetener and boil for 15 to 20 minutes.

Reduce heat to a simmer (gentle bubbles), add chicos, Red Chile Roux, pork meat and chopped chile pods.

Simmer with pot cover off or longer. (The longer, the tenderer the meat will become.)

If the stew is too thin, you may add some additional Red Chile Paste or roux until it thickens to a light gravy consistency. You may substitute mashed potato mix as a thickener.

Suggested Complementary Dishes: Tortillas, bread, fry bread.

Servings: 4–6 people

CHILE STEW (CARNE)—RED OR GREEN

Complexity Code: Cook   Origin: New Mexico
Cooking Method: Boil, Simmer

About the Recipe: Chile stew defines the Chilenista cuisine. The combination of chile, meat, potatoes and tomatoes forms the perfect meal. You choose the heat level. If there is one recipe to try in this book this is it.

Essential Recipe: Slow roasted Brisket, (p.60), Slow Roasted Pork (p.58) or Taco Ground Beef (p.62), Rehydrated Red Chile pods (p.40), Red Chile Paste, (p.33), OR Roasted Green Chile (p.46), Green Chile Paste (p.43).

Ingredient	Measure	Ingredient	Measure
Brisket or Pork shoulder or Taco Ground Beef	2 lb. cubed	Adobo Spice Mix (p.83)	2 Tbsp.
Potatoes	2 cups chopped	Sweetener (p.85)	2 Tbsp.
Red or Green Chile Paste	3–4 cups	**VARIATION:**	
Rehydrated red chile pods Ancho, Pasilla, Chipotle or Chile Seco SHU to taste	2 cups chopped	Masa harina	½–1 cup
Roasted green chile. Anaheim, Poblano, Jalapeño SHU to taste	8 cups chopped		
Water or Beef broth	8 cups		

Prep Instructions

Cut brisket or pork into 1-inch cubes.
Cut peeled potatoes into ½-inch cubes.
Chop chile into ¼-inch squares.
Place 8 cups water in 3- to 4-quart stockpot and bring to boil.

Cooking Instructions

Place meat, potatoes, chile paste, sweetener and Adobo Spice Mix into boiling water for 30 to 45 minutes until meat is tender.
Add chile paste.
Add chopped chile.
Reduce heat to simmer (gentle bubbles) for 1 hour. Stir occasionally.

Suggested Complementary Dishes: Tortillas, bread, a side of beans, posole, garbanzos.
Servings: 6–8 people

Variation:
Hearty Red or Green Chile Stew (Carne)
Add ½–1 cups masa harina to stew while boiling to thicken.

CHILE STEW (VEGGIE)—RED OR GREEN

Complexity Code: Cook
Cooking Method: Boil, Simmer

Origin: New Mexico

About the Recipe: Red or Green Chile Veggie Stew is the basis for most Feast Day, Sunday dinners and a hearty leftover breakfast.
Essential Recipe: Calabacitas (p.330), Rehydrated Red Chile pods (p.40), Red Chile Sauce (p.36), Red Chile Roux (p.35) OR Roasted Green Chile (p.46), Green Chile Sauce (p.50), Green Chile Roux (p.49).

Ingredient	Measure	Ingredient	Measure
Calabacitas or fresh squash	4 cups	Adobo Spice Mix (p.83)	2 Tbsp.
Red or Green Chile Sauce	2 cups	Sweetener (p.85)	2 Tbsp.
Rehydrated red chile pods, Ancho, Pasilla, Chipotle or Chile Seco SHU to taste	2 cups chopped	Corn	1 cup
Roasted green chile, Anaheim, Poblano, Jalapeño SHU to taste	2 cups chopped	Tomatoes (fresh or canned)	1 can 2 cups chopped
Beans: Pinto, kidney, black (canned and drained okay)	1–2 cups	Red or Green Chile Roux	½ cup
		Water	8 cups

Prep Instructions

Prepare calabacitas.
Chop Rehydrated Red Chile pods into ¼-inch squares. (Remove stem and seeds.)
Chop roasted chile into ¼-inch squares. (Remove stem and seeds.)
Place 8 cups of water in 3- to 4-quart stockpot.
Prepare red or green chile roux.

Cooking Instructions

Bring water in the stockpot to a slow boil. Add chile paste, Adobo Spice Mix, sweetener and boil for 15 to 20 minutes.
Reduce heat to a simmer (gentle bubbles); add calabacitas, beans, corn, tomatoes.
Simmer for 15 to 20 minutes. Stir occasionally.
If the stew is too thin, add Red Chile Roux until it thickens to a light gravy consistency.
Suggested Complementary Dishes: Tortillas, bread, fry bread.
Servings: 6–8 people

SOUPS

ALBONDIGAS (MEATBALL) SOUP RED OR GREEN

Complexity Code: Cook   Origin: New Mexico
Cooking Method: Boil

About the Recipe: Ablondigas Soup is a favorite winter food, providing a stick-to-your-ribs meal that you can make anytime.

Essential Recipe: Red Chile Sauce (p.36). OR Green Chile Sauce (p.50),

Ingredient	Measure	Ingredient	Measure
Ground beef	1 ½ lbs.	Adobo Spice Mix (p.83)	2 Tbsp.
Ground pork or sausages stripped of casing	½ lb.	Garlic or garlic powder	2 Tbsp. chopped
Red or Green Chile Sauce	4 cups		
Cilantro	½ cup	Annatto or Achiote Paste	1 Tbsp.
Onion	½ cup chopped	Sweetener (p.85)	2 Tbsp.
Breadcrumbs	½ cup	Diced potatoes	1 cup
Water	8 cups	Diced zucchini	½ cup
		Beans, pinto, white, black, or kidney (Canned okay)	2 cup

Prep Instructions

Place 8 cups of water in a 3- to 4-quart stockpot and bring to a boil.
Place ground beef and ground pork in a mixing bowl.
Finely chop an onion and cilantro and place in bowl.
Add 4 Tbsp. of chile sauce, 1 Tbsp. of garlic powder and bread crumbs and mix all ingredients until thoroughly blended.
Form meatballs about 1-inch in diameter and place on plate.
Dice potatoes and zucchini into ½-inch cubes.

Cooking Instructions

Place red chile sauce, Adobo Spice Mix, garlic powder, achiote powder, sweetener, diced potatoes, diced zucchini and beans in stockpot. Wait until water boils again and reduce heat to a medium boil (slow rolling bubbles). Add meatballs and boil until firm, 20 to 30 minutes.

Suggested Complementary Dishes: A meal in itself or as an opening course.

Servings: 6–8 people

BEAN SOUP (CALDILLO)—RED OR GREEN

Complexity Code: EZ   Origin: New Mexico
Cooking Method: Sauté / Boil

About the Recipe: This is a quick and easy recipe that can feed a whole
family and have them coming back for more   .
Essential Recipe: Rehydrated Red Chile pods (p.40), OR Roasted Green
Chile (p.46).

Ingredient	Measure	Ingredient	Measure
Ground Beef (Chile-ground if possible)	1 lb.	Adobo Spice Mix (p.83)	4 Tbsp.
Rehydrated red chile pods Ancho, Pasilla, Chipotle or Chile Seco SHU to taste	2 cups chopped	Beef broth or water	8 cups
OR Roasted green chile, Anaheim, Poblano, Jalapeño SHU to taste	2 cups chopped	Beef bouillon cube	2
Beans (garbanzo, pinto, kidney) canned will do	2 cups	Vegetable oil	2 Tbsp.

Prep Instructions

Mix ground beef and adobo dry spices.
If using canned chile or beans, drain and rinse to remove additives and
preservatives.
Combine chopped chile, beans and beef broth in a 4- to 6-quart stockpot.
Sauté ground beef in a heavy skillet until brown. (Do not mince the meat
to fine.)
Place stockpot on stove and bring to boil, reduce heat to a medium simmer
(gentle bubbles), add sautéed ground beef and simmer for 30 minutes until
potatoes are tender.

Suggested Complementary Dishes: Tortillas, crema and shredded
cheddar on top.

Servings: 6–8 people

CABBAGE SOUP—RED OR GREEN

Complexity Code: EZ   Origin: Original
Cooking Method: Boil, Simmer

About the Recipe: On a cold winter night nothing warms up the body and soul like this recipe.

Essential Recipe: Rehydrated Red Chile pods (p.40) OR Roasted Green Chile (p.46)

Ingredient	Measure	Ingredient	Measure
Cabbage (Medium size)	1 head	Adobo Spice Mix (p.83)	2 Tbsp.
Mexican squash, yellow squash or zucchini (Mix okay for color)	6–8 pieces	Sweetener (p.85)	2 Tbsp.
Rehydrated Red Chile Pods Ancho, Pasilla, Chipotle or Chile Seco SHU to taste	2 cups chopped	Butter	2 oz.
OR Roasted green chile, (frozen or canned okay)	2 cups chopped		
Water	8 cups		

Prep Instructions

Place 8 cups of water into a 3- to 4-quart stockpot and bring to a boil.
Cut head of cabbage into 4 quarters.
Chop squash into bite-size pieces approx. 1-inch cubes.
Chop Rehydrated Red Chile pods and Fresh Green Chile into ½-inch squares.

Cooking Instructions

Boil cabbage for approximately 1 hour until it is completely limp.
With a hand blender shred all of the cabbage until it is liquefied. (Add some additional water to compensate for evaporation.)
Add chopped chile, squash, Adobo Spice Mix, sweetener and butter; bring to a boil until the squash is soft (approx. 20 to 30 minutes).
Let cool and serve.

Suggested Complementary Dishes: Tortilla, tortilla chips, bread and butter.

Servings: 6–8 people

CHICKEN SOUP—RED OR GREEN

Complexity Code: EZ

Origin: New Mexico / Mexico

Cooking Method: Boil, Simmer

About the Recipe: Chicken soup is supposed to have medicinal qualities and is good for the soul. This recipe kicks it up a notch to make it a Chilenista's favorite as a starter or a complete meal.

Essential Recipe: Rehydrated Red Chile pods (p.40), OR Roasted Green Chile (p.46), Tortilla Chips (p.117), Slow Cooked Chicken (p.56).

Ingredient	Measure	Ingredient	Measure
Slow Cooked Chicken or if in a hurry, a rotisserie chicken (deboned)	2 lbs. +	Adobo Spice Mix (p.83)	2 Tbsp.
Chicken broth	4–6 cups	Cilantro	½ cup chopped
Rehydrated red chile pods, Ancho, Pasilla, Chipotle, or Chile Seco, SHU to taste	2 cups chopped	Shredded cheese blend, Asadero, cheddar, Jack, queso quesadilla	½ cup
OR Roasted green chile, Anaheim, Poblano, Jalapeño SHU to taste	2 cups chopped	Scallion (garnish)	¼ cup chopped
Corn (frozen okay)	1 cup	Tortilla chips	1 cup
Pinto beans (canned okay)	1 cup		

Prep Instructions

Place chicken broth into a 3- to 4-quart stockpot and bring to a boil.
Debone one rotisserie chicken and cut into bite-size strips.
Chop Rehydrated Red Chile pods into ½-inch squares.
Chop Roasted Green Chile into ½-inch squares.
Defrost corn and drain and rinse pinto beans.

Cooking Instructions

Add chicken, chopped chile and Adobo Spice Mix into stockpot, bring to boil and reduce heat to simmer. Add corn, pinto beans, cilantro and simmer for 15 to 20 minutes.

Suggested Complementary Dishes: Tortilla chips, garnish with avocado, shredded cheese mix, scallion.

Servings: 6–8 people

MENUDO

Complexity Code: Cook   Origin: New Mexico
Cooking Method: Boil, Simmer

About the Recipe: Every major holiday in the traditional New Mexico chile kitchen is celebrated with a bowl of menudo. Its unique and hearty taste is acquired and hard to forget once you have had a bowl of "menudo and red." I guarantee you will like it.

Essential Recipe: Red Chile Sauce (p.36).

Ingredient	Measure	Ingredient	Measure
Honeycomb tripe	2–4 lb.	Adobo Spice Mix (p.83)	4 Tbsp.
Red Chile Sauce SHU to taste	4 cups	**OPTIONAL:** Annatto or Achiote Paste	2 Tbsp.
Salt pork	4 oz.	Bay leaves	2–3
Water	8 cups	Onion	1 cup fine chopped
Posole (canned) or garbanzos	2 cups	Oregano	½ cup
		Lime (quartered)	1–2
		Crema	1 cup

Prep Instructions

Wash tripe thoroughly and cut into 1-inch squares.
Drain and rinse posole.
Put 8 cups of water into a 3- to 4-quart stockpot; add Adobo Spice Mixture and bay leaves.

Cooking Instructions

Bring stockpot to a boil, add tripe and salt pork, reduce heat to a simmer (gentle bubbles) and simmer for 3 to 4 hours until tripe is tender. (Make sure to add more water to keep tripe covered.) Stir every 20 to 30 minutes until tripe is tender. Remove tripe from stockpot using a slotted spoon or small strainer and place in a bowl or storage container to cool.
(You can also use a pressure cooker to cook the tripe and cut the boiling time to 1 hour.)
If you wish you can continue to boil the tripe stock to reduce it and intensify the flavor.
(There should be about 6 cups of tripe stock in the stockpot.)
Add 4 cups red chile sauce and 6 cups of tripe. Bring to a simmer, add posole and annatto paste; blend all ingredients, 5 to 10 minutes.
Any extra menudo will freeze well or store in refrigerator.

Suggested Complementary Dishes: Garnish with chopped onion, oregano, lime and a dollop of crema. Serve with tortillas, toast or crackers.
Servings: 4–6 people

RED CHILE BONE SOUP

Complexity Code: Cook   Origin: New Mexico
Cooking Method: Boil / simmer

About the Recipe: Hungry? This soup will fix you and satisfy your chile craving at the same time. This recipe is not for dainty eaters.
Essential Recipe: Red Chile Sauce (p.36)

Ingredient	Measure	Ingredient	Measure
Beef shank, beef ribs (bone-in), Soup bones with marrow	2 lbs.	Adobo Spice Mix (p.83)	4 Tbsp.
Chuck steak or shoulder steak (Fatty meat)	1 lbs.	Annatto or Achiote Paste	1 Tbsp.
Potatoes	1 lbs.	Red Chile Sauce SHU to taste	2 cups
Carrots (mini carrots okay)	2 cups	Garlic powder	2 Tbsp.
Onion	1 cup chopped	Bay leaves	2–3
Chopped Tomato (can okay)	2 cups	Sweetener (p.85)	2 Tbsp.
Zucchini	2 cups	Water	12 cups
Corn (frozen okay)	2 cups		

Prep Instructions
Add 12 cups of water into a 4- to 5-quart stockpot and start to boil.
Cut chuck steak into 1-inch cubes, cut beef ribs into 1-inch pieces (have your butcher do this), trim beef shank.
Chop potatoes and zucchini into 1-inch cubes.

Cooking Instructions
Add beef, potatoes, carrots and bay leaves into boiling water. Boil for 60 minutes until meat is very tender and then reduce heat to simmer (gentle bubbles).
Add zucchini, corn, red chile sauce, Adobo Spice Mix, achiote paste red chile sauce, garlic, tomatoes and sweetener into simmering water. Gently boil for 15 to 20 minutes.

Suggested Complementary Dishes: Tortillas, bread and butter.

Servings: 6–8 people

RED CHILE CHEESE SOUP

Complexity Code: EZ Origin: New Mexico
Cooking Method: Simmer / Sauté

About the Recipe: Red Chile Cheese Soup can be attributed to a dream and must be a staple among the angels whenever they wish to have a taste of the warmer side.
Essential Recipe: Red Chile Sauce (p.36).

Ingredient	Measure	Ingredient	Measure
Cheddar cheese	4 cups shredded	Red Chile Sauce SHU to taste	1 cup or more
Milk or half-and-half	2 cups	Balsamic vinegar	1 Tbsp.
Crema or sour cream	1 cup	Sweetener (p.85)	2 Tbsp.
Corn (frozen okay)	1 cup	Cilantro (garnish)	½ cup
Tomato (canned okay)	1 cup diced	**OPTIONAL:** Chorizos, sausage, ground beef to taste	1 lb.
Pinto beans (canned okay)	1 cup		

Prep Instructions

Place 2 cups milk in a 3- to 4-quart stockpot, heat over a low flame (simmer).
Add can of diced tomatoes and pinto beans. (Drain and strain can of beans to get rid of preservatives and canning liquid.)
Defrost and cook corn in microwave 2 to 3 minutes.
OPTIONAL: Sauté chorizos, sausage and ground beef; drain off all fat.

Cooking Instructions

Pour cheddar cheese into saucepan and stir vigorously to melt and blend with milk.
Pour crema into saucepan and stir to blend.
Add corn, tomato and optional sautéed meat; stir until all ingredients are blended.
If the soup is too thin, add some more cheese and if it is too thick add some more milk.

Suggested Complementary Dishes: Can be served as a meal or as a starter course with tortillas, tostadas or tortilla chips.

Servings: 4–6 people

RED CHILE TOMATO SOUP

Complexity Code: EZ   Origin: Original

Cooking Method: Boil, Simmer
About the Recipe: You can supercharge your tomato soup with this
easy recipe that gives a new meaning to a soup and sandwich.
Essential Recipe: Red Chile Sauce (p.36).

Ingredient	Measure	Ingredient	Measure
Tomato juice (with or without vegetable) 32 oz. can	8 cups	Adobo Spice Mix (p.83).	2 Tbsp.
Red Chile Sauce SHU to taste	2 cups	Sweetener (p.85)	2 Tbsp.
Tomatoes (Canned okay)	2 cup Chopped	Lime juice	¼ cup
		Cilantro (garnish)	½ cup chopped
		Crema or sour cream	½ cup

Prep Instructions
Pour tomato juice into a 3- to 4-quart stockpot and bring to a slow boil 3
to 4 minutes.
Cooking Instructions
Add Red Chile Sauce, chopped tomatoes, Adobo Spice Mix, sweetener
and lime juice and reduce heat to a slow simmer 10 to 15 minutes.

Suggested Complementary Dishes: Garnish with cilantro and a
dollop of crema. Serve with a sandwich or tortilla.

Servings: 6–8 people

TOMATILLO SOUP—RED OR GREEN

Complexity Code: Cook   Origin: Original
Cooking Method: Boil, Simmer

About the Recipe: The piquant sour and aromatic taste of tomatillo combined with pungent red chile will satisfy the most discriminating Chilenista. Have a second bowl handy.

Essential Recipe: Shredded Chicken (p.56), OR Taco Ground Beef (p.62). Red Chile Sauce (p.36), OR Green Chile Sauce (p.50)

Ingredient	Measure	Ingredient	Measure
Tomatillos (large) 4–6	2 cups	Sweetener (p.85)	2 Tbsp.
Shredded Chicken or Taco Ground Beef. (Substitute: roasted chicken)	2 cups	Cilantro	½ cup chopped
Chicken stock or water with (2) Tbsp. bullion.	4 cups	Garlic powder	1 Tbsp.
Red or Green Chile Sauce SHU to taste	2 cup	Crema or sour cream (garnish)	½ cup
Tomato	1 cup chopped		
Onion	1 cup chopped		

Prep Instructions

In a 3- to 4-quart stockpot bring 4 cups water or chicken broth to a boil. Clean and chop tomatillos, onion, tomatoes and cilantro into ¼-inch squares.

Cooking Instructions

Place chopped tomatillos, onion and tomatoes into boiling stockpot and boil for about 5 minutes. Shred chopped ingredients with a blender or blender stick (leaving a few chunks in soup base).
Add shredded chicken or taco ground beef, chile sauce, sweetener and garlic powder and reduce heat to simmer for 15 to 20 minutes.

Suggested Complementary Dishes: Garnish soup with cilantro and a dollop of crema. Serve with tortilla or tortilla chips.

Servings: 6–8 people

TORTILLA SOUP (RED OR GREEN—CARNE)

Complexity Code: Cook   Origin: New Mexico
Cooking Method: Boil

About the Recipe: Carne tortilla soup is a hearty soup that combines all
the flavors that a Chilenista loves and provides the meat and chile taste for
a complete meal.

Essential Recipe: Red Chile Sauce (p.36), OR Green Chile Sauce (p.50)

Ingredient	Measure	Ingredient	Measure
Brisket or Pork shoulder or Chicken	1–2 lbs. cubed	Adobo Spice Mix (p.83)	2 Tbsp.
Red or Green Chile Sauce SHU to taste	4 cups	Garlic or garlic powder	2 Tbsp. chopped
Tomato (canned)	2 cups chopped	Achiote powder	1 Tbsp.
Water	4 cups	Sweetener (p.85)	2 Tbsp.
Tortilla chips or tostada	4 cups crumbled	Crema or sour cream	1 Tbsp. per serving
Shredded cheese blend, Asadero, cheddar, Jack, queso quesadilla	1cup	Red chile powder (garnish)	

Prep Instructions

Cut brisket, pork or chicken into 1-inch cubes.
Place 4 cups (1 quart) of water in 3- to 4-quart stockpot.

Cooking Instructions

Boil water in stockpot and add brisket, pork or chicken, for 30 to 45
minutes until meat is very tender and reduce heat to simmer (gentle
bubbles).
Add Red Chile Paste, Adobo Spice Mix, garlic, achiote powder, tomatoes
and sweetener into simmering water. Gently boil red chile mixture for 15
to 20 minutes,
Add crushed tortilla chips, stir and remove from heat. (Do not let tortilla
chips get too soggy.)
Scoop soup into soup bowls, garnish with Shredded cheese and place 1
Tbsp. of crema in center.
Sprinkle red chile powder over the top to add color.

Suggested Complementary Dishes: Tortilla, bread with butter.
Servings: 4–6 people

TORTILLA SOUP (RED OR GREEN—VEGGIE)

Complexity Code: Cook
Cooking Method: Boil

Origin: New Mexico

About the Recipe: Veggie tortilla soup is a hearty soup that combines all the flavors that a Chilenista loves and provides the chile needed for a quick fix.

Essential Recipe: Calabacitas (p.330), Red Chile Sauce (p.36), OR Green Chile Sauce (p.50).

Ingredient	Measure	Ingredient	Measure
Calabacitas	4 cups	Adobo Spice Mix (p.83).	2 Tbsp.
Red or Green Chile Sauce SHU to taste	4 cups	Garlic or garlic powder	2 Tbsp. chopped
Tomato (Canned)	2 cups chopped	Achiote powder	1 Tbsp.
Water	4 cups	Sweetener (p.85)	2 Tbsp.
Tortilla chips or tostada	4 cups crumbled	Crema or sour cream	1 Tbsp. per serving
Shredded cheese blend Asadero, cheddar, Jack, queso quesadilla	1 cup	Red or Green chile powder (garnish)	

Prep Instructions

Prepare calabacitas.
Place 4 cups of water into a 3- to 4-quart stockpot and bring to slow boil (gentle rolling bubbles).
Add chile paste, tomato, Adobo Spice Mix, garlic, achiote and sweetener.

Cooking Instructions

Gently boil red chile mixture for 15 to 20 minutes.
Add calabacitas and simmer for 5 to 10 minutes.
Add crushed tortilla chips, stir and remove from heat. (Do not let tortilla chips get too soggy.)
Scoop soup into soup bowls, garnish with shredded cheese and place 1 Tbsp. of crema in center.
Sprinkle red or green chile powder over the top to add color.

Suggested Complementary Dishes: Tortilla, bread with butter.

Servings: 4 -6 people

CHOWDERS

CREAMY GREEN CHILE CHOWDER

Complexity Code: Cook
Cooking Method: BOIL / Simmer

Origin: New Mexico

About the Recipe: Creamy Green Chile Chowder has to be experienced as it is one of the highlighted recipes of this book.
Essential Recipe: Roasted Green Chile (p.46), Tortilla chips or strips (p.117),

Ingredient	Measure	Ingredient	Measure
Roasted green chile (Anaheim, Poblano, Jalapeño SHU to taste	4 cups chopped	Adobo Spice Mix (p.83)	1 Tbsp.
Potato (diced)	2 cups	Chicken bullion	1 Tbsp.
Half-and-half or milk	4 cups	Shredded cheese blend, Asadero, cheddar, Jack, queso quesadilla	2 cups
Heavy cream or crema	1 cup	Sweetener (p.85)	1 Tbsp.
Butter	2-3 Tbsp.	Cilantro (garnish)	

Prep Instructions

Boil milk or half-and-half in 3- to 4-quart saucepan.
Chop Roasted Green Chile into ½-inch squares.
Peel and dice potatoes.
Prepare Tortilla Chips or strips or use high-quality, store-bought chips.

Cooking Instructions

Place diced potatoes into boiling milk until tender (10–15 minutes).
Add Adobo Spice Mix, chicken bouillon, Fresh Green Chile, heavy cream, 1 cup shredded cheese mix and reduce boil to a low simmer (slow bubbles).
Stir soup mixture to blend all ingredients and prevent burning of bottom (15 to 20 minutes).
When all of the cheese and cream is thoroughly blended and smooth it is ready to serve.
If your simmer heat is too high the cheese can burn or curdle.

Suggested Complementary Dishes: Garnish with shredded cheese, cilantro and tortilla chips.
Servings: 4–6 people

GREEN CHILE CLAM CHOWDER

Complexity Code: Cook   Origin: New Mexico
Cooking Method: Boil, Simmer

About the Recipe: Every time I have made this recipe, it has received a standing ovation and second helpings. There is something magical that happens between the chile, cheese and clams that can make a Chilenista salivate.

Essential Recipe: Roasted green chile (p.46), Green Chile Sauce (p.50)

Ingredient	Measure	Ingredient	Measure
Chopped clams fresh or canned With clam broth* (16 oz.)	4 cups	Cilantro	1 cup chopped
Roasted green chile, Anaheim, Poblano, Jalapeño SHU to taste	2 cups chopped	Adobo Spice Mix (p.83)	1 Tbsp.
Green Chile Sauce	1 cup	Shredded sharp cheddar	1 cup
Half-and-half or milk	2 cups		
Heavy cream or crema	1 cup	**OPTIONAL:** Corn (frozen ok)	1 cup
Butter	2Tbsp.	**OPTIONAL:** Potato (diced)	2 cups

*If you cannot get chopped clams in a 32-oz. can, you can substitute a 16-oz. bag of frozen seafood mix, or assortment of shrimp, whitefish, squid and mussels. Purchase 16 oz. of clam broth.

Prep Instructions

Drain clam broth into a 3- to 4-quart stockpot and set clam strips aside.
OPTIONAL: Dice potatoes into ½-inch squares, boil in water until tender, drain and set aside.
OPTIONAL: Defrost corn and set aside.

Cooking Instructions

Bring clam broth and half-and-half to a boil.
Add clam strips or seafood mix, for 5 to 10 minutes until tender. (Stir to prevent scalding or burning.)
Reduce heat to a simmer and add heavy cream, butter, chopped green chile, Adobo Spice Mix, shredded sharp cheddar and chopped cilantro, add optional corn or diced potatoes, stir constantly until all of the ingredients are blended (10 to 15 minutes).
(If you wish to make a thicker broth, add 2–4 Tbsp. crema or sour cream.)

Suggested complementary Dishes: Tortillas, bread,

Servings: 6–8 people

GREEN CHILE CORN CHOWDER

Complexity Code: Cook   Origin: New Mexico
Cooking Method: Boil, Simmer

About the Recipe: Chile and corn combined are a marriage made in heaven, easy to make and can serve as a main dish or first course.

Essential Recipe: Roasted Green Chile (p.46), Green Chile Sauce (p.50)

Ingredient	Measure	Ingredient	Measure
Roasted green chile, Anaheim, Poblano, Jalapeño SHU to taste	4 cups chopped	Adobo Spice Mix (p.83).	1 Tbsp.
Green Chile Sauce	1 cup	Shredded cheese blend, Asadero, cheddar, Jack, queso quesadilla	2 cups
Corn kernels, fresh, frozen or canned	2 cup	Sweetener (p.85)	1 Tbsp.
Half-and-half or milk	4 cups	Cilantro (garnish)	chopped
Heavy cream or crema	1 cup		
Butter	2–3 Tbsp.	**OPTIONAL:** Potato (diced)	2 cups

Prep Instructions
OPTIONAL: Dice potatoes into ½-inch cubes, boil until tender, drain and set aside.

Cooking Instructions
In a 3- to 4-quart stockpot bring half-and-half to a boil.
Add corn, green chile, heavy cream, butter, adobo mix, shredded cheese, and sweetener and reduce heat to a simmer. Stir constantly until all of the cheese is melted and ingredients blended.
Add optional diced potatoes.
Reduce heat to a simmer. Add heavy cream and chopped cilantro, stir and allow to simmer for 15 to 20 minutes until it thickens a bit. If you wish to make a thicker broth, add 2 to 3 Tbsp. crema or sour cream.

Suggested Complementary Dishes: Tortillas, bread.

Servings: 6–8 people

GREEN CHILE GAZPACHO

Complexity Code Cook   Origin: New Mexico / Mexico
Cooking Method: Blender

About the Recipe: There is nothing more refreshing than a cool, fresh gazpacho served on a hot summer day. Add green chile and the vacation begins.

Essential Recipe: Fresh Green Chile (p.44)

Ingredient	Measure	Ingredient	Measure
Cucumber	1 large	Garlic	2 cloves
Tomato sauce or juice	2 cups	Olive oil	¼ cup
Onion	1 small sliced	Vinegar (cider or balsamic)	¼ cup
Tomatillo (if available)	1	Sweetener (p.85)	2 Tbsp.
Lime juice	¼ cup	Scallion	2 sprigs
Celery stalk	1 cup chopped	Cilantro	¼ cup fine chopped
Fresh Green Chile Anaheim, Poblano, Jalapeño SHU to taste	2 cups Chopped	Salt Cumin (ground) Oregano	1 tsp. ½ tsp. ½ tsp.
Tomatoes (Canned will work fine)	2 cups	Fresh Tomato	1 cup chopped
Green bell pepper	1 cup chopped	Hot sauce to taste	
		Basil (garnish)	
		Crema (garnish)	

Prep Instructions

Peel a large cucumber, remove the seeds, cut into quarters and place in blender.

Place tomato juice, onion, tomatillo, lime juice, celery, garlic, olive oil, vinegar and sweetener in blender and blend in the (mince / grate) mode, until all of the ingredients are finely chopped.

Place 1 cup green chile, chopped tomatoes, green bell pepper, scallion, salt, cumin and oregano into blender and blend in the (mince /grate) mode until all of the ingredients are blended.

Taste the Gazpacho blend and add additional hot sauce, sweetener or lime juice if required. Stir in the fresh chopped tomatoes and 1 cup of chopped fresh green chile. Stir and you are ready to serve.

Suggested Complementary Dishes: Garnish with basil and crema, serve with crackers, tortilla chips or tostadas. Hot sauce on the side.

Servings: 4–6 people

Chapter 9–RED OR GREEN CHILE ENTRÉE RECIPES

Chile is New Mexico's state vegetable, although it is technically a fruit. It does not really matter however, because chile rules. Once you have had red or green chile you will keep coming back for more. The recipes in this chapter provide a reason to keep eating chile for breakfast, lunch or dinner.

From a simple enchilada to an essential bowl of Green chile stew to a red chile BBQ that can knock your socks off, the recipes in this chapter are the main event.

BEANS, CHICO, GARBANZO, OR POSOLE CASSEROLE—RED OR GREEN

Complexity Code: EZ   Origin: New Mexico
Cooking Method: BAKE

About the Recipe: A New Mexico version of Mac & Cheese, only a lot easier to make and far better tasting.
Essential Recipe: Beans, Chicos, Garbanzos, Posole (p.304), Rehydrated Red Chile pods (p.40), OR Roasted Green Chile (p.46).

Ingredient	Measure	Ingredient	Measure
Beans, Chicos, Garbanzos, or Posole (from scratch or canned). Use frozen corn for Chicos	(4) 15-oz. cans	Red chile powder	4 Tbsp.
Crema or sour cream	2 cups	Oil, butter or lard	2 Tbsp.
Rehydrated Red Chile pods Ancho, Pasilla, Chipotle or Chile Seco SHU to taste	2 cups chopped	Cheddar cheese	4 cups shredded
OR Roasted Green Chile, Anaheim, Poblano, Jalapeño SHU to taste	2 cup chopped		

Prep Instructions
Grease bottom of 9-by-14-inch baking pan.
Rinse and strain 4 cans of beans, chicos, garbanzos, or posole to get rid of preservatives.
Pour veggies into the baking pan and spread evenly across bottom.
Pour crema or sour cream on top of veggies, layer chopped red chile on top of crema and layer shredded cheddar cheese on top of red chile.
Sprinkle red chile powder on top of cheddar cheese.

Cooking Instructions
Preheat oven to 350°F. Place baking pan into center of oven for 30 minutes until cheddar turns golden brown.
You can crust the top of the casserole by placing it under the broiler for 5 minutes.

Suggested Complementary Dishes: Tortilla chips, tostadas, salad

Servings 6 -8

BBQ BRAISED PORK RED CHILE

Complexity Code: Cook   Origin: Original
Cooking Method: Bake / Broil

About the Recipe: If you like red chile, this recipe will bring out the purist Chilenista in anyone; however, if BBQ is truly your thing, use the Red Chile BBQ Sauce instead of the Red Chile Sauce. In either case, you will be in for a Chilenista gourmet experience.

Essential Recipe: Slow Roasted Pork (p.58), Red Chile Sauce (p.36), Red Chile BBQ Sauce (p.73), Rehydrated Red Chile pods (p.40).

Ingredient	Measure		Measure
Slow roasted pork	2 lbs.	Adobo Spice Mix (p.83)	4 Tbsp.
Red Chile Sauce or Red Chile BBQ Sauce SHU to taste	2 cups	Onion	1 cup chopped
Rehydrated Red Chile pods Ancho, Pasilla, Chipotle or Chile Seco SHU to taste	1 cup chopped	Corn tortillas	8

Prep Instructions

Preheat oven to 350^{0}F.
Shred pork with a fork and place in a mixing bowl.
Chop red chile pods into ¼-inch squares (remove all seeds).
Chop onion into ¼-inch squares.
Mix Red Chile Sauce or BBQ Sauce, Shredded pork, Adobo Spice Mix, Chopped Red Chile Pods and onion, and stir and let sit for ½ to 1 hour for all flavors to blend.
Grease a 9-by-13-inch baking pan and place pork into baking pan.

Cooking Instructions

Place baking pan in center of oven and bake for 30 to 45 minutes until red chile bubbles.
Turn on broiler and broil pork until top starts to brown 10 to 15 minutes.
Remove pan from oven and let cool for 5 to 10 minutes.

Suggested Complementary Dishes: Serve on top of a corn tortilla, with beans, refried beans, cole slaw, salsa, rice and potatoes; make a burrito or a bolillo sandwich.

Servings 6–8

BBQ BEEF, PORK OR CHICKEN RED CHILE

Complexity Code: Cook
Cooking Method: Grilling / Baking

Origin: New Mexico

About the Recipe: BBQ can be prepared on a year-round basis with this recipe and served either in slices or shredded, depending on how you wish to serve it.

Essential Recipe: Slow Cooked, Beef, Pork, Chicken (p. 56,58,60), Red Chile BBQ Sauce (p.73)

Ingredient	Measure		Measure
Beef, Pork, Chicken (whole brisket, pork butt or chicken)	1 cut	Adobo Spice Mix (p.83)	4–8 Tbsp.
Red Chile BBQ Sauce SHU to taste	3–4 cups	Red chile powder SHU to taste	1–2 cups
		Smoker wood chips (for grill) Apple, cherry, hickory	2–3 cups

Prep Instructions

Cool slow-cooked meat recipe where it can be easily handled and stays firm.

Rub the Adobo Spice Mix and red chile powder on surface of brisket, pork or chicken.

Place meat on a cooking rack on top of a flat baking sheet to catch drippings and to make it easy to transport. Brush BBQ sauce on entire surface of meat.

Soak wood chips in water bowl. (Cherry, apple and hickory chips will give you a sweet smoky taste; mesquite will give a heavy smoky taste.)

Cooking Instructions

Grilling

Heat BBQ grill to low heat, add soaked wood chips in smoker box or open flame to start smoking.

Place meat in grill with drip pan (to prevent flare-ups) and smoke on low heat for 20 to 30 minutes. Brush additional BBQ sauce as needed to create a glazed coating on the meat.

Baking

Heat oven to 350^{0}F, place baking sheet in oven and immediately reduce the heat to 250^{0}F. Bake for 30 to 45 minutes. Brush additional BBQ sauce as needed to create a glazed coating on the meat.

Remove meat from grill or oven, let cool for 10 to 15 minutes and cut into slices or shred for your desired serving presentation.

Suggested Complementary Dishes: BBQ sauce, cole slaw, beans, refried beans, rice, tortillas, tacos, burritos.

Servings: 8–12

BBQ RIBS RED CHILE

Complexity Code: Cook   Origin: New Mexico
Cooking Method: Slow cooked BBQ / grilling / oven

About the Recipe: BBQ Ribs are an all-time favorite; this recipe will
allow you to cook BBQ ribs year-round.
Essential Recipe: Red Chile BBQ Sauce (p.73).

Ingredient	Measure	Ingredient	Measure
Slab of ribs Baby back, spare ribs, country ribs, riblets	1–2 slabs	Adobo Spice Mix (p.83)	¼ cup
Red Chile BBQ Sauce SHU to taste	3–4 cups	Red chile powder SHU to taste	1–2 cups
		Smoker wood chips (for grill), Apple, cherry, hickory	2–3 cups

Prep Instructions

Preheat oven 400^0F. Place ½ inch water in a Dutch oven with a rack.
Wash slab of ribs and dry off with a paper towel. Rub Adobo Spice Mix
and red chile powder to cover both top and bottom of ribs.
Soak wood chips in a bowl of water. (Cherry, apple and hickory chips will
give you a sweet smoky taste; mesquite will give a heavy smoky taste.)

Cooking Instructions

Slow cooked / Barbecue
Place covered Dutch oven in center of oven and immediately reduce heat
to 250^0F Cook for 2 to 3 hours until ribs are soft. (Use a toothpick to test
softness). Riblets will only require 45 to 60 minutes. Remove ribs from
oven and let cool.
Place meat on a cooking rack on top of a flat baking sheet to catch
drippings and to make it easy to transport. Brush BBQ sauce on entire
surface of ribs.
Grilling
Heat BBQ grill to low heat, and add soaked wood chips in smoker box or
open flame to start smoking.
Place meat in grill with drip pan (to prevent flare-ups) and smoke in low
heat for 20 to 30 minutes. Brush additional BBQ sauce as needed to
create a glazed coating on the meat.
Oven
Heat oven to 350^0F, place baking sheet in oven and immediately reduce
the heat to 250^0F Bake for 30 to 45 minutes. Brush additional BBQ sauce
as needed to create a glazed coating on the meat.
To crisp glaze, place ribs under broiler for 5 to 10 minutes. Remove meat
from grill or oven and let cool for 10 to 15 minutes.
Cut into slices or shred for your desired serving presentation.
Suggested Complementary Dishes: BBQ sauce, cole slaw, beans,
refried beans, rice, tortillas,
Servings: 8–12

BURRITO—RED OR GREEN

Complexity Code: EZ   Origin: New Mexico
Cooking Method: Microwave or Broil

About the Recipe: Burritos when served as a main entrée are best when smothered with red chile sauce, chopped red chile and topped with cheese. It does not get any better than this.

Essential Recipe: Red Chile Sauce (p.36), Rehydrated Red Chile pods (p.40), OR Green Chile Sauce (p.50), Roasted Green Chile (p.46), Sautéed Beef, Chicken or Pork (p.64), any Slow Cooked Beef, Pork, Chicken (p.56,58,60).

Ingredient	Measure		Measure
Tortilla (Burrito size) Thin if available	4–6	Shredded cheese blend, Asadero, cheddar, Jack, queso quesadilla or cheddar only	2–3 cups (split)
Red or Green Chile Sauce, SHU to taste	3–4 cups	Leaf lettuce: Romaine, iceberg, bibb	4–6
Rehydrated red chile pods. Ancho, Pasilla, Chipotle, or Chile Seco SHU to taste	2 cups chopped		
Roasted green chile Anaheim, Poblano, Jalapeno. SHU to taste	2 cups chopped		
SUGGESTED FILLINGS:			
Onion	2 cup chopped	Shredded Beef, Pork or Chicken	2 cups
Cilantro	1 cup chopped	Taco Ground Beef	2 cups
Tomato	1 cup chopped	Sautéed Beef, Chicken or Pork	2 cups
Any cold cut meat	1 lb.	Whitefish cooked	2 cups

Prep Instructions

Chop Rehydrated Red Chile pods (optional) into ¼-inch squares (removing stem and seeds) and place into a 2–3 qt. mixing bowl.

Chop Roasted green chile (optional) into ¼-inch squares (removing stem and seeds) and place into a 2–3 qt. mixing bowl.

Place a burrito tortilla on a flat surface and spread the tortilla with chile sauce. Leave a 2-inch ring from the edges with no sauce. Place a 1-inch row of chopped chile pods; spread a 1- to 1 ½-inch row of cheese on top of the chopped red chile.

Cover cheese with any of the optional meat ingredients,

Place a leaf of lettuce on top of meat.

Roll the tortilla toward the far end, and moisten the edge of the burrito to seal the tortilla or place a toothpick to hold it closed. Cut in half diagonally, plate and serve.

VARIATION

Smothered Burrito

Place burrito(s) seam side down on a microwaveable pan or baking pan. Smother the tortilla with the Red or Green Chile Sauce and cover with balance of cheese.

Place burritos in a microwave or broiler for 2 to 3 minutes until cheese melts, removing from oven and plate.

Suggested Complementary Dishes: Refried beans, rice, corn, salsa, crema, tortilla chips.

Serves 4–6 people

BBQ CHICKEN WINGS RED CHILE

Complexity Code: EZ   Origin: New Mexico
Cooking Method: Deep-fry / Pan-fry / Broil

About the Recipe: Chicken wings have become the number one finger food in the USA and for good reason—they taste great. This recipe gives a New Mexico version of a tried-and-true favorite that will be enjoyed by your guests and family for parties, special occasions or just good eating.

Essential Recipe: Red Chile BBQ Sauce (p.73)

Ingredient	Measure		Measure
Chicken wings, winglets and drummettes	2 lbs. (about 20)	Rice flour, masa or corn flour (not starch)	2–3 cups
Red Chile BBQ sauce	3–4 cups	Adobo spice mix	4–6 Tbsp.
Red chile powder	½–1 cup	Vegetable oil deep fry	1 quart

Prep Instructions

Mix rice flour and Adobo Spice Mix in a mixing bowl. Wash and rinse chicken wings dry with a paper towel.

Drag chicken wings through rice flour and place in a 1-gallon resealable plastic bag. Place plastic bag in refrigerator for 20 to 30 minutes.

Warm Red Chile BBQ Sauce in a small saucepan or microwave 1 to 2 minutes before use.

Preheat deep-fat fryer or large heavy skillet to 360^0F. (Skillet must have 2–3 inches of oil.)

Preheat oven to 225^0F.

Cooking Instructions

Deep Fry

Place 6–10 chicken wings into deep fat fryer for 7 to 10 minutes until golden brown. (Do not crowd fryer.) Remove chicken wings with a tong and place on a paper towel to drain excess oil. Sprinkle red chile powder and/or salt on wings; place in on a flat pan in oven to keep warm.

Pan-fry

Place 6–10 chicken wings into heavy skillet and flip wings over after 5 minutes to fry other side until golden brown. (Do not crowd fryer.) Remove chicken wings with a tong and place on a paper towel to drain excess oil. Sprinkle red chile powder and/or salt on wings; place on a flat pan and keep warm in oven.

Broil

You can serve the fried chicken wings from the oven and dip them into the BBQ sauce as desired (for maximum crunch) or you can brush the chicken wings with the BBQ sauce while in the oven and broil them for 5 to 10 minutes (for maximum glaze and stickiness).

Suggested Complementary Dishes: Cole slaw, salsa, refried beans.

Servings: 20 wings.

CARNE ADOVADA (RED CHILE) XXX

Complexity Code: Cook   Origin: New Mexico
Cooking Method: Bake

About the Recipe: Red chile adovada is usually for the experienced Chilenista that prefers hot to mild. Adovada can also be made in a mild variety by using a mild chile powder to make the chile paste. The taste of the aromatic red chile and pork combine into a sweetness that only red chile can impart.

Essential Recipe: Slow-Cooked Pork (p.58), Red Chile Roux (p.35), Red Chile Adovada Marinade (p.67), Red Chile Sauce (p.36), NOTE: look at additional marinade recipes (p.65) to flavor-infuse your meat.

Ingredient	Measure		Measure
Slow-cooked pork (cubed)	2 lbs.	Adobo spice mix (p.83)	4 Tbsp.
Red Chile Adovada Marinade	2 cups	Garlic powder	2 Tbsp.
Sweetener (p.85)	1 cup	Lard, butter or oil	2 Tbsp.
Red Chile Sauce	1 cup	Cilantro	1 cup

Prep Instructions

Preheat oven 325^{0}F.
Cut slow-cooked pork into 1-inch squares. Place 4 cubes into 3–4 qt. mixing bowl.
Pour Red Chile Adovada Marinade into mixing bowl; add sweetener, Red Chile Sauce, Adobo Spice Mix and softened butter; mix all ingredients until all are thoroughly coated.
Place carne adovada into a baking pan or casserole.

Cooking Instructions

Place casserole into oven and bake for 35 to 40 minutes until red chile sauce starts to bubble.
Remove from oven and let cool 10 to 15 minutes.

Suggested Complementary Dishes: Refried beans, rice, corn, beans, tortillas.

Serves: 4–6 people

CHIMICHANGA —RED OR GREEN

Complexity Code: COOK
Cooking Method: Pan Fry

Origin: New Mexico

About the Recipe: The ever popular burrito can be supercharged as a chimichanga that has been given a New Mexico chile cuisine make over as a delicious meal or appetizer.

Essential Recipe: Red Chile paste (p.33), OR Green Chile paste (p.43), Refried Beans (p.304), Chicken (p.56), Taco Ground Beef (p.62), Sautéed Beef, Chicken or Pork (p.64), Slow cooked Beef, Pork or Chicken (p.56,58,60), Calabacitas (p.330), Rehydrated Red Chile pods (p.40) OR Fresh Green Chile Pods (p.44) (Optional).

Ingredient	Measure		Measure
Thin 12–14" tortillas (Burrito wraps)	6	Adobo Spice Mix	2 Tbsp.
Choose Main ingredient, Beef, Chicken, Chorizo, Pork, Taco Ground Beef, Calabacitas	1 lb.	Shredded cheese blend Asadero, cheddar, Jack, queso quesadilla	1cup
Red or Green Chile paste SHU to taste	½ cup	Refried Beans	1 cups
Rehydrated Red Chile pods Ancho, Pasilla, Chipotle, or Chile Seco or Fresh Green Chile pods, Anaheim, Poblano, Jalapeno. SHU to taste	½ cup (chopped)	Sweetener (p.85)	2 Tbsp.
Red chile powder	SHU to taste	Balsamic or wine vinegar	2 Tbsp.
Crema (Garnish)		Oil (for frying)	4+ cups

Prep Instructions

Heat heavy skillet with oil to 360°F. There should be at least 2 to 3 inches of oil in the skillet.)

Place meat, chile sauce, chopped chile pods, Adobo Spice Mix, shredded cheese and refried beans, sweetener and vinegar in a 3–4 qt. mixing bowl. Mix all ingredients until well blended into a thick sticky paste.

Place tortilla on a flat surface, leaving a 2-inch edge around the tortilla for folding and wrapping. Spread a 2-inch wide by 1-inch high strip of meat blend on the tortilla (edge nearest you).

Roll the bottom of the tortilla over the top and roll toward the front. (Make sure the sides are folded to seal the meat in.) Wet the top of the tortilla to make it stick as a roll. Place a toothpick in the center to hold it together. Roll 3 to 4 tortillas at a time.

Cooking Instructions

Remove toothpick and place rolled tortillas into heated oil, seam side down for 3 to 5 minutes, and with a tong roll the chimichanga over and fry other side for 3 to 5 minutes. Tortilla should be golden brown. Remove chimichanga from pan and place on a paper towel to absorb any excess oil and sprinkle the top with red chile powder. Place tortillas in a warm oven until all the frying is complete.

Suggested Complementary Dishes: Garnish with red chile sauce, crema, cheese, and serve with cole slaw, beans, rice.

Serves: 6 people

CHIMICHANGA CHINESE STYLE RED OR GREEN

Complexity Code: COOK   Origin: Original
Cooking Method: Sauté / Fry

About the Recipe: The ever popular egg roll has been given a New Mexico chile makeover for a delicious meal or appetizer. You can use egg roll skins available at most supermarkets to make a perfect complement to chicken wings, tacos, sliders and finger food events.

Essential Recipe: Red Chile paste (p.33), Rehydrated Red Chile pods (p.40),OR Green Chile Paste (p.43, Fresh green Chile Pods (p.44) (Optional), Sautéed Beef, Chicken or Pork (p.64), Slow cooked Chicken, Pork, Beef (p.56,58,60), Taco Ground Beef (p.62), Calabacitas (p.330),

Ingredient	Measure		Measure
Egg Roll wraps (available at most groceries)	8	Red or Green Chile Paste (SHU to taste)	½ cup
Coleslaw Mix	1 cups	Soy Sauce	2 Tbsp.
Bean Sprouts	1 cups	Vinegar	1 Tbsp.
Rehydrated Red Chile pods Ancho, Pasilla, Chipotle, or Chile Seco or Fresh Green Chile pods, Anaheim, Poblano, Jalapeno. SHU to taste	½ cup chopped	Sweetener (p.85)	1 Tbsp.
Green Onion	½ cup chopped	Garlic powder	1 Tbsp.
Sliced Celery	½ cup	Coriander	1 tsp.
Choose Main ingredient, Beef, Chicken, Chorizo, Pork, Taco Ground Beef, Calabacitas	1 lb.	Oil, Pan or Deep-fry (recommended)	
Eggs	2	Red or Green chile powder	2 Tbsp.

Prep Instructions

Combine coleslaw, bean sprouts, green onion, chopped celery, garlic powder, chile paste, soy sauce, vinegar, sweetener and coriander in a mixing bowl and mix.
Prepare meat filling as per the ESSENTIAL RECIPE or your own recipe.
Lightly whip 2 eggs.

Place an egg roll wrap on a flat surface in a diamond shape away from you.

Place Veggie mix (1–2 oz.) on egg roll wrap leaving 1 inch from the bottom and 1 ½ inches from the sides (as if you were making a burrito). Place meat filling on top of veggies (1–2 oz.) and fold the sides over the mixture (about 1 ½-inch round). Roll the bottom of the egg roll wrap over the top and roll toward the front. (Make sure the sides are closed.) You can wet the top of the roll to make sure that the roll holds together. Place egg rolls on a plate ready to fry.

Cooking Instructions

In a large fry pan coat bottom with oil, heat and sauté vegetables until they are soft but not cooked. Place vegetables back into mixing bowl.

Place eggs in the heated fry pan as if you were making an omelet. Do not scramble.

Place the cooked eggs in the mixing bowl and mix with vegetables.

Prepare the filling as per the ESSENTIAL RECIPE or your own recipe.

Shred meat. Cut fish and shrimp into ½-inch squares.

Frying:

In a large skillet or fryer heat oil to at least 360°F.

Place egg rolls into hot oil and fry for about 2 to 3 minutes per side until golden brown, 3 to 4 at a time. Place fried egg rolls on a plate with some paper napkins to absorb any excess oil and sprinkle the top with red or green chile powder.

Suggested Complementary Dishes: Hot sauce, duck sauce, cole slaw.
Serves: 8 people

CARNE ASADA —RED OR GREEN

Complexity Code: Cook   Origin: New Mexico
Cooking Method: Sear / BBQ

About the Recipe: Carne Asada literally means grilled meat; usually it is
a flank steak, flap steak or skirt steak that is cut into strips across the grain.
The Asada marinade is based on fruit nectar and lime juice, which impart a
tart sweetness to the meat.
Essential Recipe: Carne Asada Marinade (p.66).
NOTE: Look at additional marinade recipes (p.65) to flavor-infuse your
meat.

Ingredient	Measure	Measure
Flank steak (cut thin)	2 lbs.	
Carne Asada Marinade	2 cups	
Fresh red chile or Fresh green chile pods (Red chile, Anaheim, Poblano)	6	
Tortillas	6	
Red chile powder SHU to taste	2 Tbsp.	

Prep Instructions

Cut flank steak into thin strips ¼ to ½ inches across the grain.
Place flank steak strips and Carne Asada Marinade into a glass bowl or
gallon plastic bag and place in refrigerator to marinate overnight.
Chop fresh chiles into ¼-inch strips.

Cooking Instructions

Grease a frying pan or comal and place on a high flame until it is very hot.
Place chopped fresh chiles on the comal and sear for 3 to 5 minutes until
softened, and place in a bowl and set aside.
Place marinated flank steak strips on comal and sear 3 to 5 minutes, turn
over with a spatula and sear second side 3 to 5 minutes until the meat is
well done.
Remove from heat; sprinkle red chile powder on meat and let cool for 5
minutes.
Combine braised chiles and meat on a serving plate. Serving suggestions:
Place meat on a tortilla and serve as a soft taco, or plate.

Suggested Complementary Dishes: Refried beans, rice, corn, salsa
and tortillas.

Serves 4-6 people

FAJITAS: CHICKEN. STEAK, FISH OR SHRIMP RED OR GREEN

Complexity Code: Cook   Origin: New Mexico
Cooking Method: Broil / Sear

About the Recipe: "You sell the sizzle and not the steak"; fajitas have made this saying famous. The aroma, sizzle and taste of fajitas have made it one of America's favorite foods. NOTE: Look at additional marinade recipes (p.65) to flavor infuse your meat.
Essential Recipes: Fajita Marinade (p.70), Fresh Red Chile (p.34), Fresh Green Chile (pp 44).

Ingredient	Measure	Ingredient	Measure
Boneless steak, (sirloin, skirt, rib eye), chicken breast, whitefish or shrimp	2 lb.	Adobo Spice Mix (p.83)	4 Tbsp.
Fajita marinade	2 cups		
Fresh red or Fresh green chile pods, Anaheim, Poblano, Jalapeno	3 pods	Guacamole (garnish) (p.131)	1 cup
Red, yellow, & green bell pepper	3 pods	Salsa (garnish) (See salsa section) (p.142)	1 cup
Onion	1 cup sliced	Tortillas	6–8

Prep Instructions
Marinate steak (1 to 2 hours), chicken (1 hour) or fish (30 minutes) in fajita marinade in a glass bowl or plastic bag.
Slice fresh chiles and bell peppers into ½-inch strips. (Remove seeds and veins). Set aside in a mixing bowl.
Slice onion into ½-inch strips. Set aside in mixing bowl.
Prepare guacamole, salsa and tortillas.
Preheat oven to 400°F.
Place a comal in oven to superheat it. (Make sure to wear gloves or use heavy potholder).

Cooking Instructions
Broil the chile, bell pepper and onion slices under broiler until they soften. Remove from oven and let cool.
Broil steak (3 to 5 minutes per side); chicken (5 to 7 minutes per side); fish 3 to 5 minutes per side; or shrimp (2 to 3 minutes) per side under the broiler 6 to 8 inches from the flame.
Remove steak, chicken, fish or shrimp; let cool for 5 minutes.
Slice steak, chicken or fish into ¼ - ½ inch thick slices across the grain.
Serving suggestions: Place meat and chile and bell pepper slices on a heated comal or cast-iron serving plates and serve while still sizzling.

Suggested Complementary Dishes: Refried beans, rice, corn, beans, salsa and tortilla.
Serves: 6–8 people.

ENCHILADA CARNE—RED OR GREEN ROLLED (BEEF, PORK, CHICKEN)

Complexity Code: Cook   Origin: New Mexico
Cooking Method: Bake

About the Recipe: Enchiladas Carne can be prepared with almost
any meat filling: Shredded slow-cooked beef, pork or chicken are my
recommendation. If you are in an extreme hurry, purchase a roasted
chicken at your supermarket, debone it and shred the meat as a filling.
Enchiladas are a food of the people that take very little time to prepare
and are nutritionally balanced for all three food groups.

Essential Recipe: Slow Cooked Beef, Pork or Chicken (p.56,58,60);
Red Chile Enchilada Sauce (p.77), Creamy Red Chile Sauce (p.38), Red
Chile Sauce (p.36), Rehydrated red chile pods(Optional) (p.40).

Ingredient	Measure		Measure
Corn Tortilla white or yellow	18	Adobo Spice Mix (p.83)	4 Tbsp.
Shredded Beef, Pork or Chicken	2 lb.	Onion	1 cup diced
Red or Green Enchilada Sauce or Creamy Red or Green Chile Sauce or Red or Green Chile Sauce SHU to Taste	6 cups (split)	Cilantro	1 cup chopped
Rehydrated red chile pods, Ancho, Pasilla, Chipotle, or Chile Seco SHU to taste	2 cups chopped	Crema or sour cream	1 cup
Roasted green chile Anaheim, Poblano, Jalapeno. SHU to taste	2 cups chopped	Vegetable oil	¼ cup
Tomatoes	1 cup chopped	Shredded cheese blend Asadero, cheddar, Jack, queso quesadilla	4–6 cups

Prep Instructions

Soften tortillas by rubbing them with water and placing them into a microwave for 15 to 20 seconds in defrost mode. You can do about 6 tortillas at a time.

Prepare the beef, pork or chicken using the Slow Cook Essential Recipe. If you are in a hurry, you can braise or pan roast the meat. If you are in a greater hurry, you can purchase a roasted chicken from a supermarket.

Shred chicken, beef or pork with a fork, place in a bowl and set aside.

Chop Rehydrated Red Chile pods (optional) into ¼-inch squares (removing stem and seeds); place into a 2–3 qt. mixing bowl.

 Chop Roasted green chile (optional) into ¼-inch squares (removing stem and seeds); place into a 2–3 qt. mixing bowl.

Chop cilantro and onion into ¼-inch squares and place in the mixing bowl.

Place 2 cups enchilada sauce, Adobo Spice Mix, onion and cilantro into mixing bowl and thoroughly blend chile filling.

Coat the bottom of a 10-by-14-inch baking pan with oil.

Cooking Instructions

Preheat oven to 350^0F. Position the softened tortilla in front to you; place a 1-inch strip of shredded beef, pork or chicken on the tortilla about 1 inch from the edge.

Spread a 1-inch row of chopped chile filling on top of the meat.

Start rolling the tortilla towards the far end as if you were making a burrito. If the edge is flying open, pin it down with a toothpick and place on the baking pan.

When you have filled the baking pan with rolled enchiladas, remove the toothpicks (if any).

Spread 4 cups of the chile sauce evenly on the top of the enchiladas and spread the shredded cheese over the top. (You can use more or less cheese as you wish.)

Bake enchilada in pan in the center of the oven for 45 minutes; remove pan let cool for 5 to 10 minutes, garnish each enchilada with a dollop of crema and get ready for the compliments.

Serves: 6–9 people. (2–3) enchiladas each.

Suggested Complementary Dishes: Refried beans, rice, corn, salsa, and crema.

ENCHILADA CHEESE—RED OR GREEN ROLLED

Complexity Code: Cook   Origin: New Mexico
Cooking Method: Bake

About the Recipe: Red Chile Cheese Enchiladas are an authentic New Mexico food. If you have only one dish to make for your family and friends, I would recommend this one. You can easily scale it up or down, prepare it ahead of time and bake it at the last minute.

Essential Recipe: Red Enchilada Sauce (p.77), Creamy Red Chile Sauce (p.38), Red Chile Sauce (p.36), Rehydrated Red Chile pods (Optional) (p.40), Green Chile Enchilada Sauce (p.76), Creamy Green Chile Sauce (p.52), Green Chile Sauce (p.50), Roasted Green Chile (Optional) (p.46).

Ingredient	Measure		Measure
Corn tortilla white or yellow	18	Adobo Spice Mix	4 Tbsp.
Red or Green Enchilada Sauce, or Creamy Red or Green Chile Sauce or Red or Green Chile Sauce to desired SHU level	6 cups (split)	Cilantro	1 cup chopped
Rehydrated red chile pods, Ancho, Pasilla, Chipotle, or Chile Seco SHU to taste	2 cups chopped	Onion	1 cup diced
Roasted green chile Anaheim, Poblano, Jalapeno. SHU to taste	2 cups chopped	Vegetable oil	¼ cup
		Crema or sour cream	1 cup
		Shredded cheese blend, Asadero, cheddar, Jack, queso quesadilla	4 –6 cups

Prep Instructions
Preheat oven to 350⁰F.
Soften tortillas by rubbing them with water and placing them into a microwave for 15 to 20 seconds in defrost mode. You can do about 6 tortillas at a time.
Chop red chile pods into ¼-inch squares (removing stem and seeds) and place in a 3–4 qt. mixing bowl.

Chop Roasted Green Chile into ¼-inch square (removing stem and seeds). Chop cilantro and onion into ¼-inch squares and place into mixing bowl. Place 2 cups Enchilada Sauce, Adobo Spice Mix, onion and cilantro into mixing bowl and thoroughly blend red chile filling.

Coat the bottom of a 10-by-14-inch baking pan with oil.

Cooking Instructions

Position the softened tortilla in front of you; spread a 1-inch strip of cheese on the tortilla about 1 inch from the edge.

Spread a 1-inch row of chile filling on top of the cheese.

Start rolling the tortilla toward the far end as if you were making a burrito. If the edge is flying open, pin it down with a toothpick and place on the baking pan seam side down.

When you have filled the baking pan with rolled enchiladas, remove the toothpicks (if any). Spread 4 cups of the enchilada sauce evenly on the top of the enchiladas and spread the balance of the shredded cheese over the top. (You can use more or less cheese as you wish.)

Bake enchilada pan in the center of the oven for 45 minutes, remove pan, let cool for 5 to 10 minutes and get ready for the compliments.

Serves: 6–9 people.

Suggested Complementary Dishes: Beans, refried beans, rice, corn.

ENCHILADA VEGGIE—RED OR GREEN ROLLED

Complexity Code: COOK   Origin: New Mexico
Cooking Method: Bake

About the Recipe: Veggie enchiladas can be prepared with almost any vegetable filling that is available; an extra flavor burst can be achieved by adding pinion nuts or other nuts to the filling mixture.

Essential Recipes: Red Chile Enchilada Sauce (p.77), Creamy Red Chile Sauce (p.38), Red Chile Sauce (p.36), Rehydrated red chile pods (Optional) (p.40), OR Green Chile Enchilada Sauce (p.76), Creamy Green Chile Sauce (p.52), Green Chile Sauce (p.50), Roasted Green Chile Pods (Optional) (p. 46). Calabacitas (p.330), Any vegetable.

Ingredient	Measure		Measure
Corn tortilla white or yellow	18	Adobo Spice Mix	4 Tbsp.
Calabacitas	2 cups	Onion	1 cup diced
Corn (Frozen or canned) Rinse and drain canned corn	2 cup	Cilantro	1 cup chopped
Beans (Pinto, kidney, black white)	2 cups	Crema or sour cream	1 cup
Red or Green Enchilada Sauce, Creamy Red or Green Chile Sauce, or Red or Green Chile Sauce. SHU to taste	6 cups (split)	Vegetable oil	¼ cup
Ancho, Pasilla, Chipotle, or Chile Seco SHU to taste	2 cups chopped	Shredded cheese blend, Asadero, cheddar, Jack, queso quesadilla	4–6 cups
Roasted green chile Anaheim, Poblano, Jalapeno. SHU to taste	2 cups chopped	Pinion nuts or sunflower seeds	1 cup or more

Prep Instructions

Soften tortillas by rubbing them with water and placing them into a microwave for 15 to 20 seconds in defrost mode. You can do about 6 tortillas at a time.

Prepare calabacitas place in a bowl and set aside.

Chop Rehydrated Red Chile pods (optional) into ¼-inch squares (removing stem and seeds); place into a 2–3 qt. mixing bowl.

Chop Roasted Green Chile Pods (optional) into ¼-inch squares (removing stem and seeds) and place into a 2–3 qt. mixing bowl
Chop cilantro and onion into ¼-inch squares and place in the mixing bowl. Place 2 cups enchilada sauce, chopped chile, Adobo Spice Mix, onion, cilantro and nuts into the mixing bowl and thoroughly blend chile filling.
Coat the bottom of a 10-by-14-inch baking pan with oil.

Cooking Instructions
Preheat oven to 350^0F. Position the softened tortilla in front to you; place a 1-inch strip of calabacitas on the tortilla about 1 inch from the edge.
Spread a 1 inch row of chopped chile filling on top of calabacitas.
Start rolling the tortilla toward the far end as if you were making a burrito. If the edge is opening, pin it down with a toothpick and place on the baking pan.
When you have filled the baking pan with rolled enchiladas, remove the toothpicks (if any).
Spread 4 cups of the chile sauce evenly on the top of the enchiladas and spread the shredded cheese over the top. (You can use more or less cheese as you wish.)
Bake enchilada pan in the center of the oven for 45 minutes. Remove pan and let cool for 5 to 10 minutes. Garnish each enchilada with a dollop of crema.
Serves: 6–9 people (2–3) enchiladas each.

Suggested Complementary Dishes: Refried beans, rice, corn, salsa, crema.

ENCHILADA THREE LAYER CARNE
RED OR GREEN

Complexity Code: Cook   Origin: New Mexico
Cooking Method: Bake

About the Recipe: Three layered carne enchilada is a favorite meal for all Chilenistas, combining chile, carne and cheese into a heavenly meal that takes very little time to prepare and cook. If you are in a real hurry to prepare a meal, pick up a roasted chicken at your grocers, debone and shred the meat.

Essential Recipe: Red Chile Enchilada Sauce (p.77), Creamy Red Chile Sauce (p.38), Red Chile Sauce (p.36), Rehydrated red chile pods(Optional) (p.40), OR Green Chile Enchilada Sauce (p.76), Creamy Green Chile Sauce (p.52), Green Chile Sauce (p.50), Roasted Green Chile Pods (Optional) (p.46), Slow Cooked (Beef, Pork Chicken) (p.56,58,60).

Ingredient	Measure		Measure
Corn tortilla white or yellow	18	Adobo Spice Mix	4 Tbsp.
Shredded (beef, pork or chicken)	1–2 lb.	Shredded cheese blend, Asadero, cheddar, Jack, queso quesadilla	4 cups (split)
Enchilada sauce, or Creamy Red Chile sauce or Red Chile Sauce SHU to taste	4 cups (split)(split)	Shredded cheddar cheese	2 cups
Rehydrated red chile pods(chopped), Ancho, Pasilla, Chipotle, or Chile Seco SHU to taste	2 cups chopped	Crema or sour cream	2 cup
Roasted green chile Anaheim, Poblano, Jalapeno. SHU to taste	2 cups chopped	Vegetable oil	¼ cup
Onion	1 cup diced		
Tomatoes	1 cup chopped		

Prep Instructions

Preheat Oven to 350⁰F.

Chop rehydrated red chile pods (optional) into ¼-inch squares (removing stem and seeds) and place into a 2–3 qt. mixing bowl.

Chop roasted green chile (optional) into ¼-inch squares (removing stem and seeds) and place into a 2–3 qt. mixing bowl.

Grease bottom of 10-by-14-inch pan.

Spread thin layer of enchilada sauce in bottom of pan

Place first layer of 6 corn tortillas on bottom of pan and rip one tortilla to cover holes in middle and sides.

Cover first layer with 2 cups enchilada sauce about ⅛ inch, sprinkle onions, tomatoes, Adobo Spice Mix and shredded meat. Spread evenly.

Place second layer of 6 corn tortillas on top of shredded meat; rip one tortilla to cover holes.

Cover second layer with 4 cups chopped chile pods, and evenly spread 2 cups crema and 2 cups enchilada sauce.

Place third layer of 6 tortillas on top of chile and cover holes with tortilla.

Spread 2 cups cheddar cheese top of third layer.

Cover pan with aluminum foil.

Cooking Instructions

Bake enchilada pan in the center of the oven for 45 minutes. Remove pan and foil, and let cool for 5 to 10 minutes.

Place enchilada under broiler for 5 to 10 minutes until cheese starts to bubble and brown.

Remove from oven, cut into 3-by-3-inch squares (about 12 squares).

Garnish with a dollop of crema and serve.

Serves: 6–9 people

Suggested Complementary Dishes: Refried beans, rice, corn, salsa and crema.

ENCHILADA THREE LAYERED CHEESE RED OR GREEN

Complexity Code EZ   Origin: New Mexico
Cooking Method: Bake

About the Recipe: When you need to make a meal in a hurry try this three layer cheese enchilada. It has the same great taste as the rolled enchilada and takes a lot less time to make.

Essential Recipe: Red Chile Enchilada Sauce (p.77), Creamy Red Chile Sauce (p.38), Red Chile Sauce (p.36), Rehydrated Red Chile pods (Optional) (p.40), OR Green Chile Enchilada Sauce (p.76), Creamy Green Chile Sauce (p.52), Green Chile Sauce (p.50), Roasted Green Chile (Optional) (p.46).

Ingredient	Measure		Measure
Corn tortilla – 6" yellow or white	18+	Adobo Spice Mix	4 Tbsp.
Enchilada Sauce, Creamy Chile Sauce or Chile Sauce. —Red or Green SHU to taste	4 cups	Shredded cheese blend, Asadero, cheddar, Jack, queso quesadilla	4 cups (split)
Rehydrated red chile pods, Ancho, Pasilla, Chipotle, or Chile Seco SHU to taste	4 cups chopped	Ground cotija cheese	1 cup ground
Fresh or Roasted green chile Anaheim, Poblano, Jalapeno. SHU to taste	4 cups chopped	Shredded cheddar cheese	2 cups
Onion	1 cup diced	Crema or Sour cream	2 cup
Tomatoes	2 cup diced	Vegetable oil	¼ cup

Prep Instructions

Preheat oven to 350⁰F.

Chop rehydrated red chile pods (optional) into ¼-inch squares (removing stem and seeds) and place into a 2–3 qt. mixing bowl.

Chop roasted green chile(optional) into ¼-inch squares (removing stem and seeds) and place into a 2–3 qt. mixing bowl.

Grease bottom of 10-by-14-inch pan.

Spread thin layer of enchilada sauce in bottom of pan.

Place first layer of 6 corn tortillas on bottom of pan and rip one tortilla to cover holes in middle and sides.

Cover first layer with 2 cups shredded cheese spread evenly, add 2 cups enchilada sauce, and sprinkle onions and Adobo Spice Mix.

Place second layer of 6 corn tortillas on top of enchilada sauce, and rip one tortilla to cover holes.

Cover second layer with 4 cups chopped chile pods, and evenly spread 2 cups crema, 1 cup cotija cheese and 1 cup enchilada sauce.

Place third layer of 6 tortillas on top of chile and cover holes with extra tortilla.

Spread 2 cups cheddar cheese on top of third layer.

Cover pan with aluminum foil.

Cooking Instructions

Bake enchilada pan in the center of the oven for 45 minutes; remove pan and foil; let cool for 5 to 10 minutes.

Place enchilada under broiler for 5 to 10 minutes until cheese starts to bubble and brown.

Remove from oven, cut into 3-by-3-inch squares (about 12 squares).

Garnish with a dollop of crema and serve.

Servings: 6–9 people.

Suggested Complementary Dishes: Refried beans, rice, corn, salsa and crema.

ENCHILADA THREE LAYER VEGGIE
RED OR GREEN

Complexity Code: Cook   Origin: New Mexico
Cooking Method : BAKE

About the Recipe: Three-layer veggie enchiladas are an excellent way to get your kids to eat their greens. Almost any vegetable can be used as the filling. If you add some nuts to the filling, they will be asking for more.

Essential Recipes: Red Chile Enchilada Sauce (p.77), Creamy Red Chile Sauce (p.38), Red Chile Sauce (p.36). Rehydrated red chile pods (optional) (p.40) OR Green Chile Enchilada Sauce (p.76), Creamy Green Chile Sauce (p.52), Green Chile Sauce (p.50), Roasted Green Chile (optional) (p.46), Calabacitas (p. 330).

Ingredient	Measure	Ingredient	Measure
Corn tortilla white or yellow	18	Adobo Spice Mix	4 Tbsp.
Calabacitas (frozen cubed squash or corn okay)	4 cups	Shredded cheese blend, Asadero, cheddar, Jack, queso quesadilla	3–4 cups
Enchilada Sauce, Creamy Chile Sauce or Chile Sauce SHU to taste	4 cups (split)	Cheddar cheese	2 cups shredded
Rehydrated Red Chile Pods, Ancho, Pasilla, Chipotle or Chile Seco (SHU to taste)	2 cups chopped	Crema or sour cream	1 cup
Fresh or Roasted green chile Anaheim, Poblano, Jalapeno. SHU to taste	2 cups chopped	Vegetable oil	¼ cup
Tomatoes	1 cup chopped	Pinion nuts or sunflower seeds	1 cup or more
Onion	1 cup diced		

Prep Instructions

Preheat oven to 350°F.

Chop rehydrated red chile pods(optional) and roasted green chile(optional) into ¼-inch squares (removing stem and seeds); place into a 2-3 quart mixing bowl

Chop roasted green chile pods (optional) ¼-inch squares (removing stem and seeds) place into a 2-3-quart mixing bowl Grease bottom of 10-by-14-inch pan.

Spread thin layer of enchilada sauce in bottom of pan

Place first layer of 6 corn tortillas on bottom of pan and rip one tortilla into pieces to cover holes in middle and sides.

Cover first layer with 2 cups enchilada sauce, and sprinkle onions, tomatoes, Adobo Spice Mix, calabacitas and pinion nuts. Spread evenly.

Place second layer of 6 corn tortillas on top of calabacitas; rip one tortilla to cover holes.

Cover second layer with 4 cups chopped chile pods; evenly spread 2 cups crema and 2 cups enchilada sauce.

Place third layer of 6 tortillas on top of chile and cover holes with pieces of another tortilla. Spread 2 cups cheddar cheese on top of third layer.

Cover pan with aluminum foil.

Cooking Instructions

Bake enchilada in pan in the center of the oven for 45 minutes. Remove pan, remove foil and let cool for 5 to 10 minutes,

Place enchilada under broiler for 5 to 10 minutes until cheese starts to bubble and brown.

Remove from oven, cut into 3-by-3-inch squares (about 12 squares).

Garnish with a dollop of crema and serve.

Serves: 6–8 people.

Suggested Complementary Dishes: Refried beans, rice, corn, salsa and crema.

GREEN CHILE CALABACITAS (THREE SISTERS)

Complexity Code: Cook   Origin: New Mexico
Cooking Method: Sauté / Bake

About the Recipe: Traditionally Native Americans consider the Three Sisters—corn, beans and squash—the perfect harvest food for every table.
Essential Recipes: Fresh Green Chile (p.44)

Ingredient	Measure	Ingredient	Measure
Yellow squash	1 cup	Crumpled mild white cheese (queso fresco, requesón, ricotta)	1 cup
Zucchini	1 cup	Olive Oil	2 Tbsp.
Corn—fresh or frozen	1 cup	Green chile powder	1-2 Tbsp.
Beans—pinto, kidney	1 cup	Sweet Onion	1 cup chopped
Fresh Green Chile pods, Anaheim, Poblano, Jalapeño SHU to taste	1 cup chopped	Garlic powder	1 tsp

Prep Instructions
Preheat oven to 350^{0}F.
Cut squash and zucchini by quartering lengthwise and then chopping into ½-inch chunks. Defrost or cut fresh corn; you can use canned corn, however make sure to rinse the corn of the preservatives in the can.
Chop a small to medium size sweet onion into ¼-inch pieces.
Chop fresh chile pods into ¼- to ½-inch chunks.

Cooking Instructions
Preheat frying pan to middle heat of 300^{0}F.
Sauté chopped onion in olive oil until onions are just threatening to brown and then add squash, zucchini and green chile. Cook until they are about half-done and add beans and corn. Move to a 9-by-9-inch casserole dish and mix in cheese, green chile powder, and garlic to taste.
Bake in preheated oven for 30 minutes.

Suggested Complementary: Any meat or entrée dish can be complemented by a side of Calabacitas.

Servings: 4-6 people

GREEN CHILES RELLENOS (CHEESE) BAKED

Complexity Code: Cook
Cooking Method: Bake

Origin: New Mexico

About the Recipe: Green Chile Rellenos (Ray-ae-nos) is a staple of the New Mexico Chilenista's cuisine and restaurant menu.
Essential Recipe: Roasted Green Chile (p.46), Green Chile Sauce (p.50) or Creamy Green Chile Sauce (p.52)

Ingredient	Measure	Ingredient	Measure
Fresh green chile pods, (Anaheim, Big Jim)	6–8 pods	Cilantro	½ cup
Roasted green chile, Anaheim, Poblano, Jalapeño SHU to taste	2 cups chopped	Garlic	1 Tbsp.
Green Chile Sauce	2 cup	Coriander	1 Tbsp.
Corn tortilla or cornmeal stuffing	½ cup	Shredded Cheese Mix, Asadero, cheddar, Jack, queso quesadilla	1 cup
		Crema or sour cream	1 cup

Prep Instructions

Wash green chiles, cut stems and tops, and scoop out seeds and veins with paring knife.
Save the tops to place on top of stuffed chile.
In a mixing bowl, moisten tortillas or cornmeal stuffing into mush with the crema; add shredded cheese, cilantro, fresh green chile and coriander.
Blend mixture into a light filling paste. Add some additional water if needed to make thinner stuffing.
Stuff chiles either by placing stuffing into the tube with your finger from the top (preferred), or cut a lengthwise slit on one side of the chile and insert stuffing.
Grease the bottom of a baking pan or dish and place chiles slit side down.
Pour 1 cup of green chile sauce over the top.

Cooking Instructions

Preheat oven to 350°F. Bake chiles for 30 minutes; remove from oven and let cool for 10 minutes. Place 1 cup of optional grated cheese on top of chiles and place back in oven under broiler for 5 minutes. Remove and serve.

Suggested Complementary Dishes: Refried beans, salsa, rice.

Serves: 4–6 hearty eaters

GREEN CHILES RELLENOS (CHEESE) FRIED

Complexity Code: Cook   Origin: New Mexico
Cooking Method: Fry

About the Recipe: Fried green chile rellenos have to be tried to be believed. They are the epitome of the green chile cuisine and can only be described as a must-have recipe in your repertoire.
Essential Recipe: Roasted Green Chile (p.46), Green Chile Sauce (p.50), Creamy Green Chile Sauce (p.52).

Ingredient	Measure	Ingredient	Measure
Fresh green chile pods, Anaheim, Big Jim, Poblano	6–8 pods	Cilantro	¼ cup chopped
Roasted green chile Anaheim, Poblano, Jalapeño SHU to taste	2 cups chopped	Garlic	1 Tbsp. chopped
Green Chile Sauce or Creamy Green Chile Sauce	1 cup	Coriander	1 Tbsp.
Corn tortilla or cornmeal stuffing	½ cup		
Batter Mix (see below)		Shredded Cheese blend Asadero, cheddar, Jack, queso quesadilla	1 cups
		Crema or sour cream	1 cup

Prep Instructions

Wash green chiles, cut stems and tops, and scoop out seeds and veins with paring knife.
Save the tops to place on top of stuffed chiles.
In a mixing bowl moisten tortillas or cornmeal stuffing (see below) into mush with the crema; add shredded cheese, chopped cilantro, roasted green chile and coriander. Blend mixture into a light filling paste. Add some additional water if needed to make thinner stuffing.
Stuff chiles either by placing stuffing into the tube with your finger from the top (preferred), or cut lengthwise slit on one side of the chile and insert stuffing.
Use a packaged corn dog pre-mix batter. (I have found this pre-mix batter very easy to use.)
To make your own batter mix: Combine 1 cup all-purpose flour, 1 tsp. baking powder, ½ tsp. salt, ¾ cup cornmeal, 1 cup milk and 2 eggs slightly beaten. (Let stand for about 5 minutes.)
Make the batter on the thick side.

Cooking Instructions

In a deep-fat fryer or frying pan heat vegetable oil at least 2 inches deep to 360°F (use a thermometer).

Dip each stuffed chile into the batter. (They should be completely covered.) Place chile into the hot oil (always away from you) slit side down. Place as many chiles into the frying pan as you can without having them touch. In about 3 minutes turn chiles over with a tong and wait another 3 minutes. The batter should be golden brown. Remove chiles and place on a rack or paper towel to absorb some of the oil.

Wait until the oil temperature rises to 360°F and fry the rest of the chiles.

Garnish the chiles relleno with green chile sauce or red chile sauce or red and green (Christmas in Santa Fe).

Serves: 4–6 hearty eaters.

Suggested Complementary Dishes: Refried beans, salsa, rice.

GREEN CHILE STUFFED (VEGGIE)

Complexity Code: Cook   Origin: New Mexico
Cooking Method: Bake

About the Recipe: This is a universal dish that is easy to make and
sure to please. You can substitute any of your favorite ingredients for the
stuffing, including the many prepared boxed stuffing mixes. You can also
use potatoes, spinach, mushrooms, tomatoes and scallions as part of the
filling.
Essential Recipe: Green Chile Sauce (p.50), Creamy Green Chile Sauce
(p.52), Roasted Green Chile (p.46).

Ingredient	Measure		Measure
Fresh chile pods (large) Poblano, Anaheim, Big Jim	8–12 Pods	Cilantro	¼ cup chopped
Corn, beans, zucchini, spinach.	4 cups	Garlic	1 Tbsp. chopped
Roasted Green Chile* Anaheim, Poblano, Jalapeño SHU to taste *Canned okay	2 cup chopped	Coriander	1 Tbsp.
Green Chile Sauce or Creamy Green Chile Sauce	2 cups	Shredded Cheese blend Asadero, cheddar, Jack, queso quesadilla	1 cups
Corn tortilla or cornbread stuffing	1 cup	Crema or sour cream	1 cup

Prep Instructions

Wash green chiles and cut stems and tops, scooping out seeds and veins
with paring knife.
Save the tops to place on top of stuffed chiles.
In a mixing bowl moisten tortillas or cornmeal stuffing into mush with the
crema; add 1 cup shredded cheese, chopped cilantro, chopped roasted
green chile, garlic and coriander. Blend mixture into a light filling paste.
Add some additional water if needed to make thinner stuffing.
Cut zucchini into ¼-inch cubes, add beans (kidney, pinto, black or white,
will do).
Chop roasted green chile into ¼-inch cubes.
If you are using canned beans, or chile make sure to rinse and strain out all
of the liquid preservatives that have been used in the canning process.)
Add chopped Fresh Green Chile, corn, chopped cilantro, garlic, and
coriander. Blend mixture into a light filling.

Stuff chiles either by placing stuffing into the tube with your finger from the top (preferred), or cut a lengthwise slit on one side of the chile and place stuffing.
Grease the bottom of a baking pan or dish and place chiles slit side down. Pour Green Chile Sauce over the top. If there is any veggie filling left over, place into pan with Green Chile Sauce. This will make a great garnish over the chiles when serving.

Cooking Instructions

Preheat oven to 350^{0}F and bake chiles for 30 minutes. Remove from oven and let cool for 10 minutes. Place 1 cup of optional grated cheese on top of chiles; place back in oven under broiler for 5 minutes. Remove and serve.

Suggested Complementary Dishes: Refried beans, salsa, rice.

Serves: 4–6 hearty eaters.

GREEN CHILE STUFFED (CARNE)

Complexity Code: Cook   Origin: New Mexico
Cooking Method: Bake

About the Recipe: This is a universal dish that is easy to make and sure to please. You can substitute any of your favorite ingredients for the stuffing, including the many prepared boxed stuffing mixes. You can also use chicken, lamb or shredded beef for stuffing

Essential Recipe: Taco Ground Beef (p.62), Sautéed Beef, Chicken or Pork (p.64), Green Chile Sauce (p.50), Creamy Green Chile Sauce (p.52).

Ingredient	Measure		Measure
Fresh chile pods (large) Poblano, Anaheim, Big Jim	8–12 Pods	Cilantro	¼ cup chopped
Taco Ground Beef or Sautéed Beef, Chicken or Pork.	1–1 ½ lb.	Pignoli nuts or other available (peanuts, walnuts)	½ cup
Cornmeal stuffing, masa or bread crumbs	½ cup	Garlic	1 Tbsp. chopped
Green Chile Sauce or Creamy Green Chile Sauce	2 cups	Coriander	1 tsp.
		Option: Shredded cheese mix. Asadero, cheddar, Monterey Jack, queso quesadilla	1–2 cups

Prep Instructions

Wash green chiles, cut stems and tops, and scoop out seeds and veins with paring knife.
Save the stems to place on top of stuffed chile.
In a mixing bowl add taco ground beef mix, chopped cilantro, nuts, chopped garlic and coriander. Blend mixture and add some additional green chile sauce or water if needed to make thinner filling.
Stuff chiles either by placing stuffing into the tube with your finger from the top (preferred), or cut a lengthwise slit on one side of the chile and placing filling.
Grease the bottom of a baking pan or dish and place chiles slit side down. Pour green chile sauce over the top. If there is any meat filling left over, place into pan with green chile sauce.
This will make a great garnish over the chiles when serving.

Cooking Instructions

Preheat oven to 350°F. Bake chiles for 30 minutes and remove from oven. Let cool for 10 minutes. Place shredded cheese on top of chiles, and place back in oven under broiler for 5 minutes. Remove and serve.

Suggested Complementary Dishes: Refried beans, salsa, rice. Serves: 4–6 hearty guests.

GREEN CHILE CHOP SUEY

Complexity Code: Cook   Origin: New Mexico
Cooking Method: Pan-fry

About the Recipe: It is told that Chop Suey originated in San Francisco
in the 1840s when some drunk and hungry miners burst into a restaurant
and demanded to be fed. The Chinese cook went into the kitchen, pulled
together all the leftovers, pan-fried them, poured soy sauce over them and
served it as "sap sui" (bits and pieces). Chop Suey has since become an
all-American dish. This is a New Mexico variation of bits and pieces that is
sure to please.
Essential Recipe: Fresh Green Chile (p.44).

Ingredient	Measure	Ingredient	Measure
Fresh Green Chile pods, Anaheim, Poblano, Jalapeño SHU to taste	2 cup	Adobo Spice Mix (p.83)	2 Tbsp.
Celery thin sliced	1 cup	Sweetener: Nectar (p.85)	2 Tbsp.
Red Bell pepper (thin sliced)	½ cup	Soy or teriyaki sauce	2 Tbsp.
Mushrooms (thin sliced)	½ cup	Oyster sauce or hoisin sauce	2 Tbsp.
Onion (thin sliced)	½ cup	Corn or tapioca starch	2 Tsp.
Water chestnuts (thin sliced)	½ cup		
Vegetable oil	2–3 Tbsp.	**OPTIONAL:** Thinly sliced beef, chicken, pork	1–2 cups.
Chinese fried noodles or rice	2 cups		

Prep Instructions

Remove stem and seeds from green chile pods and cut into thin slices
⅛-inch across. Slice 2 to 3 stalks of celery on a diagonal of ⅛ inch.
Remove stem and seeds from red bell pepper and cut into thin slices ⅛
inch. Cut mushrooms, onion and water chestnuts into thin slices.
In a mixing bowl blend sweetener, soy sauce, oyster sauce, Adobo Spice
Mix and corn starch. Stir well to blend all ingredients.
If using meat in your chop suey, slice it as thin as you can (⅛-inch slices)
and dip into the soy sauce blend for 10 to 15 minutes to marinate.
Preheat heavy skillet with vegetable oil on high heat.

Cooking Instructions

Place marinated meat in skillet and stir fry until cooked about 2 minutes.
Push meat to side of skillet. Add vegetables into skillet and stir fry until
they sizzle for about 2 minutes. Pour soy sauce marinade into skillet and
bring to a boil. Stir meat and vegetables until corn starch starts to thicken.
Suggested Complementary Dishes: Serve over Chinese noodles or
rice.
Servings: 4–6 people

MAC & CHEESE CASSEROLE—RED OR GREEN

Complexity Code: EZ   Origin: UNIVERSE
Cooking Method: Boil, Bake

About the Recipe: It would be hard to find anyone on planet earth that does not like a mac & cheese casserole, and by adding green chile, we can include the universe.

Essential Recipe: Rehydrated Red Chile Pods (p.40), OR Roasted Green Chile (p.46).

Ingredient	Measure	Ingredient	Measure
Elbow macaroni	½ lb.	Egg	1
Rehydrated red chile pods, Ancho, Pasilla, Chipotle or Chile Seco SHU to taste	2 cups chopped		
Roasted green chile(fresh or frozen) Anaheim, Poblano, Jalapeño SHU to taste	2 cups chopped	Sweetener (p.85)	2 Tbsp.
Milk or half-and-half	3 cups	Cheddar Cheese	1 cup shredded
Shredded Cheese Mix Asadero, cheddar, Jack, queso quesadilla,	1 cup	Vegetable oil or butter	2 Tbs.

Prep Instructions

Preheat oven to 350°F. Boil elbow macaroni until firm al dente (do not overcook); drain and rinse macaroni under cool water to stop cooking.
Chop Rehydrated Red Chile Pods and Roasted Green Chile into ¼-inch squares; removing stems and seeds, place in mixing bowl.
Beat egg in mixing bowl. Add cooked macaroni, chopped chile pods, milk, shredded cheese blend and sweetener. Mix until all ingredients are blended together.
Grease the bottom of a 9-by-13-inch baking dish or pan with oil or butter, pour macaroni blend into baking dish and sprinkle shredded cheddar cheese on top of the macaroni.

Cooking Instructions

Place baking dish in oven and bake 30 minutes.
Place under the broiler to form a crust (optional).
Remove baking dish from oven and let cool for 5 minutes before serving.

Suggested Complementary Dishes: Nothing else needed

Serves: 4–6 people.

MISH-MASH GROUND BEEF—RED OR GREEN

Complexity Code: Cook   Origin: New Mexico
Cooking Method: Fry / Sauté

About the Recipe: Mish-Mash can be defined as the Southwest poor boy. The taco meat, red chiles, corn and beans make it a complete meal that can be served in a bowl with tortillas, nachos or tostadas.

Essential Recipe: Rehydrated Red Chile pods (p.40), Red Chile Sauce (p.36), OR Roasted Green Chile (p.46), Green Chile Sauce (p.50), Taco Ground Beef. (p.62) OR Sautéed Beef, Chicken or Pork (p.64).

Ingredient	Measure	Ingredient	Measure
Taco Ground Beef or Sautéed Beef, Chicken or Pork	2 lbs.	Adobo Spice Mix	1 Tbsp.
Rehydrated Red Chile Pods Ancho, Pasilla, Chipotle or Chile Seco SHU to taste	1 cup chopped	Sweetener (p.85)	2 Tbsp.
Roasted Green Chile Anaheim, Poblano, Jalapeño SHU to taste	1 cup chopped	Cilantro	½ cup chopped
Corn (frozen or canned)	2 cups	Onion	½ cup chopped
Pinto or black beans	2 cups	Tomato sauce	1 cup
		Oil or lard	½ cup

Prep Instructions

Preheat large skillet with oil or grease. 360^0
Place taco ground beef, Adobo Spice Mix, chopped chile pods, chopped cilantro, tomato sauce and sweetener into a mixing bowl and blend all ingredients.

Cooking Instructions

Drop small ½ " chunks of blended ground beef mixture into skillet and fry, stirring and placing more chunks to fry, push cooked meat to edge of frying pan. (A wok works very well if available.)
When all of the meat is cooked, place chopped chile pods, tomato sauce, sweetener, corn, beans and cilantro into frying pan and sauté until all ingredients are blended.

Suggested Complementary Dishes: Mish-mash can be served in a bowl, or as a topping for tacos, a burrito, or salad.

Servings: 4–6 cups.

MEATBALLS—RED OR GREEN

Complexity Code: Cook   Origin: New Mexico
Cooking Method: Bake / Fry

About the Recipe: This is a New Mexico family recipe that will provide instant accolades.
The meatball can be used with any pasta, potato, stew or casserole or just by itself with a bowl of chile. You could say that meatballs are the perfect companion to any recipe.

Essential Recipe: Taco Ground Beef Mix (p.62), Rehydrated Red Chile pods (p.40), OR Roasted Green Chile (p.46).

Ingredient	Measure	Ingredient	Measure
Taco ground beef mix	2 lbs.	Adobo Spice Mix	2 Tbsp.
Rehydrated red chile pods, Ancho, Pasilla, Chipotle or Chile Seco SHU to taste	1 cup chopped	Cilantro	¼ cup chopped
Roasted green chile(canned okay) SHU to taste	1 cup	Ketchup or tomato sauce	¼ cup
Bread crumbs, masa, or Rice flour	½ cup	Green chile powder	1Tbsp.
		Rice flour, Masa harina, unbleached flour.	1 cup

Prep Instructions

Baking:
Preheat oven to 400⁰F.
Chop Rehydrated Red Chile Pods and Roasted Green Chile to ¼-inch squares (removing stems and seeds).
If using canned chile, drain and rinse all preservatives from can.
Mix ground beef and sausage in a mixing bowl, add roasted green chile, Adobo Spice Mix, cilantro, ketchup, green chile powder and bread crumbs. Mix ingredients well.
Coat bottom of a 10-by-15-inch baking pan with vegetable oil.
Place flour in a deep bowl.
Form meatballs 1-inch round in the palm of your hand; roll meatballs in flour mix to coat entire surface and place on baking pan in even rows not touching each other.
Place baking pan in heated oven and lower the temperature to 350⁰F. This will create a thin crust on the meatball and keep all the juices in. Bake for about 30 minutes. Take out and let cool. Sprinkle any chile powder on top to give the meatball an extra flavor burst.

Frying:
Preheat a frying pan with about ¾ inches of oil to 350⁰F. Place coated meatballs in the oil and fry until the surface turns a brownish color. You will have to turn the meatballs every 3 minutes until all sides are evenly done. They should be cooked in about 15 to 20 minutes. Place cooked meatballs on a paper towel to absorb extra oil and sprinkle with salt, green chile powder or garlic powder to give an extra burst of flavor.

Suggested Complementary Dishes: Pasta, tacos, green chile stew.

Servings: 24 meatballs

NEW MEXICO CHICKEN ROLL—RED OR GREEN

Complexity Code: CHEF   Origin: Original
Cooking Method: Sear / Braise

About the Recipe: New Mexico chicken rolls chicken rolls are an original recipe with traditional roots that is sure to please any Chilenista.
Essential Recipe: Red Chile Sauce (p.36), or Red Chile Tomato Sauce, Rehydrated Red Chile pods (p.40) OR Green Chile Sauce (p.50), or Creamy Green Chile Sauce (p.52) Roasted Green Chile (p.46)

Ingredient	Measure	Ingredient	Measure
Chicken breast, (boneless skinless)	6 pieces	Sweetener marinade: (Guava, Papaya, Tamarind) Nectar	2 cups
Rehydrated Red Chile Pods Ancho, Pasilla, Chipotle or Chile Seco SHU to taste	1 cup chopped	Adobo Spice Mix	2 Tbsp.
Roasted green chile pods Anaheim, Poblano, Jalapeño SHU to taste	1 cup	Bread Crumbs, masa or cornmeal stuffing	1 cup
Asadero cheese (thinly sliced)	½ lb.	Cilantro	½ cup chopped
Prosciutto ham or ham slices	½ lb.	Pinion nuts or walnuts	¼ cup crushed
Chile sauce SHU to taste	2 cups (split)	Oil	¼ cup
Red chile powder	¼ cup		
Tomatoes	1 cup chopped		

Prep Instructions
Pound chicken breast to ¼-inch thick.
Place chicken and nectar sweetener in a 1-gallon Ziploc bag, to marinate 2 to 4 hours in refrigerator. (Overnight will also work if you do not have the time to prep during the day.)
Chop rehydrated red chile pods to ¼-inch squares (removing stems and seeds).
Chop roasted green chile pods to ¼-inch squares (removing stems and seeds).
Chop tomatoes into ¼-inch squares.
Chop cilantro.
Combine bread crumbs, oil, and 1 cup chile sauce, chopped chile pods, pinion nuts, Adobo Spice Mixture, chopped tomatoes and chopped cilantro in a mixing bowl and blend all ingredients to create a bread crumb filling. (It should be a little sticky.)

Place the marinated chicken breast on a cutting board lengthwise (grain left to right).

Spread bread crumb filling over chicken breast (thin layer) and cover with thin slices of asadero cheese and prosciutto ham.

Roll the chicken breast away from you as if you were making a burrito. Make sure that you do not squeeze the filling out the sides. Secure the roll with some toothpicks.

Cooking Instructions

Searing is optional to seal the flavor in. In a heavy skillet, place enough oil to cover the bottom and heat to almost smoking.

Place the chicken breasts into the hot oil to sear the outside, turning often to avoid burning.

To braise (slow cook), oil the bottom of a glass Pyrex dish or 9-by-13-inch baking pan.

Place the chicken breast rolls in the pan and pour the chile sauce to cover the bottom.

Cover the top with aluminum foil.

Depending on the time you have available, you can braise the chicken breasts for 1 hour at 350^0F, 2 hours at 250^0F, or 3 hours at 210^0F. The longer the cooking time, the more tender the meat. I always prefer a longer cooking time at lower temperatures. The internal temperature is more important than the external. The flank steak will be done when the internal temperature reaches 160^0F degrees.

Remove the chicken breasts from the oven and let cool for about 10 minutes. If you want to brown the top, place the chicken under the broiler for 5 minutes and remove when the top is brownish.

Cut the chicken breast rolls into 1-inch, 1 ½-inch thick pinwheels on the diagonal.

Garnish with 1 cup red chile sauce and sprinkle with red chile powder.

Suggested Complementary Dishes: Beans, garbanzos, refried beans, calabacitas, corn, posole, rice and salsa.

Serves: 4–6 people.

NEW MEXICO FLANK STEAK ROLL-RED OR GREEN

Complexity Code: CHEF   Origin: Original
Cooking Method: Sear / Braise

About the Recipe: Flank steak has been a staple for many New Mexican dishes. Flank steak is a meat eater's cut of beef that is chewy, flavorful and can be used in many recipes such as enchiladas, tamales, burritos and fajitas. This recipe takes flank steak to its ultimate destination. It is the fillet mignon of all flank steak recipes. Take your time to marinate it and slow cook it. You will be getting compliments and praises for a long time to come.

Essential Recipe: Red Chile Sauce (p.36), or Red Chile Tomato Sauce (p.37), Rehydrated Red Chile pods (p.40), OR Green Chile Sauce (p.50), Creamy Green Chile Sauce (p.52), Roasted Green Chile (p.46)

Ingredient	Measure	Ingredient	Measure
Flank Steak shoulder (thin cut)	2 lbs.	Lime juice(Marinade)* 1 cup Lime juice 1 cup orange juice or mango nectar	2 cups
Rehydrated Red Chile Pods Ancho, Pasilla, Chipotle or Chile Seco SHU to taste	1 cup chopped	Adobo Spice Mix	4 Tbsp.
Roasted green chile pods Anaheim, Poblano, Jalapeño SHU to taste	1 cup	Masa, bread crumbs, or Cornmeal stuffing	1 cup
Asadero Cheese (thinly sliced)	½ lb.	Pinion nuts	½ - 1 cup
Red Chile Sauce or Green Chile Sauce or Creamy Green Chile Sauce SHU to taste	2 cups (split)	Oil	¼ cup
Red or green chile powder	¼ cup		
Tomatoes	1 cup chopped		
Cilantro	1 cup		

*Mix 1 cup lime juice with 1 cup orange juice

Prep Instructions

Butterfly cut flank steak ¼-inch thick and tenderize by pounding flat. Combine lime juice, 2 Tbsp. Adobo Spice Mix, in a 1 gallon zip lock bag, shake and place flank steak in bag to marinade 2-4 hours in refrigerator. (Overnight will also work if you do not have the time to prep during the day).

Chop rehydrated red chile pods to ¼-inch square (removing stem and seeds).
Chop roasted green chile pods to ¼-inch square (removing stem and seeds).
Chop tomatoes into ¼-inch squares
Chop cilantro into ¼-inch squares
Combine bread crumbs, oil, 1 cup Red Chile Sauce, chopped chile pods, pinion nuts, Adobo Spice Mixture, chopped tomatoes and chopped cilantro in a mixing bowl blend all ingredients to create a bread crumb filling. (It should be a little sticky).
Place the marinated flank steak on a cutting board lengthwise (grain left to right).
Spread bread crumb filling over top of flank steak (thin layer) and cover with thin slices of asadero cheese.
Roll the flank steak away from you as if you were making a burrito. Make sure that you do not squeeze the filling out of the sides. Secure the roll with some tooth picks.

Cooking Instructions

Searing (Optional) to seal the flavor in.
In a heavy skillet place enough oil to cover the bottom and heat to almost smoking.
Place the flank steak into the hot oil to sear the outside turn often to avoid burning.

Braising: (slow cook)
Oil the bottom of a glass baking dish or baking pan to cover bottom.
Place the flank steak roll in the pan and pour the chile sauce to cover the bottom.
Cover the top with aluminum foil.
Depending on the time you have available you can braise the Flank steak for 1 hour at 350^0, 2 hours at 250^0, 3 hours at 210^0.
The longer the cooking time to more tender the meat, I always prefer a longer cooking time at lower temperatures. The internal temperature is more important than the external. The flank steak will be done when the internal temperature reaches 145 degrees.
Remove the flank steak from the oven and let cool for about 10 minutes. If you want to brown the top, place the steak under the broiler for 5 minutes remove when the top is brownish.
Cut the flank steak into 1- to 1 ½-inch thick pin wheels on a diagonal.
Garnish with 1 cup Red Chile Sauce and sprinkle with red chile powder.

Suggested Complementary Dishes: Beans, garbanzos, refried beans, calabacitas, corn, posole, rice and salsa.
Serves: 4–6 people.

VARIATION:
New Mexico Pork Shoulder Roll—Red or Green
The pork shoulder cut is the equivalent of flank steak, a chewy and tasty cut of pork that provides a lot of meaty flavor. You can fillet the pork shoulder cut into a ¼ " slab and follow the flank steak recipe.
The pork will be a lot tenderer with a melt in your mouth deliciousness.

PAN-ROAST CHICKEN
RED OR GREEN OR CHRISTMAS

Complexity Code: Cook   Origin: New Mexico
Cooking Method: Pan-roast, roast

About the Recipe: Pan-roasted chicken is probably the way chicken was
meant to be cooked, as it preserves the entire delicate flavor of the chicken
and the crunch that many of us expect. Smother it with Red or Green or
Christmas in between. Food does not get much better than this.
Essential Recipe: Red Chile Sauce (p.36), Rehydrated Red Chile pods
(p.40), Red Chile Mole Sauce (p.81), OR Green Chile Sauce (p.50),
Roasted Green Chile (p.46), Creamy Chile Sauce (p.52)

Ingredient	Measure	Ingredient	Measure
Chicken breast or thighs (Deboned)	4 -6 pieces	Adobo Spice Mix	2 Tbsp.
Rehydrated red chile pods Ancho, Pasilla, Chipotle or Chile Seco SHU to taste	1 cup chopped	Red Chile Sauce, Red Chile Mole Sauce, Green Chile Sauce or Creamy Green Chile Sauce	2 cups
Roasted green chile pods Anaheim, Poblano, Jalapeño SHU to taste	1 cup chopped	Rice flour (Harina de Arroz), Corn flour or unbleached flour	1 cup
Carrots (baby)	½ lb.	Olive oil	3–4 Tbsp.
Yellow squash	2 pieces		

Prep Instructions
Preheat oven to 400^0F.
Debone chicken breast or thigh.
Combine rice flour and Adobo Spice Mix in a mixing bowl. Dredge
chicken parts in flour mixture; shake off excess flour. (I prefer rice flour, as
it is crunchier and will not burn as easily.)
Cut yellow squash into 1-inch pieces (quartered).
Place ¼ cup olive oil in iron skillet. Preheat oil to 375^0F (high heat).

Cooking Instructions
Place chicken breast or thighs skin side down in preheated skillet to sear
and brown skin 4 to 5 minutes. Flip chicken skin side up and sear bottom
3 to 4 minutes. Remove chicken from skillet and place into a roasting pan
skin side up.
Surround chicken with chopped chile, carrots and squash. Place roasting
pan into oven.

Bake for 15 to 20 minutes (internal temperature 160°F).
Remove chicken from oven and let cool for 5 to 10 minutes.
Place chicken on serving plate. Surround chicken with red chile and
carrots and squash. Pour Red Chile or Red Chile Mole Sauce on top of
chicken and serve. (You may wish to serve the sauces on the side as a
garnish.)

Suggested Complementary Dishes: Refried beans, calabacitas, rice,
salsa, crema.

Serves: 4 - 6 people.

POTATO AU-GRATIN—RED OR GREEN

Complexity Code: EZ   Origin: New Mexico
Cooking Method: Bake / Broil
About the Recipe: This potato recipe can highlight or be the center of
your meal. It is easy to make and will please all.
Essential Recipe: Rehydrated Red Chile Pods (p.40), OR Roasted
Green Chile (p.46).

Ingredient	Measure		Measure
Potatoes (large baking)	4	Adobo Spice Mix (p.83)	1 Tbsp.
Rehydrated red chile pods Ancho, Pasilla, Chipotle or Chile Seco SHU to taste	2 cups chopped	Shredded Cheese Mix Asadero, cheddar, Jack, queso Quesadilla	1 ½ cups
Roasted green chile pods (fresh or frozen)	2 cups chopped	Cheddar cheese	1 ½ cups shredded
Crema or sour cream	1 cup	Sweetener (p.85)	2 Tbsp.
		Half-and-half or milk	½ cup
		Vegetable oil	2 Tbsp.

Prep Instructions

Preheat oven to 400°F. Wash potato, cut into 4 quarters and thinly slice
potatoes in ⅛- to ¼-inch slices.
Chop Rehydrated Red Chile Pods and Roasted Green Chile into ¼-inch
squares; removing stem and seeds, place in mixing bowl.
Add crema, Adobe Dry Spice Mix and sweetener into bowl. Mix green
chile, until all ingredients are blended.
Grease bottom of 9-by-13-inch baking dish or pan.
Layer potatoes in baking pan. Top first layer with 1 ½ cups shredded
cheese mix cheese, top second layer of potatoes with chile blend and top
third layer of potatoes with 1 ½ cups cheddar cheese.
Pour half-and-half over cheddar cheese and gently squeeze potato layers to
remove any air between layers.
Cover baking dish with aluminum foil.

Cooking Instructions

Place baking pan in oven and reduce heat to 375°F for 30 to 45 minutes
until potatoes are soft. Test softness with a toothpick or fork.
Remove foil. Turn on broiler and broil to form a crust 5 to 10 minutes.

Suggested Complementary Dishes: Bacon, chorizos, sausage, tortilla,
any chicken or meat dish.

Servings: 6–8 people

POTATOES STUFFED—RED OR GREEN

Complexity Code: Cook   Origin: New Mexico
Cooking Method: Bake / Broil

About the Recipe: This recipe is one of the easiest to make and can be served as a main or side dish.
Essential Recipe: Rehydrated Red Chile Pods (p.40), OR Roasted Green Chile (p.46).

Ingredient	Measure		Measure
Potatoes (large baking)	4	Crema or sour cream	2 cups
Rehydrated red chile pods, Ancho, Pasilla, Chipotle or Chile Seco SHU to taste	2 cups chopped	Shredded Cheese Blend Asadero, cheddar, Jack, queso quesadilla	2 cups shredded
Roasted green chile(fresh or frozen) Anaheim, Poblano, Jalapeño SHU to taste	2 cups chopped		

Prep Instructions

Preheat oven to 400°F. Wash 4 large potatoes and poke some holes on the top with a fork; cover with tin foil.
Place potatoes in oven for 45 to 60 minutes until semi-soft.
Reduce heat to 350°F.
Remove foil from potato;, let cool. Cut top ¼ of potato off (horizontally) with a knife. Scoop most of the potato meat out and place in a mixing bowl. (Leave a minimum of a ¼-inch wall on the potato.)
Mash potato in mixing bowl, add crema and blend together. You can use a hand blender stick. Fold chopped Fresh Green Chile and shredded cheese blend into the mashed potato blend. Save ½ cup of cheese for broiling.
Stuff filling into potato shells. Place potatoes on a baking dish or pan.
Sprinkle shredded cheese on top of potato and place in oven for an additional 15 minutes, or broil for 5 minutes to create a cheesy crust.

Suggested Complementary Dishes: Chorizos, sausage, tortilla, crema.

Servings 4 people

QUESADILLA—RED OR GREEN

Complexity Code: EZ   Origin: New Mexico / Mexico
Cooking Method: Fry / Bake

About the Recipe: Quesadillas are an instant meal that can be a snack, appetizer or meal. Your imagination is the only limitation on what to use as a filling to top the cheese.

Essential Recipe: Rehydrated Red Chile pods (p.40), OR Roasted Green Chile (p.46), Taco Ground Beef (p.62), Sautéed Beef, Chicken or Pork (p.64), Slow cooked Beef, Pork,or Chicken (p.56,58,60).

Ingredient	Measure	Ingredient	Measure
Tortilla (burrito size)	8	Green chile powder	To taste
Shredded Cheese blend, Asadero, cheddar, Jack, queso Quesadilla	2 cups or more	Sautéed Beef, Chicken or Pork OR Shredded Beef, Pork, or Chicken	2 cups
Rehydrated red chile pods, Ancho, Pasilla, Chipotle or Chile Seco SHU to taste	2 cups chopped	Taco Ground Beef	2 cups
Roasted green chile Anaheim, Poblano, Jalapeño SHU to taste	2 cup chopped	Shrimp	2 cups
Onion	2 cup chopped		
Cilantro	1 cup chopped		

Prep Instructions

Prepare filling (see suggestions below).
Preheat heavy skillet with oil.
Preheat oven to 350°F.
Prepare a flat baking pan with a cooling rack on top.

Cooking Instructions

Fry tortillas 15 to 20 seconds on each side until crispy.
Place fried tortillas on the baking pan rack to drain the oil. Sprinkle green chile powder (to taste) on top of tortilla and place in preheated oven.
Spread ⅛-inch cheese layer or more on tortilla. You can use cheddar or cotija cheese to sharpen the taste. Place a layer(s) of fillings from the suggested list on top of the cheese. Cover fillings with a tortilla. Place quesadilla on a flat baking pan.
Place quesadillas into center of oven for 10 to 15 minutes to melt cheese and blend fillings.
Cut tortilla in 4 pieces and plate.
Suggested Complementary Dishes: Crema, salsa, guacamole, refried beans and rice.

Servings: 16 pieces

RED CHILE EGGPLANT PARMESAN (BAKED)

Complexity Code: EZ   Origin: Original
Cooking Method: Bake

About the Recipe: Baked Eggplant Parmesan with a Chilensta variation is one of the greatest red chile recipes that you can prepare and serve. Chilenistas will embrace it and ask for more.
  Essential Recipes: Enchilada Sauce (p.77), Red Chile Tomato Sauce (p.37), Rehydrated Red Chile pods (p.40)

Ingredient	Measure		Measure
Eggplant (large)	12 slices	Adobo Spice Mix	2 Tbsp.
Enchilada Sauce or Red Chile Tomato Sauce	2 cups	Shredded cheese blend, Asadero, cheddar, Jack, queso Quesadilla	2 cups
Rehydrated red chile pods, Ancho, Pasilla, Chipotle or Chile Seco SHU to taste	1 cup chopped	Cotija cheese or Parmesan cheese	2 cups grated
Masa harina, rice flour, flour unbleached	½ cup	Queso quesadilla or mozzarella (or any melting) cheese	½ lb. sliced
Bread crumbs	½ cup		

Prep Instructions

Preheat oven to 450°F.
Clean and cut eggplant in circles 1- to 1 ½-inch thick (12 slices).
Mix flour and Adobo Spice Mix on a flat plate.
Chop red chile pods into ¼-inch squares (removing stem and seeds).
Dredge eggplant slices though flour mix and place in a greased baking pan 9-by-13-inch baking pan.
Place in oven for 30 minutes until eggplant starts to turn brown and is soft yet firm.
Remove eggplant from oven. Reduce heat to 350°F. Let eggplant cool 15 to 20 minutes.
Pour 2 cups enchilada sauce on top of eggplant slices.
 Pour 2 cups of shredded cheese blend on top of enchilada sauce
Pour 2 cups Cotija cheese on top of shredded cheese.
Place one slice of queso quesadilla on top of each eggplant slice.
Pour a few bread crumbs on top of queso quesadilla.

Cooking Instructions

Place baking pan in oven and bake for 30 -45 minutes until the cheese is melted.
Remove baking pan from oven; let cool 10 -15 minutes and serve while hot.
Suggested Complementary Dishes: Vinaigrette salad, refried beans, spinach and crema.

Serves: 6–9 people.

RED CHILE EGGPLANT PARMESAN (FRIED)

Complexity Code: EZ   Origin: Original
Cooking Method: Fry / Bake

About the Recipe: Fried Eggplant Parmesan with a Chilensta variation is one of the greatest red chile recipes that you can prepare and serve.

Essential Recipes: Enchilada Sauce (p.77), Red Chile Tomato Sauce (p.37), Rehydrated Red Chile pods (p.40).

Ingredient	Measure	Ingredient	Measure
Eggplant (2 large)	24 slices	Adobo Spice Mix (p.83)	4 Tbsp.
Enchilada Sauce or Red Chile Tomato Sauce	3 cups	Shredded cheese blend, Asadero, cheddar, Jack, queso quesadilla	2–4 cups
Rehydrated red chile pods, Ancho, Pasilla, Chipotle or Chile Seco SHU to taste	1 cup chopped	Cotija cheese or Parmesan cheese	2 cup grated
Masa harina, rice flour, flour unbleached	1 cup	Queso quesadilla or mozzarella or any melting cheese.	½ lb. sliced
Bread crumbs	2 cups	Frying oil	4 cups
Eggs	3		

Prep Instructions

Preheat oil in deep-frying pan or fryer at 360°F.
Clean and cut eggplant in circles ½-inch thick (24 slices).
Mix flour and Adobo Spice Mix on a flat plate.
Chop red chile pods into ¼-inch squares (removing stem and seeds).
Whip eggs and add 2 Tbsp. water to thin out; place in a bowl.
Place bread crumbs on a plate.
Dredge eggplant slices though flour mix.
Soak eggplant slices into egg wash and dredge eggplant slices though bread crumbs.
Place eggplant slices into heated oil and fry 3 minutes per side. (Do not overcrowd frying pan.)
Pour 1 cup of enchilada sauce on the bottom of a greased baking pan.

Layer fried eggplant slices on baking pan (approx. 9–12 slices).
Pour 1 cup of enchilada sauce onto first layer; spread chopped red chile pods on top of enchilada sauce.
Pour 2 cups of shredded cheese blend on top of chopped red chile.
Place second layer of fried eggplant slices on top of shredded cheese.
Pour 1 cup enchilada sauce on top of eggplant slices.
Spread Cotija cheese on top of enchilada sauce.
Cover top of Cotija cheese with slices of queso quesadilla (mozzarella).
Preheat oven 350°F.

Cooking Instructions

Place baking pan in oven and bake for 30 to 45 minutes until cheese melts.
Remove baking pan from oven; let cool 10 to 15 minutes and serve while hot.

Suggested Complementary Dishes: Vinaigrette salad.

Serves: 6–9 people.

RED CHILE LASAGNA (CARNE)

Complexity Code: EZ   Origin: Original
Cooking Method: Bake

About the Recipe: Red Chile Lasagna is sure to please any Chilenista by incorporating all of the favorite tastes into a tried and true favorite recipe. If you are truly adventurous, substitute green chiles for the red.
Essential Recipes: Enchilada Sauce (p.77), Red Chile Tomato Sauce (p.37), Taco Ground Beef (p.62), Sautéed Beef, Chicken or Pork (p.64), Rehydrated Red Chile Pods (p.40) (optional).

Ingredient	Measure	Ingredient	Measure
Lasagna 12 pieces	1 box	Adobo Spice Mix (p.83)	2 Tbsp.
Enchilada Sauce or Red Chile Tomato Sauce	2 cups (each)	Panela or ricotta cheese	2 cups
Taco Ground Beef or Sautéed Beef, Chicken or Pork	4 cups	Crema	2 cups
Tomato	2 cups chopped or canned	Shredded cheese blend Asadero, cheddar, Jack, queso Quesadilla	2 cups
Cilantro	1 cup chopped	Queso quesadilla or mozzarella (sliced) or any melting cheese	½ lb. sliced
OPTIONAL: Rehydrated red chile pods. Ancho, Pasilla, Chipotle or Chile Seco SHU to taste	2 cups chopped	Oil	¼ cup

Prep Instructions

Preheat oven to 350^0F.
Fill a large stockpot with water and bring to a boil.
Place (12) lasagna pieces into boiling water. Boil for 15 to 20 minutes until lasagna is limp and firm.
Strain lasagna and cool under cold water to stop cooking. Place cooked lasagna in a bowl.
Chop tomatoes into ¼-inch squares or used canned chopped tomatoes. Place in small bowl.
Chop Rehydrated Red Chile Pods into ¼-inch squares. Removing stem and seeds, place in small bowl.
Chop cilantro and place in a small bowl.
Grease the bottom of a 9-by-14-inch baking pan and pour 1 cup enchilada sauce on bottom.

Place first layer of 4 lasagna pieces to cover bottom.
Place 2 cups panela cheese and evenly spread on bottom layer.
Place chopped red chile on top of cheese optional).
Pour 1 cup enchilada sauce on top of chopped red chile.
Place second layer of 4 lasagna pieces on top of enchilada sauce.
Spread taco ground beef on top of second layer.
Spread 2 cups of crema on top of taco ground beef.
Spread chopped cilantro on top of crema.
Pour 1 cup of enchilada sauce on top of cilantro.
Place third row of 4 lasagna pieces on top of enchilada sauce.
Spread shredded cheese blend on top of lasagna slices.
Pour 1 cup enchilada sauce on top of shredded cheese.
Cover with queso quesadilla (6–8 slices) on top of enchilada sauce.

Cooking Instructions

Place baking pan in preheated oven and bake for 60 minutes until sauce is bubbling and cheese has melted.

Remove from oven, let cool for 10 to15 minutes and cut into 3-by-3-inch squares. Serve hot.

Suggested Complementary Dishes: Vinaigrette salad.

Serves: 6–9 people.

RED CHILE TEXAS STYLE

Complexity Code: Cook   Origin: Texas / New Mexico
Cooking Method: Boil, Simmer

About the Recipe: From aromatic to blistering hot when some people think of chile this is it—a total meal in a bowl.
Essential Recipe: Taco Ground Beef (p.62), Red Chile Sauce (p.36).

Ingredient	Measure	Ingredient	Measure
Taco Ground Beef	1 lb.	Balsamic vinegar	¼ cup
Red Chile Sauce (XXXX) SHU to taste	1 cup	Oregano	2 Tbsp.
Tomato sauce	1 cup	Garlic powder	2 Tbsp.
Oil, butter, or lard	¼ cup	Sweetener (p.85)	2 Tbsp.
Hot Sauce (SHU) To taste	¼ cup	Salt	1 Tbsp.
Onion	1 medium chopped	Coriander	1 Tbsp.
Cilantro	1 cup garnish	Clove powder	½ tsp.
Chipotle Chiles Canned or Rehydrated	1 cup (garnish)	Caraway seeds	¼ tsp.
Shredded cheese blend	1 cup (garnish)	Parsley, sage, rosemary & thyme	¼ tsp. each
		OPTIONAL: Beans, pinto or kidney, canned okay	2 cups

Prep Instructions
Mix Taco Ground Beef, Red Chile Sauce, tomato sauce, oil, chopped onion, vinegar and sweetener in a 2- to 3-quart stockpot.
Mix spices oregano, garlic powder, salt, coriander, clove, caraway seeds, parsley, sage, rosemary and thyme in a small mixing bowl.

Cooking Instructions
Bring red chile meat mixture to a boil, stir to blend all ingredients, lower the heat to a simmer and add spices to red chile mixture.
OPTIONAL: To give the chile a heartier taste, stir in 2 cups of beans.
Let simmer for 15 minutes. Taste and add additional hot sauce if desired.
Serve in chile bowls and garnish with a chipotle chile.

Suggested Complementary Dishes: Crackers, tortillas, baked potato, fresh chopped onion, shredded cheese blend, cerveza and a slice of lime.
Serves 4–8 people

SANTA FE CHICKEN RED & GREEN (CHRISTMAS)

Complexity Code: Cook   Origin: New Mexico
Cooking Method: Steam or Parboil / Deep-fry

About the Recipe: Santa Fe chicken is a variation of deep-fried chicken
in that it is can be prepared in advance and flash-fried to create a crispy
outside and juicy inside. Garnish with Red or Green or both and you can
have Christmas year-round.
Essential Recipe: Red Chile Sauce (p.36), or Green Chile Sauce (p.50).

Ingredient	Measure	Ingredient	Measure
Chicken (halved or quartered bone in)	1 fryer chicken	Rice flour (Harina de Arroz), corn flour or unbleached flour	2 cup
Red Chile Sauce SHU to taste	1 cup	Adobo Spice Mix	4 Tbsp.
Green Chile Sauce SHU to taste	1 cup	Vegetable oil	1 qt. for frying

Prep Instructions

Rinse and dry chicken, either in half or quarters.
Optionally remove breast plate bone from chicken breast.
Place flour in a shallow bowl, add adobo spices and blend well.

Cooking Instructions

Place chicken in steamer and steam for 15 to 20 minutes (preferred) or
place chicken in boiling water for 20 minutes. Remove chicken and cool
for 10 to 15 minutes. (Save broth from steamer for use in any recipe that
calls for broth). Dry chicken with a paper towel.
Place chicken in the flour; blend and cover all sides. Shake off any excess
flour. You can now place chicken in a plastic bag to cool in refrigerator
for 30 to 60 minutes or freeze for future use. (To defrost, place on a
microwave defrost cycle for 5 to 6 minutes until chicken parts are warm.)
When chicken is warm, you are ready to fry. Heat oil in a heavy skillet
or deep fryer to 360°F. Carefully place chicken in the hot oil (going away
from you) and fry for 5 to 10 minutes until thin crust is golden brown. For
pan-frying, fry 3 to 5 minutes per side. (Do not crowd the fryer).
Remove the fried chicken and place on a paper towel or rack for oil to
drain and dry.
(If you are frying a lot of pieces, place fried chicken in oven at 200°F to
keep warm until all the pieces of chicken are fried).
Plate the chicken and pour the Red Chile Sauce on half of the chicken and
Green Chile Sauce on the other and you will have Santa Fe's Christmas
Chile.

Suggested Complementary Dishes: Roasted chile, beans, refried
beans, rice, red chile, cole slaw, salsa, tortillas and sopapillas.
Servings 2–4 people

STUFFED SOPAPILLA—RED OR GREEN

Complexity Code: EZ   Origin: New Mexico
Cooking Method: Deep fat-fry

About the Recipe: Sopapillas are synonymous with New Mexico's chile cuisine. The fry bread concoction is served with almost any dish forming a pocket for honey to be eaten with the hottest of chile dishes or stuffed with meats to make it a meal.
Essential Recipe: Rehydrated Red Chile Pods (p.40), OR Roasted Green Chile (p.46), Taco Ground Beef (p.62), Sautéed Beef, Chicken or Pork (p.64), Slow cooked Beef, Pork, or Chicken (p.56,58,60), Calabacitas (p.330), any other filling.

Ingredient	Measure	Ingredient	Measure
Unbleached flour	4 cups	Baking powder	2 Tsp.
Shortening or lard	4 Tbsp.	Salt	1 Tsp.
Warm milk	1½ cups	Lard or vegetable oil for frying	4 cups
Rehydrated red chile pods Ancho, Pasilla, Chipotle or Chile Seco SHU to taste	2 cups	Prepare filling from Essential Recipes	3–4 cups
Roasted green chile Anaheim, Poblano, Jalapeño SHU to taste	2 cups chopped		

Prep Instructions

Prepare filling you wish to use from the Essential Recipes. Taco Ground Beef, Chile Ground-Beef, shredded beef, pork, chicken, calabacitas or beans.
Preheat oil or lard in a deep-fat fryer or heavy skillet with at least 2–3" of oil to 375°F.
In a 3- to 4-quart mixing bowl, mix flour, baking powder and salt.* (Premixed sopapilla flour is available.)
Pour 1 ½ cups of milk and lard into a small microwaveable mixing bowl and use the microwave on the defrost cycle for 1 to 2 minutes. (Do not bring to a boil.)
Mix the liquefied lard and milk well and slowly pour in the flour, mixing well until a dough ball is formed.
Place the dough ball on a well-floured, flat surface and knead the dough, folding it in half from all sides and pushing it together until the dough ball is soft and no longer sticky.
Cover the dough ball with a wet towel and let it rest for 15 to 20 minutes.

Cut the dough ball in half and roll out a flat strip of dough ⅛-inch thick on a floured surface. Work fast so that the dough will not dry out.
With a sharp knife or pizza cutter cut the dough into 8-inch squares; place 2–4 Tbsp. of filling in the center of the front half of the dough. Fold one edge of the dough over the center. You can use a triangular or square shape and seal the edges of the dough by using your thumb. (Make sure there are no holes.) Gently squeeze any air out of the sopapilla. (Cover the stuffed dough sopapillas with a wet towel to keep the squares moist until ready to fry).

Cooking Instructions

Carefully place sopapilla dough into the fryer and fry for about one minute per side until golden brown. Place sopapilla on a paper towel or rack to drain, keep warm in an oven at 200^{0}F until all of the sopapillas are fried and ready to serve.

Suggested Complementary Dishes: Garnish sopapilla with Red or Green Chile Sauce, crema, lettuce, refried beans and rice.

Serves 8–10 people

TACOS—RED OR GREEN

Complexity Code: EZ   Origin: New Mexico
Cooking Method: Prep ingredients

About the Recipe: Tacos, soft and hard, are an ideal do-it-yourself dinner
that everyone can enjoy. By placing all of the ingredients in a bowl, you
can have everyone create their own tacos.
Essential Recipe: Taco Ground Beef (p.62), Sautéed Beef, Chicken or
Pork (p.64), OR Slow cooked Beef , Pork or Chicken (p.56,58,60), Red
chile salsa (p.134), or Green Chile Salsa (p.140).

Ingredient	Measure		Measure
Corn Tortilla white or yellow, or Tortilla shells	12	Chopped onion	2 cup
Taco Ground Beef or other meat filling Beef, Pork, Chicken Sauteed or shredded	4 cups	Chopped Tomato	2 cups
Rehydrated red chile pods, Ancho, Pasilla, Chipotle or Chile Seco SHU to taste	2 cups chopped	Shredded cheese blend, Asadero, cheddar, Jack, queso Quesadilla	2-3 cups or more
Roasted green chile Anaheim, Poblano, Jalapeño SHU to taste	2 cups chopped	Cilantro	1 cup
Chile salsa	2 cups	Red or green chile powder (Optional)	To taste
Crema or sour cream	2 cups		
OPTIONAL: Canned chipotle in adobo sauce		Optional Fillings: Hot dog, spam, ham, chorizos Whitefish, shrimp, crabmeat	

Prep Instructions
Prepare fillings and place them in small bowls (Taco Ground Beef,
shredded beef, pork or chicken). If you are in a big hurry you can purchase
a prepared broiled chicken from your grocery store or use cold cuts or
prepared meat. Cut into small cubes or shred.
Chop rehydrated red chile pods into ¼-inch squares (removing stem and
seeds) and place into a 2- to 3-quart mixing bowl.
Chop roasted green chile pods (optional) ¼-inch squares (removing stem
and seeds) place into a 2- to 3-quart mixing bowl.

Chop canned chile pods (chipotle in adobo sauce), tomato and onion (¼-inch squares), shred cheese and chop cilantro.

Salsa homemade or store bought
Crema or sour cream
Chopped onions ¼-inch squares
Chopped tomato ¼-inch squares
Shredded cheese
Chopped cilantro

Cooking Instructions

Fill each taco with layers of meat, chopped red chile, salsa, crema, chopped onion, chopped tomato, and shredded cheese, and top with cilantro and red chile powder as you wish.

Suggested Complementary Dishes: Crema, salsa, guacamole, refried beans and rice.

Servings: 12 pieces.

TAMALES CARNE—RED OR GREEN

Complexity Code: Cook   Origin: New Mexico
Cooking Method: Steam / Boil

About the Recipe: Tamales are a traditional favorite. The phrase "hot tamale" did not arise by accident: Tamales represent the best in the Chilenista cuisine. You can make one as hot or mild as you wish.
Essential Recipes: Slow Cooked Beef, Pork or Chicken (p.56,58,60), Taco Ground Beef (p.62), Sautéed Beef, Chicken or Pork (p.64), Red Chile Paste (p.33), Enchilada Sauce (p.77), Red Chile Sauce (p.36), or Green chile paste (p.43), Red Chile sauce (p.36), Rehydrated Red Chile Pods (optional) (p.40), Fresh Green Chile Pods (p.44).

Ingredient	Measure	Ingredient	Measure
Slow Cooked or Sauteed Beef, Pork or Chicken) or Taco Ground Beef (or store-bought roasted chicken)	1 lb. shredded	Adobo Spice Mix (p.83)	4 Tbsp.
Masa harina	2 cups	Red Chile Paste (XXXX) for hot tamales SHU to taste	1 cup
Water or beef broth	2 cups	Green chile Paste (XXXX) for hot tamales	
Butter lard or shortening	½ cup		
Dried corn husks	18+	Crema or sour cream (garnish)	1 cup
Baking powder	1 tsp.	Red Chile Sauce (garnish)	1–2 cups
Rehydrated red chile pods Ancho, Pasilla, Chipotle Chile Seco SHU to taste	1 cup chopped		
Roasted green Chile Pods Anaheim, Poblano, Jalapeño SHU to taste	1 cup chopped		

Prep Instructions

Soak corn husks in a large mixing bowl until they are soft and pliable. Place masa harina in a 3- to 4-quart mixing bowl, add 1 tsp. baking powder, butter or lard (softened), 2 cups of water or beef broth (warm). Gently knead the dough mixture until it is soft and spongy, cover with a wet cloth and let sit for 10 to 15 minutes.

Shred beef, pork, chicken and set aside in a small bowl.

Chop rehydrated red chile pods (optional) ¼-inch squares (removing stem and seeds) and place into a 2- to 3-quart mixing bowl.

Chop roasted green chile(optional)¼-inch squares (removing stem and seeds) and place into a 2- to 3-quart mixing bowl.

Prepare red chile paste, add Adobo Spice Mix, stir to blend and set aside in a small bowl.

Assembly

Place one corn husk on a flat surface, spread masa 1-2 Tbsp. masa dough ¼-inch thick 1" from the edge toward the center of the corn husk, in 3 to 4-inch strips. (Allow enough room to fold the corn husk to completely cover the masa and filling.)

Coat the masa with Red or Green Chile Paste. Place a strip of meat on top of the masa. Place a strip of the chopped chile pods on top of meat. (Optional)

Roll the corn husk and filling like you would roll up a burrito. Fold the ends over and tie with a small strip of corn husk so they will not unfold during cooking.

Cooking Instructions

Place tamales into a steamer basket, preferable vertically so steam can surround each tamale. Steam for 90 minutes. (Make sure that steamer does not run out of water.)

You can place tamales into a pot of boiling water if you do not have a steamer basket. Boil for 90 minutes.

Remove tamales from steamer and let cool for 5 to 10 minutes before serving.

Suggested Complementary Dishes: Refried beans, rice, corn, salsa, crema, Red or Green Chile Sauce

Servings: 18 tamales.

TAMALES VEGGIE—RED OR GREEN

Complexity Code: Cook   Origin: New Mexico
Cooking Method: Steam / Boil

About the Recipe: Tamales are a traditional favorite. You can make them as hot or mild as you wish.
Essential Recipes: Calabacitas (p.330), Refried beans (p.304), Red Chile Paste (p.33), Red Chile Enchilada Sauce (p.77) Red Chile Sauce (p.36), Rehydrated red chile pods (optional) (p.40) OR Green chile paste (p.43), Green Chile Enchilada Sauce (p.76) or Green Chile Sauce (p.50), Roasted Green Chile (optional) (p.46).

Ingredient	Measure	Ingredient	Measure
Calabacitas	2 cups	Adobo Spice Mix	4 Tbsp.
Refried beans	2 cups		
Masa harina	2 cups	Red Chile Paste (XXXX) for hot tamales SHU to taste	1 cup
Water or beef broth	2 cups	Green Chile Paste (XXXX) for hot tamales SHU to taste	
Butter lard or shortening	½ cup	Rehydrated raisins or craisins	1 cup
Dried corn husks	18+	Crema or sour cream (garnish)	1 cup
Baking powder	1 tsp.	Red Chile Sauce (garnish)	1-2 cups
Rehydrated red chile pods, Ancho, Pasilla, Chipotle or Chile Seco SHU to taste	1 cup chopped	Pinion nuts or sunflower seeds	1 cup or more
Roasted green chile pods Anaheim, Poblano, Jalapeño SHU to taste	1 cup chopped		

Prep Instructions

Soak corn husks in a large mixing bowl until they are soft and pliable. Place masa harina in a 3- to 4-quart mixing bowl, add 1 tsp. baking powder, butter or lard (softened) and 2 cups of water or beef broth (warm). Gently knead the dough mixture until it is soft and spongy, cover with a wet cloth and let sit for 10 to 15 minutes.
Chop calabacitas into ¼-inch squares and place into 2- to 3-quart mixing bowl.

Chop Rehydrated red chile pods(optional) into ¼-inch squares (removing stem and seeds) and place into a 2-3-quart mixing bowl.

Chop Roasted Green Chile Pods (optional) into ¼-inch squares (removing stem and seeds) and place into a 2- to 3-quart mixing bowl

Place refried beans, raisins and pinion nuts into mixing bowl and blend all ingredients.

Prepare chile paste, add Adobo Spice Mix, stir to blend and set aside in a small bowl.

ASSEMBLY:

Place one corn husk on a flat surface, spread masa 1–2 Tbsp. masa dough ¼-inch thick 1 inch from the edge toward the center of the corn husk, in 3 to 4-inch strips. (Allow enough room to fold the corn hush to completely cover the masa and filling.)

Coat the masa with chile paste. Place a strip of veggie filling on top of the masa. Place a strip of the chopped chile pods on top of the filling.

Roll the corn husk up with the filling (as if you were making a burrito). Fold the ends over and tie each with a small strip of corn husk so they will not unfold during cooking.

Cooking Instructions

Place tamales into a steamer basket, preferable vertically so steam can surround each tamale. Steam for 90 minutes. (Make sure that steamer does not run out of water).

You can place tamales into a pot of boiling water if you do not have a steamer basket. Boil for 90 minutes.

Remove tamales from steamer let cool for 5 to 10 minutes serve.

Suggested Complementary Dishes: Refried beans, rice, corn, salsa, crema, Red Chile Sauce.

Servings: 18 tamales.

Chapter 10—SIDE DISHES:
Beans, Corn, Rice, Vegetables

The fruit of the land reigns supreme in side dishes, with an endless variety of legumes, maize, rice and vegetables that are a part of the Chilenista cuisine. The side dishes set the stage for every entrée recipe. Can you imagine an enchilada without rice or beans, or a chile relleno without rice or vegetables? Beans, corn, rice and vegetables are the orchestra that plays for the main chile symphony. The following recipes will orchestrate your meals into a full taste experience.

BEANS

There are thousands varieties of beans and like chiles they are technically flowers. In the chile cuisine the primary varieties include pinto, kidney, black, white and garbanzo beans. All have a distinct flavor and texture but are used interchangeably in the following chile recipes.

Beans are considered by many nutritionists to be the perfect food, supplying all of the proteins, minerals, vitamins and fiber needed for a balanced diet.

Black Beans go well with smoky flavors such as chipotle chile and with fatty foods such as brisket and pork. Their bright, black color also gives a contrast to salsas and vegetable side dishes. They are available canned or can be made from scratch.

Garbanzo Beans are one of the world's most popular beans and are used in almost every kitchen. Their nutty taste and firm meat make an excellent complement for any chile stew.

Kidney Beans are known for their bright, reddish-brown skin and white meat. They make any dish look good, and their firm texture and nutty taste make them ideal for chile stews and an excellent companion for meat recipes. They are also one of the most nutritionally balanced of all beans.

Pinto Beans and their earthy flavor and smooth texture are the perfect companions for any chile recipe or can be eaten alone, refried into a paste and mixed in stews. They are the most used and abundantly available of all beans in the Chilenista cuisine

White Beans and their buttery flavor, smooth texture and white color make them an excellent side dish or addition to any salsa, stew or soup. All raw beans should be soaked in water over night to soften them and release their gasses.

BEANS (FROM SCRATCH)

Complexity Code: EZ   Origin: Global / Original
Cooking Method: Boil, Simmer

About the Recipe: The origin of beans is said to trace back to pre-Columbian times in Central and South America. Beans are one of the oldest cultivated foods on our planet. In the 1500s the Spanish exported beans to Europe and in turn spread the seeds throughout the world. Today, beans are used in every cuisine through the world and provide a staple ingredient for every kitchen.
Essential Recipe: Beans (p.304).

Ingredient	Measure	Ingredient	Measure
Black beans, garbanzo beans, kidney beans, pinto beans, white beans*	1 lb.	Adobo Spice Mix (p.83)	2 Tbsp.
Ham hock or Salt pork ¼ lb.	1 Piece	Vegetable oil or lard	¼ cup
		Red or Green chile powder	1-2 Tbsp.

Prep Instructions
Soak beans overnight to soften and de-gas them.
Pour soaking water out, and rinse beans to remove debris or film that may have formed on surface.

Cooking Instructions
Cover beans with cold water; add ham hock or salt pork. Boil beans over medium flame (slow boil); stir occasionally until the beans are soft 1 to 2 hours. Preheat oven to 235°F.
Slow Cook
Place covered beans in oven same as above and slow cook for 4 to 6 hours or overnight. You will have the best tasting beans you have ever had. (No fuss no muss.) Slow cooking keeps all of the flavors in and heats the beans evenly. You can also use a crockpot to slow cook the beans.

Suggested Complementary Dishes: Any meat, fish, chicken or vegetable dish or just beans.

Serves 4–6 people

REFRIED BEANS FROM A CAN OR DRY MIX
RED OR GREEN

Complexity Code: EZ
Origin: Original
Cooking Method: Sautee

About the Recipe: Refried bean mix is available in both dry and canned versions and with a little bit of TLC can taste homemade with this recipe. Canned or dried refried beans are an easy alternative to serving a small amount of beans with relative ease. Choose whatever variety you wish. **Essential Recipe:** Rehydrated Red Chile pods (p.40), OR Roasted Green Chile (p.46).

Ingredient	Measure	Ingredient	Measure
Refried Beans, canned or dry mix	16 oz. can	Adobo Spice Mix (p.83)	2 Tbsp.
Rehydrated red chile pods Ancho, Pasilla, Chipotle or Chile Seco SHU to taste	1 cup	Butter, vegetable oil or lard	¼ cup
Roasted green chile Anaheim, Poblano, Jalapeño SHU to taste	1 cup chopped	Red or green chile powder SHU to taste	1–2 Tbsp. To taste
Onion	1 cup chopped		

Prep Instructions
Rehydrate dried beans as per the instructions on the package or open a can.
Chop rehydrated red chile pods into ¼-inch squares; removing stem and seeds, place in mixing bowl. Chop roasted green chile into ¼-inch squares; removing stem and seeds, place in mixing bowl.

Cooking Instructions
In a heavy skillet sauté chopped chile pods and onions in vegetable oil or lard. (I have found that lightly sautéed onions work better then caramelized onions.) Add refried beans, Adobo Spice Mix and chile powder to taste. Stir until all ingredients are blended.

Suggested Complementary Dishes: Any New Mexico entrée.

REFRIED BEANS HOMEMADE—RED OR GREEN

Complexity Code: Cook   Origin: New Mexico
Cooking Method: Boil, Sautee

About the Recipe: Refried beans are a staple for any red chile recipe and are usually served as a side dish to garnish and enhance the main entrée. Homemade refried beans are the best. You can select the type of beans to use (p.304) the ingredients you use and the heat level.
Essential Recipe: Beans (p.304), Rehydrated Red Chile Pods (p.40), OR Roasted Green Chile Pods (p.46).

Ingredient	Measure	Ingredient	Measure
Pinto beans, black beans, kidney beans or garbanzo beans	1 lb.	Adobo Spice Mix (p.83)	2 Tbsp.
Rehydrated red chile pods Ancho, Pasilla, Chipotle or Chile Seco SHU to taste	1 cup chopped	Vegetable oil or lard	¼ cup
Roasted green chile Anaheim, Poblano, Jalapeño SHU to taste	1 cup chopped	**OPTIONAL:** Ham hock	
Onions	1 cup chopped	**OPTIONAL:** Salt pork	
Red or Green Chile powder SHU to taste	1–2 Tbsp.		

Prep Instructions
Soak beans overnight to soften and de-gas them.
Pour soaking water out; rinse beans to remove debris or film that may have formed on surface.
Chop rehydrated red chile pods into ¼-inch squares; removing stem and seeds, place in mixing bowl. Chop Roasted green chile into ¼-inch squares, removing stem and seeds, and place in mixing bowl.

Cooking Instructions
Cover beans with cold water; boil beans over medium flame (slow boil). Stir occasionally until the beans are soft 2 to 3 hours. (Place ham hock or salt pork into boiling water (optional).
Drain water from beans and place in a 3- to 4-quart mixing bowl; let cool 30 to 45 minutes. You can also cool by rinsing under cold water.

Mash beans with a potato masher or blender, leaving some chunks. The beans should have a mashed potato texture.

In a food processor chop/blend ham hock or salt pork and add to mashed beans.

In a large heavy skillet sauté chopped chile pods and onions in vegetable oil or lard. (I have found that lightly sautéed onions work better than caramelized onions.)

Add mashed beans, Adobo Spice Mix and chile powder to taste (1 Tbsp. at a time).

Stir until all ingredients are blended.

Suggested Complementary Dishes: Any New Mexico Entrée.

CREAMY REFRIED BEANS—RED OR GREEN

Complexity Code: EZ   Origin: New Mexico Original
Cooking Method: Sautee

About the Recipe: Creamy refried beans add a richness and flavor to
refried beans and give them a silky consistency that will allow you to use
the refried beans as a topping, dip or base for any recipe.
Essential Recipe: Rehydrated Red Chile pods (p.40), OR Roasted
Green Chile (p.46).

Ingredient	Measure	Ingredient	Measure
Refried beans (Homemade, dry mix or canned)	2 cups	Crema or sour cream	1 cup
Rehydrated red chile pods Ancho, Pasilla, Chipotle or Chile Seco SHU to taste	1 cup	Butter, vegetable oil or lard	¼ cup
Roasted green chile Anaheim, Poblano, Jalapeño SHU to taste	1 cup chopped	Red or green chile powder (garnish) SHU to taste	1-2 Tbsp. To taste
Onion	1 cup	Cilantro (garnish)	To taste

Prep Instructions
Rehydrate dried beans as per the instructions on the package or open a
can.
Chop Rehydrated red chile pods into ¼-inch squares; removing stem
and seeds, place in mixing bowl. Chop Roasted green chile into ¼-inch
squares; removing stem and seeds, place in mixing bowl.

Cooking Instructions
In a heavy skillet sauté chopped chile pods and onions in vegetable oil or
lard. (I have found that lightly sautéed onions work better then caramelized
onions.) Add refried beans, Adobo Spice Mix, crema and chile powder to
taste. Stir until all ingredients are blended.
Garnish with cilantro.

Suggested Complementary Dishes: Any New Mexico entrée.

NEW MEXICO GREEN CHILE BAKED BEANS

Complexity Code: EZ   Origin: Original
Cooking Method: Bake

About the Recipe: New Mexico Green Chile Baked Beans are very easy
to make and always are enjoyed as a side dish.
Essential Recipe: Beans From Scratch (p.304), Creamy Green Chile
Sauce (p.52), Roasted green chile((p.46), Mole Verde (p.81).

Ingredient	Measure	Ingredient	Measure
Beans From Scratch or canned, Pinto, black, kidney, white	4 cups	Adobo Spice Mix (p.83)	1 Tbsp.
Creamy Green Chile Sauce	2 cup	Mole Verde	2 Tbsp.
Roasted green chile SHU to taste	2 cups chopped	Sweetener (p.85)	1 cup
Onion	1 cup chopped	Bacon	6–8 strips
Tomatoes	1 cup chopped		
Cilantro	1 cup chopped		

Prep Instructions
Preheat oven to 375°F.
Drain can of beans of all liquid, rinse canned beans and place in 3-quart
casserole dish or baking pan. Mix Creamy Green Chile Sauce, Fresh
Green Chile, chopped onion, chopped tomato, Mole Verde and sweetener
until all ingredients are blended.
Cover top of pan with bacon strips.

Cooking Instructions
Place baking pan in center of oven and bake for 45 to 60 minutes until
beans start to bubble heavily and bacon starts to brown.
Increase oven heat to 425°F for 5 to 10 minutes to crisp bacon. Remove
from oven and let cool for 10 to 15 minutes.

Suggested Complementary Dishes: Shredded cheese, Fresh Green
Chile, tortilla, tortilla chips, any meat, chicken or fish dish or as a meal by
itself.

Servings: 8–12 cups.

NEW MEXICO RED CHILE BAKED BEANS

Complexity Code: EZ   Origin: Original
Cooking Method: Bake

About the Recipe: New Mexico Red Chile Baked Beans are very easy to
make and are always enjoyed as a side dish.
Essential Recipe: Beans From Scratch (p.304), Red Chile Sauce (p.36),
Rehydrated red chile pods (optional) (p.40), Red Chile Tomato Sauce
(p.37).

Ingredient	Measure		Measure
Beans From Scratch or canned, Pinto, black, kidney, white	4 cups	Adobo Spice Mix (p.83)	1 Tbsp.
Red Chile Sauce	2 cups	Annatto paste	1 Tbsp.
Rehydrated red chile pods, Ancho, Pasilla, Chipotle or Chile Seco SHU to taste	2 cups chopped	Sweetener (p.85)	1 cup
Red Chile Tomato Sauce	1 cup	Bacon	6 -8 strips
Onion	1 cup chopped		
Cilantro chopped	1 cup chopped		

Prep Instructions
Preheat Oven to 375°F.
Drain can of beans of all liquid, rinse canned beans and place in 3- to
4-quart casserole dish or baking pan. Mix Red Chile Sauce, chopped red
chile, chopped onion, chopped cilantro, Adobo Spice Mix, annatto paste
and sweetener until well blended.
Cover top of pan with bacon strips.

Cooking Instructions
Place baking pan in center of oven and bake for 45 to 60 minutes until
beans start to bubble heavily and bacon starts to brown. Increase oven heat
to 425°F for 5 to 10 minutes to crisp bacon.
Remove from oven and let cool for 10 to 15 minutes.

Suggested Complementary Dishes: Shredded cheese, Fresh Green
Chile, tortilla, tortilla chips, any meat, chicken or fish dish or as a meal by
itself.

Servings 8–12 cups.

CORN—MAIZE

Corn can trace it roots to ten thousand years ago in the ancient South American cultures and has provided the sustenance in fresh, dried, milled and now frozen varieties. There are thousands of ways to prepare and cook corn. We have a brief sampling in the corn recipes as it is used in the chile cuisine from on-the-cob to pan-roasted to baked.

CHICOS—RED OR GREEN

Complexity Code: EZ   Origin: New Mexico
Cooking Method: Sauté, Boil, Simmer

About the Recipe: Chicos are dried corn kernels that were stored as a food mainstay for the winter months. They can be ground to make corn flour and rehydrated for soups, stews or a mix with other vegetables. This recipe is about rehydrating chicos for soups or stews.
Essential Recipe: Red Chile Sauce (p.36), Rehydrated Red Chile (p.40),OR Fresh Green Chile (p.44), Green Chile Sauce (p.50).

Ingredient	Measure	Ingredient	Measure
Chicos (rehydrated)	2 cups	Adobo Spice Mix (p.83)	2 Tbsp.
Water or chicken broth	8 cups	Chicken bouillon (if using water)	2 Tbsp.
Fresh Green Chile or Chopped Red Chile SHU to taste	1 cup		
Onion	1 cup chopped	**OPTIONAL:** Green Chile Sauce or Red Chile Sauce	1 cup
Vegetable oil	2 Tbsp.		

Prep Instructions
Wash and rinse chicos. Soak in a stockpot overnight until chicos are soft; drain soaking water.
Place oil, onion and Fresh Green Chile into a 3- to 4-quart stockpot.

Cooking Instructions
Sauté onion until it becomes translucent.
Add 8 cups of water and bullion to stockpot and bring to a boil.
Add chicos, red or green chile and lower heat to a simmer (gentle bubbles).
Simmer chicos in an uncovered pot for 2 hours or until chicos are soft and most of the liquid has evaporated.
Optionally add Green Chile or Red Chile Sauce for additional flavor.

Suggested Complementary Dishes: Chicos can be served as a soup or added to a stew or served as a side dish that goes with any recipe.
Servings: 6–8 cups.

CORN ON THE COB

Complexity Code: EZ   Origin: Ancient
Cooking Method: Barbecue (dry-heat) / Bake

About the Recipe: Corn on the cob is a complete package onto itself; it does need any enhancement, however, a bit of chile powder red or green is sure to please any Chilenista.
Whether you BBQ, bake, steam, or boil. The result is the same: the greatest food on the planet.

Ingredient	Measure
Corn on the Cob	4 ears of corn, one per person

Cooking Instructions

Barbecue
Preheat BBQ to medium heat 325^0F- to 350^0F.
Fold corn husks back from ears of corn, remove silk, snap husks from the ear at the base and recover ear with the husk and soak in water for about 5 to 10 minutes.
Shake off excess water, place in BBQ rack and cook for 20 to 25 minutes, turning corn every 5 minutes to make sure that each side is evenly cooked. Corn does not get better than this.

Bake
Pre-heat oven to 350^0F.
Place ears of corn on a flat baking pan with a rack and follow instructions for BBQ. (No need to turn, the oven disperses the heat more evenly.)

Steam (Wet Heat)
Place a steamer basket in a 3- to 4-quart stockpot, pour 2 inches of water to cover bottom and heat to boil.
Remove husk and silk from corn and place in stockpot, cover and steam for 20 to 30 minutes. Remove corn and it is ready to eat. (This is my favorite.)

BOIL: (Wet Heat)
Bring a stockpot to a boil with enough water to cover the corn.
Remove husk and silk from corn and place in stockpot, cover and steam for 20 – 30 minutes. **OPTIONAL:** Put milk in stockpot with or without any water and bring to a boil. The milk will bring an additional sweetness to the corn.

Suggested Complementary Dishes: Sprinkle red or green chile powder, butter, salt and enjoy.

GREEN CHILE CHEESE & CORN BAKE

Complexity Code: EZ   Origin: Original
Cooking Method: Bake

About the Recipe: Green chile, cheese, and corn sounds like a recipe made in heaven, and you can make it in your kitchen with this easy recipe **Essential Recipe:** Roasted Green Chile (p.46).

Ingredient	Measure		Measure
Corn (Fresh, frozen or canned)	4 cups	Adobo Spice Mix (p.83)	1 Tbsp.
Roasted green chile Anaheim, Poblano, Jalapeño SHU to taste	1 cup chopped	Sweetener (p.85)	2 Tbsp.
Heavy cream	½ cup	Baking powder	1 tsp.
Shredded cheese blend Asadero, cheddar, Jack, queso quesadilla	1 cup	Cornmeal or crushed tortilla chips	1 cup
Eggs	2	Vegetable oil	2 Tbsp.

Prep Instructions

Preheat oven 350°F.
Grease a 9-by-13-inch roasting pan or casserole dish with vegetable oil.
Place eggs in a medium mixing bowl; add heavy cream, Adobo Spice Mix, sweetener and baking powder. Whip until bubbles form; you can use a blender stick.
Fold in cornmeal and mix until totally blended with egg mixture. Fold in green chile and shredded cheese and mix until totally blended. Pour mixture into roasting pan.

Cooking Instructions

Place roasting pan in center of oven; Bake for 45 to 60 minutes.
Remove pan from oven and let cool for 5 to 10 minutes.

Suggested Complementary Dishes: Burrito, tamale, BBQ, sausage.
Serves: 6–8 people.

GREEN CHILE CORN PAN-ROAST

Complexity Code: EZ   Origin: Original
Cooking Method: Pan-roast

About the Recipe: This is a great simple recipe that combines the flavors of corn and green chile.
Essential Recipe: Roasted Green Chile (p.46), Creamy Green Chile Sauce (p.52), Mole Verde (p.81).

Ingredient	Measure	Ingredient	Measure
Corn kernels	2 cups	Adobo Spice Mix (p.83)	1 Tbsp.
Roasted green chile Anaheim, Poblano, Jalapeño SHU to taste	2 cups chopped	Mole Verde	2 Tbsp.
Creamy Green Chile Sauce	1 cup	Sweetener (p.85)	2 Tbsp.
		Vegetable oil or butter	2 Tbsp.

Prep Instructions
Use preferably fresh or frozen corn. If using canned, strain and rinse. Chop chile. Blend sweetener, Adobo Spice Mix, mole verde and butter over low heat. (Do not boil.)

Cooking Instructions
Coat heavy skillet bottom with oil; add corn, Fresh Green Chile and Creamy Green Chile Sauce. Sauté for 2 to 3 minutes. Add sweetener and bring to a boil; immediately reduce heat to a simmer for 5 to 10 minutes.
OPTIONAL: Place pan-roasted Green Chile Corn into a small roasting pan and place in a 350°F oven for 10 to 15 minutes to crisp the corn and green chile.

Suggested Complementary Dishes: Any dish will be enhanced by this recipe on the side.

Serves: 4 people.

POSOLE OR HOMINY—RED OR GREEN

Complexity Code: EZ   Origin: Ancient
Cooking Method: Sauté, Boil, Simmer

About the Recipe: Hominy or posole is one of the most ancient
processed foods consisting of corn that has been treated in a lime or lye
mixture to remove the husk and make the corn more digestible.
Hominy can be ground into flour to create masa harina, the basic
ingredient for almost all tortillas, enchiladas and chips. Hominy is also used
in soups and stews and is called "posole" in the Chilenista cuisine.
Essential Recipe: Rehydrated Red Chile (p.40), Red Chile Sauce (p.36),
OR Roasted Green Chile (p.46), Green Chile Sauce (p.50).

Ingredient	Measure	Ingredient	Measure
Posole, (Dry-Rehydrated) Canned or frozen	2 cup 4 cups	Adobo Spice Mix (p.83)	2 Tbsp.
Water or chicken Broth	8 cups	Chicken bouillon (if using water)	2 Tbsp.
Roasted green chile or Chopped Rehydrated Red Chile	1 cup chopped		
Onion	1 cup chopped	**OPTIONAL:** Green Chile Sauce or Red Chile Sauce	1 cup
Vegetable oil	2 Tbsp.		

Prep Instructions
Wash and rinse hominy; Soak in a stockpot overnight until chicos are soft;
drain soaking water.
If using canned posole, rinse to get rid of any preservative. If using frozen
posole defrost thoroughly until soft.
Place oil, onion and chopped Roasted Green Chile into a 3- to 4-quart
stockpot.

Cooking Instructions
Sauté onion until it becomes translucent.
Add 8 cups of water and bullion to stockpot and bring to a boil.
Add posole, red or green chile and lower heat to a simmer (gentle
bubbles).
Simmer chicos in an uncovered pot for 2 hours or until chicos are soft and
most of the liquid has evaporated.
Optionally add Green Chile or Red Chile Sauce for additional flavor.

Suggested Complementary Dishes: Posole can be served as a soup,
added to a stew or served as a side dish that goes with any recipe.

Servings: 6–8 cups.

RICE

Rice is the most ancient of all cultivated foods dating back thousands of years. It has over 10,000 varieties and was introduced to the New World by the Spanish in the 1500s and has been part of the chile cuisine ever since.

Rice comes in three basic varieties: long grain, medium grain and short grain, all with differing cooked characteristics. Long grain rice is less starchy and usually more aromatic and offers a discreet grain that does not stick to the other ingredients. It is great as a side dish with almost any recipe.

Medium grain rice is starchier and sticks to the other ingredients around it. It is great for recipes that combine ingredients such as rice and beans or rice and vegetables.

Short grain rice is very starchy and will stick to itself as well as absorb any of the ingredients that are cooked with it. It is great with stews and is the favorite of the Chilenista cuisine, as it will absorb the chile around it.

The main cooking techniques for rice are boiling, roasting and steaming in a rice cooker. The recipes in this chapter illustrate a few methods and recipes that you can use to make the perfect rice with the perfect dish.

BOILED, ROASTED OR STEAMED WHITE RICE

Complexity Code: Cook   Origin: Ancient
Cooking Method: Sauté, Pan-roast (Chilenista favorite)

About the Recipe: Boiled or steamed rice forms the platform for any recipe as a main meal or side dish. Roasting short grain rice is the choice for most traditional New Mexico kitchens, giving it a roasted, sticky quality for any chile to coat the rice kernels. If you are in a hurry, a rice cooker offers a great alternative.

Ingredient	Measure
Rice (Short, medium or long grain)	1 cup
Water or chicken broth	2 cups
Vegetable oil	2 Tbsp.

Prep Instructions

Soak rice in cold water to remove any dirt and excess surface starch that will make your rice stick while cooking. Strain rice with a colander or strainer and place in a mixing bowl for 2 to 3 minutes to soak up moisture.

Pan-roast
Heat 2 Tbsp. of oil in heavy skillet (high heat). Place washed rice into skillet and stir vigorously to slightly toast rice. (It will crackle.) Pour water into skillet and bring to a boil. Reduce heat, cover skillet and simmer (low heat) for 20 to 30 minutes. (Resist the urge to peek into the pan, as the rice needs the steam to cook.) At the end of 20 minutes, dry, add water (¼ to ½ cup) and simmer for another 10 minutes.
Pour rice in a 9 x 13-inch baking pan and place in preheated oven for 15 minutes. If the rice is too moist, leave in oven for an additional 10 minutes.
Boiling
Prep and sauté rice as above.
Boil water in a 2-quart, pan, add toasted rice, reduce heat, cover pot and simmer for 20 to 30 minutes. (Resist the urge to peek into the pan, as the rice needs the steam to cook.)
At the end of 20 minutes, if the rice is too dry, add water (¼ to ½) cup and simmer for another 10 minutes. Place rice into baking pan as above and place in oven.
Rice Cooker
(A rice cooker assures that you will have perfect rice every time.)
Prep and sauté rice as above.
Place toasted rice into rice cooker, cover and turn it on. The rice will be ready in 30 to 40 minutes. Place rice into baking pan as above and place in oven.

Suggested Complementary Dishes: Any dish can be enhanced by adding rice or serving it with beans. Rice and beans are said to be a totally balanced meal and are a staple food for many.

NEW MEXICO TOASTED RICE

Complexity Code: Cook   Origin: New Mexico
Cooking Method: Pan Roast

About the Recipe: Toasted rice is the foundation of the Chilenista cuisine as a main meal or side dish. Pan-roasting short grain rice is the choice for most traditional New Mexico kitchens, giving it a roasted, sticky quality for any chile to coat the rice kernels. If you are in a hurry, a rice cooker offers a great alternative. The Adobo and Achiote will give the rice a nutty, aromatic flavor that does not need any other spices.
Essential Recipe: Adobo Spice Mix (p.83)

Ingredient	Measure	Ingredient	Measure
Rice (short, medium or long grain)	1 cup	Adobo Spice Mix (p.83)	1 Tbsp.
Water or chicken broth	2 cups	Achiote or Annatto powder or paste	1 Tbsp.
Tomato boullion	1 tsp.	Vegetable oil	2 Tbsp.

Prep Instructions

Soak rice in a mixing bowl of cold water for 2 to 3 to remove any dirt and excess surface starch that will make your rice stick while cooking. Strain rice with a colander or strainer and place in a dry bowl.
Dissolve achiote or annatto paste, Adobo Spice Mix and tomato boullion into 2 cups of water or chicken broth. (Spiced water)

Sauté, Pan-roast
Heat 2 Tbsp. of oil in heavy skillet (high heat). Place washed rice into skillet and stir vigorously to slightly toast rice. (It will crackle.) Pour spiced water into skillet and bring to a boil. Reduce heat, cover skillet and simmer (low heat) for 20 to 30 minutes. (Resist the urge to peek into the pan, as the rice needs the steam to cook.) At the end of 20 minutes, if the rice is too dry, add water (1/4 to 1/2) cup and simmer for another 10 minutes. Pour rice in a 9-by-13-inch baking pan and place in preheated oven for 15 minutes. If the rice is too moist, leave it in the oven for an additional 10 minutes.

Rice Cooker, Pan-roast
A rice cooker assures that you will have perfect rice every time. Prep and sauté rice as above. Place toasted rice in a rice cooker, pour spiced water into rice cooker, cover and turn it on. The rice will be ready in 20 to 30 minutes. Place rice into baking pan as above and place in oven.

Boiling
Prep and sauté rice as above.
Boil spiced water in 2-quart, pan, add toasted rice, reduce heat, cover pot and simmer for 20 to 30 minutes. (Resist the urge to peek into the pan, as the rice needs the steam to cook.) At the end of 20 minutes, if the rice is too dry, add ¼ to ½ cups of water and simmer for another 10 minutes. Place rice into baking pan as above and place in oven.

Suggested Complementary Dishes: Any dish can be enhanced by adding New Mexican rice.

NEW MEXICO DIRTY RICE

Complexity Code: Cook   Origin: New Mexico
Cooking Method: Sauté, Pan-roast

About the Recipe: Dirty rice is a recipe without a known origin; I would imagine that having some leftover beans and vegetables had something to do with its evolution. It has however, become a staple in almost every kitchen. I would recommend adding a bit of chile to spice it up.
Essential Recipe: Roasted Green Chile (p.46)

Ingredient	Measure	Ingredient	Measure
Rice	1 cup	Adobo Spice Mix (p.83)	1 Tbsp.
Water	2 cups	Achiote or Annatto powder or paste	1 Tbsp.
Roasted green chile, Anaheim, Poblano, or Jalapeño SHU to taste	1 cup chopped	Tomato boullion	1 tsp.
Onion	1 cup chopped	Cilantro	¼ cup
Tomato	1 cup chopped	Pignola or walnuts	¼ cup
Beans (Pinto, black, kidney)	1 cup	Vegetable or olive oil	2 Tbsp.
Corn (frozen or canned)	1 cup		

Prep Instructions
Soak rice in a mixing bowl of cold water for 2 to 3 to remove any dirt and excess surface starch that will make your rice stick while cooking. Strain rice with a colander or strainer and place in a dry bowl.
Dissolve achiote or annatto paste, Adobo Spice Mix and tomato boullion into 2 cups of water or chicken broth. (Spiced water)
Preheat oven to 250°F.

Cooking Instructions
Heat oil (high heat) in a large skillet add chopped roasted green chile, onion and sauté for 2 to 3 minutes. Add rice and stir to toast rice 1 to 2 minutes.
Add water to skillet and bring to a boil. Cover pan and lower heat to simmer for 20 to 30 minutes until rice is soft. (Resist the urge to peek into the pan, as the rice needs the steam to cook.) At the end of 20 minutes, if the rice is too dry, add water (¼ to ½ cups) and simmer for another 10 minutes.

Mix tomato, beans, corn, nuts, cilantro and any other ingredients that you may have around into a lightly greased baking pan. Add cooked rice into the pan; mix all ingredients.

Place baking pan in center of oven for 15 minutes to blend all ingredients. (If the rice is a bit moist, leave in oven for an additional 5 to 10 minutes.) Remove pan from oven, let cool for 5 minutes and serve.

Suggested Complementary Dishes: Any recipe is complemented with dirty rice on the side, or have it as a main meal.

Serves: 6–8 people.

FRIED RICE—RED OR GREEN

Complexity Code: EZ   Origin: Original
Cooking Method: Sauté, Pan-fry

About the Recipe: Everything tastes better fried and rice is no exception. Choose any rice recipe and pan-fry it.
Essential Recipe: Rice recipe (p.317), Roasted Green Chile (p.46), OR Rehydrated Red Chile pods (p.40)

Ingredient	Measure	Ingredient	Measure
Cooked rice	2–4 cups	Vegetable oil or lard	2–3 Tbsp.
OPTIONAL: Ground beef, chorizos, shrimp or scrambled eggs		Roasted green chile or Rehydrated Red Chile Pods	chopped
		Celery	chopped
		Squash	chopped
		Corn	
		Peas	
		Tomato	chopped
		Cilantro	chopped

Prep Instructions
Prepare any rice recipe and allow rice to cool to room temperature.

Cooking Instructions
Heat oil (very hot) to 360^{0}F in a heavy skillet.
Place rice in skillet and stir fry with any additional ingredients that you may wish to add such as meat, fish or vegetables.
Sauté for 5 to 10 minutes until all ingredients are blended.

Suggested Complementary Dishes: Any dish or serve as a full meal.

Serves: 4–6 people.

NEW MEXICO RICE—RED OR GREEN

Complexity Code: EZ   Origin: New Mexico
Cooking Method: Sauté / Boil / Rice cooker

About the Recipe: Chile rice will enhance any dish either as a side or
main meal.
Essential Recipe: Rice (p.317), Rehydrated Red Chile pods (p.40), OR
Roasted Green Chile (p.46).

Ingredient	Measure	Ingredient	Measure
Rice (medium or long grain)	1 cup	Adobo Spice Mix (p.83)	1 Tbsp.
Water	2 cups	Mexican saffron or turmeric	1 Tbsp.
Rehydrated red chile pods, Ancho, Pasilla, Chipotle or Chile Seco SHU to taste	1 cup	Onion	½ cup chopped
Roasted green chile. Anaheim, Poblano, Jalapeño SHU to taste	1 cup chopped	Tomato	½ cup chopped
		Vegetable oil	2 Tbsp.

Prep Instructions
Rinse rice in a bowl, drain and repeat until all white powder (starch) is
removed.
Chop Rehydrated Red Chile Pods into ¼-inch squares; removing stem
and seeds, place in mixing bowl. Chop Roasted Green Chile into ¼-inch
squares, removing stem and seeds, and place in mixing bowl. Chop, onion
and tomato into ¼-inch squares.
Heat oil in a large heavy skillet 3- to 4-quart stockpot.

Cooking Instructions
Place one grain of rice to test if it sizzles. Add rest of rice and constantly
stir until it is lightly roasted (3 to 5 minutes until it starts to lightly brown.)
Add water to skillet and bring to boil, adding chopped chile pods, onion,
tomatoes, Adobo Spice Mix and saffron; lower heat, cover pan and
simmer rice until tender 15 to 20 minutes.
Rice Cooker (If you have one)
Place rice, adobe spice mix, saffron and water in rice cooker and turn on.
When most of the water has been absorbed, add chopped chile pods,
onion, tomato and stir to mix all ingredients.
When rice cooker completes its cycle, fluff rice and serve.

Suggested Complementary Dishes: Any recipe in this book as a side
or main meal.
Serves: 4–6 people.

QUINOA—RED OR GREEN

Complexity Code: EZ   Origin: Ancient
Cooking Method: Sauté, Pan-roast

About the Recipe: Quinoa is a native plant to the Aztec and Mayan cultures that has a cultural legacy similar to beans and can provide all the nourishment necessary for a healthy diet. Although it is not very popular in the United States, it is very popular and a staple of the traditional Mexican kitchen. Prepared like rice, it can be pan-roasted, cooked in a rice cooker or boiled. Quinoa has a nutty taste and consistency, is gluten-free and feels good to eat. "The real thing" is the best way to describe it. Once you have served it, you will surely want to make it over and over again.
Please look at the rice recipes for additional ways to prepare quinoa.
Essential Recipe: Rice (p. 317), Rehydrated Red Chile pods (p.40), Roasted Green Chile (p.46)

Ingredient	Measure	Ingredient	Measure
Quinoa	1 cup	Adobo Spice Mix (p.83)	1 Tbsp.
Water or chicken broth	2 cups	Vegetable oil	2 Tbsp.
Rehydrated red chile pods, Ancho, Pasilla, Chipotle or Chile Seco SHU to taste	1 cup	Onion	½ cup chopped
Roasted green chile Anaheim, Poblano, Jalapeño SHU to taste	1 cup chopped	Tomato	½ cup chopped

Prep Instructions

Rinse quinoa under water to clean and remove any foreign matter.
Chop rehydrated red chile Pods into ¼-inch squares; removing stem and seeds, place in mixing bowl.
Chop roasted green chile into ¼-inch squares, removing stem and seeds, and place in mixing bowl. Finely chop onion and tomato into ¼-inch squares.
Finely chop onion and tomato into ¼-inch squares.
Heat 2 Tbsp. of oil in heavy skillet (high heat). Place washed rice into skillet and stir vigorously to slightly toast quinoa. Pour water into skillet and bring to a boil. Reduce heat, add red or green chile, onions, tomato and Adobo Spice Mix, stir and cover skillet, and simmer (low heat) for 20 to 30 minutes. (Resist the urge to peek into the pan, as the quinoa needs the steam to cook.) At the end of 20 minutes, if the quinoa is too dry, add water (¼ to ½ cups) and simmer for another 10 minutes.
Pour quinoa into a 9-by-13-inch baking pan and place in preheated oven for 15 minutes. If the quinoa is too moist, leave in oven for an additional 10 minutes.

Rice Cooker, Pan-roast
(A rice cooker assures that you will have perfect quinoa every time.)
Prep and sauté quinoa as above.
Place toasted quinoa in a rice cooker, pour water into rice cooker, add red or green chile, onions, tomato and Adobo Spice Mix and stir. Cover rice cooker and turn it on. The rice will be ready in 20 to 30 minutes.
Place rice into baking pan as above and place in oven.

Boil
Prep and sauté quinoa as above.
Boil water in 2-quart pan, add toasted quinoa, red or green chile, onions, tomato and Adobo Spice Mix, stir and reduce heat, cover pot and simmer for 20-30 minutes. (Resist the urge to peek into the pan, the quinoa needs the steam to cook.) At the end of 20 minutes, if the rice is too dry, add water (¼ to ½ cups) and simmer for another 10 minutes.
Place quinoa into baking pan as above and place in oven.

Suggested Complementary Dishes: Any dish can be enhanced by adding quinoa, or serve it with beans.

VEGETABLES

The Chilenista cuisine is a seasonal cuisine that uses any vegetable available with a variety of chile choices. Although chile is technically a flower, it is often used and referred to in recipes as a vegetable. Please look at the ESSENTIAL RECIPES Chapter (p.32) for ways to prepare Red or Green chile.

Fresh Chile Pods
Anaheim, poblano and jalapeño can be cleaned and sliced into strips and incorporated into any of your vegetable recipes to add the Chilenista touch. The delicate flavors, aroma and capsaicin will enhance all of your vegetable dishes. If fresh chile pods are not available, frozen or canned chiles will do.

Leafy Greens
Chard, chicory, collard, kale or spinach fresh or frozen are the ultimate side dishes for many of the chile recipes; they provide a garden-fresh taste to any chile recipe.

Vegetables
Asparagus, broccoli, green beans, squash and zucchini will provide a refreshing texture and taste to any chile dish. If fresh vegetables are not available frozen or canned will do.

CREMA AGRIA—RED OR GREEN

Complexity Code: EZ   Origin: New Mexico

About the Recipe: Crema Agria and Crema Mexicana are the most subtle tastes that exist in the Chile palate. A cross between sour cream and yogurt, slightly fermented and mildly sweet, they can be used as a topping to add sparkle and color to any chile dish or as a condiment to enhance the taste. Most importantly, they cut down the capsaicin of way-too-hot chile and allow you to take the next bite. This recipe belongs in every chile first-aid kit.

Essential Recipe: Rehydrated Red Chile pods (p.40), Roasted Green Chile (p.46), Crema (p.353).

Ingredient	Measure		Measure
Sour cream	1 cup	Rehydrated Red Chile pods	¼ cup chopped
Buttermilk	¼ cup	Roasted green chile	¼ cup chopped
*Stored bought Crema can be used.			

Prep Instructions

Blend sour cream and buttermilk in a small saucepan with a whisk or stick blender. (You can use store bought prepared Crema Agria or Crema Mexicana).

Chop Rehydrated Red Chile Pods into ¼-inch squares; removing stem and seeds, place in mixing bowl.

Chop Roasted green chile into ¼-inch squares, removing stem and seeds, place in mixing bowl.

Simmer the blend over low heat. Do not let it bubble.

Pour contents into a glass jar and let cool at room temperature 70 degrees overnight.

You now have made your own red or green chile crema. Use it liberally and often for any chile recipe.

BLANCHED GREEN CHILE
LEAFY GREENS OR VEGETABLES

Complexity Code: EZ   Origin: New Mexico
Cooking Method: Steam

About the Recipe: Blanching and boiling are the same process.
Blanching is boiling the vegetables just enough to break down some of the
fibers and immediately stopping the boiling under cold water to preserve
the taste, texture, vitamins and minerals that prolonged boiling would
destroy.
Simply put, you leave the flavor in the vegetable, prior to its leaching into
the water as you would in a soup.
Chard, chicory, collard, kale and spinach are among my favorite greens.
Asparagus, broccoli, green beans, squash and zucchini are among my
favorite vegetables. Green chile combines to turn any veggie into a
Chilenista favorite.
Essential Recipe: Fresh Green Chile Pods (p.44)

Ingredient	Measure	Ingredient	Measure
LEAFY GREENS: Chard, Chicory, Collard, Kale, or Spinach. Fresh or frozen	8 cups	**OPTIONAL:** Seasoning	
VEGETABLES: Asparagus, broccoli, green beans, squash and zucchini.	4 cups	Green chile powder	1-2 Tbsp.
Fresh Green Chile Pods Anaheim, Poblano, Jalapeño SHU to taste	2 cups	Garlic powder	1 tsp.
Water (Steaming)	12 cups	Butter	¼ cup
Salt	2 Tbsp.	Lime or lemon juice	¼ cup
		Salt	To taste

Prep Instructions
Bring a pot of water to a brisk boil and add salt. (The salt will preserve the
green color and keep the veggies crisp.)
Cut leafy greens into halves, removing stems and tops, or cut vegetables
into 1-inch squares.
Clean chile pods, cut in half, removing stem and seeds, and cut into strips.

Cooking Instructions
Place stems and Fresh Green Chile Pods into bottom of steamer and cover
pot 3 to 4 minutes.
Add leaf tops into steamer and cover pot 3 to 4 minutes.

Or

Place cut vegetables into the boiling water. The vegetables should turn a bright green when ready. (Do not overcook, no one likes mushy vegetables.)

Place pot under cold water to stop boiling and cool vegetables to warm. Drain pot and add optional seasonings to taste. Serve immediately or place vegetables in a baking pan to keep warm in a 175^0F oven until ready to serve.

Suggested Complementary Dishes: Any main dish.

Serves: 4–6 people.

CALABACITAS (THREE SISTERS)

Complexity Code: Cook   Origin: New Mexico
Cooking Method: Sauté, Bake

About the Recipe: Traditionally many Native Americans consider the
Three Sisters, corn, beans and squash the perfect harvest food.

Ingredient	Measure	Ingredient	Measure
Yellow squash	1 cup	Mild white cheese Asadero	½ cup
Zucchini	1 cup	Olive oil	2 Tbsp.
Corn (fresh or frozen)	1 cup	Garlic powder	1tsp
Beans – Pinto, kidney	1 cup	Salt	To taste
Mild onion	½ cup chopped		

Prep Instructions

Preheat frying pan to middle heat 300^0F. Preheat oven to $350F^0$.
Cut squash and zucchini by quartering lengthwise and then chopping into
½-inch chunks.
Defrost or cut fresh corn; you can use canned corn, however make sure to
rinse off the preservatives in the can.
Chop a small to medium size sweet onion into ¼-inch pieces.

Cooking Instructions

Sauté chopped onion and garlic in olive oil until onions are just threatening
to brown and then add squash and- zucchini until they are about half done.
Add beans and corn.
Place sautéed veggies into a 9-by-9-inch casserole dish and mix in cheese.
Bake in preheated oven for ½ hour.

Suggested Complementary Dishes: As a side dish to any recipe or
main dish with tortillas.

Servings: 4 cups.

GREEN CHILE CALABACITAS (THREE SISTERS)

Complexity Code: Cook   Origin: New Mexico
Cooking Method: Sauté, Bake

About the Recipe: Three Sisters is a traditional staple for many Native Americans.
Essential Recipe: Roasted Green Chile (p.46).

Ingredient	Measure	Ingredient	Measure
Yellow squash	1 cup	Mild white cheese Asadero	½ cup
Zucchini	1 cup	Olive oil	2 Tbsp.
Corn (fresh or frozen)	1 cup	Green chile powder	1–2 Tbsp.
Beans – Pinto or kidney	1 cup	Garlic powder	1 tsp.
Roasted green chile Anaheim, Poblano, Jalapeño SHU to taste	1 cup chopped	Salt	To taste
Chopped mild onion	½ cup		

Prep Instructions

Preheat frying pan to middle heat 300^0F. Preheat oven to $350F^0$.
Cut squash and zucchini by quartering lengthwise and then chopping into ½-inch chunks.
Defrost or cut fresh corn; you can use canned corn, however, make sure to rinse.
Chop a small to medium size sweet onion into ¼-inch pieces.
Chop roasted chile pods into ¼- to ½-inch chunks.

Cooking Instructions

Sauté chopped onion in olive oil until onions are just threatening to brown and then add squash, zucchini and green chile. Cook until they are about half-done and add beans and corn.
Move to a 9-by-9-inch casserole dish, mix in cheese, green chile powder and garlic to taste.
Bake in preheated oven for ½ hour.

Suggested Complementary Dishes: As a side dish to any recipe or main dish with tortillas.

Servings: 4 cups.

GREEN CHILE NAPOLITOS CON PAPAS

Complexity Code: Cook   Origin: Mexico
Cooking Method: Sauté

About the Recipe: Napolitos are the pads of the prickly pear cactus that grows throughout the Southwest and Mexico. It can be used in almost any dish as an ingredient, garnish or side dish. This recipe combines napolitos, green chile and potatoes into a tasty addition to the chile cuisine
Essential Recipe: Roasted green chile (p.46).

Ingredient	Measure	Ingredient	Measure
Napolitos (Fresh or canned)	1 lb.	Adobo Spice Mix (p.83)	2 Tbsp.
Roasted green chile Anaheim, Poblano, Jalapeño SHU to taste	1 cup chopped	Vegetable oil	2 Tbsp.
Potatoes or frozen hash browns	1 cup chopped	Cilantro	½ cup chopped
Onion	½ cup chopped	Vegetable oil	2–3 Tbsp.
Tomato	½ cup		
Tomato sauce	¼ cup		

Prep Instructions
Drain and rinse napolitos if using canned.
Chop green chile, potatoes, onion and tomato into ¼- to ½-inch cubes.
Grease bottom of medium skillet or sauté pan.

Cooking Instructions
Heat sauté pan (high heat), brown chopped potatoes until crispy, and add green chile, onions and tomatoes for about 3 to 4 minutes. Reduce heat to medium, add napolitos, Adobe Dry Spice Mix and tomato sauce. Gently stir all ingredients while simmering, add cilantro and blend. Simmer 15 to 20 minutes until napolitos are tender.

Suggested Complementary Dishes: Cheese, Chopped fresh green chile burritos, tamales and any meat, chicken or fish recipe.

Servings 4-6 people

MASHED POTATOES—RED OR GREEN

Complexity Code: EZ
Cooking Method: Boil

Origin: New Mexico

About the Recipe: Mashed potatoes are the universal food for any cuisine; add red or green chiles as flavor chunks and you have a match made in heaven. Try it. You will like it.
Essential Recipe: Rehydrated Red Chile pods (p.40), Creamy Red Chile Sauce (p.38), OR Roasted Green Chile (p.46), Creamy Green Chile Sauce (p.52).

Ingredient	Measure	Ingredient	Measure
Potato (medium size)	6	Butter	4 Tbsp.
Rehydrated Red Chile Pods, Ancho, Pasilla, Chipotle or Chile Seco SHU to taste	2 cups	Adobo Spice Mix (p.83)	1 Tbsp.
Roasted green chile Anaheim, Poblano, Jalapeño SHU to taste	2 cups chopped	**OPTIONAL:** gravy: Creamy Red Or Green Chile Sauce	2 cups
Half-and-half or heavy cream	½ cup		
		Crema or sour cream (garnish)	1 cup

Prep Instructions

Peel potatoes and place in cold water until ready to boil.
Boil water in a 4-quart stockpot.
Chop Rehydrated Red Chile Pods into ¼-inch squares; removing stem and seeds, and place in mixing bowl. Chop Roasted Green Chile into ¼-inch squares, removing stem and seeds, and add.

Cooking Instructions

Boil potatoes until tender about 20 to 30 minutes. (Stick a toothpick into potato to test tenderness.) Drain water and potatoes into a mixing bowl.
Add heavy cream, butter and adobo mix.
Mash potatoes with a masher, fork or blender or blender stick to the consistency that you wish. I always like to leave a few lumps to give me that homemade feeling.
If you do not have the time to boil the potatoes, you can use a mashed potato mix.

Suggested Complementary Dishes: Mashed potatoes will complement any meat, fish or chicken dish. You can top the mashed potatoes with the creamy chile sauce as an extra chile treat or use crema as a topping.
Servings: 6–8 people

GREEN CHILE POTATOES

Complexity Code: EZ   Origin: Original
Cooking Method: Sauté / Pan-roast

About the Recipe: Green chile potatoes are the perfect complement for any dish for breakfast, lunch or dinner.
Essential Recipe: Roasted Green Chile, (p.46), Green Chile Sauce, (p.50), Creamy Green Chile Sauce (p.52).

Ingredient	Measure	Ingredient	Measure
Potatoes (or frozen home fries)	4 cups chopped	Adobo Spice Mix (p.83)	2 Tbsp.
Roasted green chile Anaheim, Poblano, Jalapeño SHU to taste	2 cups chopped	Onion	½ cup chopped
Green Chile Sauce or Creamy Green Chile Sauce	2 cups	Oil	4 Tbs.

Prep Instructions
Chop or slice potatoes into ¼-inch cubes. Chop green chiles and finely chop onion.
Preheat heavy skillet with oil.

Cooking Instructions
Pan-fry potatoes, green chile and onion until tender.
Add Green Chile Sauce, Adobo Spice Mix and pan-roast under medium heat until all ingredients have blended (4 to 5 minutes) and Green Chile Sauce starts to bubble.

Suggested Complementary Dishes: cheddar cheese topping, any meat dish

Servings: 4–6 people

GREEN CHILE POTATO AU-GRATIN

Complexity Code: EZ   Origin: Original
Cooking Method: Bake / Broil

About the Recipe: This potato recipe will highlight any meal or can be the center of your meal. It is easy to make and will please all.
Essential Recipe: Roasted Green Chile (p.46), Green Chile Sauce (p.50) OR Creamy Green Chile Sauce (p.52)

Ingredient	Measure	Ingredient	Measure
Potatoes (large baking)	4	Crema or sour cream	1 cup
Roasted green chile Anaheim, Poblano, Jalapeño SHU to taste	2 cups chopped	Adobo Spice Mix	2 Tbsp.
Green Chile Sauce or Creamy Green Chile Sauce	1 cup	Sweetener (p.85)	2 Tbsp.
Shredded cheese blend Asadero, cheddar, Jack, queso Quesadilla	2 cup	Half-and-half or milk	½ cup
Cheddar cheese	2 cup shredded	Vegetable oil	2 Tbsp.

Prep Instructions
Preheat oven 350°F.
Wash potatoes, cut into 4 quarters and thinly slice into ⅛-inch slices.
Chop green chile into ¼-inch squares and place in mixing bowl. Add crema, adobo spice mix, green chile sauce and sweetener into bowl. Mix until all ingredients are coated. Grease bottom of 9-by-13-inch baking dish or pan.
Layer potatoes in baking pan. Top first layer with shredded cheese blend. Top second layer of potatoes with green chile. Top third layer of potatoes with 1 cup cheddar cheese.
Pour half-and-half over cheddar cheese and gently squeeze potato layers to remove any air between layers.
Cover baking dish with aluminum foil

Cooking Instructions
Place baking pan in oven for 30 to 40 minutes until potatoes are soft.
Remove foil. Turn on broiler and broil to form a crust (5 to 10 minutes).

Suggested Complementary Dishes: Bacon, chorizos, sausage, tortilla, any chicken, fish or meat dishes.

Servings: 6–8 people

RED CHILE POTATOES

Complexity Code: EZ   Origin: Original
Cooking Method: Sauté, Pan-roast

About the Recipe: Red chile potatoes make the ideal accompaniment for any chile dish.
Essential Recipe: Red Chile Sauce (p.36), or Creamy Red Chile Sauce (p.38), Rehydrated red chile pods (optional) (p.40).

Ingredient	Measure	Ingredient	Measure
Chopped potatoes (or frozen home fries)	4 cups	Adobo Spice Mix (p.83)	2 Tbsp.
OPTIONAL: Rehydrated Red Chile Pods Ancho, Pasilla, Chipotle SHU to taste	2 cups chopped	Onion	½ cup chopped
Red Chile Sauce or Creamy Red Chile Sauce	2 cups	Oil	4 Tbs.

Prep Instructions
Chop or slice potatoes into ¼-inch cubes. Chop red chiles and finely chop onion.
Preheat heavy skillet with oil.

Cooking Instructions
Pan-fry potatoes and onions until tender.
Add red chile sauce, Adobo Spice Mix, rehydrated chopped red chile and pan-roast under medium heat until all ingredients have blended (4 to 5 minutes) and Red Chile Sauce starts to bubble.

Suggested Complementary Dishes: cheddar cheese topping, any meat dish.

Servings: 4–6 people

RED CHILE POTATO AU-GRATIN

Complexity Code: EZ   Origin: Original
Cooking Method: Bake / Broil

About the Recipe: This potato recipe can highlight or be the center of your meal. It is easy to make and will please all.
Essential Recipe: Red Chile Sauce (p.36), or Creamy Red Chile Sauce (p.38), Rehydrated red chile pods (optional) (p.40).

Ingredient	Measure	Ingredient	Measure
Potatoes (large baking)	4	Crema or sour cream	1 cup
Red Chile Sauce or Creamy Red Chile Sauce	1 cup	Adobo Spice Mix (p.83)	2 Tbsp.
Rehydrated red chile pods, Ancho, Pasilla, Chipotle or Chile Seco SHU to taste	1 cup chopped	Sweetener (p.85)	2 Tbsp.
Shredded cheese blend Asadero, cheddar, Jack, queso Quesadilla	2 cup	Half-and-half or milk	½ cup
Cheddar cheese	2 cups shredded	Vegetable oil	2 Tbsp.

Prep Instructions
Preheat oven 350°F.
Wash potatoes, cut into 4 quarters and cut into ⅛-inch slices.
Chop green chile into ¼-inch squares and place in mixing bowl. Add crema, Adobo Spice Mix and sweetener into bowl. Mix until all ingredients are coated.
Grease bottom of 9-by-13-inch baking dish or pan.
Layer potatoes in baking pan; top first layer with shredded cheese blend. Top second layer of potatoes with green chile. Top third layer of potatoes with 1 cup cheddar cheese.
Pour half-and-half over cheddar cheese and gently squeeze potato layers to remove any air between layers.
Cover baking dish with aluminum foil.

Cooking Instructions
Place baking pan in oven for 30 to 40 minutes until potatoes are soft.
Remove foil. Turn on broiler and broil to form a crust (5 to 10 minutes).

Suggested Complementary Dishes: Bacon, chorizos, sausage, tortilla, any chicken, fish or meat dishes.
Servings: 6–8 people

ROASTED GREEN CHILE LEAFY GREENS

Complexity EZ
Cooking Method: Bake.

Origin: New Mexico

About the Recipe: Roasting leafy greens or vegetables is one of the cooking techniques that master chefs use to impress. The leafy greens come out crispy and retain their inner taste, while asparagus, broccoli, carrots, green beans, potatoes, squash, sweet potatoes and zucchini come out crispy on the outside and soft and tasty inside. Combined with roasted green chile, they can create a Chilenista masterpiece.

Essential Recipe: Fresh green chile pods (p.44).

Ingredient	Measure		Measure
Chard, chicory, collard, kale, or spinach. fresh or frozen	8 cups	**OPTIONAL:** Seasonings	
Fresh green chile pods, Anaheim, Poblano, Jalapeño SHU to taste	2 cups	Green chile powder	1-2 Tbsp.
Olive oil or melted butter	1 cup	Garlic powder	1 tsp.
		Butter	¼ cup
		Lime or lemon juice	¼ cup
		Salt	To taste

Prep Instructions

Preheat oven 450⁰F. (This may take 15 to 20 minutes, so make sure the oven racks are properly positioned.)
Clean chile pods and cut in half, removing stem and seeds, and cut into strips.
Wash leafy greens to get rid of any pesticides or preservatives; shake dry and place on a well-greased baking pan.
Sprinkle olive oil on top of leaves. Salt leaves to taste.

Cooking Instructions

Place baking pan(s) under broiler in center of oven; Bake for 15 to 20 minutes until the leaf edges start to crisp. Each leafy green will cook differently, so monitor cooking time. If you would like to add extra crispiness to the leaves, turn on the broiler for 3 to 5 minutes.
Remove vegetable from the oven add optional seasonings and place in a serving bowl; the drippings can be used as a sauce.

Suggested Complementary Dishes: With any main dish or use as a main dish with rice or beans. The vegetable will have a chewy quality that can replace meat.

Servings: 4-6 people

ROASTED GREEN CHILE VEGETABLES

Complexity EZ
Cooking Method: Bake

Origin: New Mexico

About the Recipe: Asparagus, broccoli, carrots, green beans, potatoes, squash, sweet potatoes and zucchini roasted with green chile are probably the tastiest way to serve vegetables, preserving the texture, color and taste unlike any other cooking method. The vegetables come out crispy and retain their inner softness and taste.. Combined with roasted green chile, you can create a Chilenista masterpiece.
Essential Recipe: Fresh Green Chile pods (p.44)

Ingredient	Measure	ingredient	Measure
Asparagus, broccoli, carrots, green beans, potatoes, squash, sweet potatoes, zucchini	8 cups	**OPTIONAL:** Seasonings	
Fresh Green Chile pods, Anaheim, Poblano, Jalapeño SHU to taste	2 cups	Green chile powder	1-2 Tbsp.
Olive oil or melted butter	1 cup	Garlic powder	1 tsp.
		Butter	¼ cup
		Lime or lemon juice	¼ cup
		Salt	To taste

Prep Instructions

Preheat oven 450°F. (This may take 15 to 20 minutes, so make sure the oven racks are properly positioned.)
Clean chile pods, cut in half, removing stem and seeds, and cut into strips.
Cut vegetable into 1-inch squares and place on a well-greased baking pan.
Sprinkle olive oil on top of the vegetables. Salt to taste.
Spread green chile evenly on top of leaves.

Cooking Instructions

Place baking pan(s) under broiler in center of oven; Bake for 20 to 30 minutes until the vegetable edges start to crisp. Each vegetable will cook differently, so monitor cooking time. If you would like to add extra crispiness to the leaves, turn on the broiler for 3 to 5 minutes.
Remove vegetable from the oven, add optional seasonings and place in a serving bowl; the drippings can be used as a sauce.

Suggested Complementary Dishes: Serve with any main dish or use as a main dish with rice or beans. The vegetables will have a chewy quality that can replace meat.

STEAMED GREEN CHILE
LEAFY GREENS OR VEGETABLES

Complexity Code: EZ   Origin: New Mexico
Cooking Method: Steam

About the Recipe: Steaming leafy greens preserve most of the taste, minerals, vitamins and digestive benefits available year-round at your grocer. Chard, chicory, collard, kale and spinach are among my favorite greens. Asparagus, broccoli, green beans, squash and zucchini are among my favorite vegetables.
Combined with green chile to turn any veggie into a Chilenista favorite.
Essential Recipe: Fresh Green Chile pods (p.44).

Ingredient	Measure	Ingredient	Measure
LEAFY GREENS: Chard, chicory, collard, kale, or spinach. fresh or frozen	8 cups	**OPTIONAL:** Seasoning	
VEGETABLES: Asparagus, broccoli, green beans, squash and zucchini	4 cups	Green chile powder	1–2 Tbsp.
Fresh green chile pods Anaheim, Poblano, Jalapeño SHU to taste	2 cups	Garlic powder	1 tsp.
Water (Steaming)	2 cups	Butter	¼ cup
Salt	1 Tbsp.	Lime or lemon juice	¼ cup
		Salt	To taste

Prep Instructions
Place steamer basket on bottom of a 3-quart pot, add salt and bring to a brisk boil. (The salt will preserve the green color and keep the veggies crisp.)
Cut leafy greens into halves (stems and tops) or cut vegetables into 1-inch squares.
Clean chile pods, cut in half, removing stem and seeds, and cut into strips.

Cooking Instructions
Place stems and Fresh Green Chile into bottom of steamer and cover pot 3 to 4 minutes.
Add leafy tops into steamer and cover pot 3 to 4 minutes or place cut vegetable into steamer basket. The vegetables should turn a bright green when ready. (Do not overcook, no one likes mushy vegetables.)
Place pot under cold water to stop steaming and cool vegetables to stop cooking. Drain pot and add optional seasonings to taste. Serve immediately or place vegetables in baking pan and keep warm in an oven at 175°F until ready to serve.
Suggested Complementary Dishes: Any main dish.

Serves: 4-6 people

Chapter 11—POSTRES (DESSERTS)

While desserts do not necessarily have red or green chile, they are a vital as the Chilenista cuisine's sweet ending.

ATOLE PORRIDGE

Complexity Code: EZ   Origin: New Mexico
Cooking Method: Boil, Simmer

About The Recipe: Atole is purported to have medicinal qualities and should be eaten daily either as a porridge or a drink at any time. Prepare as a drink before, during or after a meal to replace soda, or thicken it up as an ice cream substitute.

Ingredient	Measure	Ingredient	Measure
Masa corn flour	1 cup	Baking powder	1 tsp.
Milk or water	4 cups	Butter (garnish)	4 pats
Unrefined or brown sugar	1 cup		

Prep Instructions
Combine masa flour with 2 cups milk and baking powder in a mixing bowl, stir until it forms a smooth paste (no lumps).
Place 2 cups milk or water in a 2- to 3-quart saucepan.

Cooking Instructions
Bring saucepan with milk to a boil and immediately turn heat down to simmer.
Add Atole flour paste to milk, simmer under low flame and stir until it gains the porridge consistency you like. Turn heat down and serve.

Suggested Complementary Dishes: Garnish with a pat of butter on top.

Servings: 4–6 people

BISCOCHITOS (ANISE SEED COOKIES)

Complexity Code: Cook   Origin: New Mexico

About The Recipe: Nothing can top biscochitos for an end-of-meal dessert that will be remembered more than the meal. This is a traditional recipe that is served during Christmas and celebrations.

Ingredient	Measure		Measure
Flour (Unbleached)	3 cups	Anise seed	2 tsp.
Unrefined sugar	¾ cups	Almond extract or vanilla	½ tsp.
Baking powder	2 tsp.	Anisette, sambuca, brandy or bourbon	½ cup +
Salt	1 tsp.	Cinnamon	1 Tbsp.
Butter, lard or shortening	1 cup	Powdered sugar	1 cup
Eggs (whipped)	2		

Prep Instructions

Combine flour, sugar, baking powder and salt, anise seed and almond extract in a 3- to 4-quart mixing bowl and stir to mix.

Add softened butter and whipped egg and start to knead, adding Anisette or brandy until you have a soft dough ball, not too sticky. Divide the dough ball into two parts and wrap with plastic wrap. Let sit in refrigerator or 4–6 hours or overnight.

Preheat Oven 350°F.

Combine cinnamon and powdered sugar in a small mixing bowl.

Roll out dough ball on a floured board ¼- to ½-inch thick. Cut various shapes with a cookie cutter (round, star, fleur-de-lis). Place cookies on a lightly greased baking pan.

Bake cookies for 10 to 15 minutes until tops are golden brown.

Dip/coat each biscochito in cinnamon sugar mixture while still hot and allow to cool.

Servings: 4 dozen small cookies.

BREAD PUDDING WITH VARIATIONS

Complexity Code: EZ   Origin: New Mexico

About The Recipe: Bread pudding is the staple dessert of the Chilenista cuisine and is made with many variations, including red or green chile, to give it an extra flavor kick. Multigrain or sprouted wheat bread will give a nuttier and firmer bread pudding. White bread or Bolillos will give a mushier and softer bread pudding.

Ingredient	Measure	Ingredient	Measure
Toasted bread slices White bread, multigrain, sprouted wheat or Bolillos	8 slices	Vanilla extract	1 Tbsp.
Eggs	4	Cinnamon	1 Tbsp.
Brown sugar	1 cup	Cheddar cheese	2 cups shredded
Raisins	1 cup	Milk or half-and-half	2 cups
Water	1 cup		

Prep Instructions

Preheat oven to 350°F.
Soak raisins in 1 cup water to rehydrate in a 2- to 3-quart mixing bowl.
Beat eggs in a small mixing bowl.
Toast 6 to 9 slices of bread lightly. (You can toast the bread on a baking pan in the preheated oven.) Cut or crumble toast into 1-inch squares.
Caramelize sugar (optional). You may use brown sugar in the recipe without caramelizing.
Caramelize sugar by placing brown sugar in a saucepan with 2 Tbsp. water and melt under a low to medium heat until it is liquefied and starting to turn a golden syrupy brown. (Stir constantly to prevent burning.)
Place eggs, caramelized sugar, vanilla extract, cinnamon, shredded cheese and milk into the mixing bowl with raisins and whip mixture until all of the ingredients are thoroughly blended.
Place toasted bread into egg mixture and stir until all ingredients are coated and blended. Allow toasted bread to absorb mixture 5 to 10 minutes and place in baking pan.
Place baking pan into oven and bake for 30 minutes until all of the liquid has been absorbed and the pudding is firm. Spoon out a portion; sprinkle some cinnamon on top.

Servings: 4-6 people

BREAD PUDDING VARIATIONS

Bread Pudding with Nuts
Place 1 to 2 cups of walnuts, pinion, pecans, sunflower seeds or other nuts into the egg mixture and pour on toasted bread as per rest of recipe. Garnish with nuts.

Bread Pudding with Cranberries
Substitute cranberries for raisins in prepping bread pudding. Garnish with hydrated cranberries.

Maple Bread Pudding
Substitute maple syrup or maple sugar for sweetener and proceed with rest of recipe. Garnish with maple sugar when baked.

Red Chile Bread Pudding
Rehydrate 3 to 4 red chile pods along with raisins in the prep instructions, chop chile into ¼ squares, place into the egg mixture and pour on toasted bread as per rest of recipe. Garnish with red chile powder to taste when baked.

Green Chile Bread Pudding
Place 1 to 2 cups of roasted green chile chopped into ¼-inch squares place into the egg mixture and pour on toasted bread as per rest of recipe. Garnish with green chile powder when baked.

Chocolate Bread Pudding
Place 1 cup shaved chocolate or chocolate syrup into egg mixture and pour on toasted bread as per rest of recipe. Garnish with shaved chocolate when baked.

FLAN WITH VARIATIONS

Complexity Code: Cook   Origin: New Mexico

About The Recipe: Flan is one of the most favorite desserts in the
Chilenista cuisine and can be prepared as individual cups or as a family-
size portion that can be cut as a cake. Endless variations run from super
sweet, by adding additional sweetener, to crema, as well as adding some
red or green chile to kick up the taste. You will love it.

Ingredient	Measure	Ingredient	
Unrefined sugar, brown sugar or piloncillo*	1 cup	Eggs	6
Sweetened condensed milk	2 cups	Vanilla extract	1 Tbsp.
Half-and-half or heavy cream	1 cup		

*Piloncillo will give the Flan a dark, super sweet taste; you may wish to use
it sparingly.

Prep Instructions

Preheat oven 350°F.
Caramelize sugar by placing unrefined sugar on a saucepan with 2 Tbsp.
water and melting under a low to medium heat until it liquefies and starts
to turn a golden syrupy brown. (Stir constantly to prevent burning.) Place
caramelized sugar on the bottom of a 9-inch glass baking dish (round or
square), cupcake baking cups or individual ramekins (6 to 7 molds). Place
2–3 Tbsp., of caramelized sugar into each mold and swish around to make
sure the bottom is coated.
Prepare flan filling in a large mixing bowl; crack eggs, place sweetened
condensed milk, and vanilla extract, and vigorously whip eggs until all
ingredients are blended.
Place molds on a large baking pan, pour flan filling mixture into each mold
(individual ramekins or baking dish) and cover each mold with aluminum
foil.
Carefully pour water into the baking pan to cover the sides of the molds.
Place baking pan into the preheated oven and bake for 60 minutes for
individual molds and 90 minutes for the large baking dish.
Remove foil and test that the flan is thoroughly cooked with a toothpick. If
it comes out dry, it's cooked. If not, bake for an additional 15 minutes.
Remove baking pan from oven, remove foil and allow each mold to cool
completely 1 to 2 hours. You may wish to put into refrigerator to cool
faster.
To serve, carefully run a knife around the edge of the mold, place a flat
plate over the mold and carefully flip the mold and the plate together.
Jiggle it and the flan will fall on the plate.

Serves: 6–8 people.

VARIATIONS: Prepare recipe as above.

Red Chile Flan
Place 2 Tbsp. red chile powder into egg mixture and whip it into flan filling.

Cream Cheese Flan
Place ¼ cup crema or softened cream cheese into egg mixture and whip it into flan filling. Garnish with dollop of crema when baked.

Coffee Flan
Melt 2 Tbsp. instant coffee with 1 Tbsp. water and place into egg mixture; whip it into flan filling. Garnish with a few coffee beans when baked.

Orange Flan
Scrape ½ cup orange zest from an orange, add ½ cup frozen concentrated orange juice into egg mixture and whip filling. Garnish with a dollop of orange marmalade when baked.

Chocolate Flan
Melt 4 oz. chocolate or add ½ cup chocolate syrup; place into egg mixture and whip it into flan filling. Garnish with shaved chocolate or sprinkles when baked.

Coconut Flan
Place 1 cup condensed coconut milk and ½ cup shredded coconut into egg mixture and whip it into flan filling. Garnish with shredded coconut when baked.

Almond Flan
Substitute 1 Tbsp. almond extract for vanilla extract into egg mixture and whip it into flan filling. Garnish with shaved almond pieces when baked.

Maple Syrup Flan
Substitute 1 cup maple syrup or maple sugar for sweetener and proceed with rest of recipe. Garnish with maple sugar when baked.

Margarita Flan
Place ¼ cup tequila and 1 Tbsp. Triple Sec into egg mixture and whip it into flan filling. Garnish with shaved lime zest.

FRUIT PIES WITH VARIATIONS

Complexity Code: EZ   Origin: New Mexico

About The Recipe: Fruit pies are one of the most popular of all desserts; they can be made ahead of time and served for any occasion.

Ingredient	Measure	Ingredient	Measure
Unbleached flour	2 cups	Fillings: Fresh, canned or frozen	To taste
Shortening	¼ cup	Prune,	
Butter	2 Tbsp.	Apricot	
Egg (whipped)	1	Cherries	
Baking powder	1 tsp.	Guava	
Salt	1 tsp.	Any jam	
Water	¼ cup +		

Prep Instructions

Preheat oven 400°F.
Combine flour, baking powder and salt in a 3- to 4-quart mixing bowl and stir to mix.
Add softened shortening and butter, whipped egg and start to knead, adding water until you have a soft dough ball, not too sticky. Cover the dough ball with a wet towel and let sit for 10 to 15 minutes.
Prepare filling by blending fresh, canned or preserved fruit into a paste, adding cinnamon and sugar to taste.
Roll out dough ball on a floured board ⅛- to ¼ -inch thick. Cut 3- to 4-inch rounds out with a coffee cup or cookie cutter. Place dough rounds on a floured plate.
Place dough round on a flat surface and scoop 1–2 Tbsp. filling on the center. Place dough round on top of filling, gently squeeze any air out from the top and bottom and crimp the edges of the two dough rounds. Place rounds on a lightly greased baking pan.
Bake fruit pies 10 to 15 minutes until the dough is crisp.

Servings: 12–18 fruit pies.

RICE PUDDING

Complexity Code: EZ   Origin: New Mexico

About The Recipe: Every celebration in the traditional home has rice pudding as a special treat. It is easy to make and loved by all.

Essential Recipe: Rice (Sticky short grain) (p.316)

Ingredient	Measure	Ingredient	Measure
Rice (Short grain sticky)	4 cups	Vanilla extract	1 tsp.
Half & half or heavy cream	2 cups	Cinnamon	½ tsp
Eggs	4	Nutmeg	¼ tsp (pinch)
Sugar (unrefined white)	1 cup	**OPTIONAL:** Nuts (walnuts, pinion, pecans)	1 cup
Raisins (Hydrated)	1 cup		

Prep Instructions

Rehydrate raisins in 1 cup water.

Preheat oven to 300°F.

Prepare Sticky Short Grain Rice. Allow to cool.

Vigorously whip eggs in a 3-quart mixing bowl, add half-and-half, sugar, raisins, vanilla extract, cinnamon, a pinch of nutmeg and rice. Stir until all ingredients are blended.

Place rice mixture in a glass baking pan and bake in a 300°F oven for 15 to 20 minutes.

To serve, spoon out a portion and place in a cup or serving glass; sprinkle some cinnamon or nutmeg.

Serves: 6–8 people.

SOPAPILLA (LITTLE PILLOWS)

Complexity Code: EZ   Origin: New Mexico
Cooking Method: Deep fat-fry

About The Recipe: Sopapillas are probably the most popular of all
Chilenista desserts and are synonymous with New Mexico's chile cuisine.
This fry bread concoction can be served with any chile dish or as a dessert
with honey poured inside.

Ingredient	Measure	Ingredient	Measure
Unbleached flour*	4 cups	Baking powder	2 Tsp.
Shortening or lard	4 Tbsp.	Salt	1 Tsp.
Warm milk	1½ cups	Lard or vegetable oil for frying	4 cups
		Honey	As desired

* Prepared sopapilla flour mixes are available at your supermarket

Prep Instructions

Preheat oil or lard in a deep-fat fryer or heavy skillet with at least 2 to 3
inches of oil to 390°F (Use thermometer).
In a 3- to 4-quart mixing bowl, mix flour, baking powder and salt.* (Premix
sopapilla flour is available.)
Pour 1 ½ cups of milk and lard into a small microwaveable mixing bowl
and use the microwave on the defrost cycle for 1 to 2 minutes. (Do not
bring to a boil.) Mix the liquefied lard and milk well and slowly pour in the
flour. Mix well until a dough ball is formed.
Place the dough ball on a well- floured flat surface and knead the dough,
folding it in half from all sides and pushing it together until the dough ball
is soft and no longer sticky.
Cover the dough ball with a wet towel and let it rest for 15 to 20 minutes.
Cut the dough ball in half and roll out a flat strip of dough ⅛-inch thick on
a floured surface. Work fast so that the dough will not dry out.
With a sharp knife or pizza cutter cut the dough into 4- to 6-inch squares
or triangles.
(Cover the stuffed dough sopapillas with a wet towel to keep the squares
moist until ready to fry.)

Cooking Instructions

Carefully place sopapilla dough into the fryer and fry for about one minute
per side until golden brown. Place sopapilla on a paper towel or rack to
drain, keep warm in an oven at 200°F until all of the sopapillas are fried
and ready to serve.

Suggested Complementary Dishes: Any chile entrée dish or as
dessert. Cut off one corner and pour honey into the sopapilla.

Servings 8–10.

Chapter 12
GLOSSARY OF THE CHILE CUISINE

BREAD, CHEESE, CONDIMENTS, HERBS, SPICES & SWEETENERS

Chile cuisine is one of the oldest foods on our planet. It has a cultural legacy that goes back thousands of years and has been evolving and changing through conquests, trade, farming, hunting, fishing and the introduction of ingredients that were incorporated into the foods and their preparation. The breads, cheeses, condiments, herbs, spices and sweeteners are all part of the chile cuisine palate.

BREADS

Blue Corn Tortilla
Tortillas made from native blue cornmeal are available in most groceries. Making tortillas from scratch is an art, consisting of blue cornmeal, hot water, kneading to a sticky consistency, pressing in a tortilla press and cooking at a very high heat on a comal (flat skillet).

Blue corn Tortillas can be purchased pre-made at your supermarket.

Blue corn tortillas have a nutty taste and can be used in any recipe.

Burrito Tortilla
Burritos are usually made from flour although they are available in a whole wheat variety, are made fresh daily and are readily available at most supermarkets. Burrito tortillas are 12-inch rounds that allow you some extra room to wrap the filling or use as flat bread with your meal.

Burrito Wraps
Burrito Wraps are made slightly thinner than regular burritos and are used to make the popular wraps for breakfast or lunch. They are available next to the regular burritos at your supermarket.

Corn Tortilla
As in blue corn tortillas, the making of corn tortillas is an art, consisting of making a batter out of white, or yellow cornmeal, pressing them on a tortilla press and cooking them on a comal.

You can purchase cornmeal and follow the recipe on the side of the box.

Corn tortillas are available pre-made at most supermarkets.
They have can be used for burritos, enchiladas, or eaten plain with any dish with a swab of butter or chile or with huevos rancheros.

Duros Mexican Chips
Duros are the original Mexican chip that comes in many shapes. Pinwheels, flat chips, round chips, that can be eaten plain or with salsa and dips. They can be either fried or microwaved as needed. Please look at (p.117) of Appetizers for Duros Chips.

Chimichanga
For a quick meal or appetizer you can use tortilla or egg roll wraps available at most groceries to make a wonderful fried burrito or rolled taco. See Appetizers (p.87)

Fry Bread
Everyone loves fry bread, and there are numerous recipes to choose from. Please look at our recipe at (p.110) of the Breads Section.

Pan Bread
The New Mexican answer to biscuits and gravy. It is easy to make and loved by everyone. For a pan bread recipe please look at (p.111).

Sopapilla
An authentic New Mexico favorite that is easy to make and delightful to serve.

Sopapillas can be served as part of the meal, dessert, or as a treat with a bit of powdered sugar or honey. Please look at (p.112).

Taco Chips
You can make fresh taco chips by cutting up a tortilla and frying the chips; however, it is best to purchase them in the potato chip section of your supermarket in yellow, white or blue corn varieties.

Taco Shells (Soft)
Soft taco shells are available at your supermarket and are usually 6-inch rounds perfect for a "real" taco with your favorite filling.

Taco Shells (Hard)
Hard taco shells are the most popular fast food and are available in many varieties on your supermarket shelf, ready to be stuffed with your favorite filling.

Tortilla
Tortilla is the staple of every New Mexican dish and almost obligatory to eat. You can make tortillas by scratch, and there are many pre-mix and flour offerings at your supermarket. You can follow that recipe printed on the bag. I would recommend purchasing pre-made tortillas either in a burrito or taco size. You can fry them to create easy fry bread. Please look at (p.114).

Tostada
A tostada is a round taco chip that can be served as a crispy flat taco or crumbled as dipping chips. Tostadas are available in most supermarkets.

CHEESE

Many farmers that have sheep, goats or cattle in New Mexico and Mexico are also cheese makers. There are as many varieties of cheese as there are regions. Some varieties are Old World dating back to the Aztec and Native Americans and some New World having been imported by the Spaniards and Europeans. Some cheeses are available in supermarkets and others are harder to get. Cheese is an integral ingredient of the chile cuisine; we offer a good substitute for the cheeses that you may not be able to readily get as well as a recipe to make your own crema—one of the most popular of all cheeses that can be used as an ingredient or garnish for any recipe.

Crema Agria and Crema Mexicana are one the most subtle tastes that exist in the chile palate. It is a cross between sour cream and yogurt, slightly fermented and mildly sweet. It can be used as a topping to add sparkle and color to any chile dish or it can be used as a condiment to enhance the taste. Most of all, it can be used to cut down the capsaicin of way too hot chile and allow you to take the next bite. It belongs in every chile first aid kit.

Crema is not really a cheese but a dairy staple in Mexican cuisine. Crema is a heavy cream similar in taste to Crème Fraiche (which is a good substitute but best to just make your own). Thicker versions of crema are used as additions to sauces, and the thinner crema is used as a topping for tostadas, tacos and enchiladas.

If you cannot purchase it at your store or mail order or it is too expensive and perishable, you can make a good substitute in your kitchen.

CREMA AGRIA (Creamy Cheese)

Ingredient	Measure
Sour Cream	1 cup
Buttermilk	¼ cup

Blend sour cream and buttermilk in a small sauce pan with a whisk or stick blender. Simmer the blend over low heat. Do not let it bubble. Pour contents into a glass jar and let cool at room temperature (70 degrees overnight). You now have made your own crema. Use it liberally and often for any chile recipe.

To use crema as a base for dips, blend it 50/50 with whipped cream cheese. Substitute Crème Fraiche, sour cream (thinned) or make your own crema as a base for dips.

Cotija
The Mexican substitute for Italian Parmesan can be sprinkled on almost everything.

Fresh Queso (Cheese)

Fresh cheeses have a crumbly texture and when they are heated; they do not melt, but they do become soft and creamy without losing their shape. You can also slice fresh cheese into sticks or cubes and fry it (without breading or anything on it) and it will become brown and crispy on the outside and soft on the inside. Fresh cheeses have a generally mild flavor and pair well with any dish that calls for cheese, especially dishes like **enchiladas** and chile relleno, since the cheese will melt but stays inside the dish. Some fresh cheeses are:

Panela

A semisoft cheese that looks like mozzarella, it is made from **whole** unpasteurized milk curds that are salted and drained in baskets. Panela is best eaten fresh as a snack or tops salads or other cold dishes. You can also use panela to crumble over tacos or chili.

Substitute: Ricotta

Queso Blanco

A moist, crumbly cheese that becomes creamy when it is heated. The cheese is very versatile, so you can use to it to fill or garnish any of your favorite chile dishes.

Substitute: Monterrey Jack

Queso Fresco

A fresh cheese that is hand pressed from milk that has been allowed to curd. It has a crumbly texture and is slightly acidic. It can be sprinkled on any chile recipe or used to stuff chiles or quesadillas. It can be mixed with any other cheese to give it a creamy texture.

Substitute: Mild Feta Cheese

Requesón

A small curd cheese that can be used in any recipe as filler or eaten as a side with spices. Requesón is a cousin of ricotta cheese.

Substitute: Ricotta

Melting Cheeses

Just as the name suggests, these cheeses were made to melt. They do not separate or get greasy when they are heated, so they are ideal for any dish that calls for a lot of cheese like burritos (http//mexicanfood.about.com/od/resources/a/mexicancheese.htm)or nachos. They are also great for American dishes like pizza and cheeseburgers.

Asadero
The traditional use for this mild, chewy cheese is a filling for chiles relleno and a popular Mexican dish called chile con queso. In Oaxaca trompillos (wild berries) are used in the cheese making process, and this imparts a distinctive flavor not found in Northern Mexico or in the U.S. versions.

Cheddar Cheese (Mild, Medium, and Sharp)
From mild to sharp, cheddar is the most widely eaten cheese in the world. Its mellow to sharp tangy taste blends well with any ingredient. You have tasted cheddar in Mac & Cheese, Potatoes Au-Gratin and a Ham & Cheese Sandwich.

Queso Quesadilla
A rich, creamy melting cheese that originated in Sinaloa in Northern Mexico. It made tortilla turnovers famous and gave them their name "quesadillas." This versatile cheese can be used in many traditional Mexican-style dishes and in place of any melting cheese. It is a part of a major group of Hispanic melting cheeses.

Monterey Jack
Monterey Jack is a traditional "American cheese" that has been adopted by the chile cuisine because of its mild flavor and low melting point that blends in with other ingredients or cheeses.

Mexican Shredded Cheese Mix
A combination of asadero, cheddar, Monterey Jack and, queso quesadilla that is sold in almost every supermarket as a mixture of cheeses that can be used to top tacos, make quesadillas and top almost any dish from a hamburger to huevos rancheros. It is readily available, easy to use and blends well.

Hard Cheeses
Hard cheeses are more tangy and flavorful than the fresh and melting cheeses and can be used both as garnishes or ingredients for almost any recipe to give it an extra dimension and zip. Hard cheeses are grated. Because of the strong flavors, it makes a perfect topping for beans, salads and even grilled meats.

Añejo
Añejo" means aged. Añejo cheese is dry and gratable or can be crumbled and used on tacos, salads or any dish where you want to add a zesty flavor. Substitute Romano

Queso Chihuahua and Queso Menonita
Hard, aged cheeses that have a mild flavor. You can compare them to an aged sharp cheddar cheese.

CONDIMENTS

The Southwest kitchen has a pantheon of tastes and textures that have ancient roots to the Aztec, Mayan and Native American palates, using local herbs and spices to enhance the flavor of any food group--- meat, fish, veggie or grain. So while red or green chile are the basis of many recipes, the condiments in turn can flavor the chile with aromatic, nutty, herbal, sweet, sour, salty, bitter, and pungent taste experiences. You do not necessarily need a recipe, just a good imagination and a willingness to experiment. Sometimes a trace amount of any of the condiments will take your dish from great to a taste experience worth repeating.

While you can formulate any of these condiments yourself, it is recommended that you first try them pre-made from any of the popular brands that you will find in the Spanish section of your supermarket.

Achiote or Annatto Recado
Used to color food with a bright reddish /yellowish cast as well as a marinade for meats. Achiote has an earthy, astringent taste and is available as a paste, oil or powder. You can use it as saffron or turmeric substitute for rice, vegetables, beans or meats to add an earthiness not found in any other spice combination.

Adobo
Adobo literally means "marinade" in Spanish, and can be used to flavor any meat, chicken, fish, bean, rice or soup recipe. The main ingredients for Adobo are garlic, oregano, cumin and coriander, and it is used in many of the Mexican, Caribbean and Latin American recipes in this book. Essential Recipe for Adobo Spice Mix (p.83)

Adobo Wet Marinade
You can add local flavor and accents to your adobo such as lime juice, vinegar or black pepper, and achiote or turmeric for color. Fruit juices are a natural sweetener that can be freely used as part of the wet marinade. By adding a little bit of olive oil, vinegar or lime juice, you can make your adobo as a wet marinade (20 to 30) minutes. You can also use the dry powder within the recipe.

Adobo can be purchased pre-made either as a liquid marinade or as a powder. It is so easy to make, however, and fresh is best. (No preservative needed.) I would recommend that you make a pre-mix of your own adobo sauce and store it alongside with your other spices in dry form or freeze the wet form in an ice cube tray that you can use at a moment's notice.

Adobo is the foundation of all spices used in the Red or Green Chile cuisine.

Adobo Spice Mix

Because so many recipes call for coriander, cumin, garlic and oregano, I have found that it is very easy to blend the four spices in equal parts and store them in a spice jar ready for use with any recipe. Use as needed 1 Tbsp. at a time. To give your adobo mix an extra taste burst you may wish to add a pinch of clove and a pinch of nutmeg.

Bouillon Cubes (Beef Chicken, Garlic and Tomato)

Bouillon cubes and soup powder can be used as an instant flavor enhancer for almost any recipe in moderation. It is important to read the label. Most cubes have salt as their primary ingredient and some include MSG and many unrecognized ingredients. (Fresh is best, however; taste is good).

Canned Chile (All Varieties)

Almost every variety of chile can be purchased in cans from chopped to whole pods that can be used in recipes when the fresh or frozen chiles are not available.
It is important to rinse and strain all of the preservatives that are used in the canning process prior to using the canned chiles in your recipe.

You can also get pickled canned chiles that are great as garnishes for almost any dish; I especially like pickled chipotle chiles that can zest up any dish or palate.

Cilantro Pesto

Cilantro is one of the most refreshing herbs to be used in the chile world and adds an aromatic blend of aroma and freshness to any palate. It can be used as a side dish or a condiment. (p. 75) Cilantro Pesto.

Ketchup

Ketchup has a universal appeal for its prepared tomato tanginess and can be used either as an ingredient or condiment to complement most any recipe. You can flavor ketchup with any other condiment or spice to give it your own unique taste. Try a bit of adobo, cilantro or chile.

Lime Juice

Fresh lime juice will kick up any recipe with its own tart and sour combination. It is also available in bottles made from concentrate.

Lemon Juice

Lemons fresh or concentrated will kick up any fish, chicken or vegetable with a mild sweet-sour taste that cannot be replicated by any other spice or condiment.

Mexican Saffron

Mexican Saffron is made from the pistils of the safflower and gives great color and a nutty taste. It is known as the poor man's saffron and can be used in any recipe that calls for saffron—especially rice dishes.

Mole

Mole is the king and queen of all condiments with roots in the Aztec and Mayan civilizations. It has captivated the taste of all royal courts and introduced cocoa into the European cuisine. Its nutty, bittersweet, tangy taste cannot be replicated by any other condiment. For many Mole sauce is addictive. Once you have had it you keep coming back.

It can be purchased at most groceries either as a paste or liquid and is easily prepared at home. (p. 78, 80, 81).

Mole Verde

Mole Verde (green) brings forth the refreshing taste of cilantro, nuts, tomatillos and herbs in a piquant sauce that will enhance the taste of any chicken or fish dish. It can be used in any recipe that calls for green chile sauce. Mole Verde can be purchased in jars or you can make it yourself. (p. 78).

Recaito or Sofrito

Recaito or sofrito is found in every Caribbean and Latin American kitchen and is a green aromatic puree of onions, cilantro, garlic, green peppers and sweet chile peppers and sometimes tomatoes. Recaito or Sofrito can be purchased in bottles; however, making the sauce fresh is easily worth the effort. See Cilantro Pesto (p. 75).

Red Chile Relish

A quick homemade relish that can add sparkle to any dish can be ready in 15 minutes. Combine chopped tomatoes, chopped onion, garlic powder, red chile powder, cilantro, sweetener and a little balsamic vinegar.

Salsa

Salsa is the perfect condiment, dip, side dish and companion to any dish. Usually it is made from chopped tomatoes, red chile paste, green chile, onion, cilantro, oregano, cumin, coriander, lime, vinegar and a sweetener (any fruit juice). It will allow you to create your own

Essential Recipe to dazzle and impress your family and guests. Salsa can be purchased in many bottled varieties in mild, medium or hot. You can use a bottled salsa as a base to add your own ingredients like fresh cilantro, chopped onion, fresh chopped chile and sweetener.
Please look at Salsa's (p. 137).

Sun-Dried Tomatoes

Chopped sun-dried tomatoes can be used in almost any recipe to deliver a chunk of flavor as an unexpected flavor burst to enhance your recipe. Simply rehydrate or chop the dried tomatoes and toss them into the recipe.

Vinegar (Balsamic, Cider, White)
A spoonful of vinegar will often pop the flavor of your food from drab to wonderful by creating a taste sensation. Used in small quantities it will not be noticeable as sour, but rather sweet, especially the balsamic vinegar.

Wine
Wine can be used as a substitute liquid in any recipe to provide a sweet/tart flavor that can enhance the taste of any recipe. The heat will get rid of most of the alcohol and leave the fruity flavor behind. Wine is the secret ingredient that many chefs use.

FLOUR, THICKENERS & COATINGS

Baking Powder
If you have ever wondered how the bubbles got in there, look no further because baking powder is the chemistry that does it all for you.

Baking powder contains sodium bicarbonate but it includes the acidifying agent already (cream of tartar) and also a drying agent (usually starch). Baking powder is available as single-acting baking powder and as double-acting baking powder. Single-acting powders are activated by moisture, so you must bake recipes which include this product immediately after mixing. Double-acting powders react in two phases and can stand for a while before baking.

With double-acting powder, some gas is released at room temperature when the powder is added to dough, but the majority of the gas is released after the temperature of the dough increases in baking.
All tortillas, fry bread and sopapilla recipes use baking powder to make them rise.

Cornmeal
Cornmeal comes in fine, medium and coarse grinds and can be used as a flour substitute to provide the sweetness and taste of corn for most baking and coating applications. Fine ground cornmeal is called corn flour and should not be confused with cornstarch. Cornmeal is available in all supermarkets in white, yellow and blue varieties based on the corn that was used.

Cornstarch
Cornstarch is a thickener for almost any recipe that needs to be thickened. It has no real taste on its own, so it will easily blend to thicken a thin red or green chile stew, gravy, sauce or soup. The best way to blend cornstarch into your recipe is to first mix it in a bit of water or natural liquid from your recipe and pour it in. With a little bit of heat, it will immediately start to thicken.

Harina de Arroz Rice Flour

Rice flour is my favorite coating for fried foods, in that it does not absorb the oil and retains a crunchiness that cannot be achieved by wheat flour, which tends to absorb the oil. Try it especially for chicken or any other meat that you would like to encapsulate in crunch. Harina de Arroz is usually found in the Hispanic section of your supermarket.

Harina de Masa Corn Flour

Masa is used in almost all tortilla recipes for its nutty corn flavor and can also be used in any dough recipe as a substitute for wheat flour. I personally like the taste of masa flour in that it gives an authenticity to the recipes.

Masa harina is readily available on your grocer's flour shelves.

Wheat Flour

Flour is the universal baking, cooking and coating ingredient. It is available in many forms, bleached, unbleached, whole wheat and gluten free. All flours have their own handling and baking characteristics. I prefer to use unbleached flour, since it has fewer additives and is more flexible in its use—especially for tortillas, fry bread and sopapillas.
There are numerous flour pre-mixes that I would also like to recommend for blue corn, fry bread, sopapilla and tortilla. The pre-mix bags or boxes usually have some reliable recipes and handling instructions.

HERBS

If the ingredients of a recipe are the canvas, herbs would be the color. It is difficult to describe taste unless you have had the experience of tasting. Fortunately, most herbs will reveal themselves through the aroma and taste that they impart to any recipe. Feel free to taste each aroma to experience the aromatic palate that is available to you as a color for your cooking prowess.

Cilantro

Cilantro is one of the most used herbs in the chile family of recipes. Fresh cilantro can be used as an ideal garnish for any chile, meat, chicken, fish or salsa recipe. Its fresh aromatic flavor will both stimulate and refresh your taste buds while enhancing the rest of the flavor.

Garlic

As any garlic enthusiast will tell you, you do not need a recipe. Garlic can be sautéed, stewed, crushed, chopped and used to flavor anything. Too much ain't enough.

Ginger

Ginger has a pungent, aromatic, astringent quality that will refresh your palate and taste buds in any sauce or salsa. Ginger can be sautéed with a vegetable or infused with any salsa or sauce. The taste, however, will dissipate with prolonged cooking, as in baking. Ginger is used most in Caribbean, tropical and Asian recipes. You can use it once or use it often; its unique taste memory is not forgotten.

Oregano

Next to garlic and cilantro, oregano imparts a nutty aromatic flavor and aroma to any recipe that is difficult to forget. It is often used in chile recipes, sauces and condiments to pop the food taste. You have to use it sparingly or it will overwhelm the other ingredients, including garlic.

Parsley, Sage, Rosemary and Thyme

A perfect blend of subtle aromatics that can sweeten any recipe with a subtle flavor to enhance its natural taste. I always pre-mix the four herbs in their dry form to use with chicken and fish. They can be the melodic additive to any of your recipes.

SPICES

The New World was mistakenly found by Columbus in his quest for a shorter route to India for the exotic spices that Marco Polo brought back during his expeditions into the Far East. It is no coincidence that the Indigenous People that Columbus met were misnamed as Indians. It is also no coincidence that the "hot" fruit that he found were named chile "peppers."

It is safe to say that the search for spices changed the world we live in and modern history.

Black Pepper

All Chilenistas need to thank the black pepper corn for the discovery of the "Chile pepper" and then use it to spice up any recipe with a mild aromatic heat. Black pepper is available in whole pepper corns or ground in coarse or fine blends.

Chile Powder (Red & Green)

Chile powder is available at almost all groceries or online either in red or green with a whole spectrum of heat units ranging from mild (500 SHU) to blistering hot (30,000 SHU).
You can also purchase dried chiles and flake them or grind them in your blender or coffee grinder. They will not be as consistent as the packaged variety.

Please look at Red Chile Essential Recipes (p.32) and Green Chile Essential Recipes (p.42) for chile recipes and additional information. Do not confuse chile powder with chili powder sold in little bottles or as Molido mix as they usually contain other ingredients to reduce the price or as pre-mix for specific recipes.

Cinnamon
Cinnamon is one of the hidden treasures of chile cooking and adds sweetness to the chile. It should be used in trace amounts (¼ tsp. or less) to evoke a taste memory.

Clove
Adds a sweet aromatic bouquet to any condiment or recipe, however, it has to be used in very small quantities (a pinch) and blended well. It is like a mystery guest invited to the party.

Cocoa Powder
Cocoa powder is used to infuse the taste of chocolate into any recipe and to infuse the royal taste of mole into ordinary dishes. It should be used sparingly and to taste. Cocoa powder has a semi-bitter, astringent quality. Do not confuse cocoa powder with the chocolate milk powder that contains sugar and additives.

Coriander
Coriander is ground seeds from the cilantro plant that is related to the carrot family and has a fruity, lemony, aromatic taste. It is one of the essential ingredients of adobo along with cumin, ground oregano and coriander. I always make enough adobo mixture to use in multiple recipes.

Cumin
Ground cumin is the second-most used spice in the world. It is related to the parsley family and has a tart, nutty, peppery taste. In some Mediterranean cuisines it is kept on the table along with salt and pepper. It is an essential ingredient for your adobo mix.

Garlic Powder / Granulated Garlic
Can't get enough? Garlic powder is an easy way to infuse garlic flavor into your recipe. Let your taste be your guide. Do not confuse garlic powder or granulated garlic with garlic salt, which is mostly salt infused or mixed with some garlic.

Nutmeg
Nutmeg has a nutty, fruity, aromatic taste that is uniquely its own. It can only be defined by itself. Used in trace amounts (¼ tsp. or less), it will infuse an unforgettable aroma to your chile recipes.

Oregano Powder / Dried Oregano
Oregano has an aromatic pungent taste that is familiar to most people and is part of the Adobo Spice Mix that is used in a lot of recipes. You can purchase Mexican oregano in a dried leaf form and crush it in the palm of your hand to add to your favorite recipe.

Onion Powder/ Granulated Onions / Onion Flakes

If you need an instant dose of onion taste and do not wish to cut or sauté an onion, onion powder is your solution and is readily available at most supermarkets (1 Tbsp. is equivalent to one medium onion). Do not confuse onion salt with onion powder. Onion salt is mostly salt infused with onion powder.

Salt

Salt is the original food flavoring and is available in many forms from gourmet sea salts
to Kosher salts to plain iodized table salt. I have found that salt can mask the taste of many subtle aromatics and overwhelm the taste buds with its own taste. I prefer to use salt as an add-on to each recipe so that individuals can use as much as they wish. Salt is salt and need not be sautéed or cooked into food during preparation. It can always be added but never removed. Try a salt-free cooking regime and you may enjoy the flavors.

SWEETENERS

Everything tastes better with a little sweetness to it.

There are many sweeteners that can be used as you are cooking, each with its own unique taste, aroma and flavor. When I refer to sweetener in many of the recipes, you have many choices. The availability and your taste buds can make the decision for you. Moderation and trace amounts are the key to a whole spectrum of taste sensations. Even a blistering chile recipe will distinguish by sweetness.

Brown Sugar

Brown sugar is unbleached white sugar that has been infused with molasses to give a deep sweet aromatic taste. It can be used sparingly with any recipe or rub to enhance the natural flavor of any ingredient.

Corn Syrup

Corn syrup is a natural sweetener extracted from cornstarch and used in many processed foods as a sweetener. It is more subtle in taste that most sugars and can be used sparingly to impart a light sweet taste in any recipe.

Fruit Nectars, Concentrates or Juices

Fruit juices, nectars and concentrates are my favorite sweeteners in that they infuse both an aromatic and sweetness to the recipe. Some popular fruit nectars are mango, orange, papaya, peach, pineapple, guava, tamarind, and tropical blend. The choice is up to you. Use the nectars sparingly or in combination with other liquids in the recipe. Imagine a mango infused green chile or papaya laced red chile. Fruit nectar is about one-quarter the sweetness potency of sugar and will not overwhelm the other ingredients being used.

Honey
The labor of love for most honey bees is their honey, which come in varying degrees of sweetness and flavor. Use sparingly, and you will be the beneficiary of all the bees' hard labor.

Maple Syrup
Maple syrup is nature's gift to man. No other sweetener has the flavor and taste memory of maple syrup. I have been using it for years as a condiment and flavor enhancer and highly recommend using it as part of your ingredients (1 Tbsp. will go a long way).

Molasses
Molasses has its own unique flavor and can be used in any recipe that calls for sweetener to give it a dark, spice flavor—especially in BBQ sauces. Caution should be used, as molasses will overwhelm other, more delicate spices or ingredients. It cannot however overwhelm an 8,000+ SHU chile.

Piloncillo, (Cane Sugar)
Piloncillo is another gift of nature to man. It is made from pure cane sugar that has not been processed and is available in liquid or cone-shaped pieces

To use the Piloncillo pieces, they must be first broken apart or diluted. Place in a small microwaveable cup. Microwave for 30 to 45 seconds. Use a fork to split apart. Or use a grater to grind off as much as you need.

You can also liquefy or caramelize piloncillo by melting it in a sauce pan with 2–3 Tbsp. of water. It is by far the best substitute for sugar and adds a sweet, molasses-like taste. Piloncillo is available in the Spanish food section of your supermarket in brown cone-shaped packages.

If you cannot find piloncillo at your supermarket, you can substitute raw cane sugar.

Sugar (Bleached, Unbleached)
Sugar is the most used sweetener and available in almost any pantry. Used in moderation and to taste, it will enhance any recipe.

Sweetener Pastes

Guava, Quince (Membrillo), Agave:
Sweetener pastes are by far my favorite for any recipe that calls for sweetener. I dissolve the paste with water on a 1:1 basis to create a sweeter sauce with about the same consistency of honey for use in any recipe as needed.
Paste sweeteners are about half the sweetness potency of sugar and will not overwhelm the other ingredients being used.

Chapter 13– RERERENCE GUIDE

GUIDE TO CHILE PEPPERS
by SCOVILLE HEAT UNITS (SHU)

Chili Pepper List by Scoville Heat Units (SHU)
NOTE: Throughout the **Red or Green Chile Bible**, the reference
"SHU to taste" is made. This list should be helpful in deciding the SHU
level that you can select for you recipes from the 0 SHU units of bell
peppers to the blistering Trinidad scorpion at 2 million SHU.

Sweet bell pepper: 0 Scovilles. The typical green bell pepper, about the
size of a large fist. Very mild.

Banana pepper: 0-500 Scovilles. Also known as the Yellow wax pepper,
the Banana Pepper has a mild, sweet taste that is very popular on many
types of foods.

Trinidad Perfume chili pepper: 0-500 Scovilles. The Trinidad
Perfume chili pepper is a mild chili pepper with very little to no heat. It is
a habanero type and produces pods similar to a typical orange habanero
pepper, about 1 to 1.5 inches in length and 1.25 inches wide.

Cubanelle chili pepper: 0–1,000 Scovilles. Capsicum Annuum. The
Cubanelle is considered a sweet pepper, although its heat can range from
mild to moderate. Cubanelles are usually picked before they ripen, while
they are a yellowish-green color, but when ripe, they turn bright red.

Pimento (or Pimiento) chili pepper: 100–500 Scovilles. Not just for
stuffing olives. Pimiento is the Spanish word for "pepper."

Cherry pepper: 100–500 Scovilles. See "Pimento" chili pepper. Not just
for stuffing olives. Pimiento is the Spanish word for "pepper."

Pepperoncini chili pepper: 100–500 Scovilles: Also known as Tuscan
Peppers. These sweet, mild chili peppers are found in Italy and Greece.

NewMex R Naky chili pepper: 250–750 Scovilles. The NuMex R Naky
chile is an Anaheim-type hybrid created by Dr. Nakayama of New Mexico
State University in 1985.

Pasilla chili pepper: 250–3,999 Scovilles: Pasilla or "little raisin"
properly refers to the dried chilaca pepper. The chilaca, when fresh, is
also known as "pasilla bajio," or as the "chile negro" or "Mexican negro"
because, while it starts off dark green, it ends up dark brown. It typically
grows from 8 to 10 inches long.

Paprika chili pepper: 250–1000 Scovilles. A large, cone-shaped chili pepper. It is dried and ground to make the more familiar powdered spice.

Sonora chili pepper: 300–600 Scovilles. The Sonora is an Anaheim variety with a very mild flavor. It grows to about 10 inches in length and up to 1 ½ inches wide, and although it matures to red, it is commonly used in its less mature, green form.

Ají Panca: 500 Scovilles. The Panca chili (or "Ají Panca" as it's known in South America) is a deep red to burgundy pepper, measuring 3–5 inches.

Santa Fe Grande chili pepper: 500–700 Scovilles. Also known as the "yellow hot chile" and the "guero chile." Approximately 5 inches long and ripens from greenish-yellow to orange-yellow to red.

New Mexican chile (formerly known as Anaheim chile) pepper: 500–1,000 Scovilles. A mild, medium size chili pepper that grows to 6H10 inches, often used when green, though it can be used when red.

Coronado chili pepper: 700–1,000 Scovilles. Originally from South America, the Coronado Pepper grows to 4 inches long and 2 inches wide with thin, waxy skin.

Poblano chili pepper: 1,000–2,000 Scovilles. The poblano is extremely popular chili peppers. Four inches long, very dark green in color, ripening to dark red or brown.

Ancho chili pepper: 1,000–2,000 Scovilles. An Ancho pepper is dried form of the poblano chili pepper.

Chilaca: 1,000-2,500 Scovilles. The Chilaca is a curved, long, thin pepper that grows to about 6–9 inches, and 1 inch wide.

Hatch chili peppers: 1,000–2,500 Scovilles. Hatch chili peppers are grown and harvested in Hatch Valley, New Mexico. They are harvested in late July and early August and have a mild to medium flavor. The peppers are long and curved, much like the Anaheim chili pepper, and are perfect for stuffing.

Cascabel chili peppers: 1,000–3,000 Scovilles. Capsicum Annuum. The Cascabel Chile is grown in several areas of Mexico. It is small and round, 2–3 cm in diameter, and matures to a deep red.

Picuante/ Peppadew chili pepper: 1,177 Scovilles. Capsicum Baccatum. The Peppadew is grown in the Limpopo province of South Africa and is actually the brand name of sweet piquant peppers.

Ají chili pepper: 1,177–75,000 Scovilles. Also known generally as the Peruvian hot pepper, "Ají" is the common name primarily in South America and areas of the Caribbean for chili peppers.

Espanola chili pepper: 1,500–2,000 Scovilles. The Espanola was developed in New Mexico in the 1980s by crossing a Sandia pepper with another New Mexico chile.

Rocotillo chili pepper: 1,500–2,500 Scovilles. There is some confusion about the rocotillo chili pepper, since some appear to be from Capsicum baccatum and some from Capsicum Chinese.

NewMex Joe E Parker chili pepper: 1,500–3,000 Scovilles. This New Mexico variety was named after Mr. Joe E. Parker, a graduate of NMSU's College of Agriculture and Home Economics, who helped to evaluate this selection of chile.

Mulato chili pepper: 2,500–3,000 Scovilles. Capsicum Annuum. The Mulato is a mild to medium dried Poblano, similar to the Ancho, but with a slightly different flavor.

New Mex Big Jim chili pepper: 2,500–3,000 Scovilles. This giant chili pepper was introduced by New Mexico State University in the 1970s as a cross between a few different types of local chiles and a Peruvian chile.

Mirasol chili pepper: 2,500–5,000 Scovilles. The name Mirasol means "looking at the sun" in Spanish, which describes the way these peppers grow on the plant. They are known as Guajillo in their dried form, which are one of the main chiles used in traditional mole sauces.

Guajillo chili pepper: 2,500–5,000 Scovilles. Capsicum Annuum. The Guajillo is one of the most common and popular chiles grown and used in Mexico. It is mild to moderately hot, and has dark, reddish brown, leathery skin.

Jalapeño chili pepper: 2,500–8,000 Scovilles. The world's most popular chili pepper! Harvested when they are green or red if allowed to ripen, about 4–6 inches long. A chipotle is a smoked jalapeño chili pepper.

Purple Jalapeño chili pepper: 2,500–8,000 Scovilles. The Purple Jalapeño is an ornamental version of the typical jalapeño pepper.

Chipotle chili pepper: 2,500–8,000 Scovilles. A chipotle is a smoked jalapeño chili pepper. You'll notice the distinctive smoky flavor of certain foods like salsas that have been prepared with chipotle peppers. Very delicious.

Morita chili pepper: 2,500–8,000 Scovilles. A smoked red jalapeño, similar to a chipotle pepper.

Fresno chili pepper: 2,500–10,000 Scovilles. Capsicum Annuum. The Fresno pepper looks and tastes almost like a jalapeño, but they can be much hotter. Fresno peppers change from green to red as they grow, and increase in hotness, but they are often harvested and sold as green.

New Mexico 6-4 Heritage chili pepper: 3,000–5,000 Scovilles. The New Mexico 6-4 Heritage chile pepper was developed around 1998 from a seed bank of the original New Mexico 6-4.

Chimayo chili pepper: 4,000–6,000 Scovilles. The Chimayo is another New Mexico chile, but it is a unique one. It is not commercially mass produced, but is more commonly grown in individual homes and gardens, making them unpredictable and unconforming, in a good way.

Sandia chili pepper: 5,000–7,000 Scovilles. Another chili from New Mexico, the Sandia grows to 6 to 7 inches and is similar to the Anaheim pepper. They start green and ripen to red, but are often used while green.

Puya chili pepper: 5,000–8,000 Scovilles. The Puya chile is similar to the Guajillo, but smaller and hotter.

Hungarian Wax: 5,000–15,000 Scovilles. The Hungarian Wax Pepper, as its name suggests, originated in Hungary.

Serrano pepper: 5,000–23,000 Scovilles. A smaller version of the jalapeño, similar in color, but smaller, about 1 to 2 inches long, 1/2 inch wide. Dark green to reddish in color. Getting spicier!

Bishop's Crown chili pepper: 5,000–30,000 Scovilles. Capsicum Baccatum. This chile is a member of the Capsicum Baccatum species, which includes the Ají pepper.

Peter pepper: 5,000–30,000 Scovilles. This very interesting little chili makes a great conversation piece in the garden or in the kitchen due to its distinctively phallic shape, hence its name.

Shipkas chili pepper: 5,000–30,000 Scovilles. Also known as the "Bulgarian Carrot Pepper," this interesting little chili pepper looks remarkably like a carrot, with its bright orange color and long, narrow body.

Hidalgo chili pepper: 6,000–17,000 Scovilles. The Hidalgo is an heirloom pepper, similar in shape and hotness to the Serrano, originally from Mexico and Central America.

Aleppo: About 10,000 Scovilles. Capsicum Annuum. The Aleppo pepper, also known as the Halaby pepper, is named after the city of Aleppo in Northern Syria. It is commonly grown in Syria and Turkey, and is usually dried and crushed.

Bolivian Rainbow chili pepper: 10,000–30,000 Scovilles. Grown for centuries in Bolivia (Central South America), the Bolivian Rainbow chile is a stunningly beautiful plant.

Baker's Hot chili pepper: 15,000–30,000 Scovilles. The Barker's Hot is an extra-hot chile, the hottest of the Anaheim/New Mexico variety, and it has great flavor.

Lemon Drop Chili Pepper: 15,000–30,000 Scovilles. This bright yellow, citrus-flavored chile is also known as "Kellu Uchu" in Peru, where it originated.

Jwala Finger Hot chili pepper: 20,000–30,000 Scovilles. The Jwala is the most popular chile in India, adding great flavor and spice to many Indian dishes.

Ají Limo: 30,000–50,000 Scovilles. The Limo chile (or Ají Limo) is another super-hot chili from Peru. ("Ají" is the term for chile pepper in South America.)

Ají Amarillo: 30,000–50,000 Scovilles. Since "Amarillo" is the Spanish word for *yellow*, and "Ají" is the term for *chile* in South America, this pepper is also appropriately known as the "yellow chile."

Chile de Árbol chili pepper: Sources rate this chile in 2 categories: 15,000–30,000 and 50,000–65,000 Scovilles. Capsicum Annuum. Chiles de Árbol are small and thin Mexican peppers, growing to 2 to 3 inches long and less than a ½ inch wide.

Tabasco pepper: 30,000–50,000 Scovilles. Yep, this is the chili pepper used in Tabasco sauce. The fruit is tapered and less than 2 inches long. The color is usually creamy yellow to red.

Cayenne pepper: 30,000–50,000 Scovilles. A thin chile pepper, green to red in color, about 2 to 3 inches long. The "cayenne pepper" spice you use is the dried, ground version of this pepper.

Chile Pequin chili pepper: 30,000–60,000 Scovilles. Capsicum Annuum. Also spelled Piquin, this chile is also called "Bird Pepper," because it is consumed and spread by wild birds.

Rocoto chili pepper: 30,000–100,000 Scovilles. AKA the Manzano pepper. This chili pepper is normally found in South America. It is among the oldest of domesticated chili peppers and was grown up to as much as 5000 years ago. It is probably related to undomesticated chili peppers that still grow in South America.

Guntur Sannam chili pepper: 35,000–40,000 Scovilles. Capsicum Annuum. The Guntur Sannam chili is grown in and around Guntur and Warangal in the state of Andhra Pradesh in India.

Super Chili chili pepper: 40,000–50,000 Scovilles. These small peppers grow upright in clusters and mature from light green to red, often with shades of orange in between.

Santaka chili pepper: 40,000–50,000 Scovilles. From Japan, the Santaka chili pepper is a hot and flavorful Asian variety, perfect for Asian cooking, especially stir-fries.

Tien Tsin pepper: 50,000–75,000 Scovilles. The Tien Tsin is named after the province in China where its harvest originally took place.

Bird's Eye: 50,000–100,000 Scovilles. The tiny Bird's Eye Chili originated in Cambodia, Vietnam, Thailand, The Philippines, and surrounding countries, but they can now be found all over the world.

Chiltepin chili pepper: 50,000 to 100,000 Scovilles. Capsicum Annuum. The Chiltepin, or Chiltepine, is a tiny, round or oval shaped, red to orange-red chile, measuring about .8 cm in diameter.

Thai chili pepper: 50,000–100,000 Scovilles. Despite the common belief, there is no single "Thai chili pepper," although most candidates for the title are small in size and high in heat or pungency. There are at least 79 separate varieties of chili that have appeared from three species in Thailand.

Dundicut chili pepper: 55,000–65,000 Scovilles. Capsicum Annuum. These small, round chili peppers from Pakistan grow to about ½ inch to 1 inch in diameter, and are dark red in color.

New Mex XX Hot chili pepper: 60,000–70,000 Scovilles. Another of the many New Mexico varieties, the New Mex XX Hot is just that—very hot.

Diablo Grande chili pepper: 60,000–100,000 Scovilles. The Diablo Grande comes from the same group that includes jalapenos, poblanos, cayenne, and Serrano peppers.

Malagueta chili pepper: 60,000–100,000 Scovilles. The Malagueta chili pepper is similar in appearance to the Bird's Eye chili or the Thai chili because of its bright red color and short, tapered body. It starts out green and matures to red, and grows to only about 2 inches.

Charleston Hot chili pepper: 70,000–100,000 Scovilles. Similar to the Carolina Cayenne, the Charleston Hot is a variety of Cayenne created by the U.S. Department of Agriculture in South Carolina.

Red Amazon chili pepper: 75,000 Scovilles. The Red Amazon is actually dried Tabasco chile, but since it is so commonly known in this form, we included it separately here.

Yatsafusa chili pepper: 75,000 Scovilles. Also known as Japanese chile. Originating in Japan, these chiles come from small plants (the name refers to a dwarf tree) and grow upward in clusters around yellow flowers.

Tabiche chili pepper: 85,000–115,000 Scovilles. Originally from India, the Tabiche pepper can now be found growing worldwide and often year-round, but it does best in hot, dry climates.

Bahamian chili pepper: 95,000–110,000 Scovilles. As its name suggests, the Bahamian pepper originates from the Bahamas, where it is still one of the major agricultural crops.

Carolina Cayenne chili pepper: 100,000–125,000 Scovilles. Similar in appearance to the original cayenne, this variety is twice as hot and appears slightly wider.

African Bird's Eye/ African Devil: 175,000 Scovilles. Also sometimes known as "Piri Piri," the African Bird's Eye is a small chile, growing to only about 1 inch, but they pack a lot of punch.

Jamaican Hot: 100,000–200,000 Scovilles. As the name suggests, these peppers are from Jamaica but have become popular around the world.

Datil: 100,000–300,000 Scovilles. The Datil packs the intense heat of a Habanero or a Scotch Bonnet, but its flavor is sweeter, and fruitier.

Scotch Bonnet: 100,000–350,000 Scovilles. This pepper is a cultivar of the Habanero and is among the hottest peppers anywhere. Its name derives from its resemblance to the Scottish Tam O'Shanter hat, although it appears primarily in the Caribbean and in Guyana and the Maldives.

Habanero chili pepper: 100,000–350,000 Scovilles. Related to the Scotch Bonnet. This one is the granddaddy of all the hot peppers in terms of heat level. Grown mainly on the Yucatan Peninsula in Mexico, its coloring is yellow-orange, orange or bright red, depending upon when it's harvested. Average size 1 to 2 ½ inches long, 1 to 2 inches in diameter and tam-shaped.

Fatalii: 125,000–325,000 Scovilles. The Fatalii comes from central and southern Africa, and is one of the hottest peppers in the world. With the heat level of a Habanero, it has a fruitier, citrus flavor, and packs an instant, intense burn, unlike the habanero, whose heat "sneaks up on you."

Devil's Tongue: 125,000–325,000 Scovilles. The Devil's Tongue is similar in color and shape to the Fatalii, but with smoother skin and smaller size.

Madame Jeanette: 225,000 Scovilles. Named after a famous Brazilian prostitute, the Madame Jeanette has the shape of a bell pepper but the intense heat of a habanero.

Tiger Paw NR chili pepper: 265,000–328,000 Scovilles. Developed in Charleston, South Carolina, the Tiger Paw NR is an extra-hot bright orange habanero variety.

Trinidad Scorpion chili pepper: 300,000+ Scovilles. These red, wrinkled peppers resemble the scorpion, hence the name, and are known for their intense heat.

Chocolate Habanero chili pepper: 300,000–425,000 Scovilles. The Chocolate Habanero, also known as "Congo Black" or "Black Habanero," is one of the hottest peppers originating from the Caribbean.

Caribbean Red Habanero: 300,000–475,000 Scovilles. This extremely hot pepper, originally from the Yucatan peninsula in Mexico, is now also cultivated in the Caribbean and around North America.

Red Savina Habanero: 200,000–580,000 Scovilles. This pepper is a cultivar of the habanero. It once held the Guinness Record for the hottest chili pepper, but the Bhut Jolokia now claims that prize.

Bhut Jolokia: 1,001,304 Scovilles. Now, truly one of the hottest chili pepper around!

Naga Jolokia—It's just another name for the Bhut Jolokia chili pepper.

Ghost Pepper or Ghost Chili—It's just another name for the Bhut Jolokia chili pepper.

7-Pot Chili Pepper: Over 1 Million Scovilles. The heat of the 7-Pot pepper is similar to the Bhut Jolokia but with a more fruity and nutty flavor, like other Caribbean peppers. It is becoming more popular and well-known among chile-heads, but the seeds are very rare and hard to find.

Gibraltar/Spanish Naga Chili Pepper: 1,086,844 Scovilles. The Gibraltar Naga, or Spanish Naga, is of course grown in Spain, but was developed in the UK from Indian chili peppers.

Infinity Chili Pepper: 1,176,182 Scovilles. Created in England by Nick Woods of "Fire Foods," the Infinity Chili pepper held the World Record for the world's hottest chili pepper for two weeks in 2011, before it was ousted by the Naga Viper chili.

New Mexico Scorpion: 1,191,595 Scovilles. A New Mexico-based team has developed a super-hot chile known as the "New Mexico Scorpion." The New Mexico Scorpion has been rated at 1,191,595 Scoville Heat Units by an independent laboratory.

Naga Viper: 1,382,118 Scovilles. The Naga Viper (Capsicum Chinese) has been rated at 1,382,118 Scoville Heat Units (SHU), according to tests conducted by the Warwick HRI Mineral Analysis Laboratory, UK, in November 2010.

Trinidad Scorpion Butch T: 1,463,700 Scovilles. The Trinidad Scorpion Butch T has been rated at 1,463,700 Scoville Heat Units (SHU), according to recent tests. It was propagated by Butch Taylor of Zydeco Hot Sauce and grown by the Chili Factory.

Dorset Naga Chili Pepper: 1 million–1.5 million Scovilles. (Capsicum Chinese) Development of the Dorset Naga began near Dorset, England, around 2001 when Joy and Michael Michaud of Peppers by Post bought a Naga Morich plant from an Oriental foods store in southern England.

Chocolate 7-Pot Chili Pepper: Recently tested between 923,000 and 1.85 million Scovilles, with an average of 1,169,058. Only the Moruga Scorpion scored higher. It is suspected that it could reach 2 million in the future.

Trinidad Moruga Scorpion: 2,009,231 Scovilles. In February 2012, the 2012 New Mexico Chile Conference, in association with Jim Duffy of Refining Fire Chiles, announced that the Trinidad Moruga Scorpion is the hottest chili pepper in the world. Clocking in at 2,009,231 Scoville Units, this chili pepper is beyond blistering.

Compiled by: Michael J. Hultquist
mike@chilipeppermadness.com
www.chilipeppermadnes.com

Capsaicin & Endorphins, It Hurts, and We Like It

Burning tongue, Watery eyes, Runny nose, and the sweats. These are the first few sensations that I think of, and experience, when dealing with truly spicy foods. As we grow as a culture in the understanding of how our diet effects how we live, and how we feel, it is important to examine the positive effects of something as unassuming as the chili pepper.

When speaking of spicy foods, and the sense of heat we feel when ingesting them, we are referring more specifically to the active compound known as capsaicin. This compound is found, in widely varying degrees, in chili peppers. There are two widely accepted systems for measuring and expressing these levels of piquancy. The first was devised in 1912 by the American chemist Wilbur Scoville, who devised the Scoville Organoleptic Test for rating the pungency of chili peppers; the resulting numbers being placed on his Scoville scale. In this method, Scoville diluted a solution of the pepper extract in increasing amounts of sugar water until the "heat" is no longer discerned by a panel of tasters; usually five. The amount of sugar water needed to dilute the pepper solution enough to render it unidentifiable to all tasters would determine its place on the Scoville scale. Thusly, a sweet, or bell pepper has a Scoville rating of zero, as the "heat" was undetectable to all of the tasters, even undiluted.

On the other end of the scale, we have peppers such as the Naga Jolokia, (a chili pepper native to India, where its various nomenclatures translate into such appetizing pet names as "ghost," "cobra snake," and "poison chili"), which rate most recently at 1,041,427 on the Scoville scale when tested by an Indian export company in 2004. To provide some relative numbers, standard US Grade pepper spray begins at the 2,000,000 mark, whereas pure capsaicin reaches in upwards of 16,000,000. The main drawback of the Scoville scale is in its imprecision, for it basically depends of human subjectivity. For this reason, a second system was created and has become the preference when speaking of the measurement of piquancy; known as high-performance liquid chromatography. This method, also known as the Gillett Method, is much more scientific, as it employs machinery and mathematical formulas to measure the heat-producing chemicals of a chili pepper. The resulting levels are expressed in ASTA pungency units, which when multiplied by 15, produce that peppers' relative placement on the Scoville scale.

In essence, when we eat a pepper containing capsaicin, we are eating that plant's deterrent against being eaten; hence the irritating sensations it produces when we eat or even touch it. Pretty ironic that the reason we eat something is for its natural defenses against being eaten in the first place. Psychologist Paul Rozin sites this phenomenon as an example of "constrained risk," something that makes our body respond with warning signals, which we ignore and enjoy, much like riding a roller coaster. It is asserted by many that prolonged stimulation from capsaicin releases B-endorphins from the brain to impede and reduce pain. It is based on this idea that capsaicin has been used as a medication to aid in the alleviation of many chronic disorders, such as rheumatoid arthritis, and viral and diabetic nerve damage. However, much like a chili-eaters tolerance increases with the frequency of their use, extended use of this chemical leads to desensitization and therefore a higher dose is needed to be effective.

The value of such foods as chili peppers and the reaction that they induce within our bodies has been known to cultures for over 400 years, but to science for just a few. Humans, the adaptive organisms that we are, continue to look to the ground for the solutions to the questions that our world poses to us.

By Mike Marcelli http://cookingdistrict.com/cd/general.nsf/

Awesome Health Benefits of Chili Peppers: Chili Peppers Are Good for Your Health

Capsaicin, the active ingredient in chili peppers, is so hot that it can make your mouth feel like it's on fire. This phytochemical exists in peppers, most likely, to deter animals from eating them, and is also the active component of pepper sprays used for self-defense. Yet for humans, when capsaicin is consumed in a somewhat diluted form, such as in hot sauce, chili peppers or cayenne peppers, it offers a myriad of health benefits.

Chili peppers come in hundreds of different varieties, each with a unique flavor, color, shape and heat factor. Generally speaking, the hotter the pepper, the more capsaicin it contains. About 80 percent of the capsaicin in a chili pepper is in its ribs and seeds, which is why much of the heat is removed when these items are taken out. For those on the daring side, look at Chili Pepper List by Scoville Heat Units (SHU) for a selection of chile peppers by Scoville Heat Units (SHU). Ready to add a little spice to your life? Here are seven reasons to turn up the heat in your next meal.

1. Fight Cancer
A study published in Cancer Research found that capsaicin caused cancer cells to commit suicide. The substance caused almost 80 percent of prostate cancer cells to die in mice, and prostate tumors treated with capsaicin were about one-fifth the size of those in untreated mice. "Capsaicin inhibits the growth of human prostate cancer cells in petri dishes and mice," says lead researcher Dr. H. Phillip Koeffler, director of hematology and oncology at Cedars-Sinai Medical Center and a professor of medicine at the University of California, Los Angeles. Further, researchers say capsaicin pills may one day be used to prevent the return of prostate cancer.

2. Provide Pain Relief
A topical form of capsaicin is a recognized treatment for osteoarthritis pain, and may also help alleviate pain from diabetic neuropathy. Capsaicin is also known to inhibit Substance P, a neuropeptide that is the key transmitter of pain to the brain. Substance P can cause swelling of nerve fibers, which may result in headaches and sinus symptoms. Studies have found that capsaicin both relieves and prevents cluster headaches, migraine headaches and sinus headaches.

3. Prevent Sinusitis and Relieve Congestion
Capsaicin has potent antibacterial properties that fight and prevent chronic sinus infections, or sinusitis. Because it is so hot, it also helps to stimulate secretions that help clear mucus from your nose, thereby relieving nasal congestion. This phytochemical may also help relieve sinus-related allergy symptoms.

4. Fight Inflammation

Capsaicin is a potent anti-inflammatory agent. It works by inhibiting Substance P, which is associated with inflammatory processes. Capsaicin is being looked at as a potential treatment for arthritis, psoriasis and diabetic neuropathy.

5. Soothe Intestinal Diseases

A Duke University study found that capsaicin may lead to a cure for inflammatory bowel disease (IBD). The substance can also help to kill bacteria such as H. pylori, which can help prevent stomach ulcers.

6. Burn Fat and Lose Weight

Capsaicin is a thermogenic agent, which means it increases metabolic activity. This, in turn, helps to burn calories and fat. Many popular "fat-burning" supplements on the market contain capsaicin, as the substance may significantly increase metabolic activity for over 20 minutes after it's eaten.

7. Protect Your Heart

Capsaicin may help to protect the heart by reducing cholesterol, triglycerides and platelet aggregation. It may also help the body dissolve fibrin, which is necessary for blood clots to form. Further, cultures around the world that use hot peppers liberally in their meals have significantly lower rates of heart attack and stroke than cultures that do not.

Recommended Reading:
by www.SixWise.com
The World's 7 Most Potent Disease-Fighting Spices

THE CHEMISTRY OF SLOW COOKING MEATS

Of all the attributes of eating quality, tenderness is rated the most important factor affecting beef palatability.
Slow cooked meals are generally easier to make and very cost effective, using cuts of meat that improve in texture and flavor when cooked for long periods of time at low temperatures. These tough cuts of meat contain large amounts of collagen, which requires long cooking times to break down into a rich gelatin.

How Does Slow Cooking Work?

When you cook, collagen begins to melt at about 160^0F and turns to a rich liquid, *gelatin*. This gives meat a lot of flavor and a wonderful silky texture. When cooking it is important to liquefy collagen. *Denaturation of the collagen molecule is a kinetic process, and hence a function of both temperature and duration of heating. Cooking at low temperatures require long periods of time to liquefy collagen.*

Cooking Meat Temperatures

105^0F/40C–122^0F/50C - Calpains begin to denature and lose activity till around 105F, cathepsains at 122F. Since enzyme activity increases up to those temperatures, slow cooking can provide a significant aging effect during cooking. Meat should however be quickly seared or blanched first to kill surface microbes.

120^0F/50^0C - Meat develops a white opacity as heat sensitive myosin denatures. Coagulation produces large enough clumps to scatter light. Red meat turns pink.
Rare Meats: 120^0F/50^0C is the early stages of juiciness in meats as the protein myosin, begins to coagulate . This lends each cell some solidity and the meat some firmness. As the myosin molecules bond to each other they begin to squeeze out water molecules that separated them. Water then collects around the solidified protein core and is squeezed out of the cell by connective tissue. At this temperature meat is considered rare and when sliced juices will break through weak spots in the connective tissue.

140^0F/60^0C - Red myoglobin begins to denature into tan colored hemichrome. Meat turns from pink to brown-grey color.
140^0F/60^0C - Meat suddenly releases lots of juice, shrinks noticeably and becomes chewy as a result of collagen denaturing, which squeezes out liquids.
Medium -- Well Meats: Collagen shrinks as the meat temperature rises to 140/60 and more of the protein coagulates and cells become more segregated into a solid core and surrounding liquid as the meat gets progressively firmer and moister. At 140-150 the meat suddenly releases lots of juices, shrinks noticeably and becomes chewier as a result of collagen shrinkage. Meat served at this temperature is considered medium and begins to change from juicy to dry.

160°F/70°C - Connective tissue collagen begins to dissolve to gelatin. Melting of collagen starts to accelerate at 160°F and continues rapidly up to 180°F.

Well Done Slow Cooked Meats: Falling apart tenderness. Collagen turns to gelatin at 160°F/70°C. The meat gets dryer, but at 160°F the connective tissues containing collagen begins to dissolve into gelatin. With time, muscle fibers that had been held tightly together begin to easily spread apart. Although the fibers are still very stiff and dry, the meat appears tenderer since the gelatins provide succulence.

NOTE: At 140°F changes are caused by the denaturing of collagen in the cells. Meat served at this temperature medium-rare is changing from juicy to dry. At 160°F/ 70°C connective tissue collagen begins to dissolve to gelatin. This however is a very lengthy process. The fibers are still stiff and dry but meat seems tenderer. Source: Harold McGee -- **On Food and Cooking**

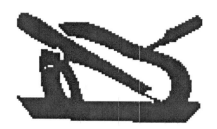

Anatomy of muscle fiber

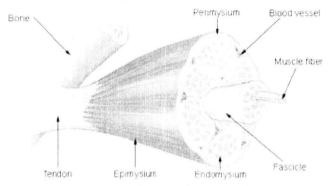

A muscle is completely enclosed by a thick sheath of connective tissue (the epimysium) and is divided into bundles of fibers by a connective tissue network (perimysium). Individual muscle fibers are bounded by a plasma membrane surrounded by connective tissue (endomysium) which consists of a basement membrane surrounded by a reticular later in which a meshwork of fine collage fibrils is embedded in a matrix. Tendons are elastic collagenous tissues.

Source: Wikipedia

Scattered among the muscle fibers are fat cells, which store energy for the muscles. Fat is crucial to meat texture. Waxy when it is cold, fat does not evaporate when you are cooking as does water. It melts and lubricates the fibers as they are getting tougher under the heat. Fat is also the source of much of the flavor in meat. As the animal ages the flavor compounds build up and get stronger. After the animal is slaughtered, the fat can turn rancid if stored improperly or too long.

The Challenge In Cooking Meat

We like our meat tender and juicy at the same time...

We therefore want our meat to be cooked tender where tough collagen is converted to gelatin but with a minimum loss of moisture. The reality is that these methods are contradictory and hence the challenge or dilemma to cooking meats. To minimize moisture loss requires temperatures less than 130^0F, however, turning collagen into gelatin requires temperatures above 160^0F and for extended time periods. As moisture evaporates, the meat begins to shrink. A slab can lose 20 percent or more of its weight in cooking due to shrinkage. Even meat cooked in liquid will dry out although not as quickly. So we are faced with a dilemma. To liquefy the collagen we need to cook the meat to 180^0F and hold it there for long periods of time. But by then it is well past well-done and the muscle fibers can be dried out. As a result, we need to add moisture.

How to Slow Loss of Moisture

Brining. Brining adds a significant amount of moisture; it helps retain moisture during cooking, contributing noticeable flavor enhancements.

Steaming. Another method of adding moisture is to cook the meat in very high humidity by wrapping it in foil with a little water or juice. This keeps moisture from escaping and some vapors penetrate the meat.

Braising or **poaching (low temperature).** Braising is a method of cooking by submerging the meat in hot liquid, but not hot enough to boil. Braising can give you juicy, tender and flavorful meat, especially if you use a flavorful braising liquid. But it tends to pull all the collagen out and rob the meat of its natural flavor. Flavor the liquid (water with pickling spices is a nice simple start), completely submerge the slab, keep the lid off, keep the temp down to about $160–180^0F$ for about 30 minutes, and let the meat cool in the liquid for 20 to 30 minutes so it will absorb some of the water before putting it on the grill.

Breakage of collagen covalent links using Acids -- (Tenderizing meats with acid). It is well known that adding a little vinegar to a stock will help tenderize meat while cooking. It is also useful to marinate meat for a few hours using vinegar to tenderize meat. Offer and Knight (1988) suggested that one of the mechanisms of pH-induced tenderization of meat could be a breakage of covalent collagen cross-links and of some specific peptide bonds.

Here are tips to keep in mind when slow-low roasting:

Develop a caramelized crust before slow cooking—by searing the meat either in a dry pan or with a small amount of oil or fat.

Place the meat or roast fat side up in the pan so it self-bastes. Tenderize your cuts of meat—e.g., pounding meat, buying aged meats (Note: meats cooked longer a 120^0F will age and be tenderer), marinating meats with acids will tenderize the meat.

Tent the resting meat with foil and allow 10 to 15 minutes before cutting it so the meat's juices will return to the center; Slice the meat against the grain.

http://www.scienceofcooking.com/meat/slow_cooking1.htm

RESOURCES & CHILE VENDORS

SOUTHWEST

Bueno Foods
201 4th Street SW
Albuquerque, NM.87102
505-243-2722
505-243-2723
1-800-95CHILE
www.buenofoods.com

Casados Farms
201 State Rd 582
Ohkay Owinegh, NM.87566
505-852-2433
505-852-2434

Chile Addict
325 Eubanks NE
Alburquerque, NM.87123
505-237-9070
www.chileaddictstore.com

The Chile Shop
109 East Water Street
Santa Fe, NM.87501
www.thechileshop.com

Chile Traditions
8204 Montgomery Blvd. NW
Albuquerque, NM.87109
505-888-3166
1-877-VERY-HOT
www.chiletraditions.com

Apple Canyon Gourmet
6025 Coronado Ave. NE, Ste. B
Albuquerque, NM. 87109
505-332-2000
1-800-866-4695
www.applecanyongourmet.com

Hobson Gardens
3656 Hobson Road
Roswell, NM. 88203
575-622-7289
Seasonal Operation

Jane Butel's Cooking School Pantry
Jane Butel's Pecos Valley Spice Co.
2655 Pan American NE
Albuquerque, NM. 87017
505-243-2622
www.janebutel.com
www.pecosvalley.com

NM Chile.com
2315 Hendola NE
Albuquerque, NM. 87110
1-888-336-4228
505-217-2105
www.nmchili.com
wholesale:
www.wholesalechili.com

Pendery's
1221 Manufacturing Street
Dallas, Texas. 75207
1-800-533-1870
214-741-1870
www.penderys.com

Santa Fe School of Cooking
125 N. Guadalupe St.
Santa Fe, NM. 87501
505-983-4511
www.santafeschoolofcooking.com

Los Chileros
309 Industrial Ave. NE
Albuquerque, NM. 87107
505-768-1100
1-888-328-1100
www.loschileros.com
Chile Pepper Emporium
2100 Louisiana Blvd. NE
Albuquerque, NM. 87110
505-881-9225
www.chilipepperemporium.com

Da Gift Basket & Bags
P.O. Box 2085
Los Lunas, NM. 87031
505-865-3645
1-877-468-2444
www.dagiftbasket.com

Graves Farms & Garden
6265 Graves Road
Roswell, NM. 88203
575-622-1889
www.gravesfarmandgarden.com

Hatch Chile Express
657 N. Franklin St.
Hatch, NM. 87937
575-267-3226
1-800-292-4454
www.hatch-chile.com

Chile Fanatic
520 W Hall St
Hatch, NM 87937
575-267-4928

Hatch Chile Sales
215 W Hall St
Hatch, NM 87937
575-267-4307

WEST & NORTHWEST

Casa Lucas Market
2934 24th Street
San Francisco, Ca. 84110
415-826-4334

La Palma
2884 24th Street
San Francisco, Ca. 94110
415-647-1500
fax: 451-647-1555
www.laplamasf.com

EAST

The Hot Shoppe
200 Water Street
Oswego, NY. 13126
www.hotshoppe.com

Mo Hotta-Mo Betta
1811 Limerick Street
Savannah, Ga. 31404
1-800-462-3220
www.mohotta.com

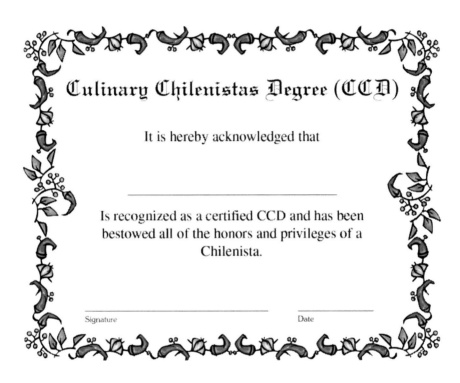

Culinary Chilenistas Degree (CCD)

It is hereby acknowledged that

_____

Is recognized as a certified CCD and has been bestowed all of the honors and privileges of a Chilenista.

_____   _____
Signature   Date

To register for your certificate please log into
www.redorgreenchilebible.com

Index

CPSIA information can be obtained
at www.ICGtesting.com
Printed in the USA
FFOW01n1235250218
45195180-45732FF